THE MISCELLANEOUS WORKS OF
JOHN BUNYAN

General Editor: Roger Sharrock

VOLUME II

THE DOCTRINE OF THE LAW
AND GRACE UNFOLDED

AND

I WILL PRAY WITH
THE SPIRIT

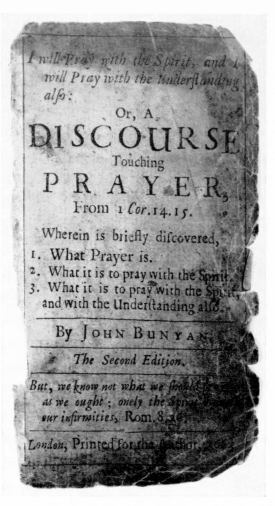

Title-page of the Bodleian copy of the second edition of
I will Pray with the Spirit

JOHN BUNYAN

The Doctrine of the Law and Grace unfolded

AND

I will pray with the Spirit

EDITED BY

RICHARD L. GREAVES

OXFORD

AT THE CLARENDON PRESS

1976

Oxford University Press, Ely House, London W. 1

GLASGOW   NEW YORK   TORONTO   MELBOURNE   WELLINGTON
CAPE TOWN   IBADAN   NAIROBI   DAR ES SALAAM   LUSAKA   ADDIS ABABA
DELHI   BOMBAY   CALCUTTA   MADRAS   KARACHI   DACCA
KUALA LUMPUR   SINGAPORE   HONG KONG   TOKYO

ISBN 0 19 811871 6

© *Oxford University Press 1976*

*Printed in Great Britain
at the University Press, Oxford
by Vivian Ridler
Printer to the University*

TO
GEOFFREY F. NUTTALL

GENERAL EDITOR'S PREFACE

SINCE the middle of the nineteenth century, there has been no complete edition of Bunyan's works. The author who is known to the world for *The Pilgrim's Progress* was a prolific preacher and writer. As his first editor and friend, Charles Doe, the comb-maker of Southwark, said: 'Here are Sixty Pieces of his Labours and he was Sixty Years of Age.' Apart from his spiritual autobiography, *Grace Abounding to the Chief of Sinners*, and the three allegorical fictions, *The Pilgrim's Progress*, *The Life and Death of Mr Badman* and *The Holy War*, these include sermons, theological treatises, biblical commentaries, and controversial works directed against the Quakers, the Latitudinarians (in the person of Edward Fowler), and the strict-communion Baptists; all these works are cast in the form of the popular sermon, with analysis of the text, abundant quotation from Scripture, a frequent employment of numbered heads and a meeting of objections by a series of questions and answers, and 'uses' or applications of the doctrine extracted from the text (these last usually conclude the work).

The purpose of this edition is to present all that Bunyan wrote in a text based on the earliest available editions, but incorporating those additions and revisions in later editions published during the author's lifetime which may reasonably be judged to have been made by Bunyan or to have received his approval. In fact, the method is that observed in the Oxford editions of *Grace Abounding* and *The Pilgrim's Progress*. As in those editions, colloquial forms and irregular grammar (such as plural subjects with singular verbs) have been retained. The punctuation, capitalization, and italicization are those of the originals, though here the editors have corrected obvious printers' errors and inconsistencies, and anything in the accidentals which might be merely confusing to the reader. A short textual introduction with title-page transcriptions precedes each work; it includes information on the printers, a list of seventeenth-century editions, and a mention of later reprints that are of any importance.

The reader of Bunyan's *Miscellaneous Works* is more likely to be a social or ecclesiastical historian, a theologian or a psychologist, than a literary student. The introductions to the various works thus aim to give an adequate account of the background of Nonconformist life in the period, as well as of Bunyan's own life and career as minister of the Bedford separatist church and visitor to its associated churches in the eastern counties and in London. Explanatory notes have been kept to a minimum. However, a good measure of individual freedom has been left to editors in respect of the introductions and notes; it seemed, for instance, that *The Doctrine of the Law and Grace Unfolded*, Bunyan's chief theological treatise, required a fairly full consideration of his particular version of the theology of the two covenants, a dialectical system which may be said to provide the basic structure informing every work in these volumes, and indeed underlying the drama of salvation and damnation in *The Pilgrim's Progress* and the other allegories.

The first attempt at a complete edition was that of Charles Doe in the Folio of 1692. This was announced in an advertisement in *Mercurius Reformatus* for 11 June 1690:

Mr. *John Bunyan*, author of *The Pilgrim's Progress*, and many other excellent Books, that have found great acceptance, hath left behind him Ten Manuscripts prepared by himself for the Press before his Death: His Widow is desired to print them (with some other of his Works, which have been already printed but are at present not to be had), which will make together a book for 10s. in sheets, in Fol. All persons who desire so great and good a work should be performed with speed, are desired to send in 5s. for their first payment to Dorman Newman, at the King's Arms in the *Poultrey*, London: Who is empower'd to give receipts for the same.

A year later, Doe issued a pamphlet, *The Struggler* (1691), telling of his efforts to bring out a collected edition of his friend's works. But when the Folio finally appeared, it contained only ten works apart from the previously unpublished ones obtained from Bunyan's widow and her son John. These were, in the order in which they appeared: *Saved by Grace, Christian Behaviour, I Will Pray with the Spirit, The Strait Gate, Gospel-Truths Opened, A Vindication of Some Gospel-Truths Opened, Light for Them that Sit in Darkness, Instruction for the Ignorant, The Holy City: Or, The New Jerusalem, The Resurrection of the Dead.* It seems likely that Doe ran into trouble over copyrights, and was therefore not able to bring out the second volume that he had planned. It is noteworthy that none of Bunyan's best-selling books are represented in the Folio; it is difficult to imagine Nathaniel Ponder, another publisher in the Poultry, surrendering his control over that valuable property *The Pilgrim's Progress*; and it is significant that the Folio was finally published by William Marshall, and not by Dorman Newman, who has issued both editions of *The Holy War*. The Folio was published by subscription, and the many copies extant suggest that the subscription-list was a long one.

A second edition of the Folio was issued in 1736–7, and this included the second volume with those writings which Doe had been unable to assemble. The edition was edited by Ebenezer Chandler and Samuel Wilson (the son of Bunyan's friend John Wilson) and published by E. Gardner and John Marshall (the son of William Marshall). Three books were still not included, but these are found in the third edition of the collected works which appeared in two volumes in 1767, and was thus the first truly complete edition. There is a preface by George Whitefield. Another collected edition in six volumes by Alexander Hogg appeared in 1780.

In 1853 the complete works were re-edited by the devoted Bunyan scholar, George Offor. In the twentieth century this has continued to be the only collected edition available to the scholar. It contains an amount of painstaking if amateurish bibliographical information, and a verbose and often melodramatic evangelical commentary; as John Brown (Bunyan's biographer and minister of Bunyan Meeting, Bedford, 1854–1903) said: 'His notes . . . are occasionally a little superfluous, sometimes indeed raising a smile by their very simplicity.' Offor's edition was revised and reissued in three volumes (Edinburgh and London, 1860–2). There was also an edition in four volumes by Henry Stebbing (1859).

The great disaster of Bunyan studies was the fire which destroyed a great part of the Offor collection when it was to be auctioned at Sotheby's in 1865 (Tuesday, 29 June). Many of the surviving volumes came into the possession of Sir Leicester Harmsworth, and at the sale of the Harmsworth Collection at Sotheby's in February 1947 passed into various public libraries. Some remained in the family or were bought back by it, and at the death of Richard Offor, George Offor's grandson and former Librarian of the University of Leeds, were presented to Elstow Moot Hall in Bunyan's birthplace. Several of the copies consulted by the present editors are badly charred books from the Offor collection.

Coleridge once drew a distinction between the Bunyan of genius and the Bunyan of the conventicle. If we accept this, the bulk of the works in this new edition represent the Bunyan of the conventicle; but Coleridge's romantic premisses, which we have in part inherited, draw a far sharper line between genius and the man rooted in his historical accidents than accuracy will admit. There is much strong, plain, effective exhortation in the awakening sermons; many of the poems in *A Book for Boys and Girls* are real poems; more important, the *Miscellaneous Works* bring us up against the raw material, the subsoil, on which the spirit of English Puritanism which we breathe in *The Pilgrim's Progress* and experience in its historical succession is founded.

ROGER SHARROCK

CONTENTS

CONTENTS

REFERENCES AND ABBREVIATIONS

[*The place of publication, unless otherwise stated, is London*]

BUNYAN'S WORKS

The Works of that Eminent Servant of Christ, Mr. John Bunyan, edited by Charles Doe (1692)	*1692 Folio*
Grace Abounding to the Chief of Sinners (1666), edited by Roger Sharrock (Oxford, 1962)	*G.A.*
The Pilgrim's Progress from This World to That Which is to Come (1678), edited by J. B. Wharey, revised by Roger Sharrock (Oxford, 1960)	*P.P.*
A Defence of the Doctrine of Justification by Faith (1672)	*Defence*
Differences of Judgment about Water-Baptism (1673)	*Differences*
Good News for the Vilest of Men (1688)	*Good News*
The Holy War (1682)	*H.W.*
Light for them that Sit in Darkness (1675)	*Light*
A Discourse upon the Pharisee and the Publicane (1685)	*Pharisee*
Peaceable Principles and True (1674)	*Principles*
Of Justification by Imputed Righteousness (1692)	*Righteousness*
Saved by Grace (1676)	*Saved*
Christ a Compleat Saviour (1692)	*Saviour*
Solomon's Temple Spiritualiz'd (1688)	*Solomon*
The Strait Gate (1676)	*Strait Gate*
Some Gospel Truths Opened (1656)	*Truths*
A Vindication of Some Gospel Truths Opened (1657)	*Vindication*

OTHER WORKS

John Brown, *John Bunyan: his Life, Times and Work*, revised edition by Frank Mott Harrison (1928)	Brown
The Church Book of Bunyan Meeting 1650–1821, a facsimile edition with Introduction by G. B. Harrison (1928)	*Church Book*
Church History	CH
Richard L. Greaves, *John Bunyan* (*Studies in Reformation Theology* II, Abingdon, 1969)	Greaves
Frank Mott Harrison, *A Bibliography of the Works of John Bunyan* (Oxford, 1932)	Harrison

Journal of the History of Ideas	*JHI*
Journal of Ecclesiastical History	*JEH*
Oxford English Dictionary	*O.E.D.*
Roger Sharrock, *John Bunyan* (1968)	*Sharrock*
M. P. Tilley, *A Dictionary of Sixteenth and Seventeenth Century Proverbs and Proverbial Phrases* (Ann Arbor, Mich., 1951)	Tilley
William York Tindall, *John Bunyan: Mechanick Preacher* (New York, 1934)	Tindall
Transactions of the Baptist Historical Society	*Trans. Bapt. Hist. Soc.*
Transactions of the Congregational Historical Society	*Trans. Cong. Hist. Soc.*

INTRODUCTION

A. THE DOCTRINE OF THE LAW AND GRACE UNFOLDED

(i) *Bunyan in the 1650s*

THE years prior to the publication of *The Doctrine of the Law and Grace Unfolded* were crucial in Bunyan's life. As the decade of the 1650s opened, Bunyan had his military service behind him and had returned to his tinker's trade. His first child, a blind daughter, was baptized in July 1650. Now began an extended period of spiritual crisis. Subsequently he encountered the Bedford Separatists, and in 1655 joined their congregation, the founder and pastor of which was John Gifford. His spiritual turmoil was not yet settled, but the following year he began preaching in public in the surrounding area. He regarded himself as unworthy of the task, and professed amazement that his preaching produced results.[1] Public proclamation quickly broadened into public disputation when Bunyan encountered the first Quakers in Bedfordshire. In successive years he attacked their doctrine, particularly that of Edward Burrough, in *Some Gospel Truths Opened* (1656) and *A Vindication of Some Gospel Truths Opened* (1657). The following year he published *A Few Sighs from Hell, or the Groans of a Damned Soul*, drawing material from his sermons. The subject-matter suited the increased expectations of the time of an imminent Last Judgement. His first wife, of whom little is known, died in 1658, leaving him with four young children.

Law and Grace was published in 1659. Like his third work, it seems to be based largely on homiletical material. His earliest sermons had been primarily concerned with human corruption and the curse of God on all men in accordance with the law. It was preaching rooted in experience, as Bunyan testifies: 'Now this part of my work I fulfilled with great sence; for the terrours of the Law, and guilt for my transgressions, lay heavy on my Conscience.

[1] *G.A.*, § 273 (pp. 84–5).

I preached what I felt, what I smartingly did feel . . .' He went as one 'in chains to preach to them in chains, and carried that fire in my own conscience that I perswaded them to beware of'.[1] Relief from this spiritual agony came around 1658, though its effects are still reflected in the pages of *Law and Grace*. His sermons then began to be concerned more with the work and benefits of Christ,[2] and this concern is also present in *Law and Grace*. The treatise also reflects Bunyan's activities in these years on behalf of the Bedford church. *The Church Book* indicates that he was sent to visit wayward brethren and probably also candidates for church membership. In the course of such activity he undoubtedly thought about the 'signs' of election and damnation, which take up a good deal of *Law and Grace*, as well as arguments aimed at directing people to consider which of the covenants they were under. The material in the treatise, drawn from sermons and pastoral activities, reflects Bunyan's work in the period 1656–9, as well as his own earlier private religious experience.

(ii) *Sources of Bunyan's Thought*

Unlike most writers of theological treatises in seventeenth-century England, Bunyan had not studied theology at Oxford or Cambridge. He apparently taught himself the essentials of Protestant theology and gleaned what he could from ministerial friends. Regrettably he rarely indicates the materials he read or the conversations that took place with ministers. His writings show that he was convinced his message would bear greater weight if it rested on Biblical authority alone. There was probably a pragmatic reason for this: in most contests characterized by appeals to divines, Bunyan would probably have been a clear loser. There is, however, one extant account of his common-sense effectiveness in extempore debate. The debate took place in a barn with Thomas Smith, Professor of Arabic at Cambridge, and University Librarian, over the authority of Scripture.[3] Nevertheless, when Bunyan set out to refute Edward Fowler's *The Design of Christianity*, he discovered

---

[1] *G.A.*, §§ 276–7 (pp. 85–6). [2] *G.A.*, § 278 (p. 86).
[3] See below, p. xxxix.

that Fowler appealed to the continental reformers John Calvin, Peter Martyr, Wolfgang Musculus, and Jerome Zanchy. Bunyan retorted that his creed was based on Scripture alone,[1] a position that would appeal directly to many unversed in theological literature. In 1675 Bunyan reaffirmed that he had not 'borrowed my Doctrine from libraries',[2] but based his faith on the Bible alone.

Two points are certain. First, Bunyan would not have asserted any doctrine which he did not believe had Scriptural authority. Like others in the Puritan tradition, he pushed to an extreme the Protestant tenet of reliance on the sole authority of the Bible. Second, Bunyan was influenced by other Protestants in the formulation of his theology, though he chose to deny it for reasons of piety and practicality. The strength of his preaching lay in a resurgent consciousness of the inner working of God expressed with effective colloquial vigour. His sermons were fortified by an appeal to Scripture alone. Just as it would have been impractical to engage in a contest of citing secondary authorities, so it would have detracted from his piety to claim reliance on anything but the Holy Spirit for his beliefs. Thus in *The Doctrine of the Law and Grace Unfolded* he piously disparages his formal education and asserts that knowledge of God is dependent on the enlightenment of man by the Holy Spirit.[3]

Some of the sources which influenced the development of Bunyan's thought are known. Bunyan mentions several in his spiritual autobiography, *Grace Abounding to the Chief of Sinners*. When he married for the first time, his bride brought him Arthur Dent's *The Plaine Mans Path-way to Heauen* and Lewis Bayly's *The Practise of Pietie*.[4] Dent's was a popular handbook of piety which influenced Bunyan's literary method (notably the use of dialogue) as well as his thought. Bayly's work was a popular manual of devotion which appears to have exercised somewhat more influence on Bunyan than did Dent's handbook. Both writers were Calvinists. Although Bunyan does not fully agree with all of their ideas, their influence

---

[1] Edward Fowler, *The Design of Christianity* (1671), p. 84; and Bunyan, *Defence*, p. 29.
[2] *Light*, sig. A4.
[3] Below, pp. 16, 149.
[4] *G.A.*, § 15 (p. 8); see the accompanying note on p. 134.

can probably be seen in various aspects of his doctrines of God, predestination, faith, and, to a lesser degree, the church.[1]

Bunyan had been sufficiently impressed with the books of Dent and Bayly to write of them, 'I . . . found some things that were somewhat pleasing to me . . .'[2] A much greater impact was made on Bunyan by Martin Luther's commentary on Paul's Epistle to the Galatians. In the course of reading Luther he discovered that his own spiritual state was accurately depicted: 'I found my condition in his experience, so largely and profoundly handled, as if his Book had been written out of my heart . . .' In the early 1670s it was Bunyan's judgement that apart from the Bible Luther's commentary was 'most fit for a wounded Conscience'.[3] Bunyan again paid tribute to Luther in *The Pilgrim's Progress*. In the course of Christian's trying journey through the valley of the shadow of death 'he thought he heard the voice of a man, as going before him . . .'[4] The direct reference is to a well-known text in the Psalms (xxiii. 4), but indirectly Bunyan was alluding to Luther. Both Bunyan and Luther underwent profound psychological experiences in the course of their conversions, and Bunyan saw in Luther not only an expositor but also a spiritual guide with whom he felt an instinctive sympathy.

Luther probably had a greater influence on Bunyan than did any other writer. Bunyan envisaged God much as Luther had. Their God was conceived above all else in terms of the dichotomy of wrath and grace experientially perceived. This conception of God is fundamental to *The Doctrine of the Law and Grace Unfolded*. Luther's religious experience as well as his Biblical exposition had led him to the conclusion that 'the doctrine of grace can by no means stand with the doctrine of the law'.[5] This is precisely the theme of Bunyan's chief theological work. Bunyan was also influenced by Luther's concept of salvation as a present possession of the believer, and by his emphasis on the necessity of justification by grace and faith alone. Luther's repeated emphasis on these doctrines is clearly echoed in Bunyan's treatise.

---

[1] See Greaves.   [2] *G.A.*, § 15 (p. 8).
[3] *G.A.*, §§ 129–30 (pp. 40–1).   [4] *P.P.*, p. 64.
[5] *A Commentarie of Master Doctor Martin Luther upon the Epistle . . . to the Galathians* (1635), f. 30ᵛ.

Law and Grace also reveals the influence of John Gifford, pastor of the Separatist church at Bedford, who was presented to the living of the parish church of St. John's in 1653 under the Cromwellian establishment. Gifford talked with Bunyan and invited him to meetings with believers at his home.[1] Bunyan subsequently wrote that Gifford's doctrine 'was much for my stability'. It was Gifford's influence that led Bunyan to adopt the sectarian belief that religious truth came from the enlightening activity of the Holy Spirit. He 'pressed us to take special heed, that we took not up any truth upon trust, as from this or that or another man or men, but to cry mightily to God, that he would convince us of the reality thereof, and set us down therein, by his own Spirit in the holy Word . . .'[2] Gifford and his successor, John Burton, also influenced Bunyan in his doctrine of the church, which was based on the principles of separation, fellowship, freedom, and holiness.[3] From his ministers Bunyan learned that the only baptism necessary for church membership was the baptism of the Holy Spirit, not baptism by water. His concept of the Separatist church and his position on baptism are both reflected in *The Doctrine of the Law and Grace Unfolded*.[4]

In this treatise Bunyan makes a marginal reference to John Dod and Robert Cleaver's *A Plain and Familiar Exposition of the Ten Commandements* (1603).[5] Like the works of Dent and Bayly, this was a popular book that went through many editions. Like them also, it was Calvinist in its theology. Bunyan urged his readers to refer to this work for an exposition of the Ten Commandments, which he did not wish to undertake. Bunyan himself was influenced by the expository work of Dod and Cleaver. He stressed their assertion that 'whosoeuer will have any true comfort by his obedience to Gods law, must not content himselfe to looke to one, or two: but must make conscience, and haue a care to keepe them all and euery one'. He also appears to have taken particular notice of their treatment of the Law in spiritual terms. Dod and Cleaver

---

[1] *G.A.*, § 77 (p. 25).
[2] *G.A.*, § 117 (p. 37).
[3] The classic treatment of these principles is found in Geoffrey F. Nuttall, *Visible Saints* (Oxford, 1957).
[4] Below, pp. 61–2, 74, 182–3.   [5] Below, p. 35.

appended a short catechism to their exposition, which contains, among other things, a brief statement of the doctrine of predestination. Bunyan accepted this doctrine, which is stated in *Law and Grace*, though others (including Bayly and Luther) besides Dod and Cleaver were very likely responsible for influencing him to accept it. The theme of Bunyan's treatise is also stated in Dod and Cleaver's catechism:

> *What are the parts of the word?*
> The law and gracious promise (otherwise called the couenant of workes, and the couenant of grace,) which from the coming of Christ is called the Gospell.[1]

Dod and Cleaver are not, however, the sole source from which Bunyan develops his scheme of covenant thought.

Before 1659, then, it is certain that Bunyan was influenced in varying degrees by Dent, Bayly, Luther, Dod and Cleaver, Gifford, and probably Burton and John Gibbs, minister at Newport Pagnell and a friend of Bunyan. He was, of course, also aware of the views of Edward Burrough, the Quaker disputant. It is probable that Bunyan was influenced by yet another work or works in these early years of his Christian life. First, a number of legal terms or allusions appear in *Law and Grace*. The best examples are 'Premunire', 'replieve', 'indenting', and 'thrown over the bar'. There is no reason to believe Bunyan derived these terms from a legal work, for he had no occasion to read such a work before his imprisonment. Rather he probably learned these usages from reading the work of another Protestant writer. Second, Bunyan's exposition of the covenant scheme was in accord with that of other strict (as distinct from moderate) Calvinists. (See the following section.) There is insufficient material in the works he is known to have read to provide him with the requisite distinctions. It can therefore be reasonably concluded that Bunyan read the views of another strict Calvinist on the covenant in the late 1650s. The same work may have provided him with the legal terminology that he uses in this treatise.

The plan of the treatise is little more than a stereotype of Puritan-

[1] (17th ed., 1628), pp. 9, 8, 24, [341].

sectarian homiletic practice. Bunyan could have derived this from the sermons of Gifford and Burton as well as from reading any published sermons of the period. He had also been exposed to the sermons of the preachers associated with the Parliamentary army in the Civil War. Moreover, much of the illustrative material and queries about his spiritual state are autobiographical. There are numerous parallels between passages in this treatise and in *Grace Abounding*. Bunyan did not have to read widely to write *Law and Grace*, but there are unmistakable indications of influence from at least six or seven sources, most of them published. Late in life Bunyan wrote: 'My Bible and Concordance are my only Library in my writings.'[1] Bunyan may very well have normally refrained from consulting other authors as he actually wrote, but there can be no denying that in theology as well as in literary devices he was not free from debt to the work of other men. In the case of his early theology this debt was certainly to Luther, contemporary English Calvinism (especially the strict variety), and the open-membership, open-communion movement in the Separatist tradition.

(iii) *Bunyan and Covenant Theology*

English Calvinist theologians in the seventeenth century were increasingly caught up in the attempt to develop Christian doctrine in the context of a covenant scheme. The first English writer to popularize this trend was William Perkins in the late sixteenth century. Perkins had a marked interest in practical divinity— the cases of conscience posed by troubled parishioners to their ministers.[2] The chief of these questions among Calvinists was that of assurance. Perkins dealt with the matter in 1589 in his *Treatise Tending unto a Declaration Whether a Man Be in the Estate of Damnation or in the Estate of Grace*. In his subsequent writings he began to treat the question by expounding Christian doctrine in a covenant context, analysing the type of conduct and belief appropriate to

---

[1] *Solomon*, sig. A8. For a discussion of Bunyan's reliance on other authors, primarily with respect to literary devices, see Tindall, pp. 190–209.

[2] See Louis B. Wright, 'William Perkins: Elizabethan Apostle of "Practical Divinity" ', *Huntington Library Quarterly*, iii (Jan. 1940), 171–96.

those living under covenants of works and grace respectively. Spiritual introspection and self-analysis were urged as means to determine the answer to the question. The value of the covenant theme to deal with the problem of assurance was subsequently recognized and developed by such men as William Ames, John Preston, and Richard Sibbes.[1] Ultimately it became something of a hallmark of most writers in the Puritan tradition.

The covenant idea had been receiving increased attention in England and on the Continent before Perkins recognized its potential value in a pastoral and psychological context. The idea of the covenant appears, of course, in the Old and New Testaments, and Christian writers made use of it from the earliest times. But Perkins caused a marked increase in the popularity of the idea. Some of those who wrote after him emphasized the contractual nature of the covenant in which the respective commitments of God and man as contracting parties were spelled out for all to perceive. The sovereignty of God and the necessity of grace were clearly recognized, but the role of man in the scheme of salvation was more strongly emphasized. Other writers, including Bunyan (whose *Law and Grace* is his principal exposition of covenant theology), minimized the reciprocal element in the covenant. Instead they treated the covenant of grace essentially as God's unilateral, absolute promise of salvation to his elect. Archbishop James Ussher, for example, emphasized that the covenant of grace was made by 'God alone, for properly man hath no more power to make a spirituall Covenant in his naturall estate, then before his creation he had to promise obedience'. Likewise John Owen insisted that 'the condition of the Covenant is not said to be required, but it is absolutely promised . . .'[2]

The development of covenant theology had important ramifications within the Puritan tradition. Recent scholarship has emphasized the significance of the experiential element in Puritanism.[3]

---

[1] See C. J. Sommerville, 'Conversion *Versus* the Early Puritan Covenant of Grace', *Journal of Presbyterian History*, xliv (Sept. 1966), 178–97; and John von Rhor, 'Covenant and Assurance in Early English Puritanism, *CH*, xxxiv (June 1965), 195–203.

[2] Ussher, *A Body of Divinitie* (1647), p. 158; Owen, *Salus electorum, sanguis Jesu: or the Death of Death in the Death of Christ* (1648), p. 103, cf. pp. 103 ff.

[3] See, e.g., James F. Maclear, ' "The Heart of New England Rent": The Mystical Element in Early Puritan History', *Mississippi Valley Historical Review*, xlii (Mar.

Yet it is essential to recognize that the covenant theme 'provided a theological consistency for experiential notions',[1] and that in many cases the nature of acceptable experience was rigidly conceived. Covenant theologians carefully depicted the soteriological process and the godly disposition requisite for it, which became controlling norms for experience. Faith did not lose its experiential quality, but the nature of that experience was determined by criteria fundamentally intellectual though they were applied to the emotional life.[2] Thus experience plays a key role in Bunyan's exposition of the covenants, but he always firmly defines the nature of what is to be experienced. Even *Grace Abounding*, a classic example of the psychological turmoil of a man struggling to determine whether he was a party to the covenant of grace, conforms to the general pattern of experience established as correct by earlier covenant writers. Ultimately, then, the seeker of assurance is faced with a series of experiences which he must personally undergo if he desires even nominal assurance of participation in the covenant of grace. Within the broad Puritan tradition there was generally nothing like experiential freedom on account of the precise and rigid accounts of spiritual experience given in authoritative expositions of the covenants.

The antecedents of covenant theology have been traced.[3] The

---

1956), 621–52; Norman Pettit, *The Heart Prepared: Grace and Conversion in Puritan Spiritual Life* (New Haven, 1966); and Geoffrey F. Nuttall, *The Holy Spirit in Puritan Faith and Experience* (Oxford, 1946).

[1] Pettit, *The Heart Prepared*, p. 11. Jerald C. Brauer observed that covenant theology was 'an ideal theological structure to bear the Puritan religiousness. It contained within it the possibility of stressing both the emotional and the rational, the subjective and the objective.' 'Reflections on the Nature of English Puritanism', *CH*, xxiii (June 1954), 104. The covenant was also used for political purposes by Puritan preachers. See John F. Wilson, *Pulpit in Parliament* (Princeton, N.J., 1969), Chap. VI.

[2] See Robert Middlekauff, 'Piety and Intellect in Puritanism', *William and Mary Quarterly*, 3rd Ser., xxii (July 1965), 457–70.

[3] L. J. Trinterud, 'The Origins of Puritanism,' *CH*, xx (Mar. 1951), 37–57; J. G. Møller, 'The Beginnings of Puritan Covenant Theology', *JEH*, xiv (Apr. 1963), 46–7; Greaves, 'The Origins and Early Development of English Covenant Thought', *Historian*, xxxi (Nov. 1968), 21–35; 'John Knox and the Covenant Tradition', *JEH*, xxiv (Jan. 1973), 23–32; and 'John Bunyan and Covenant Thought in the Seventeenth Century', *CH*, xxxvi (June 1967), 151–69. Perry Miller's works are still classics. Especially relevant are *The New England Mind: The Seventeenth Century* (New York, 1939) and various pieces in *Errand into the Wilderness* (Cambridge, Mass., 1956). For a recent discussion of Miller's theses, see Michael McGiffert, 'American

view of the covenant that stresses its reciprocal element and the responsibility incumbent on man as the result of the essentially legalistic vows taken in baptism can be traced back to William Tyndale and the Swiss Reformers Ulrich Zwingli and Heinrich Bullinger. The sacraments are important for their interpretation of the covenants. The sacraments are signs and seals of the covenant of grace, but are also ceremonies in which vows to God are undertaken. The condition of the covenant on man's part is to worship and obey God; failure to fulfil this condition means the failure to receive God's blessing. In the words of Tyndale, 'God bindeth himself to fulfil that mercy unto thee only if thou wilt endeavour thyself to keep his laws . . .'[1] This interpretation of the covenant can be traced through the writings of such Englishmen as John Bale, John Hooper, and the Separatist Robert Browne. In the seventeenth century the emphasis on a reciprocal covenant was continued by writers such as Richard Baxter, John Ball, Thomas Blake, Anthony Burgess, Samuel Rutherford, and Stephen Geree.

The view of the covenant emphasizing its promissory nature can be traced back to John Calvin. Certainly Calvin did not deny man's responsibility in the covenant with God, but the emphasis was placed on the belief that 'the covenant is at the outset drawn up as a free agreement, and perpetually remains such'.[2] Calvin's marked concern with divine sovereignty is manifested in his treatment of the covenant of grace as fundamentally a unilateral promise from God, with the contractual element subordinated but not obliterated. From the publication of the Genevan translation of the Bible in 1560, Calvin's concept of an essentially promissory covenant became increasingly popular in Calvinist circles in England. His influence can be seen in the writings of John Robinson, William Perkins, and numerous contemporaries of Bunyan, including John Owen, Thomas Goodwin, Samuel Petto, John Tombes, and Archbishop James Ussher. Those who carried this tradition to its ex-

---

Puritan Studies in the 1960's', *William and Mary Quarterly*, 3rd Ser. xxvii (Jan. 1970), 36–67.

[1] *Doctrinal Treatises and Introductions to Different Portions of the Holy Scriptures*, ed. Henry Walter (Cambridge, 1848), p. 403.

[2] *Institutes of the Christian Religion*, ed. John T. McNiell and trans. Ford Lewis Battles (Philadelphia, 1960), III. xvii. 5.

treme became Antinomians. They included John Saltmarsh, Tobias Crisp, Vavasor Powell, and Walter Cradock.

The covenant tradition to which numerous contemporaries of Bunyan adhered provides a convenient means of classifying them. Those who adhered to the reciprocal-covenant emphases of Zwingli and Tyndale may be designated 'moderate Calvinists', whereas those who followed Calvin in his emphasis on a promissory covenant may be designated 'strict Calvinists'. Those who pushed beyond the strict Calvinists were Antinomians, and those who emphasized human responsibility to the extent of accepting man's free will were, of course, Arminians. In *Law and Grace* Bunyan demonstrates his basic adherence to the strict Calvinist tradition, though on occasion he evinces Antinomian influence. The moderate Calvinist, Richard Baxter, in fact attacked Bunyan's treatise in 1690 as Antinomian and a book which 'ignorantly subverted the Gospel of Christ'.[1]

Key areas of debate for these groups were the nature of the covenants of works and grace, and the place of law in the latter. With respect to the covenant of works Bunyan was firmly a strict Calvinist. Unlike the moderate Calvinists and Arminians, Bunyan did not believe the covenant of works was that established initially by God. The first covenant entered into was the covenant between the Father and the Son, which was a covenant of grace. Nevertheless the first covenant manifested to man was the covenant of works, the chief task of which was to make man aware of his need for the covenant of grace. The covenant of works was initially made with Adam, stipulating that he render perfect obedience to the Law of God. Adam's sin violated that ordinance and, according to Bunyan, corrupted all mankind. Man became depraved and unable to fulfil any of the divine commands. The covenant of works as a means of attaining eternal life was for ever lost to all men. Man—specifically the elect—could be saved from damnation only through the covenant of grace.

For Bunyan the covenant of grace was God's gracious promise of the forgiveness of sins. With Antinomians and strict Calvinists

---

[1] Baxter, *The Scripture Gospel Defended, and Christ, Grace and Free Justification Vindicated against the Libertines* (1690), sig. A2.

Bunyan conceived of this covenant as first formed between the Father and the Son. It was thus so firmly established that nothing could shake it. It was entered into before the creation of man, and was the groundwork upon which the eternal salvation of the elect perpetually rested. As developed in *Law and Grace*, the covenant between the Father and the Son is used by Bunyan to assure struggling Christians of the permanence of their faith and the unquestionable reality of their ultimate salvation. Because the parties to the original contract were divine, and because the implications of that contract for man were promissory in nature, nothing could be more certain than the ultimate triumph of all the elect.

The certainty of salvation in a covenant context is indicated by Bunyan in yet another way. In this treatise he informed his readers that it was God who brought sinners into the covenant of grace. Subsequently, in *The Pilgrim's Progress*, he made the same point in dramatic imagery when he had Good-Will (divine grace) open the wicket gate for Christian.[1] Scrutiny of this scene reveals that Christian had first to ask Good-Will whether he could gain admittance, but this squares with Bunyan's exhortations in *Law and Grace* to the sinner to seek faith from God. The main point is incontrovertible: just as Good-Will was the only one who could open the gate, so God alone could bring the sinner into the covenant of grace. Bunyan subsequently made this explicit in the commentary on the first part of Genesis (which remained unpublished during his lifetime):

We read not here [Gen. ix. 15, where the covenant is manifested to Noah] of any Compact or Agreement between Noah and God Almighty; wherefore such Conditions and Compacts could not be the Terms between him and us; What then? why that Covenant that he calls his, which is his gift to us, I will give thee for a Covenant; this is the Covenant which is between God and us: There is one God, and one Mediator between God and Man, the Man Christ Jesus.[2]

The elect covenant with God only as their mediator has covenanted for them. The conditions required by the Father are not conditions

<hr />

[1] *P.P.*, p. 25.   [2] *1692 Folio*, p. 67.

fulfilled by man but by the Son. In *Law and Grace*, therefore, the reader discovers that Bunyan is primarily occupied with the Son's fulfilment of the Father's covenant conditions rather than with man's responsibilities. Even with respect to the faith required of man, that faith is a gift of God implanted in the elect by the Holy Spirit. One is reminded that in *The Holy War* Captain Credence (faith) is not a resident of Mansoul (the elect individual) but one of Emanuel's officers. Bunyan would not agree that man had the natural capacity to believe effectually, and so fulfil a covenant condition by himself. Neither would he accept the thesis that divine grace was given to all men to enable them to believe if they so decided. All must be done by the Son for the elect. This does, of course, assure the acceptability of the covenant conditions fulfilled for the elect by Christ.

Bunyan's analysis of the covenant of grace does not make much of the contractual relationship between God and man. The conditions are fulfilled for man by the Son; the agreement is essentially completed. Bunyan's interpretation, unlike that of the moderate Calvinists, did not provide ample opportunity to develop a set of obligations to be fulfilled by man, even when aided by grace. The gulf between Bunyan's position and that of the Arminians was sharply delineated. The noted Arminian Independent John Goodwin repeatedly stresses that the 'proper and immediate end' of the covenant of grace is 'to give Assurance unto ... Men, that upon *their* Faith and Repentance, and *their* Perseverance in both unto the end, they shall have Salvation and Eternal Life conferred upon them'. The element of human responsibility is also underscored by the moderate Calvinist Stephen Geree: Man 'must doe something, he must give his consent, and agree to the Articles, before the Covenant can actually be made'.[1] For Bunyan, however, the sovereignty of God in salvation had to be preserved without hint of compromise. But why, then, speak in terms of a covenant relationship at all? The Antinomian preacher John Saltmarsh asked himself this question and concluded that 'it were good, that we did not rest

---

[1] John Goodwin, Ἀπολύτρωσις ἀπολυτρώσεως or *Redemption Redeemed* (1651), p. 456; Geree, *The Doctrine of the Antinomians by Evidence of Gods Truth Plainely Confuted* (1644), p. 98.

too much in the notion of a Covenant . . .' The covenant, Saltmarsh believed, was only an allusion; the promise was fact.[1] Bunyan, however, retained the covenant concept not only because it had Biblical precedent, but also because his emphasis was on the contractual relationship between the Father and the Son, which (as he described it) had all the basic characteristics of a legal covenant.

Bunyan's position on baptism by water, briefly stated in this treatise, was particularly conducive to his exposition of covenant thought. For Calvinists, especially of the strict variety, the covenant of grace was made with the elect only. For those who believed that water baptism was a sign and seal of the covenant of grace, a disturbing enigma occurred when baptized persons strayed from a profession of Christianity. One solution to the problem (advocated by Baptists) was to baptize only adults who had firmly confessed adherence to Christian beliefs. Even these people could, however, stray from the church. Alternatively, one could distinguish between those really in the covenant of grace and those only apparently in the covenant. In this case baptism was sometimes only an apparent sign or seal. Bunyan, however, did not require baptism by water for church membership. Consequently he was not faced with the problem of baptism as a sign or seal of the covenant of grace. The only essential baptism for Bunyan, as he suggests in this treatise, is the baptism of the Holy Spirit.

To be baptized with the Holy Spirit was to be brought into the covenant of grace. Once in the covenant of grace there was no way for that covenant to be broken and the individual eternally damned. The reason was simple. Fulfilment of the conditions had been undertaken by the Son for the elect. Nothing man could do could alter what the Son had already accomplished. Whether he obeyed God or whether he sinned had no effect on the permanence of the covenant. Once Good-Will had opened the wicket gate, eternal destiny with God was assured. Those, however, who had clambered over the wall rather than passed through the gate had no such assurance and security. Bunyan never simplistically identified church membership or the profession of Christianity with involvement in the covenant of grace.

---

[1] *Free-grace: Or, the Flowings of Christs Blood Freely to Sinners* (1645), p. 153.

The recurring theme of *Law and Grace* is that those party to the covenant of grace are no longer subject to the consequences decreed for violation of the covenant of works (the Mosaic Law). The theme is distinctly Pauline (Rom. vi. 14), though the Apostle had not cast his discussion of law and grace in covenant terms. Paul had not intended his doctrine to be construed as an invitation to licentiousness. Apart from a few extremists, seventeenth-century writers agreed that freedom under grace had limitations. The difficulty arose in attempting to give concrete expression to those limitations. In *The Holy War* Bunyan portrayed Emanuel granting Mansoul 'the holy Law, and my Testament, with all that therein is contained, for their everlasting comfort and consolation'.[1] This law provided the elect with limitations on their freedom as parties to the covenant of grace. The covenant had, in other words, a legal aspect. This did not mean that the believer was bound to obey the Mosaic Law or face damnation. It meant instead that there existed a 'Law of Grace', and that the saint was 'not without Law to God, but under the Law to Christ'.[2] This was Pauline teaching (1 Cor. ix. 21), and was commonly accepted. Even the Antinomian Walter Cradock admitted that 'Christ hath lift up a standard & expects that every one should submit to his blessed Law.'[3]

Difficulty arose, however, in trying to determine the precise nature of the law of grace. For Bunyan the essence of the law was expressed by Jesus (Mark xii. 29–31) in his commands to love God and one's neighbour as oneself. This was the essence of the Ten Commandments, the heart of the Mosaic Law. Saints were not exempt from the Mosaic Law in this sense, but they were exempt from the 'ministration' of the Mosaic Law as given in the Old Testament. Moderate Calvinists rejected such a distinction, contending that the Mosaic prescriptions were still in force for believers. Anthony Burgess accuses those making a distinction such as Bunyan's of being Antinomians,[4] but Bunyan stops short of

---

[1] *H.W.*, p. 214.

[2] *The Work of Jesus Christ as an Advocate* (1688), p. 105; and *1692 Folio*, p. 191.

[3] Cradock, *Gospel-Libertie, in the Extensions [and] Limitations of It* (1648), p. 38; but cf. pp. 18 and 43. See Geoffrey F. Nuttall, *The Welsh Saints 1640–1660* (Cardiff, 1957), p. 69.

[4] *Vindiciae Legis* (2nd ed., 1647), p. 214.

Antinomianism (cf. below, p. 174). The difference between the strict Calvinist and the Antinomian on the place of the Law in the believer's life was largely one of emphasis. John Saltmarsh states the Antinomian case:

Though the Law be a beam of Christ in substance and matter, yet we are not to live by the light of one beam now when the Sun of righteousnesse is risen himself. . . . What need we light up a Candle for the children of the day to see by? . . . Nor doth it become the glory of Christ revealed, to be beholding to any of the light upon Moses face.[1]

Bunyan, on the other hand, carefully sought to impress his readers that the Mosaic Law or Ten Commandments was a guide for saints, a rule for the Christian life. A holy life was a life lived in accordance with the precepts of the Law. The Law was viewed appropriately when it informed the believer of his transgressions, but not when it pronounced judgement on him. The Law could serve as guide, but not saviour or judge.

Bunyan was closest to the Antinomians when he sought to interpret Romans viii. 2, which contrasts the law of the Spirit with the law of sin and death. In this sense Bunyan referred to the law of grace as a new law—a phrase popular with the Antinomians. He believed this new law was 'written and preserv'd' in 'the Heart spiritual', a statement not too far removed from Saltmarsh's Antinomian assertion that the Holy Spirit makes the believer 'the very Law of Commandments in himself, and his heart the very two Tables of Moses . . .'[2] Such views prompted Richard Baxter to warn his readers about those sectaries who asserted that 'the first Covenant is Moral as a Law, and the second Covenant is the very in-being of a Divine Nature . . .'[3] Bunyan, however, shied from Antinomian subjectivity, associating the new law of grace with the essence of the old law. 'The whole Law, as to the morality of it, is delivered into the hand of Christ, who imposes it now . . . as a Rule of life to those that have believed in him . . .'[4] Those party

[1] *Free-grace*, pp. 146–7.
[2] Bunyan, *Questions about the . . . Seventh-day-sabbath* (1685), p. 35; and Saltmarsh, *Free-grace*, p. 146.
[3] Baxter, *Catholick Theologie* (1675), Book I, part 1, chap. ccliv.
[4] *Questions about the . . . Seventh-day-sabbath*, p. 38.

to the covenant of grace therefore had a stringent set of ethical standards to strive for, but continuation in the covenant was not based on attaining the full standard of obedience prescribed by Christ.

According to his exposition of the covenants, with the corollary doctrines of divine sovereignty, predestination, and salvation, Bunyan should logically have contented himself with caring for the spiritual needs of professed believers or simply stating God's ways to man to those outside the church. Yet repeatedly in *Law and Grace* and elsewhere he encourages his readers to take action themselves. They cannot open the wicket gate; they cannot fulfil a covenant condition without effectual grace, which few men were given; all covenant conditions are in the hands of the Son, not men. But Bunyan in a sense advocates his own practical 'doctrine' of preparation.[1] Those who would be clean in God's sight are

[1] The basic study of the doctrine of preparation is Pettit's *The Heart Prepared*, especially Chaps. I and III. Bunyan did not develop his incipient concept of preparation into a regular doctrine, although it was so developed elsewhere, especially in New England. Nor did he conceive of it as did William Perkins, John Preston, Richard Sibbes, and William Ames (see below), who developed the idea of preparation in conjunction with man's responsibilities in the covenant of grace. That line of thought ultimately weakened Calvinism seriously: 'The federal theology circumscribed providence by tying it to the behavior of the saints; then with the extension of the field of behavior through the elaboration of the work of preparation, the destiny of New England was taken out of the hands of God and put squarely into the keeping of the citizens.' Bunyan's theology avoided such a development by its emphasis on the covenant of grace being between the Father and the Son. Cf. Perry Miller, ' "Preparation for Salvation" in Seventeenth-Century New England', *JHI*, iv (June 1943), 286; cf. pp. 257–63.

William Perkins (1558–1602) studied under Lawrence Chaderton at Christ's College, Cambridge, and was appointed Lecturer at Great St. Andrew's. As Fellow of Christ's, his noted pupils included William Ames and John Robinson. He vacated his fellowship in 1594, and died in 1602. His principal works include *De Praedestinationis modo et ordino* (Cambridge, 1598), *A Treatise of God's Free Grace and Man's Free Will* (Cambridge, 1602), and *The Whole Treatise of the Cases of Conscience* (Cambridge, 1606 and 1608).

William Ames (1576–1633) studied under Perkins at Christ's College, Cambridge. He was forbidden to preach at Colchester by the Bishop of London, and went to Leyden. There he engaged in doctrinal controversies. He attended the Synod of Dort. He was appointed to the chair of theology at Franeker, taking up duties in 1622. Four years later he became Rector of the University. Ill health caused his removal to Rotterdam, where he was to become pastor of an English congregation. He died shortly after his move. His major works include *Medulla Theologia* (an exposition of Calvinism published in Latin and subsequently in English) and *De Conscientia* (Amsterdam, 1631), a major work on casuistry.

John Preston (1587–1628) studied at King's College, Cambridge, and Queens,

encouraged to discover their spiritual filth by reading the Bible, especially the Mosaic Law. They are told to reckon themselves the greatest sinners in the world. They must let feelings of guilt seize on their hearts. Then they must approach Christ and 'plunge thy self into his Merits, and the vertue of his Blood . . .' Bunyan assumes that the sinner, in spite of his depraved state, is able to 'flye in all haste to Jesus Christ . . .'[1] Curiously, man can do nothing to save himself, but apparently he cannot be saved unless he makes the trek from the City of Destruction to the wicket gate as the preparation for his salvation. The grace of God is like a flowing river, and the would-be saint must do his utmost to place himself in the river's path.

(iv) Law and Grace, Grace Abounding, *and* The Pilgrim's Progress

The strongly personal character of Bunyan's early writing is revealed in the amount of autobiographical material which he included in *Law and Grace*, and which is consummated in *Grace Abounding*. The parallels extend from accounts of his schooling to the nature of his religious experience and indications of personal preferences. In *Law and Grace*, Bunyan reports that he was raised at his father's house and was never educated in the writings of Plato and Aristotle (p. 16). This account is somewhat modified in his spiritual autobiography, where he indicates that his parents sought

---

College, Cambridge. He was markedly moved by a sermon preached by John Cotton *c.* 1611, and thereafter studied divinity. He was appointed Dean and Catechist of Queens', and succeeded John Donne as preacher at Lincoln's Inn in 1622. The same year he was elected Master of Emmanuel College, Cambridge. Two years later he was appointed Lecturer at Trinity College, Cambridge. Among his writings are *The New Covenant* (1629) and numerous sermons.

Richard Sibbes (1577–1635) was educated at St. John's College, Cambridge, where he was appointed a Fellow in 1601. He was deprived in 1615 of his fellowship and his position as Lecturer at Holy Trinity Church, Cambridge, because of his Puritan views. Two years later he became preacher at Gray's Inn. In 1626 he was appointed Master of St. Catharine's Hall, Cambridge. From 1626 to 1633 he was also a Feoffee for Impropriations. His published works include numerous devotional pieces and sermons, many of them published posthumously and edited by such leading Puritans as Thomas Goodwin and Philip Nye.

[1] Below, p. 17; cf. pp. 198–9, 218.

to put him to school despite their humble background (§ 3). In both works he portrays himself in youth as one who was a thorough-going sinner and much inclined to the company of evil companions (p. 157 and §§ 11, 43). The young Bunyan was given to swearing (p. 156 and § 26) and a love of sin (p. 157 and § 23). Both works likewise reveal some of his preferences: for games (p. 157 and § 21), for dancing (p. 157 and § 35), and for music (pp. 70, 124 and § 298).

Law and Grace contains a variety of references to Bunyan's conversion experience that were subsequently amplified in *Grace Abounding*. Both works record the Sabbath incident when a heavenly voice interrupted his game of cat (p. 157 and § 22). In *Law and Grace* Bunyan testifies to the fruitlessness of trying to find religious peace by obeying the law (p. 55); his efforts are explained more fully in his autobiography (§§ 28–36). His initial turning to religion is recorded in *Law and Grace* (pp. 157–8) and amplified in *Grace Abounding* (§ 30). The Ranters are warned of their erroneous beliefs in *Law and Grace* (pp. 209–10), but in his autobiography Bunyan reveals that he himself was almost enticed by those beliefs in his search for inner peace (§§ 44–5). The pressing question of assurance of election is noted in both works (pp. 214–15 and § 59). Virtually Arminian in its implications is Bunyan's continuing concern with the 'day of grace'—the period during which God's grace was extended to an individual (pp. 211–13 and § 66). Firmer footing was established through his psycho-visual perception of Christ and his work for man, which was verified for Bunyan through Biblical testimony (p. 158 and § 120). Then came the traumatic experience associated with the dread of the unpardonable sin (p. 201 and §§ 148 ff.). The subsequent conviction of the nature of the believer's righteousness, which Bunyan believed was inspired, is recorded in both works (p. 147 and §§ 229–30). His bout of consumption and the accompanying spiritual crisis is also recorded in both works (pp. 147–8 and §§ 255–9). Above all, the intensive nature of Bunyan's conversion experience is revealed in *Law and Grace* as well as in *Grace Abounding* (cf., e.g., p. 159 and § 276). Finally, Bunyan's interest in recording his religious experience is revealed in *Law and Grace* before it finds an outlet in his spiritual autobiography (p. 156; cf. §92). *Law and Grace* is consequently important not only for Bunyan's thought but also for his biography.

Law and Grace is also essential for a fuller understanding of *The Pilgrim's Progress* for which it provides a theological foundation. Moreover *Law and Grace* anticipates *The Pilgrim's Progress* in certain respects: the occasional use of typology (e.g. pp. 91, 93, 94, 97) foreshadows its more extensive use in the allegory just as the questions and answers in *Law and Grace* anticipate the use of dialogue in *The Pilgrim's Progress*. The autobiographical element is also present in both works. Of greatest significance, however, is the parallel structure of the believer's experience as it is portrayed in the two works.

At the outset of *The Pilgrim's Progress*, Christian is depicted as a man clothed in rags with a great burden on his back. He is a man, according to *Law and Grace*, who is living under the covenant of works. Although the treatise devotes much space to depicting the condition of man under this covenant, Bunyan spends little time in the allegory moving Christian from the covenant of works to the covenant of grace. Throughout the pilgrimage, however, he has Christian confront characters who often manifest attitudes characteristic of those living under the covenant of works. The states of mind of Mr. Worldly-Wiseman, Atheist, and Talkative, for example, are signs of reprobation. It matters not whether they are, as Bunyan explains in *Law and Grace*, openly profane or more refined sinners (pp. 52 ff.). Equally damned is the man who seeks to avoid sin by adhering to the precepts of the law. Bunyan portrays him as Mr. Legality of the village of Morality. Christian, attracted to this possibility before he entered the wicket gate, was prevented from reaching the village by his fear of the overhanging hill—Mount Sinai, the law. If Christian had arrived at Mr. Legality's house and taken up residence in Morality, he would still have remained under the covenant of works and been subject to damnation. Bunyan emphasizes this point in *Law and Grace* (e.g. pp. 54 ff.). Ignorance of this fact, he warns, will be no excuse.

Christian is saved from damnation only because he is brought by Good-Will (divine grace) into the new covenant, the covenant of grace. But the manner of entrance in *The Pilgrim's Progress* is more in keeping with Bunyan's experience as recorded in *Grace Abounding* than it is with Bunyan's theology as it is set forth in *Law and Grace*. According to the latter, the covenant of grace was made between God the Father and his Son, and all the elect were part of the covenant before creation (pp. 88 ff.). In this sense entering the wicket gate was merely a recognition of a *fait accompli*, though it was a requirement for all pilgrims. Those entering via other routes, such as Formalist and Hypocrisy, were reprobates. Once in the gate, however, Bunyan requires Christian to plod yet further until he arrives at the cross, where he is relieved of his burden (sin) and receives new clothing (the righteousness of Christ imputed to the sinner, p. 86). Theologically the delay between entering the gate and the activities at the cross is intolerable, but it is experientially verifiable for Bunyan (cf. p. 157) and various fellow Calvinists. The early stages of the pilgrimage do not bring unrelieved assurance. Even after the burden was removed from Christian's back there were spiritual crises. The Hill Difficulty had to be climbed; Mistrust and Timorous had to be encountered; Doubting Castle had to be endured. Perhaps with unconscious insight Bunyan was revealing to his readers that the pilgrim *had* to doubt and undergo temptation; these were the signs of election, and thus in a sense marks of assurance. Such was one of the prime paradoxes of the Puritan tradition. (The intensity of the experience, however, could and did vary. This is a primary theme of the story of Christiana and Great-heart in the second part of *The Pilgrim's Progress*.)

For Christian the key to the successful overcoming of these trials was the promises. The importance attributed to them in *The Pilgrim's Progress* is a reflection of the role allotted them in *Law and Grace* in accordance with the nature of the new covenant. Because the conditions of that covenant were fulfilled for the elect by Christ, the covenant blessings come to the elect as promises (pp. 128-9, 153-4). Christian's trials are doubtful in outcome only as long as he neglects to rely on the promises. Their usefulness for the elect is manifested even before Christian passes through the wicket gate. It is the promises that provide the exit from the Slough of Despond, underscoring Bunyan's conviction that the covenant of grace is first and foremost a contract between the Father and the Son. Christian is a beneficiary of covenant promises even before he has individually covenanted with God.

After recollecting certain phases of his conversion experience (pp. 143–6), Bunyan anticipates Christian's visit to the Interpreter's House by referring to the enlightened understanding bestowed on the elect following their justification by imputed righteousness (pp. 147–8). Justification and enlightenment do not mean peace but the furious onslaught of the forces of evil. The onslaught comes from within as well as from without (pp. 150–1), just as it does in *The Pilgrim's Progress*. Apollyon, Vanity Fair, and Giant Despair await Christian. The Calvinist knows, though he sometimes forgets, that perseverance is assured to those in the new covenant (pp. 192–200). Thus Christian is shown that no amount of water can quench the fire in the believer as long as it is fuelled with the oil of divine grace. Hopeful was more mindful of this than Christian when the two were imprisoned in the Doubting Castle of Giant Despair. Bunyan was in that Castle more than once in his religious experience, as he relates in *Law and Grace* (pp. 158–60). As always, release came by recollection of the promises. There was an apparently easier way, as Christian discovered on Mount Caution. The rough road of the pilgrim could be avoided, but only at the cost of passing through the stile into the meadow that led back to Doubting Castle, and ultimately to a blind wandering among tombstones.

Perseverance did not rule out the possibility of slipping back into sin during the pilgrimage (p. 166). One such sin was becoming too assured of election. Christian, with Hopeful following, was victimized in this manner by Mr. Vain-confidence. But the covenant could not be broken, and Christian and Hopeful were preserved, though not without suffering the suitable tribulation of despair (pp. 166–7). Meditating on the problem of despair in *Law and Grace*, Bunyan anticipated the figure of Little-faith when he explained to his readers that the ups and downs of the pilgrimage were due primarily to the failure of the pilgrim to realize that the continuity of the covenant was not dependent on his performance

(p. 167). Thus Bunyan used the covenant notion as an exhortation to assurance rather than an admonition to perform reciprocal conditions in order to keep the covenant in force.

One of the gravest doubts that could plague the pilgrim was the fear of committing the unpardonable sin. As Christian wandered in the valley of the shadow of death, a wicked creature suggested grievous blasphemies to him in such a manner that Christian believed they were his own. Quite possibly Bunyan was recalling his own fears that he had committed the unpardonable sin (*G.A.*, § 148). That fear is dealt with extensively in *Law and Grace* (pp. 201–10). The space accorded to it reflects the impact which it had on Bunyan's religious experience. But by 1678 the memory had waned, and the unpardonable sin was not accorded a major role in *The Pilgrim's Progress*.

The figure of Ignorance, which dominates the closing pages of the first part of *The Pilgrim's Progress*, is paralleled in a major dialogue towards the end of *Law and Grace*. In both cases Bunyan is dealing with those who are not averse to religion—indeed they have a modest knowledge of Christian doctrine (as does Talkative); yet they persist in being blind to the only acceptable path to salvation. For this they must be eternally damned, even if they persist in their belief throughout their lives and remain religious if not Christian (pp. 172–6). What a man does is basically inconsequential; what matters is the spirit in which he acts and believes (pp. 179 ff.).

Finally, it is worth noting that the role accorded to the church is more pronounced in *The Pilgrim's Progress* than in *Law and Grace*. Christian enters the House Beautiful, but not until he has passed through the wicket gate and received new clothing at the cross. The House Beautiful has no soteriological significance, though it clearly reflects Bunyan's experience with the Bedford congregation. In *Law and Grace* Bunyan states that he is not opposed to churches governed in accordance with Gospel principles (e.g. p. 183), but unlike most covenant theologians he persistently refuses to associate the covenant of grace with either the church or the sacraments. In both works the church and sacraments are clearly incidental to the primary thrust of the believer's experience.

B. I WILL PRAY WITH THE SPIRIT

(i) Bunyan's First Imprisonment

The year 1659 was an eventful year in Bunyan's life. Early in 1659, he married Elizabeth, about whom virtually nothing is known before her marriage to Bunyan. Throughout the year he continued preaching and disputing, undoubtedly aware of the dangers involved. Two years earlier he had been indicted for preaching at Eaton Socon, though the case was dropped. Despite the freedom of the Commonwealth and Protectorate, a conservative reaction was setting in.

In 1659 Bunyan was also involved in a controversy with the Quakers on the matter of witchcraft. A Margaret Pryor, who occasionally attended Quaker meetings, claimed to have been temporarily turned into a mare by a Quaker 'witch' known as Widow Morlin. Bunyan believed the alleged victim and wrote a pamphlet or broadside attacking the Quakers for practising witchcraft. Bunyan's pamphlet has been lost, but the original charges are contained in *The Strange & Terrible Newes from Cambridge Being a True Relation of the Quakers Bewitching of Mary Philips* [i.e. Margaret Pryor] (1659). Bunyan's pamphlet was attacked by a Quaker alderman from Cambridge, James Blackley, in *A Lying Wonder Discovered, and the Strange and Terrible Newes from Cambridge Proved False* (1659).[1]

On Christmas day 1659 Bunyan was invited to preach at Yelden, Bedfordshire, by the rector of the parish church, William Dell, who was also Master of Gonville and Caius College, Cambridge.[2]

---

[1] In addition to Blackley's pamphlet and *The Strange & Terrible Newes from Cambridge*, see Tindall, Appendix; H. G. Tibbutt, 'John Bunyan and the Witch', *Bedfordshire Magazine*, ix (Winter 1963–4), 89–90. Bunyan's notorious reputation with the Quakers, due also in part to his earlier pamphlet controversy with Edward Burrough, is reflected in a letter from Alexander Parker to George Fox, the '4th day of the 3rd month 1659', in which the Bedford congregation is referred to as 'Bunian his society' and 'Bunyan's people'. Friends' House, Swarthmore MSS., iii. 144 (*Transcripts*, iii. 45). For Bunyan's relation to the Quakers, see T. L. Underwood's introduction to vol. i of *The Miscellaneous Works of John Bunyan* (forthcoming).

[2] Dell (*c.* 1607–69), a graduate of Emmanuel College, Cambridge, became rector of Yelden in 1641, and later (*c.* 1644) a chaplain in the New Model Army. He was appointed Master of Gonville and Caius College in 1649, but, anticipating ejection, resigned in 1660. He was ejected from Yelden in 1662. His remaining years were

Earlier in the year, however, Bunyan had not fared as well with another Cambridge man, Thomas Smith, Professor of Arabic and University Librarian.[1] In May Bunyan had been preaching in Daniel Angier's barn at Toft, Cambridgeshire, when Smith challenged his right to preach.[2] The challenge was subsequently reiterated in print in Smith's *The Quaker Disarm'd* (1659). Bunyan defended himself by claiming that he had been called by the church at Bedford. He was also defended in print by the influential General Baptist, Henry Denne, noted for his evangelistic activities in the eastern counties.[3] Denne taunted Smith about Bunyan's ability to mend souls as well as pots and pans in *The Quaker No Papist* (1659).

Presumably Bunyan continued with similar preaching and debating the following year; it is very likely that the time consumed by his preaching prevented him from becoming a deacon in the Bedford church. Of the greatest moment for Bunyan in 1660 was the Restoration of Charles II and the consequences that followed. The Bedford congregation sensed trouble and set apart days of prayer even before Charles was restored. Although aware of the dangers of continuing to preach Bunyan accepted an invitation from some of his friends to preach at Lower Samsell, Bedfordshire, on 12 November 1660. Before the service he learned that a warrant had been issued for his arrest, under an Elizabethan statute for nonconformity (35 Eliz. c. 1), but he refused to flee, convinced that his cause was good. He was seized and taken before a local magistrate, Francis Wingate, who had signed the warrant. Bunyan refused to

marked by his acquisition of considerable land and an interest in lumber. See Eric C. Walker, *William Dell: Master Puritan* (Cambridge, 1970); Leo F. Solt, *Saints in Arms: Puritanism and Democracy in Cromwell's Army* (Stanford and London, 1959).

[1] Thomas Smith, M.A., B.D., was also vicar of Caldecote, Cambs., and lecturer in rhetoric at Christ's College. See John Peile, *Biographical Register of Christ's College, 1505–1905* (Cambridge, 1910), i. 468.

[2] Bunyan's retorts were successful enough to provoke Smith to defend his position in *A Letter to Mr E. Toft* (1659). See Brown, pp. 114–17, and Tindall, pp. 48–9.

[3] Henry Denne (d. 1660?) was educated at Cambridge, served as curate of Pirton, Herts., from 1630 to 1640, and joined the Baptists in 1643. He attacked paedobaptism from the pulpit and in the press, for which he suffered brief imprisonment. Subsequent opposition caused him to join the parliamentary army in 1646, though he resumed his controversial preaching after the war and served as a Messenger for the General Baptists.

give an assurance that he would not preach again and was committed to the county gaol in Bedford. He was sentenced at the quarter-sessions in January 1661 by Sir John Kelynge (Keeling), who is probably the prototype for Lord Hategood in *The Pilgrim's Progress*.[1]

After three months Bunyan was visited by the Clerk of the Peace, John Cobb, who tried in vain to persuade him to give up his preaching. He was unaffected by the amnesty promised in connection with Charles's coronation in April 1661. The pleadings of his wife at the Midsummer Assizes in August were likewise of no avail. Yet until April 1662 Bunyan had considerable freedom for a prisoner. He advised troubled believers from the surrounding area who visited him in prison. He even travelled to London to consult the Baptists there. In September 1661 he and three fellow believers were sent by the Bedford church to visit lapsed members. There was also an opportunity to preach as well as to read and write in prison. In addition to the Bible, his primary reading during his early imprisonment was John Foxe's *Actes and Monuments*,[2] which he had cited twice in his tract on prayer. Probably his first writing in prison was his *Profitable Meditations* (1661), a collection of verses. At about the same time he wrote the pastoral letters in which he gave an account of his imprisonment; they were first published in 1765, as *A Relation of the Imprisonment of Mr. John Bunyan*.

(ii) *Contents of the Tract*

I Will Pray with the Spirit was written between these works and *Christian Behaviour* (1663). There is no surviving copy of the first edition, but the second edition is dated 1663. Some writers follow Charles Doe's dating of the work in 1663,[3] but it was probably written before 1663. Early in 1662 Bunyan wrote:

I had, by my Jailor, some liberty granted me, more than at the first, and . . . I followed my wonted course of preaching, taking all

---

[1] For further information on Bunyan's imprisonment see Joyce Godber, 'The Imprisonments of John Bunyan', *Trans. Cong. Hist. Soc.* xvi (Apr. 1949), 23–32; W. T. Whitley, 'Bunyan's Imprisonments: A Legal Study', *Trans. Bapt. Hist. Soc.* vi (1918–19), 1–24.

[2] The influence of Foxe's *magnum opus* is examined by William Haller, *Foxe's Book of Martyrs and the Elect Nation* (New York, 1963).

[3] e.g. Brown, p. 470; Harold E. B. Speight, *The Life and Writings of John Bunyan* (New York and London, 1928), p. 88.

occasions that was put into my hand to visit the people of God, ex-
horting them to be stedfast in the faith of Jesus Christ, and to take
heed that they touched not the Common Prayer, &c. but to mind
the word of God, which giveth direction to Christians in every
point . . .[1]

This preaching led to the writing of *I Will Pray with the Spirit*,
which is an expanded version of a sermon.[2] Since the preaching was
done before April 1662, it is probable that the writing took place at
that time or later in 1662 when Bunyan had greater leisure. The
issue of extempore prayer was crucial with Bunyan in this period.[3]
In one sense the tract can be read as a justification of the position
he maintained before Sir John Kelynge, a staunch advocate of the
Book of Common Prayer. He informed Kelynge that 'those prayers
in the Common Prayerbook, was such as was made by other men,
and not by the motions of the Holy Ghost, within our Hearts; and
as I said the Apostle saith, he will pray with the spirit and with
understanding; not with the spirit and the Common Prayerbook.'[4]
The issue was most burning for Bunyan in 1661 and 1662; by 1663
Bunyan's attention shifted to matters of family relations and ethical
concerns, probably reflecting the questions that had been posed to
him as a spiritual counsellor.

At the outset of Bunyan's examination by Kelynge and his
fellow justices, Bunyan asserted that Christians are not commanded to pray according to the forms of the Book of Common
Prayer. Instead they are to pray with the Spirit and the understanding, as Paul indicated in 1 Corinthians xiv. 15, which Bunyan
made the basic text for *I Will Pray with the Spirit*. The principles

---

[1] *A Relation of the Imprisonment of Mr. John Bunyan*, in *G.A.*, p. 129.

[2] The structure of Bunyan's sermons, which is typical of those in the Puritan
tradition, can be traced back in English literature to John Hooper. See, e.g., J. W.
Blench, *Preaching in England in the Late Fifteenth and Sixteenth Centuries* (New York,
1964), pp. 94, 101–2. The normal form of the sermon consists of the reading and
exposition of a Scriptural passage, the development of doctrines or lessons from the
passage, and the addition of moral applications or 'uses'. See also Caroline Francis
Richardson, *English Preachers and Preaching, 1640–1670* (New York, 1928); and
Horton Davies, *Worship and Theology in England from Cranmer to Hooker, 1534–1603*
(Princeton, N.J., 1970), pp. 304–8.

[3] The importance of prayer in Elizabethan religious literature is analysed by
Faye L. Kelly, *Prayer in Sixteenth-Century England* (Gainesville, Fla., 1966). Prayer
continues to receive significant attention in the literature of the seventeenth century.

[4] *A Relation of the Imprisonment*, in *G.A.*, p. 114.

asserted by Bunyan in the ensuing argument with Kelynge are developed in the tract on prayer, which provides a commentary on his defence. His key principle was that he could do nothing in religion that was not required by Scripture, a manifestation of the insistence of those in the Puritan tradition on *sola scriptura* as the criterion for worship.[1] The Book of Common Prayer could not be used 'because it was not commanded in the word of God, and therefore I could not do it'.[2]

There had been considerable dissatisfaction with the Book of Common Prayer from the second half of the sixteenth century on. The Puritans, for example, had criticized the prayers both for their type and for their content. Yet conservative Puritans acknowledged the value and legitimacy of set forms of prayers, whereas more liberal Puritans ('proto-Independents') and Separatists favoured extempore prayer. Dispute over read versus extempore prayers continued throughout the Civil War, Commonwealth, and Protectorate, with the Presbyterians maintaining a strong preference for read prayers. Richard Baxter is representative of moderates who valued both liturgical and extempore prayer. Bunyan was more extreme, expressing a position on extempore prayer akin to that of such sectarian contemporaries as John Saltmarsh and William Erbury. Bunyan even took pains in his tract on prayer to warn of the dangers of reciting the Lord's prayer without the Spirit and enlightened understanding, a principle earlier advanced by the Barrowists and the Brownists. The tract, therefore, reflects the virtual culmination of the trend away from liturgical prayer toward reliance on the inner working of the Spirit alone. Bunyan stopped short, however, of stressing the silent waiting upon the Spirit characteristic of the Seekers and the Quakers.[3]

In place of set forms of prayer Bunyan developed the idea of prayer as 'a sincere, sensible, affectionate pouring out of the heart or soul to God through Christ, in the strength and assistance of the

---

[1] See Davies, *Worship and Theology in England, 1534–1603*, pp. 258–61.

[2] *A Relation of the Imprisonment*, in *G.A.*, p. 116. See above, pp. xvi ff.

[3] *The Acts and Monuments of John Foxe*, ed. George Townsend, vi (AMS reprint, New York, 1965), 704; cf. the numerous references to Bonner's persecuting activity throughout vol. vii.

holy Spirit . . .' The emphasis was on the free working of the Spirit in the believer, who is admonished to submit to the will of God. It reflects an increased attention devoted to the Holy Spirit by seventeenth-century Puritans. Bunyan did not believe that the Spirit could work effectually if it was impeded by set forms of prayer. He buttressed his opposition to the Book of Common Prayer with the reminder that its lineage could be traced in part to the Catholic tradition. Moreover, he likened those who persecuted him for his failure to conform to the practices of the Church of England to Bishop Edmund Bonner and the Catholic persecutors of heretics in Marian England. In view of Bunyan's strong interest in the martyrology of John Foxe, this work may well have been the source of Bunyan's reference to the persecuting Bishop and 'his murdering office'.[1]

Placing himself squarely in the tradition of the persecuted is only one example of the way in which Bunyan used his personal experience to support and illustrate his exposition of prayer. On several occasions he writes of 'my own Experience' concerning prayer. The inner spiritual struggles he was later to describe in *Grace Abounding* are hinted at here. On the basis of his experience he tells his readers that genuine prayer is not external but 'experimental'. The understanding with which the believer is to pray does not come from education but from spiritual enlightenment. Bunyan castigates the doctors of divinity who, because of their theological training, presume to establish a human institution and require obedience to it. From his prison cell he pointedly notes that those who do not accept such human contrivances are branded as seditious and heretical. (The accusation of sedition was true; that of heresy was not.) Bunyan clinched his argument by urging his readers to 'look into the Goals in *England*, and into the Alehouses of the same: and I believe, you will find those that plead for the Spirit of Prayer in the Goal, and them that look after the Form of mens Inventions only, in the Alehouse'.

[1] See especially Horton Davies, *The Worship of the English Puritans* (1948), Chap. VIII; Geoffrey F. Nuttall, *The Holy Spirit in Puritan Faith and Experience* (Oxford, 1946), pp. 65–72; also Davies, *Worship and Theology in England, 1534–1603*, pp. 261–73; Gordon Stevens Wakefield, *Puritan Devotion: Its Place in the Development of Christian Piety* (1957), pp. 68–70.

Despite the occasional lapse into invective, the tract as a whole reflects the spirit of a man who speaks warmly in the 'of' mood, not the 'about' mood.[1] His language is the language of faith, not the language of the academic. Essentially he describes what he has experienced, and urges others to have a similar experience: 'When I say, *believingly*, I mean, for the soul to believe, and that from good experience, that the work of Grace is wrought in him . . .' His quest for the experiential rather than the formal did lead him to a manifestation of hostility to the established clergy,[2] but it also led him to a belief in religious toleration. The Spirit had to be free to work in men, and men were not to impose barriers to impede the Spirit's freedom. This is the essence of Bunyan's message in *I Will Pray with the Spirit*.

[1] I am indebted to Professor Paul Holmer of the Yale University Divinity School for this phrasing.

[2] On this subject see James Fulton Maclear, 'Popular Anticlericalism in the Puritan Revolution', *JHI*, xvii (Oct. 1956), 443–70.

THE DOCTRINE OF THE LAW
AND GRACE UNFOLDED

THE DOCTRINE OF THE LAW AND
GRACE UNFOLDED

Note on the Text

Two editions of *Law and Grace* were published in Bunyan's life-time, the first in 1659 and the second in 1685. There is no evidence of a second edition earlier than 1685, in spite of Frank Mott Harrison's conjecture that there was one.[1] The 1685 edition is not numbered on the title-page, which gives no indication of any intervening edition.

The first edition was printed for both M. Wright of London and Matthias Cowley of Newport Pagnell. A variant imprint appears on the title-page of that part of the printing assigned to Cowley: '*London*, Printed for *Matthias Cowley* Book-seller in | *Newport-Pannell*, 1659.' Wright had published Bunyan's previous tract, *A Few Sighs from Hell*. He was probably the son of John Wright, a bookseller at the King's Head in Old Bailey, and the brother of the John Wright of the same name. The younger John Wright was the publisher of Bunyan's first two tracts, *Some Gospel Truths Opened* and *A Vindication of Some Gospel Truths Opened*. These too were printed jointly for John Wright and Cowley with differing London and Newport Pagnell imprints. Although no copies of *A Few Sighs from Hell* with a Newport imprint have survived there is a likelihood that M. Wright began his relationship with Cowley with that book in order to distribute the work in both Bedfordshire and London. He thus succeeded his brother. Cowley was over-looked by Henry Plomer, but printings of Bunyan's first two (and probably the third) tracts were made for him to sell at Newport Pagnell. It seems likely that Bunyan first met Cowley during the course of his military service at Newport Pagnell. M. Wright, incidentally, had published the works of other Calvinist authors, including Daniel Cawdrey and Thomas Gouge.[2]

---

[1] Harrison, pp. 8–10.

[2] See H. R. Plomer, *A Dictionary of the Booksellers and Printers . . . from 1641 to 1667* (1907), pp. 197–8; and Brown ,p. 123.

The publisher of the second edition, Nathaniel Ponder, had already published many books by Bunyan and became his regular publisher. These books included *The Pilgrim's Progress*, *Grace Abounding*, and *The Life and Death of Mr. Badman*.[1]

THE FIRST EDITION

Title-page: [within rules] THE DOCTRINE | OF THE | LAVV and GRACE | UNFOLDED: | OR, | A Discourse touching the LAW and GRACE. The | nature of the one, and the nature of the other: shewing | what they are, as they are the two Covenants, and like- | wise who they be, and what their Conditions are, that be | under either of these two Covenants. | WHEREIN, | For the better understanding of the Reader, there | is several Questions answered, touching the LAW and | GRACE, very easie to be read, and as easie to be under- | stood, by those that are the Sons of Wisdom: the Chil- | dren of the second Covenant. | ALSO, | Several Titles set over the several Truths contain- | ed in this Book, for thy sooner finding of them, which | are those following the Epistle. | [rule] | Published by that poor and contemptible Creature, | *John Bunyan of Bedford*. | [thin rule] | *The Law made nothing perfect, but the bringing in of a bet- | ter hope did; by the which we draw nigh to God*, Heb. 7. 19 | *Therefore we conclude, that a man is justified by Faith*, | *without the deeds of the Law*, Rom. 3. 28. | *To him therefore that worketh not, but believeth on him | that justifieth the un- | godly, his faith is counted for righ- | teousness*, Rom. 4. 5. | [tapered rule] | *London*, Printed for *M. Wright*, at the Sign of the Kings- | Head in the *Old Bailey*, 1659.

Title-page variants: The last two lines of the Elstow Moot Hall[1] copy read: '*London*, Printed for *Matthias Cowley* Book-seller in | *Newport-Pannell*, 1659.' The last line of the title-page is missing in the Bunyan Meeting copy.

Collation: 8⁰: A–Z⁸, Aa–Cc⁸, Dd⁴. Dd3 and Dd4 are not signed. Q3 is signed P4 in the Bunyan Meeting copy. Q4 is signed P4 in the Moot Hall[2] copy. Pages: 28+396. Both Moot Hall copies are badly charred and incomplete. Moot Hall[1]: A1–E8 ⟨F1–F8⟩ G1–H8 ⟨I1–R8⟩ S1 ⟨S2–S7⟩ S8–Y8 ⟨Z1–Cc8⟩ Dd1–Dd4. Moot Hall[2]: ⟨A1⟩ A2–G8 ⟨H1–H2⟩ H3–N2 ⟨N3–N6⟩ N7–O8 ⟨P1⟩ P2–Z8 ⟨Aa1⟩ Aa2–Cc4 ⟨Cc5–Cc8⟩ Dd1–Dd4. A4 is missing in the Bunyan Meeting copy.

[1] See Plomer, *A Dictionary of the Printers and Booksellers . . . from 1668 to 1725* (1922), pp. 240–1.

Contents: A1ʳ title-page, A1ᵛ blank, A2ʳ–B5ʳ 'THE EPISTLE | TO THE | READER.' B5ᵛ–B6ᵛ list of subtitles, B7ʳ–Dd4ʳ text, Dd4ᵛ blank. No illustrations. Double row of ornaments at head of A2ʳ and B5ᵛ. B5ʳ is signed '*JOHN BUNYAN*.' On B5ᵛ a thin medium rule precedes 'The First Part.' A thin medium rule follows the abbreviated title on B7ʳ. K2ʳ has the signature and the catchword 'The' between a medium rule and a thin medium rule. A medium rule precedes the Scripture text on K2ᵛ. The seven lines of text on Dd4ʳ are followed by '*The End.*' between two thin medium rules. Page 363 is numbered 353; pp. 370 and 371 are numbered 270 and 271; pp. 389–95 are numbered 383–389. Moot Hall¹ has the uncorrected state of signature Dd (see below, p. 224, l. 16). Moot Hall² was extensively repaired by A. F. Cirket at the Bedfordshire County Record Office in 1956. As presently bound, this copy includes the engraving from *The Pilgrim's Progress* depicting Bunyan dreaming while Christian ascends the Hill Difficulty.

Running titles: Running title of the Epistle: '*The Epistle | to the Reader.*' There are multiple running titles for the text, with the following variants (excluding the numerous uses of the wrong fount of type and mistakes in punctuation): *N* in '*New*' is lower case on pp. 133–41; '*sacrfice*' for '*sacrifice*' on p. 169; *t* in '*Saints*' is inverted on p. 189; *c* in '*compleatly*' is upper case on pp. 192, 208; *G* in '*Grace*' is lower case on pp. 212, 220; *h* in '*brought*' is inverted on p. 233; *S* in '*Sin*' is lower case on p. 361. The running titles from p. 365 to the end are in smaller type.

Catchwords: (selected) A8ᵛ derstand B8ᵛ Christ) C8ᵛ abide D8ᵛ deed, E8ᵛ a man F8ᵛ is G8ᵛ Lord H8ᵛ able I8ᵛ great K8ᵛ firmed L8ᵛ thus; M8ᵛ tisfaction N8ᵛ fore O8ᵛ wrinkle P8ᵛ *rit* Q8ᵛ ry R8ᵛ that S8ᵛ rience T8ᵛ backt V8ᵛ hope X8ᵛ no Y8ᵛ and Z8ᵛ here, Aa8ᵛ lieve, Bb8ᵛ trou- Cc1ᵛ apert; Cc8ᵛ If Dd3ᵛ writ-

Copies collated: British Museum; Bunyan Meeting, Bedford; Moot Hall¹, Elstow (Dr. Richard Offor's Catalogue, 46|1); Moot Hall², Elstow (Dr. Richard Offor's Catalogue, 46|2).

THE SECOND EDITION

Title-page: [within rules] THE DOCTRINE | OF THE | LAW and GRACE | UNFOLDED: | OR, | A Discourse touching the *Law* and *Grace*. The | nature of the one, and the nature of the other: shewing | what they are, as they are the two Covenants; and like-| wise who they be, and what their Conditions are, that | be under either of these two Covenants. | WHEREIN, | For the better Understanding of the Reader, | there is several Questions answered touching the *Law* | and *Grace*, very easie to be read, and as easie to be un- | derstood, by those that are the Sons of Wisdom, the |

Children of the second Covenant. | ALSO, | Several Titles set over the several Truths con- | tained in this Book, for thy sooner finding of them; | which are those following the Epistle. | [thick rule] | Published by that Poor and Contemptible Creature, | *John Bunyan* of *Bedford*. | [rule] | *The Law made nothing perfect, but the bringing in of a better* | *Hope did; by the which we draw nigh to God*, Heb. 7. 19. | *Therefore we conclude, that a man is justified by Faith, with-* | *out the Deeds of the Law*, Rom. 3. 28. | *To him therefore that worketh not, but believeth on him that* | *justifieth the ungodly, his Faith is counted for Righteous-* | *ness*, Rom. 4. 5. | [thin rule] | *LONDON*, Printed for *Nath. Ponder* at the *Peacock* | in the *Poultry*. 1685.

Collation: 8⁰: A–Y⁸. O3 is unsigned. P4 is signed P2. A8 is missing in the Pierpont Morgan copy. Y8 is missing in the Folger Shakespeare copy. Pages: 16+336.

Contents: A1ʳ title-page, A1ᵛ blank, A2ʳ–A6ᵛ 'The Epistle to the Reader.', A7ʳ–A8ʳ list of subtitles, A8ᵛ blank, B1ʳ–Y7ᵛ text, Y8ʳ&ᵛ blank. No illustrations. Double rule at head of A2ʳ. A6ᵛ is signed '*JOHN BUNYAN*.' There is a thick rule on A6ᵛ, a double rule at the head of A7ʳ, a rule preceding 'The First Part.' on A7ʳ, a thick rule preceding the catchword 'THE' on A8ʳ, a rule preceding the Scripture text on B1ʳ, a double rule preceding the continuation of the text on H2ᵛ, a rule preceding the Scripture text on H2ᵛ, and, following the fifteen lines of text on Y7ᵛ, a rule preceding '*The End*.'

Running titles: Running title of the Epistle: '*The Epistle* | *to the Reader*.' As in the first edition there are multiple running titles for the text, with the following variants (excluding uses of the wrong fount of type and mistakes in punctuation): *t* in '*to*' is upper case on A4ʳ; *M* in '*Messenger*' is lower case on pp. 128, 132; *S* in '*Sacrifice*' is lower case on p. 136; *N* in '*New*' is lower case on p. 165; '*fulled*' for '*fulfilled*' on p. 162; '*the*' omitted on p. 174; *A* in '*Answered*' is lower case on p. 240; *c* in '*comfort*' is upper case on p. 314.

Catchwords: (selected) A8ʳ THE B4ʳ thouhgh B8ᵛ in C8ᵛ nity, D8ᵛ *shall* E2ʳ an (for 'and') E8ᵛ Thirdly, (wrongly placed in text) F8ᵛ *end* G8ᵛ *Answ.* H8ᵛ God I8ᵛ *seek*, K8ᵛ Secondly, L8ᵛ how M8ᵛ 8. He N8ᵛ as O8ᵛ of P8ᵛ so Q7ᵛ Fightly, Q8ᵛ because R8ᵛ Secondly, S8ᵛ And T8ᵛ man V8ᵛ *powers* X8ᵛ that Y1ʳ *Answ* (followed by various misprints instead of a full stop) Y7ʳ thy

Copies collated: British Museum; Bodleian, Oxford; Regent's Park College, Oxford; Bedford Public Library; Folger Shakespeare Library; Pierpont Morgan Library; Philip H. & A. S. W. Rosenbach Foundation. A copy at Bunyan Meeting, Bedford, has been misplaced.

Most of the changes in the second edition are corrections of misprints in the first, or fresh misprints. Occasionally the second edition mistakenly omits an entire phrase. The Scriptural references found in the margin in the first edition are placed in the text in the second edition. Several of the highly personal marginal comments in the first edition are omitted entirely, as are the marginal numbers. Bunyan may have been responsible for pointing out the misprints in the first edition to Nathaniel Ponder, but it could be the work of a printing-house corrector. Bunyan did not take the opportunity afforded by a new edition to make any alterations (at least of substance) in the text. He was either satisfied with the first as it stood, or lacked the time to make alterations or additions. Certainly he was occupied in 1685 with other writing. In the previous year he had published *A Holy Life*, *Seasonable Counsel*, the second part of *The Pilgrim's Progress*, and *A Caution to Stir Up*. In 1685 he published *The Pharisee and the Publicane* and *Questions about the . . . Seventh-day-sabbath*. That *Law and Grace* went essentially unaltered may be indicative of the consistency of Bunyan's theology throughout his adult life, but it seems more likely that as with other theological works and sermon treatises he found no occasion to supervise the printing of editions subsequent to the first.

The text that follows is based on the British Museum copy of the first edition, checked against the other known first edition copies. The modest number of obvious printer's errors are silently corrected. Alterations of any substance in the 1685 edition are noted in the textual apparatus. When, however, the 1685 edition corrects an obvious mistake in the 1659 edition, the correct reading is placed in the text and the earlier version is noted in the apparatus. Accidentals have been preserved, except in those few cases where corrections in spelling and punctuation were essential to understand the author's meaning. Where Scriptural references are omitted, they have been supplied in the Notes to the text. Erroneous Scriptural references have been corrected in the text, and the original references noted in the apparatus. Biblical quotations have been left as Bunyan cited them. The guiding principle has been fidelity to the 1659 text, except where such fidelity would hinder the understanding of Bunyan's obvious meaning.

Numerous editions of *Law and Grace* were published after the author's death. Two issues of a 'second' edition were published in

London in 1701, followed by a 'third' in 1708. The latter was re-issued *c.* 1735, again in London. A 'fourth' edition appeared in London in 1736. In 1742 an edition described as the 'third' was published in Boston, the seventh of Bunyan's works to be published in America. (The earlier works were *The Pilgrim's Progress*, 1681; *The Heavenly Foot-man*, 1716; *Grace Abounding*, 1717; *Come and Welcome*, 1728; *The Jerusalem Sinner Saved*, 1733; and *The Holy War*, 1736?[1])

[1] David E. Smith, 'Publication of John Bunyan's Works in America', *Bulletin of the New York Public Library*, lxvi (Dec. 1962), 644–52.

THE DOCTRINE 1632
OF THE
LAW and GRACE
UNFOLDED:
OR,

A Difcourfe touching the LAW and GRACE. The nature of the one, and the nature of the other: fhewing what they are, as they are the two Covenants, and likewife who they be, and what their Conditions are, that be under either of thefe two Covenants.

WHEREIN,

For the better underftanding of the Reader, there is feveral Queftions anfwered, touching the LAW and GRACE, very eafie to be read, and as eafie to be underftood, by thofe that are the Sons of Wifdom: the Children of the fecond Covenant.

ALSO,

Several Titles fet over the feveral Truths contained in this Book, for thy fooner finding of them, which are thofe following the Epiftle.

Publifhed by that poor and contemptible Creature,
Ꝛ *John Bunyan* of *Bedford.*

The Law made nothing perfect, but the bringing in of a better hope did; by the which we draw nigh to God, Heb. 7. 19
Therefore we conclude, that a man is juftified by Faith, without the deeds of the Law, Rom. 3. 28.
To him therefore that worketh not, but believeth on him that juftifieth the ungodly, his faith is counted for righteoufnefs, Rom. 4. 5.

London, Printed for *M. Wright,* at the Sign of the Kings-Head in the *Old Bailey,* 1659.

Title-page of British Museum copy of *The Doctrine of the Law and Grace Unfolded* (1659)

THE EPISTLE TO THE *READER*.

If at any time there be held forth by the Preacher, the freeness and fulness of the Gospel, together with the readiness
of the Lord of peace, to receive those that have any desire
5 thereto; presently it is the spirit of the world to cry out, sure
this man disdains the Law, slights the Law, and counts that
of none effect; and all because there is not together with the
Gospel, mingled the Doctrine of the Law (which is not a
right dispensing of the Word according to truth and know-
10 ledge). Again, if there be the terror, horror, and severity of
the Law, discovered to a people by the Servants of Jesus
Christ (though they do not speak of it, to the end people
should trust to it, by relying on it as it is a Covenant of
Works; but rather that they should be driven further from
15 that Covenant, even to embrace the tenders and priviledges
of the second), yet poor souls, because they are unacquainted
with the natures of these two Covenants, or either of them;
therefore, say they, here is nothing but preaching of the Law,
thundering of the Law; when alas, if these two be not held
20 forth (to wit) the Covenant of Works, and the Covenant of
Grace, together with the nature of the one, and the nature of
the other; souls will never be able neither to know what they
are by Nature, nor what they lie under. Also, neither can they
understand what Grace is, nor how to come from under the
25 Law, to meet God, in, and through that other most glorious
Covenant; through which, and onely through which, God
can communicate of himself, grace, glory, yea, even all the
good things of another world.

I having considered these things, together with others, have
30 made bold to present yet once more to thy view (my Friend)
something of the minde of God, to the end, if it shall be but
blessed to thee, thou mayest be benefitted thereby. For
verily these things are not such as are ordinary, and of small

concernment, but do absolutely concern thee to know, and
that experimentally too, if ever thou do partake of the glory
of God through Jesus Christ, and so escape the terrour and
unsupportable vengeance, that will otherwise come upon thee
through his Justice, because of thy living and dying in thy ₅
transgressions against the Law of God. And therefore while
thou livest here below, it is thy duty (if thou wish thy self
happy for the time to come) to give up thy self to the studying
of these two Covenants, treated of in the ensuing Discourse;
and so to study them, untill thou through grace, do, not ₁₀
onely get the notion of the one and of the other in thy head;
but until thou do feel the very power, life, and glory of the
one and of the other. For take this for granted, he that is
dark as touching the scope, intent, and nature of the Law,
is also dark as to the scope, nature, and glory of the Gospel: ₁₅
And also he that hath but a notion of the one, will hardly
have any more then a notion of the other.

And the reason is this, because, so long as people are
ignorant of the nature of the Law, and of their being under
it, that is, under the curse and condemning power of it, by ₂₀
reason of their sin against it; so long they will be careless, and
negligent as to the enquiring after the true knowledge of the
Gospel. Before the Commandement came (that is in the
spirituallity of it), *Paul* was alive, that is, thought himself
safe, which is clear, *Rom.* 7. 9, 10. compared with the 3. of ₂₅
Phil. the 5, 6, 7, 8, 9, 10, 11. *ver.* &c. but when that came and
was indeed discovered unto him by the Spirit of the Lord,
then *Paul* dies (*Rom.* 7.) to all his former life (*Phil.* 3.) and that
man which before could content himself to live, though
ignorant of the Gospel, cryes out now, *I count all things but* ₃₀
loss, for the excellency of the knowledge of Jesus Christ my Lord, v. 8.
Therefore I say, so long they will be ignorant of the nature of
the Gospel, and how glorious a thing it is to be found within
the bounds of it; for we use to say, that man that knoweth
not himself to be sick, that man will not look out for himself ₃₅
a Physician; and this Christ knew full well where he saith,

29 which before] before which *1659*

the whole have no need of a Physician, but them that are sick; that is, none will in truth desire the Physician, unless they know they be sick. That man also, that hath got but a notion of the Law (a notion, that is the knowledge of it in the head, so as to
5 discourse and talk of it) if he hath not felt the power of it, and that effectually too, he, it is to be feared, will at the best be but a notionist in the Gospel, he will not have the experimental knowledge of the same in his heart; nay he will not seek, nor heartily desire after it, and all because as I said
10 before, he hath not experience of the wounding, cutting, killing nature of the other.

I say therefore, if thou wouldest know the authority and power of the Gospel, labour first to know the power and authority of the Law; for I am verily perswaded that the want
15 of this one thing, namely, the knowledge of the Law, is one cause why so many are ignorant of the other. That man that doth not know the Law, doth not know indeed and in truth, that he is a sinner; and that man that doth not know he is a sinner, doth not know savingly that there is a Saviour.

20 Again, that man that doth not know the nature of the Law, that man doth not know the nature of sin; and that man that knoweth not the nature of sin, will not regard to know the nature of a Saviour. This is proved, *John* 8. 31, 32, 33, 34, 35, 36. ver. this people were professors, and yet did not know
25 the truth (the Gospel), and the reason was, because they did not know themselves, and so not the Law. I would not have thee mistake me Christian Reader, I do not say, that the Law of it self will lead any soul to Jesus Christ; but the soul being killed by the Law, through the operation of its severity
30 seizing on the soul, then the man, if he be enlightened by the Spirit of Christ, to see where remedy is to be had, will not thorow grace, be contented without the real and saving knowledge through faith of him.

If thou wouldest then wash thy face clean, first take a glass
35 and see where it is durty; that is, if thou wouldest indeed have thy sins washed away by the blood of Christ, labour first to see them in the glass of the Law (*Jam.* 1.) and do not be

afraid to see thy besmeared condition, but look on every spot thou hast; for he that looks on the foulness of his face by the halfs, will wash by the halfs: even so he that looks on his sins by the halfs, he will seek for Christ by the halfs. Reckon thy self therefore, I say, the biggest sinner in the world, and be perswaded that there is none worse then thy self; then let the guilt of it seize on thy heart, then also go in that case and condition to Jesus Christ, and plunge thy self into his Merits, and the vertue of his Blood; and after that thou shalt speak of the things of the Law, and of the Gospel, experimentally; and the very Language of the Children of God shall feelingly drop from thy lips, and not till then.

Let this therefore learn thee thus much, he that hath not seen his lost condition, hath not seen a safe condition; he that did never see himself in the Devils snare, did never see himself in Christs bosom. *This my son was dead, and is alive again. Was lost and is found, with whom we all had our conversation in time past. But now are* (so many of us as believe) *returned to Jesus Christ the Chief Shepherd and Bishop of our souls.*

I say therefore if thou do finde in this Treatise, in the first place, something touching the nature, end, and extent of the Law, do not thou cry out therefore all on a sudden, saying, Here is nothing but the terrour, horrour, and thundering Sentences of the Law.

Again, if thou do finde in the second part of this Discourse, something of the freeness and fulness of the Gospel, do not thou say then neither, here is nothing but Grace, therefore surely an undervaluing of the Law. No, but read it quite thorow, and so consider of it; and (I hope) thou shalt finde the two Covenants (which all men are under either the one or the other) discovered, and held forth in their natures, ends, bounds, together with the state and condition of them that are under the one, and of them that are under the other.

There be some that through ignorance do say, how that such men as preach terrour and amazement to sinners, are besides the Book, and are Ministers of the Letter, the Law, and not of the Spirit, the Gospel; but I would answer them,

citing them to the 16. of *Luke*, from the 19. ver. to the end:
and the 1 *Cor*. 6. 9, 10. and *Gal*. 3. 10. *Rom*. 3. from the 9.
Verse to the 19. onely this caution I would give by the way,
how that they which preach terror, to drive souls to the
5 obtaining of salvation, by the works of the Law, that preaching is not the right Gospel preaching. Yet when Saints speak
of the sad state that men are in by Nature, to discover to
souls their need of the Gospel, this is honest preaching (see
Rom. the 3. the 9, 10, 11, 12, 13, 14, 15, 16, 17, 18, 19, 20, 21,
10 22, 23, 24, 25, &c.) and he that doth do so, he doth the work
of a Gospel Minister.

Again, there are others that say, because we do preach the
free, full, and exceeding Grace discovered in the Gospel,
therefore we make void the Law; when indeed, unless the
15 Gospel be held forth in the glory thereof without confusion,
by mingling the Covenant of Workes therewith, the Law
cannot be established. *Do we through faith*, or preaching of the
Gospel, *make void the Law*? Nay, stay saith *Paul*, *God forbid*.
We do thereby establish the Law, Rom. 3. 31.

20   And verily, he that will indeed establish the Law, or set it
in its own place (for so I understand the words), must be
sure to hold forth the Gospel in its right colour and nature;
for if a man be ignorant of the nature of the Gospel, and the
Covenant of Grace, they, or he, will be very apt to remove the
25 Law out of its place, and that because *they are ignorant*, *not
knowing what they say*, *nor whereof they affirme*.

And let me tell you, if a man be ignorant of the Covenant
of Grace, and the bounds and boundlesness of the Gospel,
though he speaks and makes mention of the Name of the
30 Father, and of the Son, and also of the Name of the new
Covenant, and the Blood of Christ: Yet at this very time, and
in these very words, he will preach nothing but the Law,
and that as a Covenant of Works.

Reader, I must confess it is a wonderful mysterious thing,
35 and he had need have a wiser spirit then his own, that can
rightly set these two Covenants in their right places, that

14 when] which *1685*

when he speaks of the one, he doth not jasle the other out of it's place. O to be so well inlightned, as to speak of the one, that is the Law, for to magnifie the Gospel; and also, to speak of the Gospel, so as to establish (and yet not to idolize) the Law, nor any particular thereof, it is rare, and to be heard 5 and found but in very few mens breasts!

If thou shouldest say, what is it to speak to each of these two Covenants; so as to set them in their right places, and also to use the terrour of the one, so as to magnifie and advance the glory of the other? 10

To this I shall answer also, read the ensuing Discourse, but with an understanding heart, and it is like thou wilt finde a reply therein to the same purpose, which may be to thy satisfaction.

Reader, if thou do finde this book empty of Fantastical 15 expressions, and without light, vain, whimsical Scholar-like terms, thou must understand, it is because I never went to School to *Aristotle* or *Plato*, but was brought up at my fathers house, in a very mean condition, among a company of poor Countrey-men. But if thou do finde a parcel of plain, yet 20 sound, true, and home sayings, attribute that to the Lord Jesus, his gifts and abilities, which he hath bestowed upon such a poor Creature, as I am, and have been. And if thou being a seeing Christian, doest finde me coming short, though rightly touching at some things, attribute that either 25 to my brevity, or, if thou wilt to my weaknesses (for I am full of them). A word or two more, and so I shall have done with this.

And the first is, friend if thou do not desire the salvation of thy soul, yet I pray thee to read this Book over with 30 serious consideration; it may be it will stir up in thee some desires to look out after it, which at present thou mayest be without.

Secondly, if thou do find any stirrings in thy heart, by thy reading such an unworthy mans Works as mine are; be sure 35 that in the first place thou give glory to God, and give way to

1 jasle] justle *1685*

thy convictions, and be not too hasty in getting them off from thy conscience; but let them so work till thou do see thy self by nature, void of all grace, as Faith, Hope, Knowledge of God, Christ; and the Covenant of Grace.

5   Thirdly, then in the next place, flye in all haste to Jesus Christ, thou being sensible of thy lost condition without him, secretly perswading of thy soul, that Jesus Christ standeth open armed to receive thee, to wash away thy sins, to clothe thee with his righteousness; and is willing, yea, heartily
10 willing, to present thee before the presence of the Glory of God, and among the innumerable company of Angels with exceeding joy. This being thus, in the next place do not satisfie thy self, with these secret and first perswasions, which do or may incourage thee to come to Jesus Christ; but be
15 restless till thou do finde by blessed experience, the glorious glory of this the second Covenant extended unto thee, and sealed upon thy soul with the very Spirit of the Lord Jesus Christ. And that thou mayest not slight this my Counsel, I beseech thee in the second place, consider these following
20 things.

First, if thou do get off thy convictions, and not the right way (which is by seeing thy sins washed away by the Blood of Jesus Christ), it is a question whether ever God will knock at thy heart again or no; but rather say, such a one, *is joyned*
25 *to Idols; let him alone.** Though he be in a natural state, *let him* *Hos. 4. 17 *alone*. Though he be in, or under the Curse of the Law, *Let him alone*. Though he be in the very hand of the Devil, *Let him alone*. Though he be a going poste haste to Hell, *Let him alone*. Though his damnation, will not onely be damnation for sins
30 against the Law, but also for slighting the Gospel, yet, *Let him alone*. My Spirit, my Ministers, my Word, my Grace, my Mercy, my Love, my Pitty, my common Providences shall no more strive with him, *Let him alone*. O sad! O miserable! who would slight convictions that are on their souls,
35 which tend so much for their good?

Secondly, if thou shalt not regard how thou do put off

25 *1685 customarily places marginal Scriptural references in the text.*

convictions, but put them off without the precious blood of Christ, being savingly applied to thy soul; thou art sure to have the mispending of that conviction to prove the hardning of thy heart, against the next time thou art to hear the Word preached, or read. This is commonly seen, that those souls, 5 that have not regarded those convictions, that are at first set upon their spirits, do commonly (and that by the just judgements of God upon them) grow more hard, more sense-less, more seared and sottish in their spirits; for some, who formerly would quake and weep, and relent under the hearing 10 of the word, do now for the present sit so senseless, so seared, and hardened in their consciences, that certainly if they should have Hell Fire thrown in their faces, as it is sometimes cried up in their ears, they would scarce be moved; and this comes upon them as a just Judgement of God, 2 *Thess.* 2. 11, 12. 15

Thirdly, if thou do slight these, or those convictions, that may be set upon thy heart, by reading of this Discourse, or hearing of any other good man preach the Word of God sincerely; thou wilt have the stifling of these, or those con-victions to account, and answer for at the day of Judgement; 20 not onely thy sins that are commonly committed by thee in thy calling, and common discourse; but thou shalt be called to a reckoning for slighting Convictions, disregarding of Convic-tions, which God useth as a special means, to make poor sinners see their lost condition, and the need of a Saviour. Now here I 25 might adde many more considerations besides these, to the end thou mayest be willing to tend, and listen to Convictions, as,

First, consider thou hast a precious soul, more worth then the whole world, and this is commonly worked upon (if ever it be saved) by Convictions.   30

Secondly, this soul is (for certain) to go to Hell, if thou shalt be a slighter of Convictions.

Thirdly, if that go to Hell, thy body must go thither too, and then never to come out again. *Now consider this, you that* (are apt to) *forget God* (and his Convictions), *lest he tear you in* 35 *pieces, and there be none to deliver,* Psal. 50. 22.

9, 11 seared] feared *1659, 1685.*

But if thou shalt be such a one, that shalt, notwithstanding
thy reading of thy misery, and also of Gods mercy, still persist
to go on in thy sins; know in the first place, that here thou
shalt be left, by the things that thou readest, without excuse;
5 and in the world to come thy damnation will be exceedingly
aggravated, for thy not regarding of them, and turning from
thy sins; which was not onely reproved by them, but also
for rejecting of that word of grace, that did instruct thee,
how, and which way thou shouldest be saved from them.
10 And so farewell, I shall leave thee, and also this Discourse
to God, who I know will pass a righteous judgement both
upon that and thee. I am yours, though not to serve your
lusts and filthy mindes, yet to reprove, instruct, and according to that proportion of faith and knowledge which God
15 hath given me, to declare unto you the way of life and salvation. Your judgeings, railings, surmizings, and disdaining of
me, that I shall leave till the fiery judgement comes, in which
the offendor shall not go unpunished, be he you or me; yet I
shall pray for you, wish well to you, and do you what good I
20 can. And that I might not write or speak in vain, Christian
pray for me to our God, with much earnestness, fervency, and
frequently, in all your knockings at our fathers door, because
I do very much stand in need thereof; for my work is great,
my heart is vile, the Devil lieth at watch, the world would
25 fain be saying, aha, aha, thus we would have it; and of my
self, keep my self I cannot; trust my self I dare not; if God do
not help me, I am sure it will not be long before my heart
deceive me, and the world have their advantage of me; and
so God be dishonoured by me, and thou also ashamed to own
30 me. O therefore be much in prayer for me, thy fellow; I trust
in that glorious grace that is conveyed from heaven to sinners,
by which they are not onely sanctified here in this world, but
shall be glorified in that which is to come. Unto which the
Lord of his mercy bring us all.

JOHN BUNYAN.

These are severall Titles which are set over the several *TRUTHS* contained in this Book, for thy sooner finding of them.

THE DOCTRINE

Of the

Law and Grace unfolded:

OR,

A discovery of the Law and Grace,
the nature of the one, and the na-
ture of the other, as they are
the two Covenants, &c.

Rom. 6. 14.

For ye are not under the Law, but under Grace.

In the three former Chapters, the Apostle is pleading for the
salvation of sinners by Grace, without the Works of the Law,
5 to the end he might confirm the Saints, and also that he
might win over all those that did oppose the truth of this
Doctrine, or else leave them the more without excuse; and
that he might so do, he taketh in hand, First, to shew the
state of all men naturally, or, as they come into the world by
10 Generation, saying in the third Chapter, *There is none righteous,*
no not one; there is none that understandeth, there is none that doth
good, &c. As if he had said, It seems there is a Generation
of men that think to be saved by the righteousness of the
Law, but let me tell them, that they are much deceived, in
15 that they have already sinned against the Law. *For by the*
disobedience of one, many, yea all, was brought into a state of con-
demnation, Rom. 5. 12, 13, 14, 15, 16, 17, 18, 19. Now in the
sixth Chapter, he doth as if he had turned him round to the
Brethren, and said, My Brethren, you see now that it is
20 clear and evident, that it is freely by the Grace of Christ, that

we do inherit eternal life. And again, for your comfort, my brethren, let me tell you, that your condition is wonderous safe, in that you are under Grace, for saith he, *Sin shall not have dominion over you*, that is, neither the damning power, neither the filthy power, so as to destroy your souls; *For you are not* 5 *under the Law*, that is, you are not under that, that will damn you for sin; *But* (you are) *under grace*, or stand thus in relation to God, that though you have sinned, yet you shall be pardoned. *For you are not under the Law, but under Grace. You are not under the Law, &c.* If any should ask what is the meaning of the word 10 [UNDER] I answer, it signifieth you are not held, kept, or shut up by it, so as to appear before God under that administration, and none but that; or thus, you are not now bound by the authority of the Law, to fulfil it, and obey it, so as to have no salvation without you so do, or thus; if you transgress against 15 any one tittle of it, you by the power of it must be condemned: No, no; for you are not so under it, that is, not thus under the Law. Again, *For you are not under the Law*; what is meant by this word [LAW?] The word Law, in Scripture, may be taken more wayes then one, as might be largely cleared. There is 20 the Law of Faith, the Law of Sin, the Law of men, the Law of Works, otherwise called the Covenant of Works; or the first, or old Covenant, *Heb.* 8. 13. *In that he saith a new Covenant* (which is the Grace of God, or commonly called the Covenant of Grace), *he hath made the first old*; that is the covenant of 25 Works, or the Law. I say therefore the word [LAW] and the word [GRACE] in this sixth of the *Romans*, do hold forth the two Covenants, which all men are under, that is, either the one, or the other. *For ye are not under the Law*; that is, you to whom I do now write these words; who are and have been 30 effectually brought into the faith of Jesus: you are not under the Law, or under the Covenant of Works. He doth not therefore apply these words to all, but to some, when he saith, *But ye*, mark [YE], *ye* Believers, *ye* Converted persons, *ye* Saints, *ye* that have been born again. *Ye, For ye are not under the* 35 *Law*, implying others are, that are in their natural state, that

have not been brought in to the Covenant of Grace, by faith
in Jesus Christ. The words therefore being thus understood,
there is discovered these two Truths in them.

First, that there are some in Gospel times, that are under Doct. 1
5 the Covenant of Works.

Secondly, that there is never a Believer under the Law (as Doct. 2
it is a Covenant of Works), but under Grace through Christ.
For ye, you Believers, you Converted persons, *Ye are not under
the Law, but under Grace*; or, for you are delivered and brought
10 into, or under, the Covenant of Grace.

For the first, that there are some that are under the Law,
or under the Covenant of Works, see I pray you that Scripture
in the third of the *Romans*, where the Apostle speaking before
of sins against the Law, and of the denunciations thereof,
15 against those that are in that condition; he saith, *What things
soever the Law saith, it saith to them that are under*; Mark, it
saith to them that are under *the Law, that every mouth may be
stopped, and all the world become guilty before God*, Rom. 3. 19.
that is, all those are under the Law, as a Covenant of Works,
20 that are yet in their sins, and unconverted, as I told you
before. Again, *Gal*. 5. 18. He saith, *But if you be led by the
Spirit, you are not under the Law*, implying again, that those
which are for sinning against the Law, or the works of
the Law, either as it is the old Covenant; these are under the
25 Law, and not under the Covenant of Grace. Again, *Gal*. the
3. the 10. Verse, there he saith, *For as many as are of the Works
of the Law are under the Curse*; that is, they that are under the
Law, are under the Curse; for mark, they that are under the
Covenant of Grace are not under the Curse. Now there are
30 but two Covenants; therefore it must needs be, that they
that are under the Curse, are under the Law; seeing those
that are under the other Covenant, are not under the Curse,
but under the Blessing. *So then, they which be of faith, are blessed
with faithful Abraham*, but the rest are under the Law, *Gal*.
35 3. 9. Now I shall proceed to what I do intend to speak unto.

First, I shall shew you what the Covenant of Works, or the Law, is, and when it was first given, together with the nature of it.

Secondly, I shall shew you what it is to be under the Law, or Covenant of Works, and the miserable state of all those 5 that are under it.

Thirdly, I shall shew you who they are that are under this Covenant, or Law.

Fourthly, I shall shew you how far a man may go, and yet be under this Covenant, or Law.   10

For the first, what this Covenant of Works is, and when it was given.

The Covenant of Works, or the Law here spoken of, is the Law delivered on Mount *Sinai*, to *Moses*, in two Tables of stone, in ten particular branches, or heads; for this see *Gal.* 15 4. the Apostle speaking there of the Law, and of some also that through delusions of false doctrine, was brought again as it were under it, or at least was leaning that way, *Ver.* 21. He saith, As for you that desire to be under the Law, I will shew you the mystery of *Abrahams* two Sons which he 20 had by *Agar* and *Sarah*; these two do signifie the two Covenants, the one named *Agar*, signifies Mount *Sinai* where the Law was delivered to *Moses* on two Tables of stone, *Exod.* 24. 12. *Chap.* 34. 1. *Deut.* 10. 1. which is that, that whosoever is under, he is destitute of, and altogether without the 25 Grace of Christ in his heart at the present, *Gal.* 5. 3, 4. *For I testifie again to every man* (saith he), speaking to the same people *that Christ is become of none effect unto you, whosoever of you are justified by the Law*, namely, that given on Mount *Sinai*. *Ye are fallen from Grace*. That is, not that any can be justified by the 30 Law: but his meaning is, that all those that seek justification by the Works of the Law, they are not such as seek to be under the second Covenant, the Covenant of Grace. Also the 2 *Cor.* 3. 7, 8. the Apostle speaking again of these two Covenants, he saith, *For if the ministration of death* (or the Law, 35 for it is all one) *written and engraven in stones* (mark that) *was*

glorious: how shall not the ministration of the Spirit (or the Covenant of Grace) *be rather glorious?* As if he had said, 'Tis true,
there was a glory in the Covenant of Works, and a very
great excellency did appear in it; namely, in that given in the
5 stones on Sinai, yet there is another Covenant, the Covenant
of Grace, that doth exceed it for comfort and glory.

But secondly, though this Law was delivered to *Moses*
from the hands of Angels in two Tables of Stone on Mount
Sinai; yet this was not the first appearing of this Law to
10 Man; but even this in substance (though possibly not so
openly) was given to the first Man *Adam,* in the garden of
Eden, in these words, *And the Lord God commanded the man,*
saying, Of every tree in the garden thou mayest freely eat. But of the
tree of knowledge of good and evil, thou shalt not eat of it; for in the
15 *day thou eatest thereof thou shalt surely dye,* Gen. 2. 16, 17.
Which commandement then given to *Adam,* did contain in it,
a forbidding to doe any of those things, that was, and is
accounted evil, although at that time it did not appear so
plainly, in so many particular heads, as it did when it was
20 again delivered on Mount Sinai: but yet the very same, and
that I shall prove thus.

God commanded *Adam* in Paradise to abstain from all evil
against the first Covenant, and not from some sins onely:
but if God had not commanded *Adam* to abstain from the sins
25 spoken against in the Ten Commandments, he had not commanded to abstain from all, but from some; therefore it must
needs be, that he then commanded to abstain from all sins
forbidden in the Law given on Mount Sinai. Now that God
commanded to abstain from all evil, or sin, against any of the
30 Ten Commandments, when he gave *Adam* the Command in
the Garden, it is evident, in that he did punish the sinnes
that was committed against those commands, that was then delivered on Mount Sinai, before they were delivered on Mount
Sinai, which will appear as followeth.

35   The first, second, and third Commandments were broken
by *Pharaoh* and his men; for they had false gods which the

Lord executed judgement against (as in *Exod.* 12. 12.), and blasphemed their true God (*Exod.* 5. 2.); which escaped not punishment (*Exod.* 7. 17. to the end): for their gods could neither deliver themselves, nor their people, from the hand of God; but in the things wherein they dealt proudly, he was 5 above them, *Exod.* 18. 11.

Again, some judge that the Lord punished the sin against the second Commandment, which *Jacob* was in some measure guilty of, in not purging his house from false gods, with the defiling of his daughter *Dinah, Gen.* 34. 2.   10

Again, we finde that *Abimelech,* thought the sin against the third Commandment so great, that he required no other security of *Abraham* against the fear of mischief that might be done to him by *Abraham,* his son, and his sons son: but onely *Abraham's* Oath (*Gen.* 21. 23.); the like we see between 15 *Abimelech* and *Isaac* (*Gen.* 31. 53.), the like we finde in *Moses* and the Israelites, who durst not leave the bones of *Joseph* in *Egypt*; because of the Oath of the Lord, whose Name by so doing, would have been abused, *Exod.* 13. 19.

And we finde the Lord rebuking his people for the breach 20 of the fourth Commandment, *Exod.* 16. 27, 28, 29.

And for the breach of the fifth, the Curse came upon *Ham, Gen.* 9. 25, 26, 27. and *Ishmael* dishonouring his Father, in mocking *Isaac,* was cast out, as we read, *Gen.* 21. 9, 10. The sons in law of *Lot,* for sleighting their father, perish in the 25 overthrow of *Sodom, Genesis* 19. 14, &c.

The Sixth Commandment was broken by *Cain,* and so dreadfull a curse and punishment came upon him, that it made him cry out, *My Punishment is greater then I can bear,* Gen. 4. 13.

Again, when *Esau* threatned to slay his brother, *Rebecca* 30 sent him away saying, *Why should I be deprived of you both in one day?* hinting unto us, that she knew murther was to be punished with death, *Genesis* 27. 45. which the Lord himself declared likewise to *Noah, Gen.* 9. 6.

Again, a notable example of the Lords justice in punishing 35 murther, we see in the Egyptians, and *Pharaoh,* who drowned

2–3 (*Exod.* 5. 2.) . . . punishment] *om. 1685*   33 45.] 54. *1659, 1685*

the Israelites children in the River, *Exod.* 1. 22. and they
themselves were drowned in the Sea, *Exodus* 14. 27.

The sin against the Seventh Commandment was punished
in the Sodomites, &c. with the utter destruction of their
5 City, and themselves, *Gen.* 19. 24, 25. Yea, they suffer the
vengeance of eternall fire, *Jude* 7. Also the male Sechemites,
for the sin committed by *Hamors* son, were all put to the
sword, *Gen.* 34. 25, 26.

Our first Parents sinned against the Eighth Commandment
10 in taking the forbidden fruit, and so brought the curse on
themselves, and their posterity, *Gen.* 3. 16.

Again the punishment due to the breach of this Commandment, was by *Jacob* accounted death, *Genesis* 31. 30, 32. and
also by *Jacobs* sons, *Gen.* 44. 9, 10.

15 *Cain* sinning against the Ninth Commandment, as in *Gen.*
4. 9. was therefore cursed from the earth, verse the 11. And
Abraham, though the Friend of God, was blamed for false wit-
nesse by *Pharaoh*, and sent out of *Egypt*, *Gen.* 12. 18, 19, 20.
and both he and *Sarah* reproved by *Abimelech*, *Gen.* 20. 9,
20 10, 16.

Pharaoh sinned against the Tenth Commandment, *Gen.*
12. 15. and was therefore plagued with great plagues, verse 17.
Abimelech coveted *Abrahams* Wife, and the Lord threatned
death to him and his; except he restored her again, *Gen.* 20. 3.
25 Yea, though he had not come near her; yet for coveting and
taking her, the Lord fast closed up the Wombs of his house,
verse 18.

I could have spoken more fully to this; but that I would
not be too tedious, but speak what I have to say with as
30 much brevity as I can. But before I pass it, I will besides this,
give you an argument or two more for the further clearing
of this; that the substance of the Law, delivered on Mount
Sinai, was before that delivered by the Lord to man in the
Garden. As first, Death reigned over them that had not sinned,
35 after the similitude of *Adams transgression* (that is, though they
did not take the forbidden fruit as *Adam* did), but had the

4 their] this *1685*   16 from] to *1685*

transgression been no other, or had their sin been laid to the charge of none but those that did eat of that fruit, then those that was born to *Adam*, after he was shut out of the Garden, had not had sin; in that they did not actually eat of that fruit, and so had not been slaves to death. But in that Death did 5 reign from *Adam* to *Moses*, or from the time of his transgression against the first giving of the Law, till the time the Law was given on Mount Sinai, it is evident, that the substance of the Ten Commandments was given to *Adam* and his Posterity under that Command, *Eat not of the tree that is in the* 10 *midst of the Garden*. But yet if any shall say, that it was because of the sin of their Father that death reigned over them: to that I shall answer, that although originall sin be laid to the charge of his Posterity, yet it is also for their sins, that they actually committed, that they were plagued. And again, 15 saith the Apostle, *For where there is no Law, there is no transgression*, Rom. 4. 15. *For sin is not imputed where there is no Law: Neverthelesse death reigned from Adam to Moses*, saith he, *Rom.* 5. 13, 14. But if there had been no Law, then there had been no transgression, and so no death to follow after, as the wages 20 thereof: for death is the wages of sin, *Rom.* 6. 23. and sin is the breach of the Law; an actual breach, in our particular persons, as well as an actual breach in our publick person, I *John* 3. 4.

Again, they are no other sins, then those against that Law 25 given on Sinai, for the which those sins before mentioned was punished; therefore the Law given before by the Lord to *Adam* and his posterity, is the same with that afterwards given on Mount Sinai.

Again, the conditions of that on Sinai, and of that in the 30 Garden are all one, the one saying, *Do this and live*, the other saying the same. Also, judgement denounced against men in both kindes alike; therefore this law, it appeareth to be the very same, that was given on Mount Sinai.

Again, the Apostle speaketh but of two Covenants (to 35 wit, Grace and Works) under which two Covenants all are; some under one, and some under the other: Now this to

Adam is one; therefore that on Sinai is one; and all one with this, and that this is a truth. I say I know that the sins against that on Sinai was punished by God, for the breach thereof, before it was given there: so it doth plainly appear to be a
5 truth; for it would be unrighteous with God for to punish for that Law, that was not broken: therefore it was all one with that on Sinai.

Now the Law given on Sinai, was for the more clear discovery of those sins that was before committed against it;
10 for though the very substance of the Ten Commandments was given in the Garden, before they were received from Sinai; yet they lay so darkly in the heart of man, that his sins was not so clearly discovered, as afterwards they were; therefore saith the Apostle, *The Law was added*, Gal. 3. 19.
15 (or more plainly given on Sinai, in Tables of Stone) *that the offence might abound*; that is, that it might the more clearly be made manifest, and appear, *Rom.* 5. 20.

Again, we have a notable resemblance for this at Sinai, even in giving the Law; for first, the Law was given twice on
20 Sinai: to signifie that indeed the substance of it was given before. And secondly, the first tables that was given on Sinai was broken, at the foot of the Mount, and the other was preserved whole: to signifie, that though it was the true Law, that was given before, with that given on Sinai, yet
25 it was not so easie to be read, and to be taken notice of, in that the stones were not whole, but broken, and so the Law written thereon somewhat defaced, and disfigured.

But if any object and say, though the sins against the one, be the sins against the other, and so in that they do agree;
30 yet it doth not appear, that the same is therefore the same Covenant of Works with the other.

Answ. That which was given to *Adam* in Paradise, you will grant was the Covenant of Works; for it runs thus. *Do this and live*; do it not, and die; nay *thou shalt surely die*. Now there
35 is but one Covenant of Works: If therefore I prove, that that which was delivered on Mount Sinai, is the Covenant of

Works, then all will be put out of doubt. Now that this is so, it is evident.

First, consider the two Covenants, are thus called in Scripture, the one the administration of death, and the other the administration of life; the one the Covenant of Works, the other of Grace, but that delivered on Sinai, is called the ministration of death; that therefore is the Covenant of Works, 2 *Cor.* 3. *For if* (saith he) *the ministration of death Written and Ingraven in stones was glorious*, &c.

Secondly the Apostle writing to the *Galatians*, doth labour to beat them off from trusting in the Covenant of Works; but when he comes to give a discovery of that Law, or Covenant (he labouring to take them off from trusting in it) he doth plainly tell them, it is that which was given on Sinai, *Gal.* 4. 24, 25. Therefore that which was delivered in two Tables of Stone on Mount Sinai, is the very same that was given before to *Adam* in Paradise, they running both alike; that in the Garden saying, *Do this and live; but in the day thou eatest thereof* (or doest not do this), *thou shalt surely die.*

And so is this on Sinai, as is evident when he saith, *The man that doth these things shall live by them*, Rom. 10. 5. and in case they break them, even any of them, it saith, *Cursed is every one that continueth not in all things that are written in the* (whole) *book of the Law to do them*, Gal. 3. 10. Now this being thus cleared, I shall proceed.

A second thing to be spoken to, is this, to shew what it is to be under the Law; as it is a Covenant of Works, to which I shall speak, and that thus.

To be under the Law, as it is a Covenant of Works, it is, *to be bound upon pain of eternal damnation, to fulfill, and that compleatly, and continually, every particular point of the Ten Commandments, by doing them; do this, and then thou shalt live*: otherwise, *Cursed is every one that continueth not in all* (in every particular thing) (or) *things that are written in the book of the Law to do them*, Gal. 3. 10. That man that is under the first Covenant stands thus, and onely thus, as he is under that Covenant, or Law.

Poor souls through ignorance of the nature of that Covenant
of Works, the Law, that they are under, they do not think
their state to be half so bad as it is: when alas there is none
in the world in such a sad condition again besides themselves;
5 for indeed they do not understand these things. He that is
under the Law, as it is a Covenant of Works, is like the man
that is bound by the Law of his King upon pain of banishment,
or of being Hanged, Drawn, and Quartered, not to transgress
any of the Commandements of the King: So here, they that
10 are under the Covenant of Works, they are bound upon pain of
eternal banishment, and condemnation, to keep within the
compass of the Law of the God of Heaven. The Covenant of
Works may in this case be compared to the Laws of the
Medes and Persians, which being once made, cannot be
15 altered, *Dan.* 6. 8. You finde that when there was a Law made,
and given forth, that none should ask a Petition of any God,
or Man, but of the King onely: this Law being established
by the King (*ver.* 9.), *Daniel* breaking of it, let all do what ever
they can, *Daniel* must into the Lions Den, *ver.* 16. So here, I
20 say, there being a Law given, and sealed with the Truth, and
the Word of God (how, that the soul that sinneth shall dye,
Ezek. 18. 4.), whosoever doth abide under this Covenant,
and dieth under the same, they must and shall into the
Lions Den: nay worse then that, for they shall be thrown into
25 Hell, to the very Devils.

But to speak in a few particulars for thy better understanding herein. Know first, that the Law of God, or Covenant of
Works, doth not contain it self in one particular branch of the
Law, but doth extend it self into many, even into all the Ten
30 Commandments, and them ten into very many more, as might
be shewed: so that the danger doth not lie in the breaking
of one, or two of these ten onely; but it doth lie, even in the
transgression of any one of them. As you know, if a King
should give forth ten particular commands to be obeyed, by
35 his subjects upon pain of death: now if any man doth transgress against any one of these ten, he doth commit treason,

as if he had broke them all; and lieth liable to have the sentence of the Law, as certainly passed on him, as if he had broken every particular of them.

2. Again, you know that the Laws being given forth by the King, which if a man keep and obey a long time; yet if at the last he slips and breaks those Laws, he is presently apprehended, and condemned by that Law. These things are clear as touching the Law of God, as it is a Covenant of Works: if a man do fulfill nine of the Commandments, and yet breaketh but one, that being broken, will as surely destroy him, and shut him out from the joyes of heaven, as if he had actually transgressed against them all; for indeed in effect so he hath: there is a notable Scripture for this, in the Epistle of *James*, 2 Chap. at the 10. ver. that runs thus. *For whosoever shall keep the whole Law, and yet offend in one point, he is guilty of all*; that is, he hath in effect broken them all, and shall have the voice of them all cry out against him: and it must needs be so saith *James*, because, *he that said* (or that Law which said) *Do not commit Adultery, said also, do not Kill. Now if thou commit no Adultery, yet if thou kill, thou art become a transgressor of the Law.* As thus: it may be thou didst never make to thy self a God of Stone or Wood, or at least not to worship them so greatly, and so openly, as the Heathen do: yet if thou hast stollen, born false witness, or lusted after a Woman in thy heart, *Mat.* 5. 28. thou hast transgressed the Law; and must for certain, living and dying under that Covenant, perish for ever by the Law: for the Law hath resolved on that beforehand, saying, *Cursed is every one that continueth not in ALL things*; mark, I pray you, *in all things*, that's the word, and that seals the Doctrine.

3. Again, though a man do not covet, steal, murther, worship gods of Wood and Stone, &c. yet if they do take the Lords Name in vain, they are for ever gone, living and dying under that Covenant. *Thou shalt not take the Name of the Lord thy God in vain*; there is the command, but how if we do? then he saith, *The Lord will not hold him guiltlesse that taketh his*

Name in vain: No, though thou live as holy as ever thou canst, and walk as circumspectly as ever any did; yet if thou doest take the Lords Name in vain, thou art gone by that Covenant; *For I will not*, mark, *I will not* (let him be in never so much 5 danger), *I will not hold him guiltlesse that takes my Name in vain*, Exod. 20. 7. and so likewise for any other of the ten, do but break them, and thy state is irrecoverable, if thou live and die under that Covenant.

4. Though thou shouldest fulfill this Covenant, or Law, 10 even all of it, for a long time, ten, twenty, forty, fifty, or threescore years, yet if thou do chance to slip, and break one of them but once before thou die, thou art also gone and lost by that Covenant; for mark, *Cursed is every one that continueth not in all things* (that continueth not in all things, mark that) 15 *which are written in the Book of the Law to do them*: but if a man do keep all the Law of God his whole life time, onely sin one time before he dye, that one sin is a breach of the Law, and he hath not continued in doing the things contained therein; (For, for to continue according to the sense of this 20 Scripture, is to hold on without any failing, either in thought, word, or deed) therefore I say, though a man do walk up to the Law all his life time, but onely at the very last sin one time before he die, he is sure to perish for ever, dying under that Covenant: For my Friends you must understand, that 25 the Law of God is (*yea*) as well as the Gospel; and as they that are under the Covenant of Grace shall surely be saved by it; so, even so, they that are under the Covenant of Works and the Law, they shall surely be damned by it, if continuing there. This is the Covenant of Works, and the nature of it; 30 Namely, not to bate any thing, no, not a mite to him that lives and dies under it; *I tell thee* (saith Christ) *thou shalt not depart thence*, that is from under the Curse, *till thou hast paid the very last mite*, Luke 12. 59.

5. Again, you must consider, that this Law doth not onely 35 condemn words and actions, as I said before; but it hath authority to condemn the most secret thought of the heart,

being evil; so that if thou do not speak any word that is evill, as swearing, lying, jeasting, dissembling, or any other word that tendeth to, or savoureth of sin, yet if there should chance to passe but one vain thought thorow thy heart but once in all thy life time, the Law taketh hold of it, accuseth, 5 and also will condemn thee for it. You may see one instance for all in the fifth of *Matthew* at the 27, 28. verses, where Christ saith, That though a man do not lie with a woman carnally; yet if he do but look on her, and in his heart lust after her, he is counted by the Law, being rightly expounded, 10 such a one that hath committed the sin; and thereby hath laid himself under the condemnation of the Law. And so likewise of all the rest of the commands; if there be any thought that is evill, do but passe thorow thy heart, whether it be against God, or against man in the least measure, 15 though possibly not discerned of thee, or by thee, yet the Law takes hold of thee therefore, and doth by its authority both cast, condemn, and execute thee for thy so doing. The thought of wickednesse is sin, *Prov.*

6. Again, the Law is of that nature and severity that it 20 doth not only enquire into the generality of thy life, as touching severall things, whether thou art upright there or no, but the Law doth also follow thee into all thy holy duties, and watcheth over thee there, to see whether thou doest do all things aright there; that is to say, whether when thou doest 25 pray, thy heart hath no wandering thoughts in it; whether thou do every holy duty thou doest perfectly, without the least mixture of sin; and if it do finde thee to slip, or in the least measure to fail in any holy duty that thou doest perform, the Law taketh hold on that, & findeth fault with that, so as 30 to render all the holy duties that ever thou didst unavailable because of that: I say, if when thou art a hearing, there is but one vain thought, or in praying but one vain thought, or in any other thing whatsoever, let it be civill or spirituall, one vain thought once in all thy life time, will cause the Law to 35 take such hold on it, that for that one thing, it doth even set open all the flood-gates of Gods wrath against thee, and

irrecoverably by that Covenant, it doth bring eternall vengeance upon thee. So that I say look which wayes thou wilt,
and fail wherein thou wilt, and do it as seldom as ever thou
canst, either in civill or spirituall things, as aforesaid; that is
5 either in the service of God, or in thy employments in the
world, as thy trade or calling, either in buying or selling any
way, in any thing whatsoever; I say, if in any particular it
findeth thee tardy, or in the least measure guilty, it calleth
thee an offender, it accuseth thee to God, it puts a stop to all
10 the promises thereof, that are joyned to the Law, and leavs
thee there as a cursed transgressor against God, & a destroier
of thy own soul.

   Here I would have thee by the way for to take notice, that
it is not my intent at this time to inlarge on the several
15 Commands in particular; for that would be very tedious
both for me to write, and thee to read: onely thus much I
would have thee to do at the reading hereof; make a pause,
and sit still one quarter of an hour, and muse a little in thy
minde thus with thy self, and say; Did I ever break the Law,
20 yea or no? had I ever in all my life time one sinful thought
passed thorow my heart since I was born, yea or no? and if
thou findest thy self guilty, as I am sure thou canst not
otherwise choose but do, unless thou shut thy eyes against
thy every dayes practice; then I say conclude thy self guilty
25 of the breach of the first Covenant. And when that is done;
be sure in the next place, thou do not straightway forget it,
and put it out of thy minde, that thou art condemned by the
same Covenant; and then do not content thy self untill thou
do finde, that God hath sent thee a pardon from heaven,
30 through the Merits of our Lord Jesus Christ, the mediator
of the second Covenant. And if God shall but give thee a
heart to take this my counsel, I do make no question but
these words spoken by me, will prove an instrument for the
directing of thy heart, to the right remedy, for the salvation
35 of thy soul.

   Thus much now touching the Law and the severity of it,

*If thou would-
est have a more
full discourse
hereof, read
Dod upon the
Command-
ments.*

25 that is] that this is *1685*

upon the person that is found under it, having offended, or broken any particular of it, either in thought, word, or action; and now before I do proceed to the next thing, I shall answer four objections that do lie in my way; and also, such as do stumble most part of the world.   5

The first
objection. And first, but you will say, methinks you speak very harsh; it is enough to daunt a body: set the case therefore, that a man after he hath sinned, and broken the Law, repenteth of his wickedness, and promiseth to do so no more; Will not God have mercy then, and save a poor sinner then?   10

1. *Answ.* I told you before, that the Covenant once broken, will execute upon the offender that which it doth threaten to lay upon him; and as for your supposing that your repenting, and promising to do so no more, may help well, and put you in a condition to attain the mercy of God by the Law: 15 these thoughts do flow from gross ignorance, both of the nature of sin, and also of the nature of the justice of God. And if I was to give you a description, of one in a lost condition for the present, I would brand him out with such a mark of ignorance as this is.   20

The first
Answer is ex-
pounded by
the second. 2. *Answ.* The Law as it is a Covenant of works, doth not allow of any repentance unto life, to those that live and dye under it; for the law being once broken by thee never speaks good unto thee, neither doth God at all regard thee if thou be under that Covenant, notwithstanding all thy repentings, 25 and also promises, to do so no more. No, saith the Law, thou hast sinned, therefore I must curse thee; for it is my nature to curse, even, and nothing else but curse every one that doth in any point transgress against me, *Gal.* 3. 10. *They brake my Covenant, and I regarded them not saith the Lord,* Heb. 8. Let them 30 cry, I will not regard them; let them repent I will not regard them; they have broken my Covenant, and done that in which I delighted not; therefore by that covenant I do curse, and not bless; damn, and not save; frown, and not smile; reject, and not embrace; charge sin, and not forgive it. *They* 35 *brake my Covenant, and I regarded them not*: So that I say if thou

break the Law, the first Covenant; and thou being found
there, God looking on thee thorow that, he hath no regard
on thee, no pitty for thee, no delight in thee.

But hath not the Law promises as well as threatnings?
5 saying, *The man that doth these things shall live* (Mark, he shall
live), *by them*, or in them.

Answ. First, to break the Commandments, is not to keep
or fulfill the same; but thou hast broken them, therefore the
promise doth not belong to thee, by that Covenant. Secondly,
10 the promises that are of the Law, are conditionall, and so
not performed, unless there be a full and continual obedience
to every particular of it, and that without the least sin. *Do
this*, mark, *do this*, and afterwards *thou shalt live*; but if thou
break one point of it once in all thy life, thou hast not done
15 the Law; therefore the promises following the Law do not
belong unto thee, if one sin hath been committed by thee.
As thus (I will give you a plain instance), 'Set the case there
be a Law made by the King, that if any man speak a word
against him, he must be put to death, and this must not be
20 revoked, but must for certain be expected on the offender;
though there be a promise made to them that do not speak a
word against him, that they shall have great love from him:
yet this promise is nothing to the offender, he is like to have
no share in it, or to be ever the better for it; but contrariwise,
25 the Law that he hath offended must be executed on him; for
his sin shutteth him out from a share of, or in the Promises.'
So it is here, there is a promise made indeed, but to whom?
Why, it is to none but those that live without sinning against
the Law: but if thou (I say) sin one time against it in all thy
30 life time, thou art gone, and not one promise belongs to thee,
if thou continue under this Covenant. Methinks the prisoners
at the bar, having offended the Law (and the charge of a
just Judge towards them) do much hold forth the Law, as it is
a Covenant of Works, and how it deals with them that are
35 under it. The prisoner having offended cries out for mercy;
good my Lord mercy (saith he) pray my Lord pitty me; the

4–5 marg. The second Objection.] *Object. 2. (placed in text) 1685*

Judge saith, What canst thou say for thy self, that sentence of
Death should not be passed upon thee? Why, nothing but this,
I pray my Lord be merciful: But he answers again, Friend, the
Law must take place, the Law must not be broken: The
prisoner saith, Good my Lord spare me, and I will never do 5
so any more: the Judge notwithstanding the mans out-cryes,
and sad condition, must according to the tenor of the Law,
pass Judgement upon him, and the Sentence of Condemnation
must be read to the prisoner, though it makes him fall down
dead to hear it, if he executes the Law, as he ought to do. 10
And just thus it is concerning the Law of God.

The third   I, but sometimes (for all your haste) the Judge doth also
objection. give some Pardons, and forgive some offenders, notwithstanding their offences, though he be a Judge.

Answ. It is not because the Law is merciful, but because 15
there is manifested the love of the Judge (not the love of the
Law), I beseech you to mark this distinction; for if a man that
hath deserved death by the Law, be notwithstanding this
forgiven his offence; it is not because the Law saith, spare
him, but it is the love of the Judge (or Chief Magistrate) that 20
doth set the man free from the condemnation of the Law:
But mark, here the Law of men and the Law of God do
differ; the Law of man is not so unrevokable, but if the
Supreme please, he may sometimes grant a Pardon, without
satisfaction given for the offence; but the Law of God is of 25
this nature, that if the man be found under it, and a transgressor, or one that hath transgressed against it, before that
prisoner can be released, there must be a full, and compleat
satisfaction given to it, either by the mans own life, or by the
blood of some other man: *For without shedding of blood there is* 30
no remission, Heb. 9. 22. that is, there is no deliverance from
under the curse of the Law of God; and therefore however the
Law of man may be made of none effect, sometimes by shewing mercy without giving of a full satisfaction, yet the Law of
God cannot be so contented, nor at the least give way, that 35

8 of] of the *1685*   9 him] them *1685*   12–13 marg. The third objection.] Object. 3. (*placed in text*) *1685*   23 unrevokable] irrevokable *1685*

the person offending that, should escape the curse, and not be damned, except some one do give a full and compleat satisfaction to it for him, and bring the Prisoner into another Covenant, (to wit) the Covenant of Grace, which is more
5 easie, and soul-refreshing, and sin-pardoning.

I say therefore, you must understand, that if there be a Law made that reaches the life, to take it away for the offence given by the offender against it; then it is clear, that if the man be spared and saved, it is not the Law that doth give the
10 man this advantage, but it is the meer mercy of the King, either because he hath a ransom, or satisfaction some other way; or being provoked thereto out of his own love to the person whom he saveth. Now thou also having transgressed and broken the Law of God, if the Law be not executed upon
15 thee, it is not because the Law is merciful, or can pass by the least offence done by thee, but thy deliverence comes another way: therefore I say, however it be by the Laws of men, where they be corrupted and perverted, yet the Law of God is of that nature, that if it hath not thy own blood, or the
20 blood of some other man (for it calls for no less) for to ransome thee from the curse of it, being due to thee for thy transgression, and to satisfie the cries, the doleful cries thereof, and ever for to present thee pure, and spotless before God (notwithstanding this fiery Law) thou art gone if thou
25 hadest a thousand souls; *For without shedding of blood there is no remission*, Heb. 9. 22. No forgiveness of the least sin against the Law.

But you will say, I do not onely repent me of my former life, The fourth and also promise to do so no more, but now I do labour to be objection.
30 righteous, and to live a holy life; and now instead of being a breaker of the Law, I do labour to fulfill the same: what say you to that?

Answ. Set the case thou couldest walk like an Angel of God; set the case thou couldest fulfill the whole Law, and live from
35 this day to thy lives end, without sinning in thought, word, or deed, which is unpossible: but, I say, set the case it should

28-9 marg. The fourth objection.] *Object. 4. (placed in text) 1685* be so, why, thy state is as bad (if thou be under the first Covenant) as ever it was. For first, I know thou darest not say but thou hast at one time or other sinned; and if so, then the Law hath condemned thee; and if so, then I am sure, that thou with all thy actions, and works of righteousness, canst 5 not remove the dreadful, and unresistible Curse that is already laid upon thee, by that Law which thou art under, and which thou hast sinned against; though thou livest the holiest life that any man can live in this world, being under the Law of Works, and so not under the Covenant of Grace, 10 thou must be cut off without remedy; for thou hast sinned, though afterwards thou live never so well.

The reasons for this that hath been spoken, are these.

First, the nature of Gods justice calls for it, that is, it calls for irrecoverable ruine on them that transgress against 15 this Law: for justice gave it, and justice looks to have it compleatly, and continually obeyed, or else justice is resolved to take place, and execute its office, which is to punish the transgressor against it; you must understand that the justice of God is as unchangeable as his love; his justice cannot change 20 it's nature, justice it is, if it be pleased, and justice it is, if it be displeased. The justice of God in this case, may be compared to fire; there is a great fire made in some place, if thou do keep out of it, it is fire; if thou do fall into it thou wilt finde it fire; and therefore the Apostle useth this as an argu- 25 ment to stir up the *Hebrews* to stick close to Jesus Christ, lest

^{Heb. 12. 29.} they fell under the Justice of God, by these words, *For our God is a consuming fire*: into which if thou fall, it is not for thee to get out again, as it is with some that fall into a material fire; no, but he that falls into this, he must lie there forever; 30 as it is clear where he saith, *Who among us can dwell with*

^{*Isa. 33. 14.} *everlasting burnings, and with devouring fire**; for justice once offended, knoweth not how to shew any pitty or compassion to the offender; but runs on him like a Lion, takes him by the throat, throws him into prison, and there he is sure to lie, 35 and that to all eternity, unless infinite satisfaction be given

21–2 if it be] be if it *1685*   22 case] place *1685*

to it; which is impossible to be given by any of (us) the sons of *Adam*.

 Secondly, the faithfulness of God calls for irrecoverable ruine, to be poured out on those that shall live and dye under
5 this Covenant. If thou having sinned but one sin against this Covenant, and shouldest afterwards escape damning; God must be unfaithful to himself, and to his Word, which both agree as one. First, he would be unfaithful to himself; to himself, that is, to his Justice, Holiness, Righteousness,
10 Wisdom, and Power, if he should offer to stop the runnings out of his Justice, for the damning of them that have offended it. And secondly he would be unfaithful to his Word (his written Word) and deny, disown, and break that, of which he hath said, *It is easier for heaven and earth to pass away, then for*
15 *one tittle of the Law to fail,** or be made of none effect; now *Luk: 16. if he should not according to his certain declarations therein, 17. take vengeance on those that fall and die within the threat, and sad curses denounced, in that, his word could not be fulfilled.

20 Thirdly, because otherwise he would disown the sayings oɪ his Prophets, and gratifie the sayings of his enemies: his Prophets say he will take vengeance, his enemies say he will not; his Prophets say he will remember their iniquities, and recompence them into their bosom; but his enemies say
25 they shall do well, and they* *shall have peace though they walk* *Deut. 29. *after the imagination of their own heart*, and be not so strict as the 19, 20. word commands, and do not as it saith: but let me tell thee, hadst thou a thousand souls, and each of them was worth a thousand worlds, God would set them all on a lightfire, if
30 they fall within the condemnings of his Word, and thou dye without a Jesus, even the right Jesus; *for the Scriptures cannot be broken*. What doest thou think that God, Christ, Prophets, and Scriptures, will all lie for thee? and falsifie their words for thee? it will be but ill venturing thy soul upon that.
35 And the reasons for it are these, First, because God is God, and secondly, because man is man.

15 *tittle*] title *1659* marg. 16. 17.] 16. 7. *1685*

First, because God is perfectly just, and eternally just, perfectly holy, and eternally holy, perfectly faithful, and eternally faithful; that is without any variableness or shadow of turning: but perfectly continueth the same, and can as well cease to be God, as to alter or change the nature of his God-head. And as he is thus the perfection of all perfections, he gave out his Law to be obeyed; but if any offend it, then they fall into the hands of this his eternal justice, and so must drink of his irrecoverable wrath, which is the execution of the same justice. I say, this being thus, the Law being broken, justice takes place, and so faithfulness followeth, to see that execution be done, and also to testifie that he is true, and doth denounce his unspeakable, unsupportable, and unchangeable vengeance on the party offending.

Secondly, because thou art not as infinite as God, but a poor created weed, that is here to day and gone to morrow; and not able to answer God in his Essence, Being, and Attributes, thou art found to fall under him, for that thy soul or body can do nothing that is infinite in such a way as to satisfie this God, which is an infinite God in all his attributes.

But to declare unto you the misery of man by this Law to purpose, I do beseech you to take notice of these following particulars, besides what hath been already spoken. First, I shall shew the danger of them by reason of the Law, as they come from *Adam*. Secondly, as they are in their own persons particularly under it.

1.   First, as they come from *Adam*, they are in a sad condition; because he left them a broken Covenant: or take it thus; because they, while they were in him, did with him break that Covenant. Oh! this was the treasure that *Adam* left to his posterity, it was a broken Covenant, insomuch that death reigned over all his Children, and doth still to this day, as they come from him, both natural and eternal death, *Rom.* the 5. It may be Drunkard, Swearer, Lier, Thief, thou dost not think of this.

2.   Secondly, he did not onely leave them a broken Covenant, but also made them (himself) sinners against it: he made them

sinners; *By one mans disobedience many were made sinners, Rom. 5.
19.* And this is worse then the first.

Thirdly, not onely so; but he did deprive them of their 3.
strength, by which at first they were enabled to stand, and
5 left them no more then dead men. Oh helpless state! Oh! how
beggarly and miserable are the sons of *Adam*!

Fourthly, not onely so; but also before he left them, he was 4.
the conduit-pipe through which the Devil did convey of his
poisoned spawn and venome nature into the hearts of *Adams*
10 sons and daughters, by which they are at this day so strongly
and so violently carried away, that they flie as fast to Hell and
the Devil, by reason of sin, as chaff before a mighty winde.

Fifthly, in a word, *Adam* led them out of their Paradise, 5.
that is one more; and put out their eyes, that is another; and
15 left them to the leading of the Devil; O sad! Canst thou hear
this and not have thy ears to tingle and burn on thy head?
Canst thou read this and not feel thy Conscience begin to
throb and dagg? If so, surely it is because thou art either possessed with the Devil, or besides thy self. But I pass this, and
20 come to the second thing, which is the cause of their being in
a sad condition, which is by reason of their being in their
Particular persons under it.

First, therefore they that are under the Law, they are in
a sad condition; because they are under that which is more
25 ready (through our infirmity) to curse then to bless: they are
under that called the ministration of condemnation, 2 *Cor. 3.*
that is, they are under that dispensation, or administration,
whose proper work is to curse, and condemn, and nothing else.

Secondly, their condition is sad, who are under the Law;
30 because they are not onely under that administration that
doth condemn, but also that which doth wait an opportunity
to condemn: the Law doth not wait that it might be gracious,
but it doth wait to curse and condemn; I, it came on purpose to discover sin, *Rom. 5. 20. The Law entred,* saith the
35 Apostle, *that the offence might abound;* or appear indeed to be
that which God doth hate; and also to curse for that which

17 feel] feel this and not feel *1685*

hath been committed, as he saith, *Cursed is every one that con-tinueth not in all things that are written in the book of the Law to do them, Gal.* 3. 10.

Thirdly, they are in a sad condition; because that ad-ministration they are under, that are under the Law, doth 5 always finde fault with the sinners obedience, as well as his disobedience (if it be not done in a right spirit, which they that are under that Covenant cannot do, by reason of their being destitute of Faith); therefore, I say, it doth controll them, saying, This was not well done; this was done by the 10 halves; this was not done freely, and that was not done perfectly, and out of love to God: and hence it is that some men, notwithstanding they labour to live as holy as ever they can, according to the Law; yet they do not live a peace-able life, but are full of condemnings, full of guilt and torment 15 of Conscience; finding themselves to fail here, and to fall short there, omitting this good which the Law commands, and doing that evil which the Law forbids; but never giveth them one good word for all their pains.

Fourthly, they that are under the Law are in a sad con- 20 dition; because they are under that administration that will never be contented with what is done by the sinner: if thou be under this Covenant, work as hard as thou canst, the Law will never say, *Well done*; never say, *My good servant*: No, but alwayes it will be driving of thee faster, hastening 25 of thee harder, giving of thee fresh commands, which thou must do; and upon pain of damnation not to be left undone. Nay, it is such a master that will curse thee, not onely for thy sins, but also because thy good works were not so well done, as they ought to be. 30

Fifthly, they that are under this Covenant, or Law, their state is very sad; because, this Law doth command im-possible things of him that is under it; and yet doth but right in it; seeing man at the first, had in *Adam* strength to stand, if he would have used it and the Law was given then (as 35 I said before), when man was in his full strength; and therefore

30 ought] oft *1659*

no unequality if it commands the same still, seeing God that gave thee strength, did not take it away. I will give you a similitude for the clearing of it; set the case that I give to my servant ten pounds, with this charge, lay it out for my best
5 advantage, that I may have my own again with profit; now if my servant contrary to my command, goeth and spends my money in a disobedient way; is it any unequality in me to demand of my servant what I gave him at first? nay, and though he have nothing to pay, I may lawfully cast him into
10 prison, and keep him there untill I have satisfaction. So here, the Law was delivered to man, at the first when he was in a possibility to have fulfilled it; now then, though man have lost his strength, yet God is just in commanding the same work to be done. I, and if they do not do the same things, I
15 say, that are impossible for them to do, it is just with God to damn them, seeing it was they themselves that brought themselves into this condition; therefore saith the Apostle, *What things soever the Law, or Commands saith, it saith to them that are under the Law; that every mouth may be stopped, and all the*
20 *world may become guilty before God*, Rom. 3. 19. and this is thy sad condition that art under the Law, *Gal*. 3. 10.

But if any should object and say, but the Law doth not command unpossible things of a natural man.

I should answer in this case as the Apostle did in another,
25 very much like unto it, saying, *They know not what they say, nor whereof they affirme*: For doth not the Law command thee to love the Lord thy God, with all thy soul, with all thy strength, with all thy might, &c. and can the natural man do this? *How can those that are accustomed to do evil, do that which is* Jer. 13. 23.
30 *commanded in this particular? Can the Ethiopian change his skin, or the Leopard his spots?*

Doth the Law command thee to do good, and nothing but good? and that with all thy soul, heart, and delight (which the Law as a Covenant of Works calleth for), and canst thou
35 being Carnal do that? But there is no man that hath understanding, if he should hear thee say so, but would say that thou wast either bewitched, or stark mad.

Sixthly, they that are under the Law, are in a sad condition; because that, though they follow the Law, or Covenant of Works, I say, though they follow it, it will not lead them to heaven; no, but contrariwise, it will lead them under the Curse. *It is not possible*, saith *Paul*, *that any should be justified by the Law* (or by our following of it), *for by that is the knowledge of sin*, and by it we are condemned for the same, which is far from leading us to life, being the ministration of death, 2 *Cor.* 3. and again, *Israel that followed after the Law of righteousness, hath not attained to the Law of righteousness: wherefore? because they sought it not by faith, but by the Law, and by the Works thereof*, Rom. 9. 30, 31, 32.

Seventhly, they that are under the Law, are in a sad condition; because they do not know whether ever they shall have any wages for their work or no; they shall have no assurance of the pardon of their sins, neither any hopes of eternal life: but poor hearts as they are, they work for they do not know what, even like a poor horse, that works hard all day, and at night hath a dirty stable for his pains; so thou mayest work hard all the dayes of thy life, and at the day of death instead of having of a glorious rest in the Kingdome of Heaven, thou mayest, nay, thou shalt have for thy sins, the damnation of thy soul and body in hell to all eternity; for as much as I said before, that the Law, if thou sinnest, it doth not take notice of any good work done by thee; but takes its advantage to destroy, and cut off thy soul for the sin thou hast committed.

Eighthly, they that are under the Law, are in a sad condition; because they are under that administration, upon whose souls God doth not smile (they dying there); for the administration that God doth smile upon his Children through, is the Covenant of Grace, they being in Jesus Christ, the Lord of life and consolation: but contrariwise to those that are under the Law; for they have his frowns, his rebukes, his threatnings, and with much severity they must be dealt withall. For *they brake my Covenant, and I regarded them not, saith the Lord*, Heb. 8. 9.

Ninthly, they are in a sad condition; because they are out of the faith of Christ: they that are under the Law, have not the faith of Christ in them; for that dispensation which they are under, is not the administration of faith, *The Law is not of* 5 *faith*, saith the Apostle, Gal. 3. 12.

Tenthly, because they have not received the Spirit; for that is received *by the hearing of faith*, and not by the Law, nor the Works thereof, *Gal.* 3. 2.

Eleventhly, in a word, if thou live and dye under that 10 Covenant; Jesus Christ will neither pray for thee, neither let thee have one drop of his Blood to wash away thy sins; neither shalt thou be so much as one of the least in the Kingdome of Heaven; for all these priviledges come to souls under another Covenant, as the Apostle saith, *For such are not under the Law*, 15 *but under Grace*, that is, such as have a share in the benefits of Jesus Christ, or such as are brought from under the first Covenant, into the second; or from under the Law, into the Grace of Christs Gospel; without which Covenant of Grace, and being found in that, there is no soul can have the least 20 hope of eternal life, no joy in the holy Ghost, no share in the priviledges of Saints, because they are tyed up from them by the limits and bonds of the Covenant of Works. For you must understand, that these two Covenants have their several bonds and limitations, for the ruling and keeping in subjection, 25 or giving of freedom to the parties under the said Covenants: now they that are under the Law, are within the compass and the jurisdiction of that, and are bound to be in subjection to that; and living and dying under that, they must stand and fall to that, as *Paul* saith, *To his own master, he shall stand or fall.* 30 The Covenant of Grace doth admit to those that are under it, also liberty and freedom, together with commanding of subjection to the things contained in it, which I shall speak to further hereafter.

But now, that the former things may be further made to 35 appear, that is, what the sad condition of all them that are under the Law is: as I have shown you something of the nature

of the Law, so also shall I shew, that the Law was added, and
given for this purpose, that it might be so with those that
are out of the Covenant of Grace.

First, God did give the Law, that sin might abound, *Rom.*
5. 20. not that it should take away sin in any, but to discover the sin which is already begotten, or that may hereafter be begotten, by lust and Satan: I say, this is one proper
work of the Law to make manifest sin; it is sent to finde fault
with the sinner, and it doth also watch that it may so do, and
it doth take all advantages for the accomplishing of its work
in them that give ear thereto, or do not give ear, if it have the
rule over them. I say, it is like a man that is sent by his Lord
to see and pry into the labours and works of other men, taking
every advantage to discover their infirmities and failings,
and to chide them; yea, to throw them out of the Lords
favour for the same.

Secondly, Another great end why the Lord did adde or give
the Law, it was that no man might have any thing to lay to
the charge of the Lord, for his condemning of them that do
transgress against the same. You know that if a man should
be had before an Officer or Judge, and there be condemned,
and yet by no Law; he that condemns him, might be very
well reprehended or reproved for passing the judgement; yea
the party himself might have better ground to plead for his
liberty, then the other to plead for the condemning of him:
but this shall not be so in the judgement day, but contrariwise; for then every man shall be forced to lay his hand on his
mouth, and hold his tongue at the Judgement of God, when
it is passed upon them; therefore saith the Apostle, *What
things soever the Law saith, it saith to them that are under the Law*
(that is, all the commands, all the curses and threatnings that
are spoken by it, are spoken saith he) *that every mouth may be
stopped*; mark, I beseech you, it saith, saith he, *that every mouth
might be stopped, and that all the world might become guilty before
God*, Rom. 3. 19. So that now in case any in the judgement day,
should object against the judgement of God, as those in the

25. of *Matthew* do, saying, Lord when saw we thee thus and thus? And why doest thou pass such a sad sentence of condemnation upon us? surely this is injustice and not equity; now for the preventing of this, the Law was given; I, and
5 that it might prevent thee to purpose, God gave it betimes, before either thy first father had sinned, or thou wast born. So that again, if there should be these objections offered against the proceedings of the Lord in justice, and judgement, saying, Lord, why am I thus condemned, I did not
10 know it was sin? now against these two, was the Law given, and that betimes, so that both these are answered. If the first come in and say, why am I judged? why am I damned? then will the Law come in, even all the Ten Commandments, with every one of their cries against thy soul, the first saying,
15 he hath sinned against me, damn him; the second saying also, he hath transgressed against me, damn him; the third also saying the same, together with the 4, 5, 6, 7, 8, 9, 10. even all of them will discharge themselves against thy soul, if thou dye under the first Covenant, saying he, or they, have trans-
20 gressed against us, damn them, damn them: and I tell thee also, that these ten great guns, the Ten Commandments, will with discharging themselves in justice against thy soul, so rattle in thy conscience, that thou wilt in spite of thy teeth, be immediately put to silence, and have thy mouth stopped;
25 and let me tell thee further, that if thou shalt appear before God, to have the Ten Commandments discharge themselves against thee, thou hadst better be tied to a tree, and have ten, yea ten thousand of the biggest pieces of Ordnance in the world to be shot off against thee; for these could go no
30 further, but onely to kill the body; but they both body and soul to be tormented in hell with the devil to all eternity.
   3. Again, if the second thing should be objected, saying, But Lord I did not think this had been sin, or the other had been sin; for no body told me so: then also will the giving of
35 the Law take off that, saying, nay, but I was given to thy father *Adam* before he had sinned, or before thou wast born, and have ever since been in thy soul to convince thee of thy

sins, and to controul thee for doing the thing that was not
right. Did not I secretly tell thee at such a time, in such a
place, when thou wast doing of such a thing, with such a
one, or when thou wast all alone, that this was a sin, and that
God did forbid it; therefore if thou didst commit it, God 5
would be displeased with thee for it? And when thou wast
thinking to do such a thing, at such a time, did not I say,
forbear, do not so? God will smite thee, and punish thee for
it, if thou doest do it? And besides God did so order it, that
you had me in your Houses, in your Bibles, and also you 10
could speak and talk of me; thus pleading the truth, thou
shalt be forced to confess it is so; nay, it shall be so in some
sort with the very Gentiles and Barbarous people, that fall
far short of that light we have in these parts of the world,
(for saith the Apostle), *The Gentiles which have not the Law, these* 15
do by nature the things contained in the Law; these having not the
Law, (that is, not written as we have, yet they) *are a Law*
unto themselves, which sheweth the works of the Law is written in
their hearts*: that is, they have the Law of works in them by
nature, and therefore they shall be left without excuse; for 20
their own consciences shall stand up for the truth of this,
where he saith, *Their conscience also bearing witness, and their*
thoughts the mean while accusing, or else excusing one another.
I but when? *Why, in the day when God shall judge the secrets of men*
by Jesus Christ according to my Gospel, Rom. 2. 15, 16. So this 25
I say is another end, for which the Lord did give the Law,
namely, that God might pass a sentence in righteousness,
without being charged with any injustice, by those that shall
fall under it, in the judgement.

   4. A fourth end, why the Lord did give the Law, it was, 30
because they that dye out of Jesus Christ, might not onely
have their mouthes stopped, but also that their persons
might become guilty before God (*Rom.* 3. 19.) and indeed this
will be the ground of silencing (as I said before), they finding
themselves guilty, their consciences backing the truth of the 35
judgement of God passed upon them, *they shall become guilty,*
that is, they shall be fit vessels for the wrath of God to be

poured out into, being filled with guilt, by reason of transgressions against the Commandments: thus therefore shall
the parties under the first Covenant *be fitted to destruction*
(Rom. 9. 22), even as wood, or straw, being well dried, is
5 fitted for the fire; and the Law was added, and given, and
speaks to this very end that sins might be shown, mouths
might be stopt from quarrelling: *And that all the world*, mark,
the world might become guilty before God, and so be in justice for
ever and ever overthrown, because of their sins.

10   And this will be so, for these reasons.

First, because God hath a time to magnifie his justice, and
holiness, as well as to shew his forbearance and mercy. We
read in Scripture that his eyes are too pure to behold iniquity*, •Hab. 1. 13
and then we shall finde it true. We read in Scripture, that he
15 will magnifie the Law, and make it honourable, and then he
will do it indeed.

Now because the Lord doth not strike so soon as he is
provoked by sin, therefore poor souls will not know, nor
regard the justice of God; neither do they consider the time in
20 which it must be advanced, (which will be) when men drop   2 Pet. 3. 9.
under the wrath of God as fast as hail in a mighty storme. Psal. 50. 21,
Now therefore look to it all you that count the long-suffering 22.
and forbearance of Gods slackness; and because for the present
he keepeth silence, therefore to think that he is like unto your
25 selves. No, no; but know that God hath his set time for every
purpose of his, and in its time, it shall be advanced most
marvellously to the everlasting astonishment and overthrow
of that soul, that shall be dealt withall by Justice and the
Law. O! how will God advance his Justice? O! how will
30 God advance his holiness? First by shewing men that he in
justice cannot, will not regard them, because they have
sinned: and secondly, in that his holiness will not give way
for such unclean wretches to abide in his sight, his eyes are
so pure.

35   Secondly, because God will make it appear that he will be
as good as his word to sinners; sinners must not look to escape
alwayes, though they may escape a while, yet they shall

not go for all adoe unpunished; no, but they shall have their due to a farthing, when every threatning and curse shall be accomplished, and fulfilled on the head of the transgressor. Friend there is never an idle word that thou speakest, but God will account with thee for it; there is never a lye thou 5 tellest, but God will reckon with thee for it; nay, there shall not pass, so much as one passage in all thy life-time, but God, the righteous God, will have it in the trial by his Law (if thou dye under it) in the judgement-day.

But you will say: But who are those that are thus under 10 the Law?

Answ. Those that are under the Law, may be branched out into three ranks of men: either, first such as are grosly prophane, or such as are more refined; which may be two wayes, some in a lower sort, and some in a more eminent way.   15

First then, they are under the Law as a Covenant of Works, who are open prophane and ungodly wretches, such as delight not onely in sin, but also make their boast of the same, and brag at the thoughts of committing of it: now as for such as these are, there is a Scripture in the first Epistle of 20 *Paul* to *Timothy*, the 1 Chap. at the 9. and 10. verses, which is a notable one to this purpose, *The Law* (saith he) *is not made for a righteous man* (not as it is a Covenant of Works), *but for the* (unrighteous or) *lawless and disobedient; for the ungodly, and for sinners, for unholy, and prophane, for murderers of* 25 *fathers, and murderers of mothers, for man-slayers, for whoremongers, for them that defile themselves with mankinde, for menstealers, for liars* (look to it liars), *for perjured persons, and* (in a word) *if there be any other thing that is not according to sound Doctrine.* These are one sort of people that are under the Law, 30 and so under the curse of the same, whose due is to drink up the brim-full cup of Gods eternal vengeance, and therefore I beseech you not to deceive your selves. *For know you not that the unrighteous shall not inherit the Kingdome of God? Neither Fornicatours, nor Idolators, nor Adulterers, nor Effeminates, nor* 35 *Abusers of themselves with mankinde, nor Theeves, nor Covetous, nor*

*Drunkards, nor Revilers, nor Extortioners shall inherit the Kingdome
of Heaven,* 1 Cor. 6. 9, 10. Poor souls, you think that you may
have your sins, your lusts and pleasures, and yet you shall do
pretty well, and be let to go free in the judgement day:
5 but see what God saith of such in that 29. of *Deuteronomy,*
at the 19. and 20. verses, *Which shall bless themselves in their
heart, saying, I shall have peace, I shall be saved, I shall do as well
as others, in the day when God shall judge the world by Jesus Christ;*
(but saith God) *I will not spare them; no, but my anger and my
10 jealousie shall smoke against them. How far? even to the executing all
the curses that are written in the Law of God upon them:* nay, saith
God, I will be even with them; *For I will blot out their names from
under Heaven.* And indeed it must of necessity be so, because such
souls are unbelievers, in their sins, and under the Law, which
15 cannot, will not shew any mercy on them; for it is not the administration of mercy and life, but the administration of death
and destruction (as you have it, 2 *Cor.* the 3 *Chap.* the 7, 9. verses),
and all those, every one of them, that are open profane and
scandalous wretches are under it, and have been so ever since
20 they came into the world to this day; and they will for certain
live and dye under the same dispensation, and then be damned
to all eternity, if they be not converted from under that
Covenant, into, and under the Covenant of Grace (of which
I shall speak in its place); and yet for all this, how brag and
25 cranck are our poor wantons, and wicked ones, in this day of
forbearance? as if God would never have a reckoning with
them, as if there was no Law to condemn them, as if there was
no hell fire to put them into: but O! how will they be deceived?
when they shall see Christ sitting upon the judgement-seat,
30 having laid aside his priestly and prophetical office, and appearing onely as a judge to the wicked. When they shall see
all the records of heaven unfolded and laid open; when they
shall see each man his name out of the book of life, and in the
book of the Law; when they shall see God in his Majesty,
35 Christ in his Majesty, the Saints in their Dignity; but themselves in their impurity, what will they say then? whither

will they flie then? where will they leave their glory? *Isa.* 10. 3. O sad state!

Secondly, they are under the Law, also, who do not onely so break and disobey the Law, but follow after the Law, as hard as ever they can, seeking justification thereby; that is, though a man should abstain from the sins against the Law, and labour to fulfill the Law, and give up himself to the Law, yet if he look no further then the Law, he is still under the Law; and for all his obedience to the Law, the righteous Law of God, he shall be destroyed by that Law. Friend, you must not understand that none but profane persons are under the Law; no, but you must understand that a man may be turned from a vain, loose, open, profane conversation, and sinning against the Law, to a holy, righteous, religious life, and yet be in the same state, under the same Law, and as sure to be damned as the other that are more profane and loose. And though you may say this is very strange, yet I shall both say it, and prove it to be true. Read with understanding that Scripture in *Romans* 9. at the 30, 31. verses, where the Apostle speaking of the very same thing, saith, *But Israel which followed after the Law of righteousness*; mark, that followed after the Law of righteousness; they, notwithstanding their earnest pursuit, or hunting after the Law of righteousness, *fell short of the Law of righteousness*. It signifies thus much to us, that let a man be never so earnest, so fervent, so restless, so serious, so ready, so apt and willing to follow the Law, and the righteousness thereof, if he be under that Covenant, he is gone, he is lost, he is deprived of eternal life; because he is not under the ministration of life (if he dye there). Read also that Scripture, *Gal.* 3. 10. (which saith) *For as many as are of the Works of the Law are under the Curse*; mark, they that are of the works of the Law; now for to be of the works ot the Law, it is to be of the works of the righteousness thereof; that is, to abstain from sins against the Law, and to do the commands thereof, as near as ever they can for their lives, or with all the might they have, and therefore I beseech you to consider it; for mens being ignorant of this, is the cause why so many go on, supposing they have a share in Christ; because they are reformed, and abstain from the sins against the Law, who when all comes to all, will be damned notwithstanding; because they are not brought out 5 from under the Covenant of Works, and put under the Covenant of Grace.

Object. But (can you in very deed make these things manifestly evident from the Word of God?) methinks to reason this is very strange, that a man should labour to walk up 10 according to the Law of God, as much as ever he can, and yet that men notwithstanding this should be still under the Curse. Pray clear it.

Answ. Truly this doth seem very strange, I do know full well, to the natural man, to him that is yet in his unbelief; 15 because he goeth by beguiled reason: but for my part I do know it is so, and shall labour also to convince thee of the truth of the same.

First then, the Law is thus strict and severe, that if a man do sin but once against it, he (I say) is gone for ever by the 20 Law, living and dying under that Covenant: if you would be satisfied, as touching the truth of this, do but read the third of the *Galatians* at the 10. verse. Where it saith, *Cursed is every one* (that is, not a man shall miss by that Covenant) *that continueth not in all* (mark, in all) *things that are written in the* 25 *book of the Law to do them*: pray mark, here is a curse in the first place; if all things written in the Book of the Law be not done, and that continually too, that is, without any failing, or one slip, as I said before. Now there is never a one in the world, but before they did begin to yield obedience to the 30 least command, they in their own persons did sin against it, by breaking of it: the Apostle methinks is very notable for the clearing of this in that 3. of the *Romans,* and also in the fifth, in the one he endeavours for to prove that all had transgressed in the first *Adam,* as he stood a common person re- 35 presenting both himself and us in his standing and falling, *Rom.* 5. 12. *Wherefore* (saith he) *as by one man sin entered into the world, and death by sin: and so death passed upon all men*; mark that, but why? *for that all have sinned*, that is, for as much as all naturally are guilty of original sin, the sin that was committed by us in *Adam*: So this is one cause why none can be justified by their obedience to the Law, because, they have in the first place broken it in their first parents. But secondly, in case this should be opposed and rejected by quarrelsome persons, though there be no ground for it, *Paul* hath another argument to back his Doctrine, saying, *For we have proved* (already) *that both Jews and Gentiles are all under sin.* First, *As it is written, there is none righteous, no not one.* Secondly, *They are all gone out of the way, they are together* (mark, together) *become unprofitable, there is none that doth good, no not one.* Thirdly, *Their throat is an open Sepulchre, with their tongues they have used deceit, the poyson of asps is under their lips.* Fourthly, *Their mouthes are full of cursing and bitterness.* Fifthly, *Their feet are swift to shed blood.* In a word, *Destruction and misery are in their wayes: And the way of peace they have not known.* Now then saith he, having proved these things so clearly, the conclusion of the whole is this, *That what things soever the Law saith* (in both shewing of sin and cursing for the same) *it saith* (All) *to them that are under the Law, that every mouth may be stopped, and all the world may become guilty before God*, Rom. 3. 9, 10, 11, 12, 13, 14, 15, 16, 17, 18, 19. So that here I say lieth the ground of our not being justified by the Law, even because in the first place we have sinned against it; for know this for certain, that if the Law doth take the least advantage of thee, by thy sinning against it, all that ever thou shalt afterwards hear from it, is nothing but curse, curse, curse him, *For not continuing in all things that are written in the book of the Law to do them.*

Secondly, thou canst not be saved by the righteous Law of God, the first Covenant, because, that (together with this thy miserable state, by original and actual sins, before thou didst follow the Law) since thy turning to the Law, thou hast committed several sins against the Law. (*In many things we offend all.*) So that now thy righteousness to the Law, being mixed with sometimes the lust of concupiscence,

fornication, covetousness, pride, heart-risings against God,
coldness of affection towards him, backwardness to good
duties, speaking idle words, having of strife in your hearts,
and such like; I say, these things being thus, the righteous-
5 ness of the Law is become too weak through this our flesh
(*Rom.* 8. 3.), and so notwithstanding all our obedience to the
Law, we are yet through our weakness under the Curse of
the Law; for as I said before, the Law is so holy, so just, and so
good, that it cannot allow that any failing or slip should be
10 done by them that look for life by the same. *Cursed is every one
that continueth not in every thing,* Gal. 3. 10. and this *Paul* knew
full well, which made him throw away all his righteousness
(But you will say that was his own. *Answer.* But it was even
that which while he calls it his own, he also calls it the
15 righteousness of the Law, see *Phil.* 3. 7, 8, 9, 10.), and to
account it but dung, but as dirt on his shoes, and that, that
he might be found in Christ, and so be saved by him without
the deeds of the Law, *Rom.* 3. 28.

But thirdly, set the case the righteousness of the Law, which
20 thou hast was pure and perfect without the least flaw, or
fault, without the least mixture of the least sinful thought;
yet this would fall far short of presenting of thee blameless in
the sight of God. And that I prove by these arguments.

The first Argument is; That that which is not Christ,
25 cannot redeem souls from the Curse. It cannot compleatly
present them before the Lord. Now the Law is not Christ;
Therefore the moral Law, cannot (by all our obedience to it)
deliver us from the curse that is due to us, *Act.* 4. 12.

The second Argument is; That that righteousness that is
30 not the righteousness of faith (that is by believing in Jesus
Christ) cannot please God. Now the righteousness of the
Law as a Covenant of works is not the righteousness of faith;
Therefore the righteousness of the Law as acted by us, being
under that Covenant cannot please God. The first is proved
35 in *Heb.* 11. 6. *But without faith it is impossible to please him,*
mark, it is impossible. The second thus. *The Law is not of
faith,* Gal. 3. 12. Rom. 10. 5, 6. compared with *Gal.* 3. 11.

*But that no man is justified in the sight of the Lord by the Law,
it is evident; for the just shall live by faith, and the Law is not of
faith.* But for the better understanding of those that are
weak of apprehension, I shall prove it thus.

First, that soul that hath eternal life, he must have it by 5
right of purchase, or redemption (*Heb.* 9. 22. *Eph.* 1. 7.).
Secondly this purchase or redemption, must be through the
Blood of Christ. *You have redemption through his Blood. Without
shedding of blood there is no remission.* Now the Law is not in a
capacity to dye, and so to redeem sinners by the purchase of 10
Blood, which satisfaction justice calls for (read the same
Scriptures, *Heb.* 9. 22.); justice calls for satisfaction, because
thou hast transgressed, and sinned against it, and that must
have satisfaction; therefore, all that ever thou canst do
cannot bring in redemption: though thou follow the Law up 15
to the nail-head (as I may say); because all this is not shedding
of blood: for believe it, and know it for certain, that though
thou hadst sinned but one sin, before thou didst turn to the
Law; that one sin will murther thy soul, if it be not washed
away by blood, even by the precious Blood of Jesus Christ, that 20
was shed when he did hang upon the Cross on Mount *Calvary.*

Object. But (you will say) methinks that giving of our
selves up to live a righteous life, should make God like the
better of us, and so let us be saved by Christ, because we are
so willing to obey his Law.   25

Answ. The motive that moveth God to have mercy upon
sinners, is not because they are willing to follow the Law, but
because he is willing to save them. *Not for thy righteousness,
or for thy uprightness of heart doest thou possess the Land,* Deut.
9. 4, 5, 6. Now understand this; if thy will to do righteousness 30
was the first moving cause why God had mercy on thee
through Christ, then it must not be freely by grace (I say
freely), but the Lord loves thee and saves thee upon free
termes, having nothing before-hand to make him accept of
thy soul, but onely the Blood of Christ; therefore to allow of 35
such a principle, it is to allow, that grace is to be obtained

22–3 of our selves up] up you selves *1685*   23–4 the better of]better on *1685*

by the works of the Law, which is as gross darkness as lies in the darkest dungeon in Popery, and is also directly opposite to Scripture. *For we are justified freely by his grace: through the redemption that is in Christ*, not through the good that is in our
5 selves or done by us (*Rom.* 3. 24.). No, *But by faith, without*; mark that, *without the deeds of the Law*, verse 28. Again, *not of works, lest any man should boast*, Eph. 2. 9. (No, no, saith he) *Not according to our works* (or righteousness), *but according to his own purpose*; mark, *according to his own purpose and grace which*
10 *was* (a free gift) *given us in Christ Jesus* (not lately, but) *before the world began*, 2 Tim. 1. 9.

Object. But you will say, then, why did God give the Law, if we cannot have salvation by following of it?

Answ. I told you before, that the Law was given for these
15 following reasons.

First, that thou mightest be convinced by it of thy sins, and that thy sins might indeed appear very sinfull unto thee; which is done by the Law these wayes. First, by shewing of thee what a holy God he is that did give the Law; and
20 secondly, by shewing thee thy vileness and wickedness, in that thou contrary to this holy God, hast transgressed against, and broken this his holy Law; therefore saith *Paul, The Law was added, that the offence might abound*, Rom. 5. 20. that is, by shewing the creature the holiness of God, and also its own
25 vileness.

Secondly, that thou mayest know, that God will not damn thee for nothing in the judgement-day.

Thirdly, because he would have no quarrelling at his just condemning of them at that day.

30 Fourthly, because he will make thee to know that he is a holy God, and pure.

Quest. But seeing you have spoken thus far: I wish you would do so much as to show in some particulars, both what men have done, and how far they have gone, and what they
35 have received, being yet under this Covenant, which you call the ministration of condemnation.

Answ. This is something a difficult question, and had need be not onely warily, but also home and soundly answered. The question consists of three particulars. First, what men have done. Secondly, how far men have gone. Thirdly, what they have received, and yet to be under the Law or Covenant 5 of works; & so in a state of condemnation.

As for the first, I have spoken something in general to that already, but for thy better understanding, I shall speak yet more particularly. First, a man hath, and may be convinced and troubled for his sins, and yet be under this Covenant, and 10 that in a very heavy and dreadful manner; insomuch that he may finde the weight of them to be intollerable and too heavy for him to bear, as it was with *Cain, Gen.* 4. 13. *My punishment* (saith he) *is greater then I can bear.*

Secondly, a man living thus under a sense of his sins, 15 may repent, and be sorry for them, and yet be under this Covenant, and yet be in a damned state, *Matth.* 27. 3. *And when he* (Judas) *saw what was done he repented.*

Thirdly, men may not onely be convinced, and also repent for their sins; but they may also desire the prayers of the 20 Children of God for them too, and yet be under this Covenant, and Curse, *Exod.* 10. 16, 17. *And Pharaoh called for Moses and Aaron, and said, I have sinned, intreat the Lord your God that he may take away from me these plagues.*

Fourthly, A man may also humble himself for his offences, 25 and disobedience against his God, and yet be under this Covenant, see 1 *Kings* 21 Chap. at the 24, 25, 26, 27, 28, 29. verses.

Fifthly, A man may make restitution unto men for the offence he hath done unto them, and yet be under this 30 Covenant.

Sixthly, A man may do much work for God in his generation and yet be under this first Covenant, as *Jehu*, who did do that which God bid him, 2 *King.* 9. 25, 26. and yet God threatneth even *Jehu*, because, though he did do the thing 35 that the Lord commanded him; yet he did it not from a right

27 Chap. at the] *om. 1685*   28 verses] *om. 1685*

principle; for had he, the Lord would not have said, *Yet a little while and I will avenge the blood of Jezreel upon the house of Jehu,* Hos. 1. 4.

Seventhly, Men may hear, and fear the servants of the Lord, 5 and reverance them very highly; yea, and when they hear, they may not onely hear, but hear and do, and that gladly too, not one or two things, but many; mark, *many things gladly*, and yet be lost, and yet be damned (see *Mark* the 6. 20.) *For Herod feared John* (why? not because he had any 10 civil power over him, but), *because he was a just man, and holy, and observed him, and when he heard him, he did many things, and heard him gladly*; it may be that thou thinkest, that because thou hearest such and such, therefore thou art better then thy neighbours: but know for certain that thou mayest not 15 onely hear, but thou mayest hear and do, and that not with a backward will, but *gladly*; mark, *gladly* and yet be *Herod still*, an enemy to the Lord Jesus *still*: consider this I pray you.

2. But secondly, to the second thing, which is this. *How far may such a one go?* to what may such a one attain? 20 whither may he arrive? and yet be an undone man under this Covenant.

Answ. First, such a one may be received into fellowship with the Saints, as they are in a visible way of walking one with another; they may walk hand in hand together (see *Matth.* 25 25 at the first verse, where he saith) *The Kingdom of Heaven* (that is a visible company of professors of Christ) *is likened to ten Virgins, which took their lamps, and went forth to meet the Bridegroom, five of them were wise, and five were foolish.* These in the first place are called Virgins; that is, such as are clear 30 from the pollutions of the world. Secondly, they are said to go forth; that is, from the rudiments and traditions of men. Thirdly, they do agree to take their lamps with them; that is, to profess themselves the Servants of Jesus Christ, that wait upon him, and for him; and yet when he came, he found half 35 of them (even them Virgins) that had Lamps, that also went forth from the pollutions of the world, and the customs of

8 the] *om. 1685*   25 25 at the first verse] 25. 1. *1685*

men, to be such as lost their precious souls (see verse 10.) which they should not have done, had they been under the Covenant of Grace, and so, not under the Law.

Secondly, they may attain to a great deal of honour in the said company of professors (that which may be accounted 5 honour) insomuch that they may be put in trust with Church Affairs, and bear the bag, as *Judas* did. I speak not this to shame the Saints: but being beloved I warne them; yet I spake this on purpose, that it might (if the Lord will) knock at the door of the souls of professors, consider *Demas*.   10

Thirdly, they may attain to speak of the word as Ministers, and become preachers of the Gospel of Jesus Christ, insomuch that the people where they dwell, may even take up a proverb concerning them, saying, *Is he among the Prophets?* his gifts may be so rare, his tongue may be so fluent, and his matter may 15 be so fit, that he may speak with a tongue like an Angel, and speak of the hidden mysteries, yea, of them *all*; mark that (1 *Cor.* 13. 1, 2, 3, 4.), and yet be nothing, and yet be none of the Lords annointed ones with the Spirit of grace savingly, but may live and dye under the Curse of the Law.   20

Fourthly, They may go yet further; they may have the gifts of the Spirit of God, which may inable them to cast out Devils, to remove the biggest Hills or Mountains in the world; nay, thou mayest be so gifted as to prophesie of things to come, the most glorious things, even the coming of the Lord 25 Jesus Christ to reign over all his enemies, and yet be but a *Balaam*, a wicked and a mad Prophet, see 2 *Pet.* 2. 16. *Numbers* 24. the 16, 17, 18, 19, 20, 21, 22, 23, 24, 25. verses.

Fifthly, they may not onely stand thus for a while, for a little season; but they may stand thus *till the coming of the* 30 *Lord Jesus Christ with his holy Angels*, I, and not be discovered of the Saints *till* that very day. *Then all those Virgins arose* (the wise and the foolish) then, when? why, when this voice was heard, *Behold the Bridegroom cometh, go ye out to meet him* (Matth. 25. 1, 2, 3, 4, 5, 6.), and yet was out of the Lord Jesus 35 Christ, and yet was under the Law.

Sixthly, nay further, they may not onely continue in a profession *till then* (supposing themselves to be under the Grace of the Gospel, when indeed they are under the Curse of the Law), but even when the Bridegroom is *come*, they may 5 still be so confident of their state to be good, that they will even reason out the case with Christ, why they are not let into the Kingdom of glory, saying, *Lord, Lord, have we not eaten and drunk in thy presence? and hast not thou taught in our streets?* Nay further, *Have not we taught in thy Name? and in thy* 10 *Name cast out devils*: nay not onely this, but, *done many*: mark, *we have done many wonderful works*; nay further, they were so confident, that they commanded *in a commanding way*, saying, *Lord open to us*. See here I beseech you, how far these went, they thought they had had intimate acquaintance with Jesus 15 Christ, they thought he could not chuse but save them, they had eat and drunk with him, sat at the table with him, received power from him, executed the same power. *In thy Name have we done thus and thus*, even wrought many *wonderful works*, see *Mat.* 7. 22. *Luke* 13. 25, 26. And yet these poor 20 creatures was shut out of the Kingdome. O consider this (I beseech you) before it be too late, lest you say, Lord, let us come in, when Christ saith, thrust him out, *ver.* 28. Hears you cry, *Lord open to us*, when he saith, *Depart I know you not*; lest, though you think of having *joy*, you have *weeping and gnashing* 25 *of teeth*.

3. But thirdly, the third thing touched in the question, was this; What may such a one receive of God, who is under the Curse of the Law?

First, they may receive *an answer to their prayers from God,* 30 at some times, for some things as they do stand in need of. I finde in Scripture that God did hear these persons, that the Apostle saith was cast out, see *Gen.* 21. 17. *And God heard the voice of the Lad* (even of cast out *Ishmael*), *and the Angel of the Lord called to Hagar out of heaven* (which was the bond- 35 woman, and under the Law, *Gal.* 4. 30.), *and said unto her, Fear not: for God hath heard the voice of the Lad where he is.* Friends, it may be you may think, because you have your prayers answered in some particular things, therefore you may suppose, that as to your eternal state, your condition is very good. But you must know that God doth hear the cry of a company of Ishmaelites the sons of the Bond-woman, who are under the Law as a Covenant of Works. I do not say he hears them as to their eternal state, but he heareth them as to several streights, that they go through in this life, I, and gives them ease and liberty from their trouble. Here this poor wretch was almost perished for a little water, and he cryed, and God heard him, yea he heard him out of *Heaven*. Read also the 107 *Psalm*, the 23, 24, 25, 26, 27, 28, 29. verses. *Psal.* 106. 15. *He gave them their desire, and sent leanness to their souls.*

But some may say, methinks this is yet more strange that God should hear the prayers, the cries of those that are under the Law, and answer them.

Answ. I told you before he doth not hear them as to their eternal state, but as to their temporal state; For God as their Creator hath a care of them, and causeth the sun to shine upon them, and the rain to distill upon their substance, *Matth.* 5. 45. Nay he doth give the Beasts in the field their appointed food, and doth hear the young Ravens when they cry, *Psal.* 147. 9. which are far inferiour to man. I say therefore, that God doth hear the cries of his Creatures, and doth answer them too, though not as to their eternal state; but may damn them nevertheless when they dye for all that.

Secondly, they may receive promises from the mouth of the Lord. There are many that have had promises made to them by the Lord, in a most eminent way, and yet (as I said before) are such as are cast out and called the Children of the Bond-woman (which is the Law) see *Gen.* 21. 17, 18. *And the Angel of the Lord called out of Heaven to Hagar* (that was the Bond-woman) *saying, fear not: for God hath heard the voice of the Lad where he is. Arise, lift up the Lad, and hold him in thine hand*: FOR I WILL MAKE OF HIM: mark, there is the promise. *For I will make of him* (of the son of the Bond-woman), *a great Nation.*

11 the²] *om. 1685*   verses] *om. 1685*   29 way] manner *1685*

Thirdly, nay they may go further; for they may receive another heart then they had before, and yet be under the Law. There is no man I think, but those that do not know what they say, that will think or say, that *Saul* was under the 5 Covenant of Grace, yet after he had talked with *Samuel*, and had turned his back to go from him, saith the Scripture, *God gave him another heart* (1 *Sam.* 10. 9.), another *heart*; mark that, and yet an out-cast, a rejected person, 1 *Sam.* 15. 26, 29. Friends, I beseech you let not these things offend you, but 10 let them rather beget in your hearts, an enquiring into the truth of your condition, and be willing to be searched to the bottom, and also, that every thing which hath not been planted by the Lords right hand, may be rejected, and that there may be a reaching after better things, even the things 15 that will not onely make thy soul think thy state is good now; but that thou mayest be able to look sin, death, hell, the curse of the Law, together with the Judge in the face with comfort, having such a real, sound, effectual work of Gods Grace in thy soul, that when thou hearest the Trumpet sound, 20 seest the graves flie open, and the dead come creeping forth out of their holes; when thou shalt see the judgement seat, the books opened, and all the world standing before the judgement seat; I say, that then thou mayest not fear, that then thou mayest stand, and have that blessed sentence spoken 25 to thy soul, *Come ye blessed of my Father, inherit the Kingdome prepared for you from before the Foundation of the world, Matth. 25. 34.*

But (you will say) for all this we cannot believe that we Objection. are under the Law; for these reasons. As first, because we 30 have found a change in our hearts. Secondly, because we do deny that the Covenant of Works will save any. Thirdly, because for our parts, we judge ourselves far from legal principles; for we are got up into as perfect a Gospel order, as to matter of practice and discipline in Church Affairs, as any 35 this day in *England*, as we judge.

Answ. First, that mans belief that is grounded upon any

23–4 not fear . . . mayest] *om.* 1685

thing done in him, or by him onely, that mans belief is not
grounded upon the death, burial, resurrection, ascension,
and intercession of Jesus Christ; for that man that hath
indeed good ground of his eternal salvation, his faith is
settled upon that object which God is well pleased, or satis- 5
fied withal, which is that man that was born of *Mary*, even
her *first-born Son*; that is, he doth apply by faith to his soul,
the vertues of his death, blood, righteousness, &c. and doth
look for satisfaction of soul no where else, then from that,
neither doth the soul seek to give God any satisfaction, as to 10
justification any other wayes: but doth willingly and chear-
fully accept of, and embrace the vertues of Christs death,
together with the rest of his things, done by himself on the
Cross as a Sacrifice, and since also as a Priest, Advocate,
Mediator, &c. And doth so really and effectually, receive 15
the glories of the same, *That thereby*; mark that, *thereby he is
changed into the same image, from glory to glory*, 2 Cor. 3. 18.
Thus in general: but yet more particular.

First, to think that your condition is good, because there is
some change in you from a loose profane life, to a more close, 20
honest, and civil life and conversation; I say to think this
testimony sufficient for to ground the stress of thy salvation
upon, is very dangerous. First, because such a soul doth not
onely lay the stress of its salvation besides the man Christ
Jesus that dyed upon the Cross: But secondly, because that 25
his confidence is not grounded upon the Saviour of sinners;
but upon his turning from gross sins, to a more refined life
(and it may be to the performance of some good duties),
which is no Saviour: I say this is very dangerous; therefore
read it, and the Lord help you to understand it; for unless 30
you lay the whole stress of the salvation of your souls upon
the merits of another man (namely Jesus) and that by what
he did do, and is a doing without you; for certain, as sure as
God is in heaven, your souls will perish: And this must not be
notionally neither, as with an assenting of the understanding 35
onely: but it must be by the wonderful, invisible, invincible
power, of the Almighty God, working in your souls by his

Spirit, such a real, saving, holy faith, that can through the operation of the same Spirit by which it is wrought, lay hold on, and apply these most heavenly, most excellent, most meritorious benefits of the man Christ Jesus, not onely to
5 your heads and fancies, but to your very souls, and consciences, so effectually, that you may be able by the same faith to challenge the power, madness, malice, rage, and destroying nature, either of sin, the Law, death, the Devil, together with hell, and all other evils, throwing your souls upon the
10 death, burial, resurrection, and intercession of that man Jesus without sin. *Rom.* 8. 32, 33, 34, 35, 36, 37, 38, 39.

But secondly, do you think that there was no change in the five foolish Virgins spoken of in *Matth.* 25. 1, 2, 3. verses? Yes, there was such a change in them very people, that the
15 five wise ones could give them admittance of walking with them, in the most purer wayes and institutions of the Gospel of Christ, and yet but foolish; nay, they walked with them, or shall walk with them, until the Lord Jesus Christ shall break down from heaven; and yet but foolish Virgins, and
20 yet but under the Law; and so under the Curse, as I said before.

Object. But (say you) we have disowned the Covenant of Works, and turned from that also.

Answ. This is sooner said then done: Alas, alas, poor souls
25 think because they can say *grace*, *grace*, it is freely by grace; therefore they are under the Covenant of Grace. A very wide mistake; you must understand thus much, that though you be such as can speak of the Grace of the Gospel, yet if you your selves be not brought under the very Covenant of
30 Grace, you are yet notwithstanding your talk, and profession, very far wide, of a *sence*, and of a *share* in the Covenant of the Grace of God, held forth in the Gospel.

The Jews were men of a clearer understanding many of them, then to conclude that the Law, and onely the Law, was
35 the way to salvation; for they, even they that received not the Christ of God, did expect a Saviour should come, *John*

11 sin] *om. 1659, 1685*   13 verses] *om. 1685*

7. 27. and the 41, 42, 43. but they were men that had not that Gospel Spirit, which alone is able to lead them to the very life, marrow, or substance of the Gospel in right terms; and so being muddy in their understandings, being between the thoughts of a Saviour, and the thoughts of the Works of the Law, thinking that they must be accomplished for the obtaining of a Saviour, and his mercy towards them; I say, between these, they fell short of a Saviour. As many poor souls in these dayes; they think they must be saved alone by the Saviour: yet they think there is something to be done on their parts, for the obtaining of the good will of the Saviour: as their humiliation for sin, their turning from the same, their promises, and vows, and resolutions to become a new man, joyn in Church-fellowship, and what not; and thus they bringing this along with them, as a means to help them, they fall short of eternal salvation, if they convert not; see that Scripture, *Rom.* 9. at the 30, 31, 32. verses. The Apostle saith there, that they that sought not did obtain, when they that did seek fell short. *What shall we say then*, saith he, *that the Gentiles, which sought not after righteousness, have attained to righteousness, (yea) even the righteousness of faith*; and what else? Why, *But Israel which followed after the Law of righteousness, have not attained to the Law of righteousness*; how came that to pass? *because* (saith he) *they sought it not by faith, but as it were*; mark, he doth not say *altogether*: no, *but as it were*, that is, because as they sought, they did a little by the by lean upon the Works of the Law. And let me tell you, that this is such a hard thing to beat men off of, that though *Paul* himself did take the work in hand, he did finde enough to do touching it; How is he fain to labour in the ten first Chapters of his Epistle to the *Romans*, for the establishing of those that did even profess largely in the Doctrine of Grace? And also in that Epistle to the *Galatians*, and yet lost many, do what he could? Now the reason why the doctrine of Grace doth go

---

1 and the] *om. 1685*   17 at the] *om. 1685*   verses] *om. 1685*   25 no, *but as it*] no, but it *1685*   30 fain] faint *1659, 1685*   34 go] *om. 1659, 1685*

so hardly down (even with professors), in truth, effectually; it is because there is a principle naturally in man, that doth argue against the same, and that thus: why? saith the soul, I am a *sinner*, and God is *righteous*, *holy*, and *just*; his holy Law
5 therefore having been broken by *me*, I must by all means, if ever I look to be saved; In the first place be sorry for my sins. Secondly, turn from the same. Thirdly, follow after good duties, and practise the good things of the Law, and or- dinances of the Gospel, and so hope that God for Christs
10 sake may forgive all my sins; which is not the way to God, as a Father in Christ, but the way, the very way to come to God by the Covenant of Works, or the Law, which things I shall more fully clear, when I speak to the second doctrine.

Again therefore, those that this day profess the Gospel,
15 for the generality of them, they are such that notwithstanding their profession, they are very ignorant of that glorious in- fluence, and lustre of the same; I say, they are ignorant of the vertue and efficacy of the glorious things of Christ held forth by, and in the Gospel; which doth argue their not being under 2 Cor. 4. 3.
20 the Covenant of Grace, but rather under the Law or old Coven- ant. As for instance, If you do come among some professors of the Gospel, in general, you shall have them pretty busie, and ripe; also able to hold you in a very large discourse in several points of the same glorious Gospel; but if you come
25 to the same people and ask them concerning heart-work, or what work the Gospel hath wrought on them, and what ap- pearance they have had of the sweet influences and vertues on their souls and consciences; it may be they will give you such an answer as this: I do finde by the preaching thereof,
30 that I am changed, and turned from my sins in a good measure, and also have learned* to distinguish between the Law and the *But onely Gospel, so that for the one, that is, for the Gospel I can plead, in tongue. and also can shew the weakness, and unprofitableness of the other; and thus far it is like they may go, which is not
35 far enough to prove them under the Covenant of Grace, though they may have their tongues so largely tipt with the

13 speak] spake *1659*

profession of the same: see 2 *Pet.* the 2 Chap. the 20. verse, where he saith, *For if after they have escaped the pollutions of the world, through the knowledge of our Lord and Saviour Jesus Christ* (which was not a saving knowledge), *they are again intangled therein and overcome, the latter end of that man is worse then his beginning.* See also *Matth.* 25. 1, 2, 3, 4, &c. and also *Matth.* 7. 22.

Object. But (you will say) is not this a fair declaring of the Work of Grace, or doth it not discover that without all gain-saying we are under the Covenant of Grace, when we are able, not onely to speak of the glorious Gospel of Jesus Christ; but also to tell, and that by experience, that we have been changed from worse to better, from sin to a holy life by leaving of the same, and that by hearing of the Word preached?

An. A man may in the first place be able to talk of all the mysteries of the Gospel, and that like an Angel of God, and yet be no more in Gods account, then the sounding of a Drum, Brass, or the tinckling of a Cimball, which are things that notwithstanding their sound, and great noise, are absolutely void of life and motion; and so are accounted with God as nothing, that is, no Christians, no believers, not under the Covenant of Grace for all that. See 1 *Cor.* 13: 1, 2, 3, 4.

Secondly, men may not onely do this, but may also be changed in reality for a season, from what they formerly were, and yet be nothing at all in the Lords account, as to an eternal blessing. Read the 2 *Pet.* 2. 20. the Scripture which I mentioned before; for indeed that one Scripture is enough to prove all that I desire to say, as to this very thing; for if you observe, there is enfolded therein, these following things; first, that reprobates may attain to a knowledge of Christ. Secondly, this knowledge may be of such weight and force, that for the present, it may make them escape the pollutions of the world, and this by hearing the Gospel. *For if after they have escaped the pollutions of the world, through the knowledge of our Lord and Saviour Jesus Christ, they are again entangled therein, and*

1 the 2 Chap. the 20. verse] 2. 20. *1685*   26 the[1]] *om. 1685*

overcome, the last end of that man is worse then his beginning. Now
that they are Reprobates,* Dogs, or Sows. Read further, *But*
(saith he) *it is happened to them according to the true proverb;*
the Dog is turned to his own vomit again, and the Sow, that was
5 *washed to her wallowing in the mire,* the 21, 22. verses.

But (say you) our practices in the worship of God shall
testifie for us, that we are not under the Law; for we have by
Gods goodness attained to as exact a way of walking in the
ordinances of God, and as near the examples of the Apostles,
10 as ever any Churches since the primitive times, as we judge.

Answ. What then? do you think that the walking in the
order of the Churches of old, as to matter of outward worship,
is sufficient to clear you of your sins at the judgement day?
or do you think that God will be contented with a little bodily
15 subjection to that which shall vanish, and fade like a flower,
when the Lord shall come from heaven in flaming fire, with his
mighty Angels? Alas, alas, how will such professors as these
are, fall before the Judgement-seat of Christ? then such a
question as this, *Friend how camest thou in hither, not having on*
20 *thy wedding garment,* will make them be speechless, and fall
down into everlasting burnings, thousands on a heap; for you
must know, that it is not then your crying Lord, Lord, that
will stand you in stead, nor your saying, We have eat and
drunk in thy presence, that will keep you from standing on
25 the left hand of Christ.

It is the principle as well as the practice, that shall be
enquired into at that day.

Quest. The principle (you will say) what do you mean by
that?

30 *Answ.* My meaning is, the Lord Jesus Christ will then
enquire, and examine, whether the Spirit from which you
acted, was Legal, or Evangelical; that is, whether it was the
spirit of adoption, that did draw you out to the thing you
took in hand, or a meer moral principle, together with some
35 shallow and common illuminations into the outward way of
the Worship of God, according to Gospel rule.

5 the 21, 22. verses] verse 21. 22. *1685*

Side notes:

Some professors take them at the best, they are but like Dogs, spuing out their filth for a time.

The last part of the objection.

2 Thess. 1. 7, 8.

Quest. But (you will say its like) how should this be made manifest, & appear?

Answ. I shall speak briefly in answer hereunto, as followeth. First then, that man that doth take up any of the ordinances of God, namely, as prayer, baptisme, breaking of bread, reading, hearing, alms-deeds, or the like; I say, he that doth practice any of these or such like, supposing thereby to procure the love of Christ to his own soul; he doth do what he doth from a Legal, and not from an Evangelical, or Gospel Spirit, as thus; for a man to suppose that God will hear him for his prayers sake, for his alms sake, for his humiliation sake, or because he hath promised to make God amends here-after, whereas there is no such thing as a satisfaction to be made to God by our prayers, or whatever we can do; I say, there is no such way to have reconciliation with God in. And so also, for men to think, because they are got into such and such an Ordinance, and have crouded themselves into such and such a *Society*, that therefore they have got pretty good shelter from the wrath of the Almighty; when alas poor souls there is no such thing; No, but God will so set his face against such professors, that his very looks will make them to tear their very flesh; yea, make them to wish, would they had the biggest Mill-stone in the world hanged about their necks, and they cast into the midst of the Sea. For friends, let me tell you, though you can now content your selves, without the holy, harmless, undefiled, perfect righteousness of Christ; yet there is a day a coming, in which there is not one of you shall be saved; but those that are, and shall be found clothed with that righteousness: God will say to *ALL* the rest, *Take them, binde them hand and foot, and cast them into outer darkness; there shall be weeping and gnashing of teeth* (Matth. 22. 13.), for Christ will not say unto men in that day, Come which of you made a *profession* of me, and walked in Church-*fellowship* with my Saints? no; but then it shall be enquired into, who hath the reality of the truth of grace wrought in their *hearts*: and for certain, he that misseth of *that*, shall surely be cast into the lake of fire; there to burn with the

devils and damned men and women; there to undergo the
wrath of the eternal God, and that not for a day, a moneth, a
year; but for ever, for ever, for ever, and ever, there is that
which cutteth to the quick; therefore look to it, and consider
5 now what you do, and whereon you hang your souls; for it is
not every pin that will hold in the judgement, nor every
foundation that will be able to hold up the house against
those mighty, terrible, soul-drowning floods, and destroying
tempests, which then will roar against the soul and body of
10 a sinner (*Luke* the 6. the three last verses), and if the principle
be rotten, all will fall, all will come to nothing. Now the
principle is this, not to do things because we would be saved,
but to do them from this, namely, because we do really
believe that we *are* and *shall* be saved; but do not mistake me,
15 I do not say we should slight any holy duties (God forbid);
but I say, he that doth look for life because he doth do good
duties, he is under the Covenant of Works, the Law: let
his duties be never so eminent, so often, so fervent, so zealous.
I, and I say, as I said before, that if any man, or men, or
20 multitudes of people, do get into never so high, so eminent,
and clear practices, and Gospel-order, as to Church-discipline,
if it be done to this end I have been speaking, from this
principle; they must and shall have these sad things fall to
their share, which I have made mention of.
25   *Object.* But (you will say) can a man use Gospel-ordinances
with a Legal spirit?
    Answ. Yes as easily as the Jews could use and practice cir-
cumcision, though not the Moral, or Ten Commandments.
For this I shall be bold to affirm, that it is not the Commands
30 of the New Testament administration, that can keep a man
from using of its self in a legal spirit; for know this for certain,
that it is the principle, not the command, that makes the subjecter to the same, either Legal or Evangelical, and so his
obedience from that command to be from Legal convictions,
35 or Evangelical principles.
    Now herein the devil is wonderous subtle and crafty, in
suffering people to practice the ordinances and commands of

*I beseech you
do not think
that because
I say this:
therefore I
am against the
Ordinances of
the Gospel;
for I do
honour them
in their
places: yet
would not
that any of
them should
be idolized, or
done in a
wrong spirit.

the Gospel, if they do but do them in a Legal spirit*, from a spirit of works; for he knows then, that if he can but get the soul to go on in such a spirit, though they do never so many duties, he shall hold them sure enough; for he knows full well, that thereby they do set up something in the room of, 5 or at the least to have some (though but a little) share with the Lord Jesus Christ in their salvation; and if he can but get thee here, he knows that he shall cause thee by thy depending a little upon the one and so thy whole dependance being not upon the other (that is Christ, and taking of him upon his 10 own terms), thou wilt fall short of life by Christ, though thou do very much busie thy self, in a suitable walking, in an outward conformity to the several commands of the Lord Jesus Christ. And let me tell you plainly, that I do verily believe, that as Satan by his Instruments did draw many of 15 the Galatians by Circumcision (though, I say, it was none of the commands of the moral Law), to be debtors to do upon pain of eternal damnation, the whole of the moral Law: So also Satan in the time of the Gospel, doth use even the commands laid down in the Gospel (some of them) to binde the 20 soul over to do the same Law; the thing being done and walked in, by, and in the same spirit: For as I said before, it is not the obedience to the command, that makes the subjecter thereto Evangelical, or of a Gospel Spirit; but contrariwise, the principle that leads out the soul to the doing of the com- 25 mand, that makes the persons that do thus practice any command, together with the command by them practised, either Legal or Evangelical.

As for instance, prayer it is a Gospel command; yet if he that prayes, doth it in a Legal spirit, he doth make that 30 which in it self, is a Gospel command, an occasion of leading him into a Covenant of Works, in as much as he doth it by, and in that old Covenant spirit.

Again, giving of alms, is a Gospel command; yet if I do give alms from a Legal principle, the command to me is not 35 Gospel, but Legal; and it bindes me over (as aforesaid) to do the whole Law, *For he is not a Jew* (not a Christian) *that is one outwardly*, that is one, onely by an outward subjection to the ordinances of prayer, hearing, reading, baptisme, breaking of bread, *&c. But he is a Jew* (a Christian), *which is one inwardly*, who is rightly principled, and practiseth the ordinances of 5 the Lord from the leadings forth of the spirit of the Lord from a true and saving faith in the Lord, *Rom.* 2. 28, 29.

Those men spoken of in the 7. of *Matthew*, for certain, for all their great declaration, did not do what they did from a right Gospel Spirit; for had they, no question but the Lord 10 would have said, *Well done good and faithful servants*: but in that the Lord Jesus doth turn them away into hell, notwithstanding their great profession of the Lord, and of their doing in his name, it is evident that notwithstanding all that they did do, they were still under the Law, and not under that 15 Covenant as true believers are (to wit) the Covenant of Grace, and if so, then all their duties that they did, of which they boasted before the Lord, was not in, and by a right Evangelical principle, or Spirit.

Again, saith the Apostle, *Whatsoever is not of faith is sin*, 20 *Rom.* 14. 23. but there are some that do even practise baptisme, breaking of bread, together with other ordinances, & yet are unbelievers; therfore unbelievers doing these things, they are not done in faith, but sin: now to do these things in sin, or without the faith, it is not to do things in an Evan- 25 gelical or Gospel Spirit; also they that do these things in a Legal Spirit, the very practising of them renders them not under the Law of Christ, as head of his Church; but the works they do are of so much contradiction to the Gospel of God or the Covenant of Grace, that they that do them thus, do 30 even set up against the Covenant of Grace; and the very performance of them is of such force that it is sufficient to drown them that are subjecters thereunto, even under the Covenant of Works; but this poor souls are not aware of, and there is their misery.

35   *Quest.* But have you no other way to discover the things of the Gospel, how they are done with a Legal principle, but those you have already made mention of?

Answ. That thou mightest be indeed satisfied herein, I shall shew you the very manner and way that a Legal, or old Covenant converted professor (bear with the terms) doth take, both in the beginning, middle, and the end of his doing of any duty, or command, or whatsoever it be that he doth do. 5

First, he thinking this or that to be his duty, and considering of the same, he is also presently perswaded in his own conscience, that God will not accept of him, if he leave it undone; he seeing that he is short of his duty (as he supposeth) while this is undone by him, and also judging that 10 God is angry with him, untill the thing be done; he in the second place sets to the doing of the duty, to the end he may be able to pacifie his conscience by doing of the same, perswading of himself that now the Lord is pleased with him for doing of it. Thirdly, having done it he contents himself, 15 sits down at his ease untill some further convictions of his duty to be done, which when he seeth and knoweth, he doth do it as aforesaid, from the same principle as he did the former, and so goeth on in his progress of profession. This is to do things from a Legal principle, and from an old Covenant 20 spirit; for thus runs that Covenant. *The man that doth these things shall live in them, or by them,* Levit. 18. 5. Ezek. 20. 11. Gal. 3. 12. Rom. 10. 5. but more of this in the use of this Doctrine.

Object. But (you will say) by these words of yours, you do 25 seem to deny that there are conditional promises in the Gospel, as is clear, in that you strike at such practices as are conditional, and commanded to be done upon the same.

Answ. The thing that I strike at is this; that a man in, or, with a legal spirit, should not, nay cannot, do any conditional 30 command of the Gospel acceptable, as to his eternal state; because he doth it in an old Covenant spirit. *No man putteth new Wine into old Bottles*: but new Wine must have new Bottles; a Gospel command must have a Gospel spirit, or else the Wine will break the Bottles, or the principle will break 35 the command.

Object. Then you do grant that there are conditional pro-

mises in the New Testament, as in the moral Law, or ten
Commands?

Answ. Though this be true; yet the conditional promises
in the New Testament, do not call to the same people, in the
5 same state of unregeneracy to fulfill them, upon the same
conditions.

The Law, and the Gospel being two distinct Covenants,
they are made in divers wayes, and the nature of the conditions also being not the same, as saith the Apostle, *The*
10 *righteousness of the Law saith one thing, and the righteousness of*
Faith saith another, Rom. 10. 4, 5, 6. that is, the great condition
in the Law is, *If you do these things you shall live by them*: but the
condition, even the greatest condition, laid down for a poor
soul to do, as to salvation (for it is that we speak of), is to
15 believe, that my sins be forgiven me for Jesus Christs sake,
without the works or righteousness of the Law, on my part,
to help forward, *Rom. 4. 5. To him that worketh not* (saith the
Apostle) (for salvation) *but believeth on him that justifieth the*
ungodly, his faith; mark, *his faith is counted for righteousness.*
20 *So that we* (saith he) *conclude, that a man is justified by faith,*
without; mark again, *without the deeds of the Law*, Rom. 3. 28.

But again, there is never a condition in the Gospel, that can
be fulfilled by an unbeliever; and therefore, whether there be
conditions, or whether there be none, it makes no matter to
25 thee, who art without the Faith of Christ; for it is unpossible
for thee in that state to do them, so as to be ever the better,
as to thy eternal state; therefore lest thou shouldest split thy
soul upon the conditions laid down in the Gospel, as thou
wilt do, if thou go about to do them, onely with a Legal
30 spirit: but I say, to prevent this, see if thou canst fulfill the
first condition; that is, to believe that all thy sins are forgiven thee; not for any condition that hath been, or can be
done by thee, but meerly for the mans sake, that did hang on
Mount *Calvary*, between two Theeves, some sixteen hundred
35 years ago and odd: And I say, see if thou canst believe that at
that time, he did (when he hanged on the Cross) give full

6 conditions] condition *1685*

satisfaction for all thy sins, before thou in thy person hadst committed ever a one. I say, see if thou canst believe this, and take heed thou deceive not thy self with an historical, notional, or traditional acknowledgement of the same. And secondly, see if thou canst so well fulfill this condition, that the very vertue and efficacy that it hath on thy soul, will ingage thee to fulfill those other conditions, really in love to that man, whom thou shouldest believe, hath frankly, and freely forgiven thee all, without any condition acted by thee, to move him thereto, according to that saying in the 2 *Cor.* 5. 14, 15. and then thy doing will arise from a contrary principle, then otherwise it will do; that is, then thou wilt not act, and do, because thou wouldest be accepted of God; but because thou hast some good hope in thy heart, that thou art accepted of him already, and not on thine, but wholly and alone upon another mans account; for here runs the Gospel Spirit of Faith; *We believe*; mark, *We believe and therefore speak*; So we believe, and therefore do. 2 *Cor.* 4. 13. *Take heed therefore that you do not do, that you may believe; but rather believe so effectually, that you may do*, even all that Jesus doth require of you from a right principle, even out of love to your dear Lord Jesus Christ, which thing I shall speak to more fully by and by.

Object. But what do you mean by those expressions, *Do not do that you may believe, but believe so effectually that you may do?*

Answ. When I say, do not do that you may believe; I mean, do not think that any of the things that thou canst do, will procure, or purchase faith from God unto thy soul; for that is still the old Covenant Spirit, the Spirit of the Law, to think to have it for thy doing. They that are saved, they are saved by Grace, through faith, and that not of themselves; not for any thing that they can do, for they are both the free gift of God, *Eph.* 2. 8. *Not of* (doing, or of) *works, lest any man should* (be proud, and) *boast*, verse the 9. Now some people be so ignorant, as to think that God will give them Christ, and so

17 Faith; *We believe*; mark] *Faith*; mark *1685*   19 *do²*] *om. 1685*
34 the] *om. 1685*

all the merits of his, if they will be but vigilant, and do something to please God, that they may obtain him at his hands;
but let me tell them they may lose a thousand souls quickly
if they had so many, by going this way to work, and yet be
5 never the better; for the Lord doth not give his Christ to
any, upon such conditions, but he doth give him freely, that
is, without having respect to any thing that is in thee, *Rev.*
22. 17. Isa. 55. 1, 2. To him that is a thirst will I give; he doth
not say I will sell, but I *will give him the water of Life freely,*
10 *Rev. 21. 6.*

Now if Christ doth give it, and that freely, then he doth
not sell it for any thing that is in the creature; but Christ
doth give himself, as also doth his Father, and that freely; not
because there is any thing in us, or done by us, that moves
15 him thereunto. If it were by doing, then saith *Paul, Grace is*
not Grace, seeing it is obtained by works; but Grace is Grace,
and that is the reason it is given to men without their works,
Rom. 11. 6. And if it be by Grace, that is, if it be a free gift from
God, without any thing foreseen, as done, or to be done by
20 the creature, *then it is not of works*, which is clear: therefore it is
grace without the works of the Law; but if you say nay, it is
of something in the man, done by him, that moves God
thereunto; then you must conclude, that either *Grace is no*
Grace, or else that *Works are Grace*, and not *Works*. Do but
25 read with understanding, *Rom. 11. 6.*

Now before I go any further, it may be necessary to speak
a word or two to some poor souls that are willing to close in
with Jesus Christ, and would willingly take him upon his
own terms, onely they being muddy in their minds, and have
30 not yet attained the understanding of the terms, and conditions of the two Covenants, they are kept off from closing
with Christ; and all is, because they see they can do nothing.
As for example, come to some souls, and ask them how they
do, they will tell you presently, that they are so bad that it is
35 not to be expressed: If you bid them believe in Jesus Christ,
they will answer, that they cannot believe; if you ask them
why they cannot believe, they will answer, because their

hearts are so hard, so dead, so dull, so backward to good
duties; and if their hearts were but better, if they were more
earnest, if they could pray better, and keep their hearts more
from running after sin, then they could believe; but should
they believe with such vile hearts, and presume to believe in 5
Christ, and be so filthy? Now all this is, because the Spirit
of the Law still ruleth in such a soul, and blindes them so that
they cannot see the terms of the Gospel. To clear this, take
the substance of the drift of this poor soul, which is this: If I
was better then I think I could believe, but being so bad as 10
I am, that is the reason that I cannot; this is just to do something that I may believe, to work that I may have Christ,
to do the Law that I may have the Gospel; or thus, to be
righteous that I may come to Christ. O man! thou must go
quite back again, thou art out of the way; thou must believe, 15
because thou canst not pray, because thou canst not do;
thou must believe, because there is nothing in thee (naturally)
that is good, or desireth after good, or else thou wilt never
come to Christ as a sinner; and if so, then Christ will not
receive thee; and if so, then thou mayest see that to keep off 20
from Christ, because thou canst not do, is to be kept from
Christ by the Law, and to stand off from him because thou
canst not buy him. Thus having spoken something by the
way, for the direction of those souls that would come to
Christ, I shall return to the former discourse wherein ariseth 25
this objection.

   Object. But you did but even now put souls upon fulfilling
the first condition of the Gospel, even to believe in Christ,
and so be saved; but now you say, it is alone by Grace, without condition; and therefore by these words, there is first a 30
contradiction to your former sayings, and also that men may
be saved without the condition of faith, which to me seems a
very strange thing. I desire therefore that you would clear
out what you have said, as to my satisfaction.

   Answ. Though there be a condition commanded in the 35
Gospel; yet he that commands the condition, doth not leave

his children to their own natural abilities, that in their own strength they should fulfill them (as the Law doth); but the same God that doth command that the condition be ful-filled, even he, doth help his children by his holy Spirit to
5 fulfill the same condition, *For it is God that worketh in you*, mark, *in you* (believers) *both to will and to do, of his own good pleasure*, Phil. 2. 13. *Thou hast wrought all our works in us, and for us*, Isa. 26. 12. So that the condition be fulfilled, it is not done in the ability of the creature.

10   But secondly, faith as it is a gift of God, or an act of ours, take it which way you will; If we speak properly of salvation, it is not the first, nor the second cause of our salvation; but the third, and that but instrumentally neither; that is, it onely layeth hold of, and applieth to us that which saveth us,
15 which is the love of God, through the merits of Christ, which are the two main causes of our salvation, without which all other things are nothing, whether it be faith, hope, love, or what ever can be done by us. And to this, the great Apostle of the Gentiles speaks fully; for saith he, *God who is rich in* •Eph. 2. 4.
20 *mercy loved us, even when we were dead in our sins* (that is, when we were without faith), and that was the cause why we be-lieve; for he thereby hath quickned us together, through the meritorious cause, which is Christ, and so hath saved us by Grace, that is, of his own voluntary love and good will; the
25 effect of which was this, he gave us faith to believe in Christ, read soberly that second of the *Ephesians*, at the 4, 5, 6, 7, 8. verses. Faith as the gift of God is not the Saviour, as our act doth merit nothing. Faith was not the cause that God gave Christ at the first, neither is it the cause why God converts
30 men to Christ: but faith is a gift bestowed upon us, by the gracious God, the nature of which is to lay hold on Christ, that God afore did give for a Ransom, to redeem sinners; this faith hath its nourishment, and supplies from the same God, that at the first did give it; and is the onely instrument
35 through the Spirit, that doth keep the soul in a comfortable frame, both to do and suffer for Christ; helps the soul to

25 effect] effects *1685*

receive comfort from Christ, when it can get none from it self, beareth up the soul in its progress heaven-wards: but that it is the first cause of salvation, that I deny; or that it is the second, I deny: but is onely the instrument, or hand, that receiveth the benefits that God hath prepared for thee before 5 thou hadst any faith: so that we do nothing for salvation, as we are men. But if we speak properly, *it was Gods Grace that moved him to give Christ a Ransom for sinners, and the same God with the same Grace, that doth give to the soul faith to believe, and so by believing to close in with him, whom God out of his love and* 10 *pitty, did send into the world to save sinners; so that all the works of the creature are shut out, as to justification and life, and men are saved freely by Grace.* I shall speak no more here, but in my discourse upon the second Covenant, I shall answer a hell-bred Objection or two, to forewarn sinners, how they turn the 15 Grace of God into wantonness.

And thus you see I have briefly spoken to you something touching the Law. First, what it is, and when given. Secondly, how sad those mens conditions are that are under it. Thirdly, who they are that be under it. Fourthly, how far they may 20 go, and what they may do, and receive, and yet be under it, which hath been done by way of answers to several questions, for the better satisfaction of those that may stand in doubt of the truth of what hath been delivered.

Now in the next place, I should come to some application 25 of the truth of that which hath been spoken; but I shall in the first place speak something to the second Doctrine, and then afterwards I shall speak something by way of Use and Application to this first Doctrine.

The second Doctrine now to be spoken to, is to shew, that the people of God are not under the Law but under Grace.

For ye are not under the Law but under Grace.

Rom. 6. 14.

You may well remember that from these words, I did observe these two great truths of the Lord. First, that there are 5 some in Gospel times, that are under the Law, or Covenant of Works.

Secondly, that there is never a believer under the Law (or Covenant of Works) but under Grace.

I have spoken something to the former of these truths 10 (to wit) that there are some under the Law, together with who they are, and what their condition is, that are under it. Now I am to speak to the second, and to shew you who they are, and what their condition is, that are under that.

But before I come to that, I shall speak a few words, to I touched upon 15 shew you what the word GRACE in this place signifies; this in the for the word Grace in the Scripture referreth sometimes to first Doctrine. favour with men (*Esther* 2. 17. *Gen*. 39. 4. Chap. 50. 4. Chap. 33. 10.), sometimes to holy qualifications of Saints (2 *Cor*. 8. 7.), and sometimes to hold forth the condescension of 20 Christ, in coming down from the glory which he had with his Father, before the world was, to be made of no reputation, and a servant to men (2 *Cor*. 8. 9. *Phil*. 2. 7.). Again, sometimes it is taken for the free, rich, and unchangeable love of God to man, through Jesus Christ; that for our cause 25 and sakes, did make himself poor: and so it is to be understood in these words. *For you are not under the Law* (to be cursed, and damned, and sent headlong to hell) *but* (you are) *under Grace*, to be saved, to be pardoned, to be preserved, *and kept by the mighty power of God, through faith* (which alone

17 17.] 7. *1659, 1685*   18 33. 10.] 4, 33, 10 *1685*

is the gift of Grace) *unto eternal glory*. This one Scripture alone proves the same, *Eph*. 2. 8. *For by Grace you are saved*, by free grace, by rich grace, by unchangeable grace. And you are saved from the curse of the Law, from the power, guilt, and filth of sin, from the power, malice, madness, and rage of the devil, from the wishes, curses, and desires of wicked men, from the hot, scalding, flaming, fiery furnace of hell, from being arraigned, as malefactors, convinced, judged, condemned, and fettered with the chains of our sins to the devils, to all eternity; and all this freely, freely by his grace (*Rom*. 3. 24.), by rich grace, unchangeable grace; for saith he, *I am God, and change not: therefore ye sons of Jacob are not consumed*, Mal. 3. 6. This is grace indeed.

The word [GRACE] therefore in this Scripture (*Rom*. 6. 14.), is to be understood of the free love of God in Christ to sinners, by vertue of the new Covenant, in delivering them from the power of sin, from the curse and condemning power of the Old Covenant, from the destroying nature of sin, by its continual workings; as is all evident, if you read with understanding the words as they lie, *For* (saith he) *sin shall not have dominion over you*, or it shall not domineer, reign, or destroy you, though you have transgressed against the Covenant of works (the Law); and the reason is rendered in these words, *For ye are not under the Law*, that is, under that which accuseth, chargeth, condemneth, and brings execution on the soul for sin, *But under Grace*; that is, under that which frees you, forgives you, keeps you, and justifies you from all your sins, adversaries, or whatsoever may come in to lay any thing to your charge, to damn you. For that is truly called grace in this sense, that doth set a man free from all his sins, deliver him from all the curses of the Law, and what else can be laid to his charge, freely without any foresight in God to look at what good will be done by the party that hath offended: and also that doth keep the soul by the same power through faith (which also is his own proper gift) unto eternal glory.

28 whatsoever] whatever *1685*   32 any] an *1659*

Again, that it is a pardon not conditional but freely given;
Consider first, it is set in opposition to works. *You are not
under the Law.* Secondly, the promise that is made to them
(saying, *Sin shall not have dominion over you*), doth not run with
5 any condition, as on their part to be done; but meerly and
alone because they were (*under*) or because they had the Grace
of God extended to them. *Sin shall not have dominion over you*;
For (mark the reason), *For you are not under the Law, but under
Grace.* The words being thus opened, and the truth thus laid
10 down, how there is never a believer under the Covenant of
Works, but under Grace, the free, rich, unchangeable love of
God; it remaineth that in the first place we prove the Doctrine,
and after that proceed.

Now in the Doctrine there is two things to be considered,
15 and proved. First, that believers are under Grace. Secondly,
not under the Law as a Covenant of works (for so you must
understand me); For these two, we need go no further then
the very words themselves, the first part of the words proves
the first part of the Doctrine, *You are not under the Law*; the
20 second part proves the other, *But* (ye are) *under Grace.*

But besides these consider with me a few things for the
demonstrating of these truths, as,

First, they are not under the Law; because their sins are
pardoned; which could not be if they were dealt withall
25 according to the Law, and their being under it; for the Law
alloweth of no repentance, but accuseth, curseth, and condemneth every one that is under it. *Cursed is every one that
continueth not in all things written in the book of the Law to do
them,* Gal. 3. 10. But I say, believers having their sins forgiven
30 them, it is because they are under another, even a New Covenant, *Heb.* 8. 8. *Behold the dayes come, saith the Lord, that I will
make a new Covenant with them: For I will be merciful to their
unrighteousnes, & their sins & their iniquities will I remember no
more,* v. 12.

35 Secondly, they are not under the Law; because their sins
and iniquities are not onely forgiven, but they are forgiven

them freely: they that stand in the first Covenant, and continue there, are to have never a sin forgiven them, unless they can give God a compleat satisfaction; for the Law calls for it at their hands, saying, *Pay me that thou owest.* O but when God deals with his Saints by the Covenant of Grace, it is not so; for it is said, *And when he saw they had nothing to pay, he frankly, and freely, forgave them all. I will heal their back-slidings and love them freely. I will blot out thy transgressions for mine own sake,* &c. Luke 7. 42. Hosea 14. 4. Isaiah 43. 25.

Thirdly, the Saints are not under the Law, because the righteousness that they stand justified before God in, is not their own actual righteousness by the Law, but by imputation; and is really the righteousness of another, namely, of God in Christ, 2. Cor. 5. 21. Phil. 3. 8, 9, 10, *Even the righteousness of God, which is by faith of Jesus Christ, which is unto all, and upon all* (that is imputed to) *them that believe,* Rom. 3. 22. But if they were under the Old Covenant, the Covenant of Works, then their righteousness must be their own*, or no forgiveness of sins. *If thou do well, shalt not thou be accepted? but if thou transgress sin lieth at the door,* saith the Law, *Gen.* 4. 7.

*But it is impossible that the righteousness of man by the Law should save him.

Fourthly, in a word, whatsoever they do receive, whether it be conversion to God, whether it be pardon of sin, whether it be faith or hope, whether it be righteousness, whether it be strength, whether it be the Spirit, or the fruits thereof, whether it be victory over sin, death, or hell, whether it be heaven, everlasting life, and glory unexpressable, or whatsoever it be, it comes to them freely, God having no first eye to what they would do, or should do, for the obtaining of the same. But to take this in pieces, 1. In a word, are they converted? God findes them first, for saith he, *I am found of them that sought me not,* Isa. 65. 1.

2. Have they pardon of sin? they have that also freely, *I will heal their back-slidings and love them freely,* Hos. 14. 4.

3. Have they faith? It is the gift of God in Christ Jesus, *and he is not onely the author* (that is the beginner thereof), *but he doth also perfect the same,* Heb. 12. 2.

4. Have they hope? It is God that is the first cause thereof. *Remember thy word unto thy servant, wherein THOU hast caused me to hope.* Psal. 119. 49.

5. Have they righteousness? It is the free gift of God, *Rom.* 5. 17.

6. Have they strength to do the work of God in their generations? or any other thing that God would have them do, that also is a free gift from the Lord; for without him, we neither do, nor can do any thing. *John* 15. 5.

7. Have we comfort, or consolation? we have it not for what we have done, but from God through Christ; for he is *the God of all our comforts and consolations,* 2 Cor. 1.

8. Have we the Spirit, or the fruits thereof? It is the gift of the Father. *How much more shall your heavenly Father give the holy Spirit to them that ask him?* Luke 11. 13. *Thou hast wrought all our works for us,* Isa. 26. 12.

And so I say, whether it be victory over sin, death, hell, or the devil, it is given us by the victory of Christ. *But thanks be to God which hath given us the victory through our Lord Jesus Christ,* 1 Cor. 15. 57. Rom. 7. 24, 25. Heaven and glory it is also the gift of him *who giveth his people richly all things to enjoy,* Matthew 25.

So that these things, if they be duly and soberly considered, will give satisfaction in this thing. I might have added many more for the clearing of these things: As first when God came to man to convert him, he found him *a dead man,* Eph. 2. 1, 2. he found him *an enemy to God, Christ, and the Salvation of his own soul;* he found him wallowing *in all manner of wickedness, he found him taking pleasure therein, with all delight and greediness.*

2. He was fain to *quicken him by putting his Spirit into him, and to translate him by the mighty operation thereof.*

3. He was fain to reveal Christ Jesus unto him, *man being altogether senseless, and ignorant of this blessed Jesus,* Mat. 11. 25, 27. 1 Cor. 2. 7, 8, 9, 10.

4. He was fain to break the snare of the devil, and to let

poor man, poor bound and fettered man, out of the chains of the enemy.

Now we are to proceed, and the things that we are to treat upon in the second place, are these.

First, *why it is a free and unchangeable grace.   5

*Besides the reasons already given.

Secondly, who they are, that are actually brought into his free and unchangeable Covenant of Grace, and how they are brought in.

Thirdly, what are the priviledges of those that are actually brought into this free and glorious grace of the glorious God of heaven, and glory.   10

For the first, *Why it is a free and unchangeable grace*; and for the opening of this, we must consider, First, how and through whom this grace doth come, to be, first free to us, and secondly unchangeable. This grace is free to us, through conditions in another; that is, by way of Covenant, or Bargain; for this Grace comes by way of Covenant or Bargain to us, yet made with another, for us.   15

First, that it comes by way of Covenant, Contract, or Bargain (though not personally with us) be pleased to con-sider these Scriptures, where it is said, *I have made a Covenant with my chosen: I have sworn unto David my servant, And as for thee also, by the blood of thy Covenant* (speaking of Christ) *have I sent forth the prisoners out of the pit, wherein was no water*, Zech. 9. 9, 10, 11. Again, *You have sold yourselves for naught, and you shall be bought without money. Blessed be the Lord* (therefore saith Zacharias), *for he hath visited and (also) REDEEMED his people. And hath raised up an horn of salvation for us, in the house of his servant* David. *As he spake by the mouth of his holy Prophets, which have been since the world began: that we should be saved from our enemies, and from the hands of all that hate us: To perform his mercy promised to our Fathers, and to remember his holy Covenant*, or Bargain, *Luke*. 1. 68, 69, 70, 71, 72. And if any should be offended with the plainness of these words as some poor souls may be through ignorance, let them be pleased to read soberly that 49. Chapter of the Prophet *Isaiah*, from the 1. verse to the 12. and there they may see that it runs as plain a Bargain, as   20   25   30   35

*Ps. 89. 3. The word *David* in this place signifieth Christ, as also in these Scriptures. Ezek. 34. 23, 24. Chap. 37. 24, 25.

I might give you more Scriptures: but pray consider the second thing.

if two should be making of a Bargain between themselves, and concluding upon several conditions on both sides. But more of this hereafter.

Now secondly, this Covenant (I say) was made with one, not with many; and also confirmed in the conditions of it with one, not with several. First, that the Covenant was made with one, see *Gal. 3. 16. Now to Abraham and to his seed was the promises made; he saith not to seeds, as of many; but as of one; and to thy seed, which is Christ*, ver. 17. *And this I say, the Covenant which was confirmed before of God in Christ*, &c. The Covenant was made with the seed of *Abraham*, not the seeds, but the seed, which is the Lord Jesus Christ, our head and undertaker in the things concerning the Covenant.

3. The condition was made with one, and also accomplished by him alone, and not by several; yet in the nature, and for the everlasting deliverance of many; even by one man Jesus Christ, as it is clear from *Rom. 5. 15, 16, 17*, &c. and in *Zech. 9. 11*. the Lord saith to Christ, *And as for thee*; mark, *as for thee also, by the blood of the Covenant*, or as for thee whose covenant was by blood; that is, the conditions of the Covenant was, that thou shouldest spill thy blood; which having been done in the account of God (saith he), I according to my condition, have let go the prisoners, or sent them out of the pit wherein was no water; those Scriptures in Galatians the 3. at the 16. and 17. verses that are above cited, are notable to our purpose, the sixteenth verse saith, It was made with Christ, and the seventeenth saith, It was also confirmed in, or with God in him, pray read with understanding. *Now* (saith *Paul*) *the promises were not made unto seeds, as of many; but as of one, and to thy seed, which is Christ.*—*The Law which was four hundred and thirty years after cannot disanul, that it should make the promise of none effect.* Not that the Covenant was with *Abraham* and Christ together, as two persons that were the undertakers of the same; the promise was made with, or, to *Abraham* afterwards: but the Covenant with Christ before. Further, that the Covenant was not personally made with *Abraham*, no, nor with any of the Fathers, neither so as that they were the

persons that should stand ingaged, to be the accomplishers thereof, either in whole or in part, which is very clear.

First, because this Covenant was not made with God and the creature; not with another poor *Adam*, that onely stood upon the strength of natural abilities: but this Covenant was 5 made with the second person, with the eternal Word of God; with him that was every wayes as holy, as pure, as infinite, as powerful, and as everlasting as God (*Prov.* 8. the 22, 23, 24, 25, 26, 27, 28, 29, 30. verses. *Zech.* 13. 7. *Rev.* 1. 16, 17. and the 22. 13, 16. *Isa.* 9. 6. *Phil.* 2. 6. *Heb.* 1.).   10

Secondly, this Covenant or Bargain was made indeed and in truth before man was in being. Oh! God thought of the salvation of man before there was any transgression of man; for then I say, and not since then, was the Covenant of Grace made with the undertaker thereof; for all the other sayings are 15 to shew unto us that glorious plot and contrivance that was concluded on before time between the Father and the Son, which may very well be concluded on for a truth from the word of God, if you consider, first, that the Scripture doth declare that the price was agreed on by the Son before time; 20 the promise was made to him by the Father, that he should have his Bargain before time, and the choice, who they were that should be saved, was made before time, even before the world began.

For the first, that the price was agreed upon before the 25 world began; Consider the word which speaketh of the price that was paid for sinners, even *The precious Blood of Christ*; It saith of him, *who verily was fore-ordained before the foundation of the world, but was made manifest in these last times for you; who by him do believe*, &c. 1 Pet. 1. 19. and 20. verses. Mark, it was fore- 30 ordained or concluded on between the Father and his Son before the world began.

Secondly, the promise from God to the Son was also made in the same manner, as it is clear, where the Apostle saith with comfort to his soul, that he had *hopes of eternal life, which* 35

God that cannot lie promised before the World began, Tit. 1. 2. which could be to none but the Mediator of the New Covenant, because there was none else to whom it should be made but he.

5   Thirdly, the choice was also made then, even before man had a being in this world, as it is evident where he saith, *Blessed be the God and Father of our Lord Jesus Christ, who hath blessed US with all spiritual blessings in heavenly places IN Christ, according as he hath chosen US in him before the foundation of the* 10 *world, that we should be holy and without blame before him in love,* Eph. 1. 3, 4. Nay, did I look upon it here to be necessary, I should shew you very largely and clearly, that God did not onely make the Covenant with Christ before the world began, and the conditions thereof: But I could also shew you 15 that the very Saints qualifications as part of the Covenant, was then concluded on by the Father and the Son, according to these Scriptures, *Eph.* 1. 3, 4. Chap. 2. 10. and *Rom.* 8. 28. which it may be I may touch upon further anon.

Did I think this would meet with any opposition, I should be in this more large.

But thirdly, this Covenant was not made with any of the 20 Fathers, neither in whole, nor in part, as the undertakers thereof; for then it must be also concluded that they are Co-partners with Christ in our salvation, and so, that Christ is not Mediator alone: but this would be blasphemy for any one to surmise. And therefore by the way, when thou readest 25 of the new Covenant in Scripture, as though it was made with *Adam, Noah, Abraham,* or *David,* thou art to consider thus with thy self; First, that God spake to them in such a way, for to shew, or signifie unto us, how he did make the Covenant, that he did make with Christ, before the world began, 30 they being types of him. Secondly, that he thereby might let them understand, that he was the same then as he is now, and now as he was then; and that then it was resolved on between his Son and He, that in after ages his Son should in their natures, from their loins, and for their sins be Born of a 35 Woman, hanged on the Cross, &c. for them: for all along you may see that when he speaketh to them of the New Covenant,

24 one] once *1659*

he mentions their seed, their seed, still aiming at Christ;

Gen. 3. 15. Christ the *Seed* of the Woman, was to break the Serpents head.

Gen. 17. Now to *Abraham* and his *Seed*, was the promise made, his seed
Ps. 89. 36. shall endure for ever, and his Throne as the dayes of heaven,
&c. still pointing at Christ. And thirdly, to stir up their 5
faith and expectations to be constant unto the end, in waiting
for that which he and his Son had concluded on before time,
and what he had since the conclusion declared unto the world
by the Prophets. Fourthly, it appeareth that the heart of
God was much delighted therein also, as is evident, in that 10
he was alwayes in every age, declaring of that unto them,
which before he had prepared for them. O this good God of
Heaven!

Object.   But (you will say perhaps) the Scriptures say plainly, that
the New Covenant was, and is made with Believers, saying, 15
*The dayes come, saith the Lord, that I will make a New Covenant
with the house of Israel, and the House of Judah, not according to
the Covenant that I made with their fathers in the day in which I
brought them out of the Land of Egypt,* &c. Heb. 8. 10, 11, 12.
Jer. 31. 33. So that it doth not run with Christ alone, but with 20
believers also. *I will make a New Covenant with the House of
Israel and Judah,* &c.

1 Answ.   First, it cannot be meant that the New Covenant was made
with Christ, and the House of *Israel* and *Judah* as the undertakers thereof: for so it was made with Christ alone, which is 25
clear in that it was made long before the House of *Israel* and
Judah had a being, as I shewed before.

2 Answ.   But secondly, these words here are spoken, first to shew
rather the end of the Ceremonies, then the beginning or rise
of the new Covenant. Minde a little, The Apostle is labouring 30
to beat the Jews (to whom he wrote this Epistle) off of the
Ceremonies of the Law, of the Priests, Alter, Offerings,
Temple, &c. and to bring them to the right understanding of
the thing and things that they held forth, which was to come,
and to put an end to those. If you do but understand the 35
Epistle to the *Hebrews*, it is a discourse that sheweth, that the

Son of God being come, there is an end put to the Ceremonies;
for they were to continue so long and no longer. *It*, saith the
Apostle, *stood in meats, and drinks, and divers washings, and carnal
ordinances imposed on them untill the time of reformation*; that is,
5 untill Christ did come. *But Christ being come an high Priest of
good things to come*, &c.—puts an end to the things and ordinances of the Levitical Priest-hood, read the 7, 8, 9, 10.
Chapters, and you will finde this true. So then, when he
saith, *The dayes come in which I will make a New Covenant*, it is
10 rather to be meant a changing of the administration, a taking
away the type, the shadow, the Ceremonies from the House of
Israel and *Judah*, and revealing, by the Birth of Christ, and the
Death of Christ, and the Offering of the Body of him, whom
the shadows and types did point out, to be indeed he, whom
15 God the Father had given for a Ransom by Covenant for the
souls of the Saints; and also to manifest the truth of that
Covenant, which was made between the Father and the Son
before the world began: for though the New Covenant was
made before the world began, and also every one in all ages
20 was saved by the vertue of that Covenant; yet that Covenant
was never so clearly made manifest, as at the coming, death,
and resurrection of Christ; and therefore saith the Scripture,
He hath brought life and immortality to light through the Gospel,
2 Tim. 1. 9, 10, *Who hath saved us, and called us with an holy
25 calling, not according to the works of righteousness which we have
done: but according to his own purpose and grace, which was given
us in Christ before the world began* (there is the Covenant): *but
it was made MANIFEST by the APPEARING of our Saviour
Jesus Christ who hath abolished death, and brought life and im-
30 mortality to LIGHT through the Gospel*. Therefore I say, these
words are rather to discover, that the time was come to
change the dispensation, to take away the type and bring in
the substance, and so manifesting that more clearly, which
before lay hid in dark sayings and figures. And this is usuall
35 with God to speak in this manner.

Again, if at any time you do finde in the Scripture, that the
Covenant of Works is spoken of, as the first Covenant that

was manifested, and so before the second Covenant; yet you must understand that it was so onely, as to manifestation, that is, it was first given to man, yet not made before that which was made Christ: And indeed it was requisite that it should be given, or made known first, that thereby there 5 might be a way made for the second by its discovering of sin, and the sad state that man was in after the fall, by reason of that. And again, that the other might be made the more

Yet the second Adam was before the first and also the second Covenant before the first. This is a Riddle. welcome to the sons of men. And in this did Christ in time most gloriously answer *Adam*, who was the figure of Christ 10 (Rom. 5.), as well as of other things: for as the first Covenant was made with the first *Adam*, so was the second Covenant made with the second; for these are and were the two great publick persons, or representators of the whole world, as to the first and second Covenants; and therefore you finde God 15 speaking on this wise in Scripture concerning the New Covenant, *My Covenant shall stand fast with HIM*; Psal. 89. 28, 34, 35. *My mercy will I keep for HIM for evermore*, saith God: *my Covenant shall stand fast with HIM* (this *HIM* is Christ, if you compare this with *Luke* 1. 32.). *My Covenant will I not* 20 *break*, namely that which was made with *HIM, nor alter the thing that is gone out of my mouth: Once have I sworn by my* *David here is to be understood Christ.* *Holinesse that I will not lie unto DAVID*, to whom this was spoken figuratively in the person of Christ: for that was Gods usuall way to speak of the glorious things of the Gospel in 25 the time of the Law, as I said before.

Secondly, The conditions also were concluded on, and agreed to be fulfilled by him, as it is clear, if you understand his saying in the 12. of *John* at the 27. verse, where he fore-☞ telleth his death and saith, *Now is my soul troubled, and what shall* 30 *I say? Father save me from this hour; but for this cause came I* (into the world) *unto this hour*: as if he had said, My business is now not to shrink from my sufferings that are a coming upon me; for these are the things that are a great part of the conditions contracted in the Covenant which stands between 35 my Father and I; therefore I shall not pray that this might be absolutely removed from me. For, *for this cause came I into the world*; even this was the very terms of the Covenant. By this you may say we are under Grace.

Now in a Covenant there is these three things to be 5 considered.

First, what it is, that is covenanted for.

Secondly, the conditions, upon which the persons, who are concerned in it, do agree.

Thirdly, if the conditions on both sides be not according to 10 the agreement fulfilled: then the Covenant standeth not, but is made void.

And this New Covenant in these particulars is very exactly fulfilled, and made out in Christ.

First, the thing or things covenanted for, was the salva-15 tion of man, but made good in Christ. *The Son of man is come to seek and save that which was lost. The Son of Man did not come to destroy mens lives, but to save them. I give my life a ransom for many. And this is the will* (or Covenant) *of him that sent me, that of all which he hath given me, I should lose nothing; but should raise* 20 *it up again at the day*, John the sixth, the thirty ninth verse.

Secondly, as touching the conditions agreed on, they run thus.

First, on the Mediatours side, that he should come into the world; and then on the Fathers side, that he should give 25 him a body. This was one of the glorious conditions between the Father and Christ. *Wherefore when he cometh into the world, he saith, Sacrifices and Offerings thou wouldest not*, that is, the Old Covenant must not stand, but give way to another Sacrifice which thou hast prepared, which is the giving up 30 my Manhood to the stroaks of thy *Justice; for a body hast thou prepared me*, Heb. 13. 20, 21. This doth prove us under Grace.

Secondly, on the Mediatours side, that he should be put to death; and on God the Fathers side, that he should raise him 35 up again; this was concluded on also to be done between God the Father, and his Son Jesus Christ. On Christs side,

20 the sixth ... verse] 6. 39. *1685*

that he should die to give the justice of his Father *satisfaction*, and so to take away the curse that was due to us wretched *sinners*, by reason of our transgressions: and that God his Father being every wayes fully and compleatly satisfied, should by his mighty power revive and raise him up again. 5 He hath *brought again—our Lord Jesus*, that is, from death to life, *through* (the vertue or effectuall satisfaction that he received from) *the blood* (that was shed according to the terms) *of the everlasting Covenant*, Heb. 13. 20, 21, 22.

Thirdly, on the Mediatours side, that he should be made 10 a curse; and on the Fathers side, that through him sinners should be inheritours of the *blessing*; what wonderfull love doth there appear by this in the heart of our Lord Jesus, in suffering such things for our poor bodies and souls, *Gal.* 3. 13, 14. This is Grace.   15

Fourthly, That on the Mediators side there should be *by him* a victory over Hell, Death, and the Devil, and the curse of the Law: and on the Fathers side, that these should be communicated to sinners, and they set at liberty thereby, *Zech.* 9. 12. *Turn to the strong hold*, saith God, *ye prisoners of hope, even* 20 *to day do I declare that I will render double unto thee*: Why so? It is because of the *blood* of my Sons *Covenant*, verse 11. which made *Paul* (though sensible of a body of death, and of the sting that death did strike into the souls of all those that are found in their sins) bold to say, *O death, where is thy sting?* 25 *O grave, where is thy victory? The sting of death is sin*, that is true, and the terrible Law of God doth aggravate, and set it home with unsupportable torment and pain: but shall I be daunted at *this*? No, *I thank my God through Jesus Christ, he hath given me the victory*; so that now, though I be a *sinner* in my self, 30 yet I can by believing in Jesus Christ the Mediatour of this New Covenant, *triumph* over the Devil, Sin, Death, and Hell; and say, do not fear, my soul, seeing the victory is obtained over all my enemies through my Lord Jesus, 1 *Cor.* 15. the 55, 56, 57. verses. This is the way to prove our selves under Grace. 35

Fifthly, That on the Mediatours side he should by thus doing bring in *everlasting* righteousness for Saints, *Dan.* 9. 24. and that the Father for this should give them an everlasting Kingdom, 1 *Pet.* 1. 3, 4, 5. *Eph.* 1. 4. 2 *Tim.* 4. 18. *Luke* 22.
5 28, 29.

But in the next place, this was not all; that is, the *Covenant* of Grace, with the conditions thereof, was not onely concluded on by both parties to be done: but *Jesus Christ*, he must be *authorized* to do what was concluded on, touching this Coven-
10 ant by way of *Office*. I shall therefore speak a word or two also, touching the *Offices* (at least some of them) that Christ Jesus did, and doth still execute as the Mediator of the New Covenant, which also was typed out by the Levitical Law, for this is the way to prove that we are not under the Law but under
15 Grace.

Christ is put into office by the Father to do all things contained in the New Covenant.

And first, his first Office, after the Covenant was made and concluded upon, was, that Jesus should become *bound* as a *Surety*, and stand ingaged upon *Oath* to see that all the conditions of the Covenant, that was concluded on between him
20 and his Father, should according to the *agreement*, be accomplished by *him*. And secondly, that after that, he should be the *messenger* from God to the world, for to declare the minde of God, touching the tenor and nature of both the Covenants, especially of the New one; the Scripture saith, that Jesus
25 Christ was not onely made a *Priest* by an *Oath*, but also a *surety*, or bonds-man, as in the 7. of *Hebrews* at the 21, 22. verses; in the 21. verse he speaking of the priesthood of Christ, that it was with an *Oath*, saith in the 22. verse. *By so much* (also) *was Jesus made the surety of a better Testament*, or
30 Covenant.

His suretiship.

Now the Covenant was not onely made on Jesus Christs side with an *Oath*: but also on God the Fathers side, that it might be for the better *ground* of stablishment to all those that are, or are to be the children of the *Promise*. Methinks it is wonder-
35 ful to consider, that the God and Father of our souls by Jesus Christ, should be so bent upon the salvation of sinners, that he would covenant with his Son Jesus for the *security* of

them; and also that there should pass an *Oath* on both sides, for the confirmation of their resolution to do good: as if the Lord had said, My Son, thou, and I, have here made a *Covenant*, that I, on my part, should do thus, and thus; and that thou on thy part, shouldest do so, and so: now that we may give these souls the best *ground* of comfort that may be, there shall pass an *Oath* on both sides, that our children may see that we do indeed love them. *Wherein God willing more ABUND-ANTLY to shew unto the heirs of promise, the immutability of his counsel* (in making of the Covenant), *confirmed it by an Oath,— That we might have strong consolation, who have fled for refuge to lay hold upon the hope set before us.* Mark, the sixth Chapter saith God confirmed his part by an *Oath*; and the seventh saith, Christ was made, or set on his *Office* also by an *Oath*. Again, *Once* (saith God) *have I sworn by my holiness that I will not lie unto David,** *nor alter the thing that is gone out of my mouth*; as was before cited.

Herein you may see that God and Christ was in good earnest about the salvation of *sinners*; for so soon as ever the Covenant was made, the next thing was, who should be *bound* to see all those things fulfilled which was *conditioned* on, between the Father and the Son: The *Angels* they would have no hand in it; The *world* could not do it; The *Devils* had rather see them damned, then they would wish them the least good; thus Christ looked, and there was none to help; though the burthen lay never so heavy upon *his shoulder* he must *bear* it himself; for there was none besides himself to uphold, or so much as to step in to be *bound*, to see the conditions (before mentioned) fulfilled, neither in whole, nor in part (*Isa.* 63. 1, 2, 3, 4, 5, 6. verses). So that he must not be onely he, with whom the Covenant was *made*: but he must also become the *bonds-man*, or surety thereof; and so stand *bound* to see that all, and every *particular* thing conditioned for, should be both in manner, and matter, at the time, and place, according to the agreement, duly, and orderly fulfilled. Is not this grace?

Margin notes:
Heb. 6. 13, 14, 15, 16, 17, 18. Heb. 7. 21.
*Psal. 89. 34, 35.

Line numbers: 5, 10, 15, 20, 25, 30, 35

30 verses] *om.* 1685

Now as touching the nature of a *surety* and his work, (in some things) it is well known to most men; therefore I shall be very brief upon it.

First, you know a *surety* is at the *bargains* making; and so 5 was Christ. *Then was I by him*, Prov. 8. 30.

Secondly, a *surety* must consent to the *terms* of the Agreement, or Covenant; and so did Christ Jesus.

Now that which he did ingage, should be done for sinners, according to the terms of the Covenant, it was this.

10 First, that there should be a *compleat* satisfaction given to God for the sins of the world, for that was one great thing that was agreed upon, when the Covenant was made, *Heb.* 10. 5.

Secondly, that Jesus Christ should (as aforesaid) bring in an everlasting righteousness to clothe (his body) the Saints 15 withall, *Dan.* 9. 24, 25. Here is grace.

Thirdly, that he should take in *charge* to see all those forthcoming without *spot* or wrinkle, at the day of his glorious appearing from heaven to judgement, and to quit them before the judgement-seat.

20 Again, thirdly in the work of a *surety*, there is required by the *creditor*, that the *surety* should stand to what he is *bound*; and on the *sureties* side there is a consenting thereunto. ^{How ever it}

First, the *creditor* looks, that in case the *debtor* proves a bankerupt, that then the *surety* should ingage the payment. 25 Is not this grace?

(in margin:) How ever it is in other ingagements, yet it is thus in this.

Secondly, the *creditor* looks that the *surety* should be an *able man*: now our *surety* was, and is, in this case every way suitable; for he is *heir of all things*.

Thirdly, the *creditor* appoints the day, and also looks that 30 the Covenant should be kept, and the debt paid according to the *time* appointed; and it is required of *sureties* (as well as stewards) that they be found *faithful*, namely, to pay the debt according to the *bargain*: and therefore it is said, *When the fulness of time was come, God sent forth his Son—made under the* 35 *Law, to redeem them that are under the Law* (according to his suretiship), *Gal.* 4. 4, 5. Thus comes grace to Saints.

22 side] *om. 1685*

Fourthly, the *creditor* looks that his *money* should be brought into his house, to his own habitation. Jesus our *surety*, in this also is faithful; for by his *own* blood, which was the *payment*, he is entred into the holy place, even into heaven it self which is Gods *dwelling* place, to render the *value* and *price* that was 5 *agreed* upon for the salvation of *sinners*; but I shall speak more of this in another head, therefore I pass it.

Though the debtor together with the surety is liable to pay the debt by the law of man, yet Christ our surety onely by the Covenant of Grace.
Again fourthly, if the *surety* stands *bound* the debtor is at liberty, and if the Law do issue out any process to take any, it will be the *surety*; and O! how wonderful true was this 10 accomplished, in that when Christ our *surety* came down from heaven, Gods Law did so seize upon the Lord Jesus, and so cruelly handle him, and so exact upon him, that it would never let him alone, untill it had accused him, and condemned him, executed him, and scrued his very heart blood out of his 15 precious heart, and side; nay, and more then this too, as I shall shew hereafter.

But secondly, in the next place, after that Jesus Christ had stood bound, and was become our surety in things pertaining to this *Covenant*, his next office was to be the *messenger* of God 20 touching his minde, and the tenour of the Covenant, unto the poor world; and this did the Prophet foresee long before, where he saith, *Behold I will send my messenger, and he shall prepare thy way before thee* (speaking of *John* the Baptist); *And he shall prepare thy way before thee:* (and then he speaketh of 25 Christ to the people, saying) *And the Lord whom ye seek shall suddenly come to his Temple,* who is he? *even the messenger of the Covenant, whom ye delight in* (that is Christ): *behold he shall come saith the Lord of hosts,* Mal. 3. 1.

Now the Covenant being made before between the Father 30 and the Son, and Jesus Christ becoming bound to see all the conditions fulfilled; this being done, he comes down from Heaven to Earth, to declare to the world what *God* the Father, and *He*, had concluded on before, and what was the minde of the Father towards the world concerning the salvation of 35 their *souls*: and indeed who could better come of such an

6 speak] spake *1659*

errand, then he that stood by when the Covenant was made; then he that *shook hands* with the Father in making of the Covenant; then he that was become a Surety in the behalf of poor Sinners, according to the terms of this Covenant.

5   Now you know a *messenger* commonly when he cometh, he doth bring some errand to them to whom he is sent, either of what is done for them, or what they would have them, whom they send unto, do for them, or such like. Now what a glorious *message* was that which our Lord Jesus Christ came 10 down from Heaven withall to *declare* unto poor sinners, and that from God his Father? I say, how glorious was it, and how sweet is it to you that have seen your selves lost by nature; and it will also appear a glorious one to you, who are a seeking after Jesus Christ; if you do but consider these 15 following things about what he was sent.

First, Jesus Christ was sent from Heaven, to declare unto the world, from God the Father, that he was *wonderfully* filled with love to poor sinners. First, in that he would *forgive* their *sins*. Secondly, in that he would *save* their *souls*. 20 Thirdly, in that he would make them *heirs* of his glory. *For God so loved the world, that he gave his onely begotten Son.—For God sent not his Son into the world to condemn the world; but that the world through him might be saved,* John 3. 15, 16, 17.

Secondly, God sent Jesus Christ to tell the poor world, 25 how that he would do this for poor sinners, and yet be *just*, and yet do his *Justice* no *wrong*; and that was to be done by Jesus Christ, his *dying* of a *cursed* death in the *room* of poor sinners; to satisfie *justice*, and make way for *mercy*; to take away the *stumbling-blocks*, and set open *Heaven-gates*; to overcome 30 *Satan*, and break off from *sinners* his chains; to set* open *Luke 4. 18. the prison doors, and to let the prisoners go free*: And this *Isa. 61. 1, 2, was the *message* that Christ was to *deliver* to the world by 3. commandment from his Father; and this did he tell us when he came of his *errand*, where he saith, *I lay down my life for my* 35 *Sheep.—No man taketh it away from me, but I lay it down of my self: I have power to lay it down, and to take it up again: and this* *commandment have I received of my Father*, John 10. 15, 16, 17, 18. even this commandment hath my Father given me, that I should both do this thing, and also tell it unto you.

Thirdly, He was not onely sent as a *messenger* to *declare* this his Fathers love; but also how dearly he himself loved sinners; 5 what a heart he had to do them good, where he saith, *All that the Father hath given me, shall come to me* (and let me tell you *my heart* too, saith Christ): *He that cometh unto me, I will in no wise cast out.* As my Father is *willing* to give you unto *me*; even so am I, as *willing* to *receive* you. As my Father is 10 *willing* to give you Heaven, so am I *willing* to make you fit for it, by washing you with my own blood: I lay down my life, that you might have life; and this I was sent to tell you of my Father.

Fourthly, His *message* was further; he came to tell them 15 how, and which way they should come to enjoy these glorious benefits: also by laying down motives, to stir them up to accept of the benefits. The way is laid down in *John* 3. 14, 15. where Christ saith, *As Moses lifted up the serpent in the wilderness; even so must the Son of Man be lifted up,* or caused to be 20 hanged on the Cross, and die the death, *That whosoever believeth in him, should not perish, but have everlasting life.* The way therefore that thou shalt have the benefit and comfort of that which my Father and I have *covenanted* for *thee*, I am come down from heaven to earth on purpose to give thee intelli- 25 gence, and to certifie thee of it: know therefore, that as I have been born of a woman, and have taken this body upon me, it is on purpose that I might offer it up upon the Cross a Sacrifice to God, to give him satisfaction for *thy sins*, that his *mercy* may be extended to *thy soul*, without any *wrong* done 30 to *justice*; and this thou art to believe, and not in the notion, but from thy very whole soul. Now the motives are many. First, if they do not leave their sins, and come to Jesus Christ, that their sins may be *washed* away by his blood, they are sure to be *damned* in hell; for the *Law* hath condemned them 35 *already*, John 3. 18, 19. Secondly, But if they do come, they

19 *up*] om. *1659*   24 for] for for *1659*

shall have the *bosome* of Christ to lye in, the *kingdom* of Heaven to dwell in, the *Angels* and *Saints* for their companions, shall *shine* there like the *Sun*, shall be there for *ever*, shall *sit* upon the *Thrones* of *judgement*, &c. Here is Grace.

5   Methinks if I had but time to speak fully to all things that I could speak to from these two heavenly Truths, and to make application thereof; surely, with the blessing of God, I think it might perswade some vile and abominable wretch to lay down his arms that he hath taken up in defiance against 10 God (and is marching hell-wards, poste haste with the Devill); I say methinks it should stop them, and make them willing to look back, and accept of salvation for their poor condemned souls, before Gods eternall vengeance is executed upon them. O therefore! you that are upon this march, I 15 beseech you consider a little. What, shall Christ become a *drudge* for you? and will you be *drudges* for the Devill? Shall Christ covenant with God for the *salvation* of sinners? and shall sinners covenant with Hell, Death, and the Devil, for the *damnation* of their souls? Shall Christ come down from 20 Heaven to Earth to declare this to sinners? and shall sinners stop their ears against this good tidings? Will you not hear the *errand* of Christ, although he *telleth* you *tidings* of peace and salvation? How if he had come, having taken a command from his Father to damn you, and to send you to the Devills 25 in Hell? Sinner hear his *message*, he speaketh *no harm*, his words are eternall *life*, all men that give ear unto them, they have eternall advantage by them. Advantage, I say, that never hath an end.

Besides, do but consider these two things, 'tis like they 30 may have some sway upon thy soul.

First, when he came on his message, he came with tears in his eyes, and did even weepingly tender the terms of reconciliation to them; I say with tears in his eyes. And when he came near the City (*i.e.*) with his message of peace, beholding 35 the hardness of their hearts, he wept over it, and took up a lamentation over it; because he saw they rejected his mercy, which was tidings of peace. (I say) wilt thou then slight a weeping Jesus, one that so loveth thy soul, that rather then he will lose thee, he will with tears perswade with thee.

2. Not onely so: but also when he came, he came all on a goar blood to proffer mercy to thee, to shew thee still how dearly he did love thee; as if he had said, sinner, here is mercy for thee, but behold my bloody sweat, my bloody wounds, my cursed death; behold and see what danger I have gone through to come unto thy soul, I am come indeed unto thee, and do bring thee tidings of salvation, but it cost me my heart blood before I could come at thee, to give thee the fruits of my everlasting love. But more of this anon.

Thus have I spoken something concerning Christ, being the messenger of the new Covenant; but because I am not willing to cut too short of what shall come after, I shall pass by these things, not half touched, and come to the other which I promised even now; which was to shew you, that as there was Levitical Ceremonies, in, or, belonging to the first Covenant, so these types, or Levitical Ceremonies, did represent the glorious things of the new Covenant. In those Ceremonies, you read of a Sacrifice, of a Priest to offer up the Sacrifice; the *place* where, and the *manner* how he was to offer it: of which I shall speak something.

First, as touching the *Sacrifice*, you finde that it was not to be *offered* up of all kinde of beasts; as of *Lions, Bears, Wolves, Tigers, Dragons, Serpents*, or such like. To signifie, that not all kinde of *Creatures* that had sinned, as *Devils*, the *fallen Angels*, should be saved: but the *Sacrifice* was to be taken out of some kinde of *Beasts* and *Birds*: to signifie, that *some* of Gods *Creatures* that had *sinned*, he would be pleased to reconcile them to himself again; as poor fallen *Man*, and *Woman*, those miserable *Creatures*: God, the God of Heaven, had a good *look* for after their fall: but not for the *cursed Devils*; though more *noble* Creatures by *Creation* then *We*. Here is grace.

Now though these *Sacrifices* were offered; yet they were not offered to the end, they should make the comers to, or offerers thereof *perfect*: but the things was to represent to the world, what God had in after ages for to do; which was even the salvation of his Creatures by *that offering* of the *body* of Jesus Christ, of which these were a *shadow* and a *type* for the accomplishing of the second Covenant. For Christ was by Covenant to offer a *Sacrifice*, and that an effectual one *too*, if he intended 5 the salvation of sinners: *A body hast thou prepared me; I am come to do thy will*, Heb. 10.

I shall therefore shew you, First, what was *expected* of God in the *Sacrifice*, in the *Type*, and then *shew* you how it was answered in the *Antitipe*. Secondly, I shall shew you the 10 *manner* of the *offering* of the *type*; and so answerable thereto, to shew you the fitness of the *Sacrifice* of the *Body* of Christ by way of answering some questions.

For the first of these.

First, God did expect that *Sacrifice* which he himself had 15 appointed, and not another. To signifie that none would serve his turn, but the body and soul of his appointed Christ, the Mediator of the new Covenant, *John* 1. 29.

Secondly, this *Sacrifice* must not be *lame*, nor *deformed*; it must have no *scar*, *spot*, or *blemish*; to signifie, that Jesus 20 Christ was to be a *compleat Sacrifice* by Covenant, 1 *Pet.* 1. 9.

Thirdly, this *sacrifice* was to be *taken* out of the *flock*, or *herd*; to signifie that Jesus Christ *was* to *come* out of the *race* of *mankinde*, according to Covenant, *Heb.* 10. 5.

But secondly, as to the *manner* of it. First, the *sacrifice*, be-25 fore it was offered, was to have all the sins of the Children of Israel confessed over it: to signifie, that Jesus Christ must* bear the sins of all his children by Covenant. *As for thee, by the blood of thy Covenant, in his own body on the tree*, Zech. 9. 10, 11. *Isa. 53. 4, 5, 6, 7. 1 Pet. 2. 24.

Secondly, it must be had to the *place* appointed, namely, 30 *without* the *Camp* of Israel: to signifie, that Jesus Christ must be *led* to the Mount *Calvary*, Luke 23. 33.

Thirdly, the *sacrifice* was to be *killed there*; to signifie, that Jesus Christ *must*, and did *suffer* without the *City* of *Jerusalem* for our salvation.

35 Fourthly, the *sacrifice* must not onely have its *life* taken away, but also some of its *flesh burned* upon the *Alter*: to

signifie, that Jesus Christ was not onely to *dye* a *natural* death, but also that he should *undergo* the *pains* and *torments* of the damned *in hell*.

Fifthly, sometimes there must be a *living* offering, and a *dead* offering; as the goat that was *killed*, and the *scape* goat; 5 the *dead* bird, and the *living* bird, *Levit*. 14. 3, 4, 5, 6. To signifie, that Jesus Christ must *dye*, and come to *life* again.

Sixthly, the goat that *was* to *dye*, *was* to be the *sin-offering*; that is, to be offered as the rest of the sin-offerings, to make an atonement as a type; and the *other goat*, was to have *all the* 10 sins of the Children of Israel *confessed* over *him**, and then to *be let go* into the wilderness, *never* to be catched again, to signifie that Christs *death*, was to make satisfaction for sin; and his coming to *life* again, was to bring in everlasting **justification*, from the power, curse, and destroying nature 15 of sin.

*Levit. 16. from the 7. verse to the 22.

*Rom. 4. 25.

Seventhly, the scape goat was to be carried by a *fit* man into the wilderness. To signifie that Jesus Christ should be both *fit* and *able*, to carry our sins quite away from us, so as they should never be laid to our charge again. Here is Grace.   20

Eighthly, the sacrifices under the Law, commonly part of them must be *eaten**; To signifie, that they that are saved, should spiritually *feed* on the *body* and *blood* of Jesus *Christ*, or else they have no *life* by him, *John*. 6. 51, 52, 53.

*Exod. 12. from the 5. to the 11.

Ninthly, this sacrifice must be eaten with *unleavened* 25 bread: To signifie, that they which *love* their *sins*, that devilish *leaven* of *wickedness*; they do not *feed* upon Jesus Christ.

Now of what hath been spoken, this is the *sum*: that there is a *sacrifice* under the *new* Covenant, as there was sacrifices under the *old*; and that this *sacrifice* did every wayes answer *that*, 30 or *those*: Indeed, they did but suffer for sin in shew, but he in reality; they as the *shadow*, but he as the *substance*. O! when Jesus Christ did come to make himself a *sacrifice*, or to offer himself for *sin*; you may understand that our sins was indeed charged to purpose upon him: O how they scared his *soul*, 35

how they break his *body*; insomuch that they made the blood
run down his blessed face, and from his precious side; therefore thou must understand these following things. First, that
Jesus Christ by Covenant did dye for sin. Secondly, that his
5 death was not a meer natural death, but a cursed death;
even such a one as men do undergo from God for their sins
(though he himself had none), even such a death, as to endure
the very pains and torments of *hell*; O sad *pains*! and inex-
pressable *torments*, that this our *sacrifice* for sin went under.
10 The pains of his *body was not all; no, but the pains of his
soul; for his *soul* was made an offering, as well as his body; yet
all but one sacrifice. *Isa.* 53. To signifie, that the suffering of
Christ was not onely a *bodily* suffering, but a *soul* suffering;
not onely to suffer what man could inflict upon him: but also
15 to suffer *soul torments*, that none but God can inflict, or suffer
to be inflicted upon him. O the torments of his *soul*! they were
the torments *indeed*; his *soul* was that that felt the *wrath* of
God. *My soul* saith he, *is exceeding sorrowful, even unto death**.
My soul is troubled, and what shall I say*? The *Rock* was not so
20 *rent*, as was his precious *soul*: there was not such a terrible
darkness on the face of the earth then, as there was on his
precious *soul*. O the *torments* of hell! and the *eclipsings* of the
divine smiles of God, were both upon him at *once*; the *Devils*
assailing of him, and *God* forsaking of him, and all at *once*.
25 *My God, my God*, saith he, *why hast thou forsaken me**? now in my
greatest extremity; now *sin* is laid upon me, the *curse* takes
hold on me, the *pains* of *hell* are clasped about me, and thou
hast *forsaken* me. O sad! Sinner, this was not done in *pretence*,
but in reality; not in *shew*, but in very *deed*; Otherwise Christ
30 had *dissembled*, and had not spoken the *truth*; but the truth of
it, his *bloody* sweat declares, his mighty *cries* declares, the
things what, and for what he suffered declares. Nay, I must
say thus much, that all the *damned* souls in *hell*, with all their
damnations, did never yet *feel* that torment and *pain*, that did
35 this blessed Jesus in a *little* time. Sinner, canst thou read that
Jesus Christ was made an *offering* for *sin*, and yet go on in sin?

As Christ did not suffer in his body without suffering in soul, nor yet in soul without his suffering in body; it was because not without the soul, but both the body and soul of the Saints should be for ever saved.

*Mat. 26. 38.

*John 12. 27.

*Mat. 27. 46.

16 the torments] torment *1685*

Canst thou hear that the *load* of thy *sins* did break the very *heart* of Christ, and spill his precious *Blood*? And canst thou finde in thy heart to labour to lay *more* sins upon his *back*? Canst thou hear that he *suffered* the pains, the fiery flames of *Hell*? and canst thou finde in thy heart, to *add* to his *groans*, by slighting of his *sufferings*? O hard hearted wretch! How canst thou deal so unkindly with such a sweet Lord Jesus?

Quest. But why did Christ offer himself in *sacrifice*?

Answ. That thou shouldest not be thrown to the very *Devils*.

Quest. But why did he spill his precious *blood*?

Answ. That thou mightest enjoy the joyes of *Heaven*.

Quest. But why did he suffer the pains of *Hell*?

Answ. That thou mightest not *fry* with the devil and *damned* souls.

Quest. But could not we have been saved if Christ had not died?

Answ. No, for without *shedding* of *blood* there is no *remission*: and besides, there was no *death*, that could satisfie Gods *justice* but his, which is evident; because there was none in a capacity to dye, or that was *able* to answer an *infinite* God by his so *suffering*, but he.

Quest. But why did God let him dye?

Answ. He standing in the room of sinners; and that in their *names* and *natures*, Gods justice must fall upon *him*; for justice takes vengeance for sin wheresoever it finds it, though it be on his dear *Son*. Nay, God favoured his *Son* no more, finding our sins upon *him*, then he would have favoured any of *us*: For, should *we* have died? so did *he*. Should we have been made a *curse*? so was *he*. Should *we* have undergone the pains of *hell*? so did *he*.

Quest. But did he indeed suffer the torments of hell?

Answ. Yea, and that in such an horrible way too, that it is unspeakable.

Quest. Could he not have suffered without his so suffering? would not his dying onely of a *natural* death have served the turn?

Answ. No, in no wise: The *sins*, for which he suffered, called for the torments of *hell*; the *condition* in which he *died*, did call for the torments of *hell*; for Christ did not dye the death of a Saint, but the death of a Sinner; of a cursed and damned sin-
5 ner (because he stood in their rooms, *Gal.* 3. 13.), the *Law* to which he was subjected, called for the torments of *hell*; the *nature* of Gods *justice* could not bate him any thing, the *death* which he was to suffer, had not *lost* its *sting*; all these being put together do *irresistibly* declare unto us, that he as
10 a *sacrifice*, did suffer the torments of *hell*.

But secondly, had he not *died* and suffered the *cursed* death, the Covenant had been made void, and his *suretiship* would have been forfeited; and *besides* this, the world *damned* in the flames of hell fire: therefore his being a *sacrifice*, was one *part*
15 of the Covenant; for the *terms* of the Covenant was, that he should spill his blood, *Zech.* 9. 10, 11. O blessed Jesus! O blessed Grace!

Quest. But why then is his death so slighted by some?

Answ. Because they are *enemies* to him, either through
20 *ignorance*, or *presumption*; either for want of *knowledge*, or out of *malice*; for surely, did they *love*, or *believe* him, they could not chuse but *break*, and *bleed* at heart, to consider and to think of him, *Zech.* 12. 10, 11.

Thus, passing this, I shall now speak something to Christs
25 *priestly* office: but by the way, if any should think, that I do here spin my thread too long in distinguishing his *priestly* office, from his being a *sacrifice*; they supposing that for Christ to be a Priest, and a sacrifice is all one and the same thing, and it may be it is; because they have not thought on this so
30 well as they should: Namely, that as he was a sacrifice, he was *passive*; that is, led, or had away as a lamb to his sufferings: Isa. 53. But as a Priest, he was active; that is, he did willingly, and *freely* give up his body to be a sacrifice. *He hath given his life a ransom for many.* This consideration being with some weight
35 and clearness on my spirit, I was, and am caused to lay them down in two particular heads. And therefore,

24 this] his *1659, 1685*

The second thing that I would speak something to, it is this; that as there were *Priests* under the first *Covenant*; so there is a Priest under this, belonging to this New *Covenant*, a high *Priest*, the chief *Priest*: as it is clear, where it is said, *We having an high Priest over the house of God*, Heb. 10. 21. 5 Chap. 3. 1. Chap. 5. 5, 10. and Chap. 7. 24, 25, 26. Chap. 8. 1, 4.

Now the things that I shall treat upon are these. First I shall shew you the *Qualifications* required of a *Priest* under the Law. Secondly, his Office; and thirdly, how Jesus Christ did accord- 10 ing to what was *signified* by those under the Law: I say, how he did answer the *Types*, and where he went beyond them.

For his Qualifications.

The first qualification. First, They must be called thereto of God; *No man takes this honour upon him, but he that is called of God, as Aaron*, Heb. 15 5. 4. Now *Aarons* being called of God to be a *Priest*, signifies, that *Jesus Christ* is a *Priest* of Gods appointment, such a one that God hath chosen, likes of, and hath set on work, *called of God an high Priest*, &c. ver. 10.

The second qualification. Secondly, The *Priests* under the Law, they must be men 20 *compleat*, not deformed; *Speak unto Aaron*, saith God to *Moses*, *saying, Whosoever he be of thy seed in their generations, that hath any blemish, let him not approach to offer the bread of his God: for whatsoever man he be that hath a blemish, he shall not approach: (if he be) a blinde man, or a lame man, or he that hath a flat nose,* 25 *or any thing superfluous, or a man that is broken footed, or broken handed, or crookt backt, or a dwarf, or he that hath a blemish in his eye, or be scurvy, or scabbed, or hath his stones broken: No man that hath a blemish of the seed of Aaron the Priest, shall come nigh to offer offerings of the Lord made by fire; he hath a blemish, he shall* 30 *not come nigh to offer the bread of his God*, Leviticus 21. 17, 18, 19, 20, 21. What doth all this signifie; but that, in the first place, he must not be *lame*, to signifie he must not go *halt- ingly* about the work of our salvation. 2. He must not be *blinde*, to signifie, that he must not go *ignorantly* to work, but 35

14 marg. The first qualification.] *om. 1685*   20 marg. The second qualification.] *om. 1685*

he must be *quick* of understanding in the things of God. 3.
He must not be scabbed, to signifie, that the Priest must not
be *corrupt*, or filthy in his office. 4. In a word, he must be every
wayes *compleat*, to signifie to us, that Jesus Christ was to be,
5 and is most *compleat*, and most perfect every way, an *accept-*
able high Priest in things pertaining to God, in reference to
this second Covenant.

Thirdly, The *Priests* under the Law were not to be *hard* The third
hearted, but *pittifull* and *compassionate*, willing and ready, with Qualification.
10 abundance of bowels to offer for the people, and to make an
atonement for them, Heb. 5. 1, 2. To signifie, that Jesus Christ
should be a *tender hearted* high Priest, able and *willing* to
simpathize, and be affected with the *infirmities* of others, to
pray for *them*, to offer up for *them* his precious bloud; he must
15 be such an one, *who can have compassion on* (a company of poor)
ignorant souls, and on them that are out of the way, to recover Heb. 4. 15.
them, and to set *them* in safety; and that he might thus do,
he must be a *man* that had experience of the disadvantages
that *infirmity* and sin did bring unto these poor creatures,
20 *Heb. 2. 17.*

Fourthly, The high *Priests* under the Law were not to be The fourth
shie, or *squemish*, in case there was any that had the *plague* or Qualification.
leprosie, *scab* or *blaunches*; but must look on them, go to them,
and offer for them (*Levit.* 13. read that whole Chapter), all
25 which is to signifie, that Jesus Christ should not *refuse* to take
notice of the *severall infirmities* of his poorest people, but to
teach them, and to see that none of them be lost, by reason of
their infirmity, for want of looking too, or tending of. This
priviledge also have we under this second Covenant. This is
30 the way to make Grace shine.

Fifthly, The high *Priests* under the *Law*, they were to be The fifth
anointed with very *excellent* Oyl, compounded by art (*Exod.* qualification.
29. 7. *Chap.* 30. 30.), to signifie, that Jesus, the great high
Priest of this New Covenant, should be in a most eminent
35 way *anointed* to his *Priestly* Office by the *Holy Spirit* of the Lord.

8 marg. The third Qualification.] *om. 1685*   21 marg. The fourth
Qualification.] *om. 1685*   31 marg. The fifth qualification.] *om. 1685*

The sixth qualification. Sixthly, The *Priests* food and livelihood in the time of his *Ministery*, was to be the *consecrated* and holy things, *Exod.* 29. 33. to signifie, that it is the very *meat and drink* of Jesus Christ, to do his *Priestly* Office, and to save and preserve his poor tempted and afflicted Saints. O what a New Covenant 5 high Priest have we!

The seventh qualification. Seventhly, The Priests under the *Law* were to be *washed* with water, *Exod.* 29. 4. to signifie, that *Jesus Christ* should not go about the work of his *Priestly* Office with the filth of sin upon him; but was *without* sin to appear as our high Priest 10 in the presence of his Father, to execute his Priestly Office there for our advantage. *For such a high Priest became us, who is holy, harmless, undefiled, separate from sinners, and made higher then the heavens,* Heb. 7. 26.

The eighth qualification. Eighthly, The high *Priests* under the *Law*, before they went 15 into the holy place, they were to be clothed with a *curious* garment, *a breast-plate, and an ephod, and a robe, and a broidered coat, a mitre, and a girdle,* and these were to be made of *gold*, and *blue*, and *purple*, and *scarlet*, and *fine linnen*; and in this *garment* and glorious *ornaments*, there must be *precious stones*, 20 and on those *stones* there must be written the *names of the children of Israel* (read the 28. of *Exodus*), and all was to signifie what a *glorious* high Priest Jesus Christ should be; and how in the *righteousness* of God, he should *appear* before God as our high *Priest*, to offer up the *sacrifice* that was to be *offered* for our 25 salvation to God his Father: but I pass that.

Now I shall speak to his Office: The Office of the high *Priest* in generall was two-fold. First, to *offer* the sacrifice *without* the Camp. Secondly, to *bring* it *within* the vail, that is, into the holiest of all, which did type out Heaven. 30

First, it was the office of the Priest to *offer* the sacrifice; and so did Jesus Christ, he did *offer* his own body and soul in sacrifice. I say, HE did OFFER it and not another, as it is written, *No man taketh away my life, but I lay it down of my self; I have power to lay it down, and I have power to take it again,* 35

John 10. 17, 18. And again it is said, *When he* (Jesus) *had offered up one sacrifice for sins for ever, sate down on the right hand of God*, Heb. 10. 12.

Secondly, The *Priests* under the *Law* must offer up the 5 sacrifice that *God* had appointed, and none else, a compleat one without any blemish: and so did our high Priest, where he saith, *Sacrifice and offerings thou wouldest not, but a body hast thou prepared me*, and that will I offer, Heb. 10. 5.

Thirdly, The *Priest* was to take of the *ashes* of the sacrifice, 10 and lay them in a *clean* place: and this signifies, that the *body* of Jesus after it had been offered, should be laid into *Josephs sepulchre*, as in a clean place, where never any man before was laid, *Levit.* 6. 11. compared with *John* 19. 41, 42.

This being one part of his office, and when this was done, 15 then in the next place he was to put on the *glorious* garment, when he was to go into the *holiest*, and take of the bloud and carry it *thither*, &c. he was to put on the *holy garment*, which signifieth the *righteousness* of Jesus Christ.

Secondly, He was in this *holy garment*, which hath in it the 20 *stones*, and in the *stones* the *names* of the *twelve* Tribes of the Children of *Israel*, to appear in the holy place, *Exodus* 28. *And thou shalt take two Onix stones, and shalt grave on them the names of the children of Israel. Six of their names on one stone, and the other six names of the rest on the other stone according to their birth,* 25 ver. 9, 10. And this was to signifie, that when Jesus Christ was to *enter* into the holiest, then he was *there* to bear the *names* of his *elect*, in the *tables* of his *heart*, before the Throne of God, and the Mercy-seat, Heb. 12. 23.

Thirdly, with this he was to take of the *blood* of the sacri- 30 fices, and carry it into the *holiest* of all, which was a type of *heaven*, and there was he to *sprinkle* the mercy-seat; and this was to be done by the high Priest onely. To signifie, that *none* but Jesus Christ must have this office, and priviledge, to be the peoples high Priest to offer for them. *Heb.* 9. 7. *But* 35 *into the second went the high priest alone once every year, yet not without blood, which he offered for himself, and for the errours of the people.*

Fourthly, He was there to make an *atonement* for the people with the *blood*, sprinkling of it upon the mercy-seat: but this must be done with much *incense*, *Levit.* 16. *And Aaron shall bring the bullock which is for a sin-offering, for himself, and for his house, and shall kill the bullock of the sin-offering, which is for himself.* *And he shall take a censer full of burning coals of fire from off the Alter before the Lord, and his hands full of sweet incense beaten small, and bring it within the vail: And he shall put the incense upon the fire before the Lord, that the cloud of the incense may cover the mercy-seat, that is upon the testimony, that he dye not. And he shall take of the blood of the bullock, and sprinkle it upon the mercy-seat east-ward, and before the mercy-seat shall he sprinkle the blood with his finger seven times. And then shall he kill the goat of the sin-offering which is for the people, and bring his blood within the vail, and do with that blood as he did with the blood of the bullock, and sprinkle it upon the mercy-seat, and before the mercy-seat,* ver. the 11, 12, 13, 14, 15. Now this was for the *priest* and the *people*; all which doth signifie, that Jesus Christ was *after* his death, to go into heaven it self, of which this holy place was a figure. *Heb.* 9. and there to carry the *sacrifice* that he offered upon the Cross into the presence of God, for to obtain mercy for the people in a way of justice. And in that he is said to take his hands full of sweet *incense*, it signifies, that Jesus Christ was to offer up his *sacrifice* in the *presence* of his Father, in a way of *intercession* and prayers.

I might have branched these things out into several particulars, but I would be brief.

I say, therefore the office of the *Priests* was to *carry* the blood *into* the holy place, and *there* to present it before the *mercy-seat*, with his heart full of *intercessions* for the people, for *whom* he was a *priest*, *Luke* 1. 8, 9, 10, 11. This is Jesus Christs work *now* in the kingdom of glory to plead his own blood, the nature and vertue of it, with a perpetual *intercession* to the God of mercy, on the behalf of us poor miserable sinners, *Heb.* 7. 24.

Now in the *intercession* of this Jesus, which is *part* of his

13 *shall he*] *he shall 1685*   16 ver. the] verse *1685*

priestly *office*, there is these things to be considered for our comfort.

First, there is a *pleading* of the vertue of his blood, *for them* that are already come in; that they may be kept from the 5 *evils* of *heresies, delusions, temptations, pleasures, profits,* or *any* thing of this world, which may be too hard for them. Father, *I pray not that thou shouldest take them out of the world* (saith Christ) *but that thou shouldest keep them from the evil,* John 17. 15.

Secondly, in case the *devil* should aspire up into the presence 10 of God, to *accuse* any of the poor *Saints,* and to *plead* their back-slidings against *them,* as he will do if he can; then there is Jesus, our Lord Jesus, ready in the Court of Heaven, at the right hand of God, to plead the *vertue* of his *blood,* not onely for the great and *general* satisfaction that he did give when he was on 15 the Cross; but also the *vertue* that is in it *now,* for the *cleansing,* and *fresh* purging, of his poor Saints, under their *several* temptations and infirmities; as saith the Apostle, *For if when we were enemies, we were reconciled to God, by the death of his Son: much more then being reconciled, we shall be saved by his life*; that 20 is, by his intercession, *Rom.* 5. 10.

Thirdly, the *maintaining* of *grace,* also, is by Jesus Christs *intercession,* being the second part of his *priestly* office. O! had we not a Jesus at the right hand of God, making *intercession* for us, and to *convey* fresh supplies of Grace unto *us,* 25 through the *vertue* of his *blood,* being pleaded at Gods right hand; how soon would it be with *us,* as it is with *those* for whom he *prayes* not at all, *John* 17. 9. But the reason why thou *standest,* while others *fall,* the reason why thou goest *through* the many temptations of the world, and shakest them 30 off from thee, while others are *ensnared,* and intangled therein; it is because thou hast an *interceding* Jesus. *I have prayed* (saith he) *that thy faith fail not,* Luke 22. 32.

Fourthly, it is partly by the *vertue* of Christs *intercession* that the *elect* are brought in; there is many that are to *come* 35 to Christ, which are not yet brought in to Christ: and it is one part of his work to *pray* for *their* salvation too. *Neither pray I for these alone, but for all those that shall believe* (though as yet they do not believe) *on me* (but that they may believe) *through their word*, John 17. 20. And let me tell thee soul for thy comfort, who art a coming in to Christ, *panting*, and *sighing*, as if thy heart would *break*; I tell thee soul, thou wouldest *never* have come to Christ, if he had not *first*, by the vertue of his blood and *intercession*, sent into thy heart an *earnest* desire after Christ: and let me tell thee also, that it is his *business* to make intercession for thee; not onely that thou *mightest* come in, but that thou *mightest* be *preserved*, when thou *art* come in. Compare *Heb.* 7. ver. 25. with *Rom.* 8. ver. 33, 34, 35, &c.

Fifthly, it is by the *intercession* of Christ, that the *infirmities* of the *Saints* in their *holy* duties are forgiven: Alas, if it was not for the *priestly* office of Christ Jesus, the prayers, alms, and other duties of the Saints, might be *rejected*, because of the *sin* that is in them: but Jesus being our high Priest, he is *ready* to take away the *iniquities* of our *holy* things, perfuming our prayers with the glory of his own *perfections*: and therefore it is, that there is an answer given to the Saints *prayers*, and also acceptance of their *holy* duties, *Rev.* 8. 3, 4. *But Christ being come an high Priest of good things to come, by a greater and more perfect Tabernacle, not made with hands, that is to say, not of this building. Neither by the blood of goats and calves: but by his own blood he entered in once into the holy place, having obtained eternal redemption for us. For if the blood of bulls and goats, and the ashes of an heifer sprinkling the unclean, sanctifieth to the purifying of the flesh; How much more shall the blood of Christ, who through the eternal Spirit, offered himself without spot to God, purge your consciences from dead works to serve the living God? And for this cause he is the Mediator of the New Testament (or Covenant) that by means of death, for the redemption of the transgressions that were under the first Testament, they which are called (notwithstanding all their sins) might receive the promise of eternal inheritance,* Heb. 9. 11, 12, 13, 14, 15.

The third thing now to be spoken to, it is to shew where, and how Jesus Christ out-went, and goes beyond these priests in all their qualifications and offices, for the comfort of poor Saints.

First, they that were called to the priesthood under the Law, were but *men: but he is both *God and man. *Heb. 7. 28. *Ver. 3.

5 2. Their qualifications were in them in a very *scanty way*: but Jesus was every way qualified in an infinite and *full way*.

3. They were consecrated but for a *time: but he for *evermore. *Heb. 7. 23. *Ver. 24.

4. They were made without an *oath: but he with an oath. *Ver. 20, 21.

10 5. They as *servants*: but he as a *Son. *Heb. 3. 6.

6. Their garments were but such as could be made with *hands: but his the very righteousness of *God. *Ex. 28. *Rom. 3. 22.

7. Their offerings were but the *body and blood of beasts, and such like: but his offering was *his own body and soul. *Phil. 3. 8. *Heb. 9. 12,13. Chap. 10. 4, 5.

15 8. Those were but at best but a *shadow or type; but he the very *substance and end of all those Ceremonies. Isa. 53. 10. Heb. 10. 5. *Verse 1.

9. Their *holy place* was but *made by men*; but his, or that which Jesus is entered, is into *heaven it self. *Heb. 9. 10,11. *Heb. 9. 24. *Heb. 5. 2, 3. Heb. 7. 26.

10. When they went to offer their sacrifice, they were 20 forced to offer for *themselves as men compassed about with *infirmity*; but he *holy, harmless, who did never commit the least transgression. *Heb. 10. 11. *Heb. 7. 26.

11. They, when they went in to offer, they were fain to do it *standing*; to signifie, that God had no satisfaction therein: 25 but he, *when he had offered one sacrifice for sin, for ever *sate down on the right hand of God*: To signifie, that God was very well pleased with his offering. *Heb. 10. 11. *Ver. 12.

12. They were fain *to offer *oftentimes the same sacrifice that could never take away sin; but he by one offering hath perfected for 30 *ever them that are sanctified*. *Heb. 10. 11. *Ver. 14.

13. Their sacrifices at the best could but serve for the cleansing of the *flesh*, but his for cleansing both body and soul: The blood of Jesus Christ doth purge the *conscience from *dead works* to live a holy life. *Heb. 9. 13. *Ver. 14.

35 14. Those high Priests could not offer but *once a year in *Ver. 7.

4 marg. Ver.] om. 1685   7 3.] om. 1685   14*] om. 1659, 1685
28 same] om. 1685

*Heb. 7. 24, the holiest of all; but our high Priest, he *ever liveth* to make
 25. intercession for us.

15. Those high Priests, notwithstanding they were Priests, they were not *always* to wear their holy garments; but Jesus *never* puts them off of him, but is in them *always*.   5

Heb. 7. 22, 16. Those high Priests *death* would be too hard for them;
Heb. 2. 15. 23. but our High Priest hath *vanquished* and *overcome* that cruell enemy of ours, and brought life and immortality to light through the glorious Gospel, 2 *Tim.* 1. 10.

17. Those high Priests were not *able* to save themselves; 10 but this is able to save himself, and *all* that come to God by him, *Heb.* 7. 25.

18. Those high Priests blood could not do away sin; but the blood of Jesus Christ, who is our High Priest, *cleanseth us from all sin*, 1 John 1. 7.   15

19. Those high Priests sometimes by sin caused God to reject their sacrifices; but this high Priest *doth always the things that please him*.

20. Those high Priests could *never* conveigh the Spirit by vertue of their sacrifices or office; but this High Priest, our 20 Lord Jesus, he can, and doth *give all* the gifts and graces that are given to the sons of men.

21. Those high Priests could never by their sacrifices bring the soul of any sinner to glory, by vertue of *it* self; but Jesus hath by one offering (as I said before) perfected *for ever* those 25 that he did die for. Thus in brief I have shewed in some particulars how, and wherein Jesus our High Priest doth go beyond those high Priests: and many more without question might be mentioned, but I forbear.

A fifth *Office* of Christ in reference to the second Covenant, 30 it was that he should be the *Forerunner* again to heaven before his Saints that were to follow after. First, he strikes *hands* in the Covenant. Secondly, he *stands* bound as a *surety* to see every thing in the Covenant accomplished, that was to be done on *his* part; then he brings the *message* from heaven to the 35 *world*; and before he goeth back, he offereth himself for the *same* sins that he *agreed* to suffer for: and so soon as this was done, he goeth poste haste to heaven again; not onely to exercise the second part of his Priestly Office; but as our forerunner, to take possession for us, even into heaven it self, 5 as you may see, *Heb.* 6. 20. where it is said, *Whither the forerunner is for us entered.*

First, he *is run* before to open heaven gates: *Be ye open ye everlasting doors, that the King of Glory may enter in.*

Secondly, He is *run* before to take possession of glory in our 10 natures for us.

Thirdly, He is *run* before to prepare *us* our *places* against we come after; *I go to prepare a place for you,* John 14. 1, 2, 3.

Fourthly, He is *run* thither to make the way *easie,* in that he hath first troden the path himself.

15   Fifthly, He is *run* thither to receive *gifts for us.* All spirituall and heavenly *gifts* had been kept from *us,* had not Christ so soon as the time appointed was come, run back to the king-dom of glory to receive them for *us.* But I cannot stand to enlarge upon these glorious things, the Lord enlarge them 20 upon your hearts by meditation.

These things have I spoken to shew you, that Saints are under Grace.

Here now I might begin to speak of his Propheticall and Kingly Office, and the priviledges that do, and shall come thereby: but that I fear I shall be too tedious, therefore at this time I shall passe them by. Thus you may see how the Coven-25 ant of Grace doth *run,* and with whom it was made, and also what was the conditions thereof.

Now then, *this* Grace, *this* everlasting Grace of God comes to be *free* to *us* through the satisfaction (according to the conditions) *given* by another for *us;* for though it be free, and 30 freely given to *us,* yet the obtaining of it did cost our *Head,* our *Publick-man* a very *dear* price (1 *Cor.* 6. 20.), *For ye are bought with a price, even with the precious blood of Christ* (1 *Pet.* 1. 9.). So it is by *another,* I say, not by *us;* yet it is as sure made over to *us,* even to so many of *us* as do, or shall believe, as if 35 *we* had done it, and obtained the grace of God *our selves:* nay *surer;* for consider, I say this grace is *free to us,* and comes upon a clear score, by vertue of the *labour* and purchase of *another* for *us*; mark, that which is obtained by *another* for *us*, is not obtained for *us* by our selves: No, *but Christ hath obtained eternall redemption for us*, Heb. 9. 12. *not by the blood of goats and calves* (which was things offered by men under the Law), *but by his own blood* (meaning Christs) *he entered into the holy* 5 *place, having obtained eternall redemption for us.*

Secondly, it comes to be *unchangeable* through the *perfection* of that *satisfaction* that was given to God through the *Son* of *Mary* for *us*; for what ever the divine, infinite, and eternal justice of God did call for at the *hands* of *man*, if ever he in- 10 tended to be a partaker of the grace of God, this *Jesus*, this one *man*, this *publick* person, did compleatly give a satisfaction to it, even so effectually; which caused God not onely to say, I am pleased, but *I am well pleased*, Mat. 3. 17. Compleatly and sufficiently satisfied with *thee* on *their* behalf; for 15 so you must understand it: Mark therefore these following words; *And having made peace* (or compleatly made up the difference) *through the blood of his Cross, by him to reconcile all things unto himself; by him, I say, whether they be things in earth, or things in heaven. And you who were sometimes alienated, and* 20 *enemies in your minde by wicked works; yet now hath he reconciled,* how, *in the body of his flesh, through death, to present you holy;* mark, *holy and unblameable, and unreproveable in his sight,* Coloss. 1. the 21, 22, 23. ver. And thus it is *Grace*, unchangeable *Grace* to *us*; because it was obtained, yea, compleatly obtained 25 for *us*, by *Jesus Christ* God-man.

Object.   But some may say, how was it possible that the one *man* Jesus by one offering, should so compleatly obtain and bring in unchangeable grace for such an *innumerable* company of sinners, as are to be saved.   30

Answ.   *Answ.* First, in that he was every wayes *fitted* for such a work. And secondly, in that, as I said before, he did *every* wayes compleatly satisfie that which was offended by our disobedience to the *former* Covenant. And for the clearing of this.

First, consider, was it *man* that had offended? He was *man* 35 that gave the satisfaction. *For as by man came death, even so also by man did come the resurrection from the dead,* 1 Cor. 15. 21.

Secondly, was it God that was offended, he was *God* that did give a satisfaction. *To us a Child is born, to us a Son is given.* 5 —*And his name shall be called the mighty God* (Isa. 9. 6.). He *thought it no robbery to be equal with God: but* (for our sakes, 2 Cor. 8. 9.) *he made himself of no reputation,* &c. Phil. 2. 5, 6, 7.

Thirdly, for the further clearing of this, to shew you that in every thing he was rightly qualified for this great work; 10 see what God himself saith of him: he calls him in the first place *man*; and secondly he owns him to be his *fellow,* saying, *Awake O sword against my shepherd, against the man*; mark, *the man that is my fellow saith the Lord of Hosts,* Zech. 13. 7.

So that now let divine and infinite Justice turn it self 15 which way it will, it findes one that can tell how to match it; for if it say, I will require the satisfaction of *man,* here is a *man* to satisfie its cry: and if it say, but I am an *infinite* God, and must and will have an *infinite* satisfaction: here is one also that is *infinite,* even fellow with God; *fellow* in his essence and 20 being, *Prov.* 8. 23. *Fellow* in his power and strength, 1 *Cor.* I. 24. *Fellow* in his wisdom, *see again the same verse. Fellow* in his mercy and grace, *Tit.* 2. 10. compared with ver. 11. together with the rest of the attributes of God; so that, I say, let justice turn it self which way it will, here is a compleat per-25 son to give a compleat satisfaction: thus much of the fitness of the person.

Secondly, for the compleatness of the satisfaction given by him for us. And that is discovered in these particulars.

First, doth justice call for the blood of *that* nature that 30 sinned? Here is the heart blood of Jesus Christ. *We have redemption through his blood,* Ephes. I. 7. 1 Pet. I. 18, 19. Zech. 9. 10, 11.

2. Doth justice say, that this blood, if it be not the blood of one that is *really,* and *naturally* God, it will not give satis-35 faction to infinite justice? Then here is God, *purchasing his Church with his own blood,* Acts 20. 28.

31 I. 7.] I. 14. *1659, 1685*   36 *with*] *with with 1659*

3. Doth justice say, that it must not onely have satisfaction for sinners; but they that are saved must be also *washed* and *sanctified* with this blood? Then here is he that so loved us, that he *washed us from our sins in his own blood*, Rev. 1. 5.

4. Is there to be a *righteousness* to clothe them with, that are to be presented before divine justice? Then here is the *righteousness* of Christ, which is, *even the righteousness of God by faith*, Rom. 3. 22. Phil. 3. 8, 9, 10.

5. Is there any sins now that will fly upon this Saviour, like so many Lions, or raging Devils, if he take in hand to redeem *man*? He will be content *to bear them all himself alone, even in his own body upon the tree*, 1 Pet. 2. 24.

6. Is there any *Law* now that will *curse*, and condemn this Saviour for standing in our persons, to give satisfaction to God for the transgression of *man*? He will be willing to be *cursed*, yea, to be *made a curse for sinners*, rather then they shall be cursed and damned themselves, Gal. 3. 13.

7. Must the great and glorious God, whose eyes are so pure that he cannot behold iniquity, I say, must he not onely have the blood, but the very *life* of him that will take in hand to be the deliverer, and Saviour of us poor miserable sinners? He is *willing to lay down his life for his sheep*, John 10. 11.

8. Must he not onely dye a natural death, but must his soul descend into hell (though it should not be left there)? He will suffer that also. *Psal.* 16. 10. and *Acts* 17. 3.

9. Must he not onely be *buried*, but *rise* again from the *dead*, and overcome *death*, that he might be the first fruits to God of them that *sleep*, which shall be saved? He will be *buried*, and also through the strength of his Godhead, he will *raise* himself out of the *grave*, though *death* hold him never so *fast*, and the Jews lay never such a great stone upon the mouth of the Sepulchre, and seal it never so fast, 1 *Cor.* 15. 2. *Luke* 24. 34.

10. Must he *carry* that *body* into the presence of his Father, to take *possession* of Heaven? *Heb.* 9. 24. *John* 14. 2, 3. And must he appear there as *Priest* (*Heb.* 6. 20.), as *forerunner*

25 17. 3.] 2. 3. *1659, 1685*

(ver. the same), as an *Advocate* (1 John 2. 1, 2.), as *Prophet*, as a *Treasure-house*, an as *Interceder*, and *pleader* of the *Causes* of his *people*? He will be all these, and much more; to the end, the grace of God by faith in Jesus Christ, might be made
5 *surer* to all the seed. *Who then can condemn? it is God that justi-fieth; because Christ hath dyed, yea, rather that is risen again. Who* (now seeing all this is so effectually done) *shall lay any thing*, the least thing? who can finde the least flaw, the least wrinkle, the least defect or imperfection *in this glorious satisfaction*?

10   But is it possible that he should so *soon* give infinite justice ᴏᵦⱼₑ꜀ₜ. a satisfaction, a compleat satisfaction? For the eternall God doth require an eternall lying under the Curse; to the end, he may be eternally satisfied.

   Answ. Indeed that which is *finite*, must have an *eternity* to
15 satisfie God in; that is, they that fall into the prison and *pit* of utter darknesse, must be there to all eternity, to the end, the justice of God may have its *full blow* at them. But now he that I am speaking of, is *God* (*Isa.* 9. 6. 2. *Tim.* 1. 16. *Heb.* 1. 8, 9. *Phil.* 2. 4, 5, 6), and so *is infinite*: Now he which is
20 true God, is *able* to give in as little a time an *infinite* satisfaction, as *Adam* was in giving the *dissatisfaction. Adam* himself might have given *satisfaction* for himself as soon as Christ, had he been very God, as Jesus Christ was: For the reason why the posterity of *Adam*, even so many of them as fall short of life,
25 must lye *broyling* in hell to all *eternity*, is this; They are not *able* to give the justice of God satisfaction, they being not *infinite*, as aforesaid. *But Christ* (that is God-man) *being come an high Priest* (that is to offer and give satisfaction) *of good things to come, by a greater and more perfect tabernacle, not made*
30 *with hands, that is to say, not of this building: Neither by the blood of goats and calves, but by his own*; mark you that, *but by his own blood he hath entered into the holy place, having* (already) *obtained eternall redemption for us*: But how? *For if the bloud of bulls and goats, and the ashes of an heifer sprinkling the unclean,*
35 *sanctifieth to the purging of the flesh, how much more shall the blood of Christ, who through the eternall Spirit* (who through the power

and vertue of his infinite Godhead) *offered himself without spot to God, purge your consciences from dead works, to serve the living God? And for this cause* (that is, for that he is God as well as man, and so able to give justice an infinite satisfaction; therefore) *he is the Mediatour of the New Covenant, that by the means of his death for the redemption of the transgressions that were under the first testament, they which are called might receive the promise of eternall inheritance,* Heb. 9. 11, 12, 13, 14, 15. as I said before.

Object. This is much; but is God *contented* with this? Is he satisfied now in the behalf of sinners by *this mans* thus *suffering?* If he is, then how doth it appear?

Answ. It is evident, yea, wonderfull evident, that this hath pleased him to the *full,* as appeareth by these following Demonstrations.

First, In that God did *admit* him into his *presence;* yea, receive him with *joy* and musick, even with the sound of a *Trumpet* at his ascension into heaven (*Psal.* 47. 5.): and Christ makes it an argument to his Children, that *his righteousness* was sufficient, in that he went to his Father, and they *saw* him *no more* (*John* 16. 10.). *Of righteousness,* saith he, *because I go to my Father, and ye see me no more:* As if he had said, My Spirit shall shew to the world, that I have brought in a sufficient *righteousness* to justifie sinners withall, in that when I go to appear in the presence of my *Father* on *their* behalf, he shall give me *entertainment,* and not throw me down from heaven, because I did not do it sufficiently.

Again, If you consider the high esteem that God the Father doth set on the death of his Son, you will finde that he hath received good content thereby. When the Lord Jesus by way of complaint told his Father, that he and his merits were not valued to the worth; his Father answered, *It is a light thing that I should give thee O my servant, to bring Jacob again; I will also give thee for a light to the Gentiles, that thou mayest be for salvation unto the ends of the earth.* As if the Lord had said, My Son, I do value thy death at a higher rate, then that thou shouldest save the Tribes of *Israel* onely; behold the Gentiles, the barbarous Heathens, they also shall be brought in as the price of thy blood. It is a

Isa. 49. 1, 2, 3, 4, 5, 6

light thing that thou shouldest be my servant (onely) to bring or redeem the Tribes of *Jacob*, and to restore the preserved of *Israel*; I will give thee for a light to the Gentiles, that thou mayest be my salvation to the ends of the earth.

5   Again, you may see it also by the carriage of God the Father to all the great sinners to whom mercy was proffered. We do not finde that God maketh any objection against them that come to him for the pardon of their sins, because he did want a satisfaction suitable to the greatness of their sins. There was 10 *Manassah*, who was one that burnt his children in the fire to the devil; that used witchcraft, that used to worship the host of heaven; that turned his back on the word that God sent unto him: nay, that did worse then the very heathen that God cast out before the children of Israel. Also those that 15 are spoken of in the nineteenth of *Acts*, that did spend so much time in conjuration, and the like (for such I judge they were); that when they came to burn their books, they counted the price thereof, to be fifty thousand pieces of silver. *Simon Magus* also that was a Sorcerer, and bewitched the whole 20 City, yet he had mercy proffered to him once and again: I say, it was not the greatness of the sins of these sinners; no, nor of an innumerable company of others that made God at all to object against the salvation of their souls, which justice would have constrained him to, had he not had satis-25 faction sufficient, by the blood of the Lord Jesus. Nay, further, I do finde that because God the Father, would not have the merits of his Son to be undervalued, I say, he doth therefore freely by his consent, let mercy be proffered to the greatest sinners in the first place, for the Jews, that were the 30 worst of men in that day for blasphemy against the Gospel: yet the Apostle proffered mercy to them in the first place. *It is necessary* (saith he) *that the Word of God should first have been spoken unto you*: And Christ gave them commission so to do: for saith he, *Let repentance and remission of sins be preached in my*

Marginal notes:

See the 2 Chron. 33. from the 1. ver. to the 12.

Acts 19. 19. Acts 8.

Acts 13. 46. Act. 3. 26. Luke 24. 47.

12 marg. the 1. ver. to the] 1. to *1685*   15 in the nineteenth of *Acts*] *Acts* 19. 19. (*the corresponding marginal reference is omitted*) *1685*   22 others] other *1659*

name among all nations: and begin; mark that, *begin at Jerusalem.*
Let them that but the other day had their hands up to the
elbows in my heart blood have the first proffer of my mercy.

1 Tim. 1. 15. And saith *Paul, For this cause I obtained mercy, that in me first,*
16. *Jesus Christ might shew forth all long-suffering, for a pattern to* 5
them that should hereafter believe on him to life everlasting. As the
Apostle saith, those sinners that were dead, possessed with
the devil, and the children of wrath, he hath quickned, de-

Ephes. 2. 1, livered, and saved, *that he might even in the very ages to come*
2, 3, 4, 5, 6, *shew forth the exceeding riches of his grace in his kindness towards us* 10
7. (and that) *through Jesus Christ.*

Secondly, it is evident that that which this man did as
a common person, he did it compleatly, and satisfactorily, as
appears by the openness (as I may so call it) which was in the
heart of God to him at his resurrection and ascension. *Ask of* 15
me (saith he), *and I will give thee the* (very) *heathen for thine*
inheritance, and the uttermost parts of the earth for thy possession.
Psal. 2. 8. And this was at his resurrection, *Acts* 13. 33. Whereas, though he had asked, yet if he had not given a full and
compleat satisfaction, *justice* would not have given him any 20
thing; for *justice*, the *justice* of God is so *pure*, that if it be not
compleatly *satisfied* in every particular, it giveth nothing but
curses, *Gal.* 3. 10.

Thirdly, it is yet far more evident that he hath indeed
pleased God in the behalf of sinners, in that God hath *given* 25
him *gifts* to distribute to sinners, yea the worst of sinners,
as a *fruit* of his satisfaction, and that at his ascension (*Psal.*
68. 18.), Christ hath so satisfied God, that he hath given
him all the treasures both of heaven and earth, to dispose of
as he seeth good; he hath so pleased God that he hath given 30

Phil. 2. 9. him a *name*, above every *name*; a *Scepter*, above every *Scepter*; a
Rev. 19. 16. *Crown*, above every *Crown*; a *Kingdome*, above every *Kingdom*;
he hath given him the *highest* place in heaven, even his own
right hand, he hath given him all the *power* of heaven, and
earth, and under the earth in his *own hand*, to *binde* whom *he* 35
pleaseth, and to set *free* whom *he* thinks meet; he hath in a
word, such an high esteem in the eyes of his Father, that he

hath put into his hand, all things that are for the profit of his people, both in this world, and that which is to *come*; and all this as the fruit of his faithfulness in doing of his work, as the *Mediator* of the new Covenant. *Thou hast ascended on high,*
5 *thou hast led Captivity Captive, thou hast received gifts*; mark, thou hast received them, *for men, even for the* (worst of men, the) *rebellious also*: And hath sent forth some, being furnished with these gifts; some I say, *For the work of the ministry*, to the edifying of them that are already called, and also for the calling
10 in of all those for whom he covenanted with his Father, *Till all come in the unity of the faith* &c. Eph. 4. 8, 9, 10, 11, 12, 13.

Fourthly, It doth still appear yet *far more* evident: For will you hear what the Father himself saith for the shewing of his well-pleasednesse, in these two particulars. First, in that
15 he bids poor souls to *hear*, and to *do as Christ* would *have them*, Mat. 3. 17. Luke 9. 35. Secondly, in that he *resolves* to make them that *turn* their *backs* upon him, that dishonour him (which is done in a very great measure by those that lay aside his merits done by himself for Justification), I say, he
20 hath *resolved* to make them his *footstool*; where he saith, *Sit thou at my right hand, untill I make thine enemies thy footstool.* Are they enemies to *thee*, saith God, I will be even with them. Do they slight *thy* merits? Do they slight *thy* groans, *thy* tears, *thy* blood, *thy* death, *thy* resurrection and intercession,
25 *thy* second coming again in heavenly glory? I will *tear* them, and *rend them*, Ile make them as *mire* in the *streets*; I will make thy enemies thy footstool (*Psal.* 110. 1. *Matth.* 22. 44. *Heb.* 1. 13. *Chap.* 10. 13.). I, saith he, *And thou shalt dash them in pieces like a potters vessell*, Psal. 2. 9. Look to it you that slight
30 the merits of the blood of Christ.

Fifthly, again further yet; God will make all the world to know, that he hath been, and is well pleased in his Son, in that God hath given (and will make it appear he hath given) the *world to come* into *his* hand, *Heb.* 2. And that
35 he shall *raise* the dead, *bring* them before his judgement-seat, *execute* judgement upon them which he pleaseth to execute

12 yet] *om. 1685*

judgement on to their damnation; and to *receive* them to eternal life whom he doth favour, even so many as shall be found to believe in his Name and merits (*John* 5. 26, 27, 28.). *For as the Father hath life in himself; so hath he given to the Son to have life in himself: And he hath given him authority to execute* 5 *judgement also; because he is the Son of man.*—*For the hour is comming, that all that are in the graves shall hear his voice, and shall come forth: they that have done good, unto the resurrection of life, and they that have done evill, unto the resurrection of damnation.* I, and the worst enemy that Christ hath now, shall come at 10 that day with a *pale* face, with a *quaking* heart, and *bended* knees *trembling* before him, *confessing* the glory of his merits, and the vertue there was in them to save, *to the glory of God the Father*, Romans 14. 11. Philippians 2. 9, 10, 11.

Much more might be added to discover the glorious per- 15 fection of this mans satisfaction: but for you that desire to be further satisfied concerning this, search the Scriptures, and beg of God to give you faith and understanding therein: and as for you that slight these things, and continue so doing, God hath another way to take with you, even to dash 20 you in pieces like a Potters vessel; for this hath Christ received of his Father to do unto you, *Revelations* 2. 27.

Thus I have shewed you in particular, that the Covenant of the Grace of God is free and unchangeable to men; that is, in that it hath been obtained for men, and that perfectly, to 25 the satisfying of justice, and taking all things out of the way, that were any wayes an hinderance to our salvation, *Col*. 2. 14.

The second thing for the discovering of this freenesse, and constancy of the Covenant of the Grace of God, it is manifested thus.   30

First, whatsoever any man hath of the grace of God, he hath it as a *free gift* of God through Christ Jesus the Mediatour of this Covenant, even when they are in a state of enmity to him (mark that *Rom*. 5. 8, 9. *Col*. 1. 21, 22.), whether it be Christ as the *foundation* stone, or *faith* to lay hold on him, Eph. 35 2. 8. *For by Grace you are saved through Faith, and that not of your*

30 manifested] manifest 1685

selves (not for any thing in you, or done by you for the purchasing of it), *but it is the free gift of God.* And that bestowed on you, *even when you were dead in trespasses and sins,* Eph. 2. 1, 2, 3, 4, 5, 6, 7, 8, 9. Nay if thou hast so much as one desire that is
5 right, it is the *gift* of God; for of our selves, saith the Apostle, *we are not able to speak a good word, or think a good thought,* 2 Corinth. 3. 5.

Was it not grace, *absolute* grace, that God made promise to *Adam* after transgression? *Gen.* 3. 5.
10 Was it not *free* grace in God to save such a wretch as *Manasseh* was, who used enchantments, witchcraft, burnt his children in the fire, and wrought much evill? 2 *Chron.* 33.

Was it not free grace to save such as those were that are spoken of in the 16. of *Ezekiel,* which *no* eye pitied?
15 Was it not *free* grace for Christ to give *Peter* a loving look after he had cursed, and swore, and denied him?

Was it not *free* grace that met *Paul* when he was a going to *Damascus* to persecute, which converted him, and made him a vessel of mercy?
20 And what shall I say of such that are spoken of in the 1 *Cor.* 6. 9, 10? Speaking there of *fornicatours, idolators, adulterers, effeminates, abusers of themselves with mankinde, theeves, covetous, revilers, drunkards, extortioners,* the basest of sinners in the world, and *yet* were washed, and *yet* were justified, was it not *freely*
25 by grace? O Saints! you that are in Heaven, cry out, We came *hither* by *grace;* and you that are on earth, I am sure you cry, if ever *we* do go *thither,* it must be *freely* by grace.

Secondly, In the next place, it appears to be unchangeable in this. First, because Justice being *once* satisfied, doth not use
30 to *call* for the *debt* again: No, let never such a sinner come to Jesus Christ, and so to God by him; and *Justice* instead of speaking against the salvation of that *sinner,* it will say, I am *just* as well as faithful to forgive him *his sins,* 1 *John* 1. 9. When Justice it self is *pleased* with a *man,* and speaks on his
35 side, instead of speaking against him, we may well cry out, *Who shall condemn?*

2. Because there is no *Law* to come in against the sinner
that believes in Jesus Christ; for he is not *under* that, and that
by right comes in against none, but those that are under it:
but Believers are not *under that, that* is not their Lord, therefore *that* hath nothing to do with them; and besides Christs 5
blood hath not onely taken away the *curse* thereof, but also
he hath in his own person compleatly fulfilled it, as a *publique*
person in our stead, *Rom.* 8. 1, 2, 3, 4.

3. The Devill that accused them is destroyed, *Heb.* 2. 14, 15.

4. *Death*, and the *grave*, and *hell* are overcome, 1 *Corinth.* 10
15. 55. *Hosea* 13. 14.

5. *Sin* that great enemy of *mans* salvation, that is washed
away, *Rev.* 1. 5.

6. The *righteousness* of God is put upon them that believe,
and given to them, and they are found in it, *Phil.* 3. 8, 9, 10. 15
Rom. 3. 22.

7. Christ is *alwayes* in heaven to *plead* for them, and to prepare a place for them, *Heb.* 7. 24. *John* 14. 1, 2, 3, 4.

8. He hath not onely *promised* that he will not leave us,
nor forsake us; but he hath also *sworn* to fulfill his promise. 20
O rich grace! free grace! Lord, who desired thee to *promise*?
Who compelled thee to *swear*? We use to take honest men
upon their bare *words*. But *God willing more abundantly to shew
unto the heirs of promise the immutability of his counsel* (hath) *confirmed it by an oath: that by two immutable things* (his promise and 25
his oath), *in which it is impossible for God to lye* (or break either
of them), *we might have strong consolation, who have fled for
refuge to lay hold upon the hope set before us* (Heb. 6. 13, 17, 18.).
Ile warrant you God will never break his *oath*; therefore we
may well have good ground to *hope* from such a good founda- 30
tion as this, that God will never leave us indeed.

Again thirdly, not onely thus: but first, God hath begotten
Believers again to himself, to be his *adopted* and *accepted*
Children, in and through the Lord Jesus, 1 *Pet.* 1. 3.

Secondly, God hath *prepared* a kingdom for them, before the 35
foundation of the world, through Jesus Christ, *Mat.* 25.

12 mans] man 1659

Thirdly, he hath given them an *earnest* of their *happiness*, while they live *here* in this world (*Eph.* I. 13, 14.). *After ye believed ye were sealed with the holy Spirit of promise, which is the earnest of our inheritance, until the redemption of the purchased pos-*
5 *session to the praise of his glory,* and that through this Jesus.

Fourthly, if his children *sin* through *weakness*, or by suddain temptation; they confessing of it, he willingly forgives, and *heals all their wounds*, reneweth his love towards *them*, waits to do *them* good, casteth *their* sins into the depths of the sea; and
10 all this freely, without any work done by *men* as *men*. *Not for your sakes do I this, O house of Israel, be it known unto you, saith the Lord,* Ezek. 36. 22, 32. but wholly and alone by the blood of Jesus.

Fifthly, in a word, if you would see it altogether, Gods
15 love was the *cause* why Jesus Christ was *sent* to bleed for sinners. Jesus Christs *bleeding* stops the *cries* of divine *justice*: God looks upon *them* as compleat in *him*, gives *them* to *him*, as his by right of *purchase*. Jesus ever lives to *pray* for them that are *thus* given unto him. God *sends* his holy *Spirit* into *them*,
20 to *reveal* this to *them*; sends his Angels to minister for *them*: and all this by vertue of an everlasting Covenant between the Father and the Son. *Thrice happy are the people that are in such a case.*

Nay, further he hath made them *Brethren* with Jesus Christ,
25 *members* of his *flesh*, and of his *bones*: the *Spouse* of this Lord Jesus; and all to shew you how *dearly*, how *really*, how *con-stantly* he loveth us, who by the faith of his operation, have laid hold upon him.

I shall now lay down a few arguments for the superaboun-
30 dant clearing of it, and afterwards answer two or three ob-jections, as may be made against it, and so I shall fall upon the next thing.

First, God *loves* the *Saints*, as he *loves* Jesus *Christ*. And God loves Jesus Christ with an *eternal* love; therefore the Saints
35 also with the *same*. *Thou hast loved them, as thou hast loved me,* John 17. 23.

24–6 marg. These things . . . more largely.] *om. 1685*

Secondly, that *love* which is God *himself* must needs be everlasting *love*. And that is the *love* wherewith God hath *loved* his Saints in Christ Jesus; therefore his *love* towards his children in Christ must needs be an *everlasting love*. There is none dare say, that the love of God is *mixed* with a *created* 5 mixture: if not, then it must needs be himself, 1 *John* 4. 16.

Thirdly, that *love* which is *always* pitched upon *us*, in an *object* as *holy* as God, must needs be an *everlasting* love. Now the love of God was, and is *pitched* upon *us*, through an object as *holy* as God himself, even our Lord Jesus: Therefore it must 10 needs be unchangeable.

You must not understand that love in God, is a passion as it is in us: but the love of God is the very essence, or nature of God. 1 John 4. 16.

Fourthly, if *he* with whom the Covenant of Grace was made, did in every thing, and condition do, even what the Lord could *desire* or *require* of him, that his love might be extended to us, and that for ever; Then his love must needs be an 15 *everlasting* love, seeing every thing *required* of *us*, was compleatly accomplished for *us* by *him*: And all this hath our Lord Jesus *done*, and that most gloriously, even on our behalf: therefore it must needs be a love that lasts for ever and ever.

Fifthly, if God hath *declared* himself, to be the God that 20 *changeth* not, and hath *sworn* to be *immutable* in his promise, then surely he will be *unchangeable*. And he hath done so: therefore it is *impossible* for God to lie; and so for his eternal love to be changeable (*Heb.* 6. 13, 14, 17, 18.). Here is an argument of the Spirits own making, who can contradict it? 25 If any object, and say, but still it is upon the condition of *believing*, I answer, the *condition* also is his own *free gift*, and not a qualification arising from the *stock of nature* (Eph. 2. 8. Phil. 1. 28, 29.). So that here is the love unchangeable, here is also the condition given by him whose love is unchangeable, 30 which may serve yet further for a strong argument, that God *will* have his love unchangeable. Sinner this is better *felt* and enjoyed, then talked of.

The first objection.

Object. But if this love of God be unchangeable in it *self*; yet it is not unchangeably set upon the *Saints*, unless they 35 behave themselves the better.

24 changeable] unchangeable *1685*   34 marg. The first objection.] *om. 1685*

Answ. As Gods love at the *first* was bestowed upon the Saints, without any thing *foreseen* by the Lord in *them*, as done by *them* (*Deut.* 9. 4, 5, 6.), So he goeth on with the same, saying, *I will never leave thee nor forsake thee,* Heb. 13. 5.

5   *Object.* But how cometh it to pass then that many *fall* off The second again, from the *grace* of the Gospel, after a profession of it objection. for some time; some to delusions, and some to their open sins again?

Answ. They are fallen away, *not* from the everlasting love of 10 God to them; *but* from the profession of the love of God to *them*: men may profess that God loves them, when there is no such *matter*, and that they are the *Children* of *God*, when the *devil* is their father (as it is in *John* 8. 40, 41, 42, 43, 44.). Therefore they that do finally *fall away* from a profession of 15 the grace of the *Gospel*: It is first, because, they are *Bastards* and not *Sons*. Secondly, because as they are not *Sons*, so God suffereth them to *fall*; to make it appear that they are not *Sons*, not of the houshold of God. *They went out from us, for they were not of us; for if they had been of us, no doubt*, mark that, 20 *no doubt*, saith he, *they would have continued with us; but they went out from us, that it might be made manifest that they were not all of us* (1 John 2. 19.). And though *Hymeneus* and *Philetus* do throw themselves headlong to hell, *Nevertheless the foundation of God standeth sure, having this seal, the Lord knoweth them* 25 *that are his,* 2 Tim. 2. 17, 18, 19.

Object. But the Scripture saith, that there are *some* that had The third *Faith*, yet lost *it*, and have made shipwrack of *it*: Now God objection. loves no *longer* then they *believe*, as is evident; *For he that believes not shall be damned.* So then, if *some* may have *Faith*, 30 and yet lose *it*, and so *lose* the love of God, because they have *lost* their *Faith*; it is evident that Gods love is not so *immutable* as you say it is to every one that believeth.

Answ. There is more sorts of Faith then *one*, that is spoken of in Scripture.

35   First, There is a Faith that men may have, and yet be

5 marg. The second objection.] *om. 1685*   26 marg. The third objection.] *om. 1685*

nothing, none of the Saints of God (1 *Cor.* 13. 1, 2, 3, 4.), and yet may do great things *therewith*.

2. There is a Faith that was wrought meerly by the operation of the miracles that was done in those dayes by Christ and his followers; *And many of the people believed on him.* How came they by their Faith? Why, by the operation of the miracles that he did among them; for said they, *When Christ cometh, will he do more miracles then this man hath done?* The great thing that wrought their Faith in them, was onely by seeing the miracles that he did (*John* 7. 31. *John* 2. 23.), which is not that saving Faith, which is called the Faith of Gods Elect, as is evident: for there must not be onely miracles wrought upon outward objects, to beget that, that being too weak a thing; but it must be by the same power that was stretched out in raising Christ from the dead; yea, the exceeding greatness of that power (*Eph.* 1. 18, 19.). So there is a believing, being taken with some marvellous work, visibly appearing to the outward sense of seeing; and there is a believing that is wrought in the heart by an invisible operation of the Spirit, revealing the certainty of the satisfaction of the merits of Christ to the soul in a more glorious way, both for certainty and for durablenesse, both as to the promise and the constancy of it (*Matthew* 16. 17, 18.).

3. There is a Faith of a mans own, of a mans self also; but the Faith of the operation of God (in Scripture) is set in opposition to that; for saith he, *You are saved by Grace through Faith, and that not of your selves*; of your own making, but that which is the free gift of God, *Eph.* 2. 8.

4. We say there is an Historicall Faith, that is, such as is begotten meerly by the history of the word, not by the co-operation of the Spirit with the Word.

5. We say there is a Traditionall Faith, that is, to believe things by Tradition, because others say they believe them; this is received by Tradition, not by Revelation; and shall never be able to stand neither at the day of death, nor at the day of judgement; though possibly men, while they live here,

may esteem themselves and states to be very good, because
their heads are filled full of it.

6. There is a Faith that is called (in Scripture) a dead Faith,
the Faith of Devils, or of the Devil; they also that have onely
5 this, they are like the Devil, and as sure to be damned as he,
notwithstanding their Faith, if they get no better into their
hearts; for it is far off from enabling of them to lay effectuall
hold of Jesus Christ, and so to put him on for eternall life
and sanctification (*Jam.* 2. 19, *&* 26.), which they must do
10 if ever they be saved.

But all these are short of the saving Faith of Gods elect,
as is manifest; I say, first because these may be wrought, and
not by that power so exceedingly stretched forth. Secondly,
because these are wrought; partly, first by the sense of seeing,
15 namely the miracles (not by hearing): and secondly, the
rest is wrought by a traditionall or historicall influence of the
words in their heads, not by an heavenly, invisible, almighty,
and saving operation of the Spirit of God in their hearts.

7. I do suppose also, that there is a Faith that is wrought
20 upon men through the influence of those gifts and abilities
that God gives sometimes to those that are not his own by
election, though by creation: my meaning is, some men
finding that God hath given them very great gifts and abilities; as to the gifts of preaching, praying, working miracles,
25 or the like; I say, they therefore do conclude, that God is
their Father, and they his Children; the ground of which confidence is still begotten, not by the glorious operation of the
spirit, but by a considering of the great gifts that God hath
bestowed upon them, as to the things before mentioned.

30 As thus, first the poor soul considering how ignorant it was,
and now how knowing it is. Secondly, considering how vain
it formerly was, and also now how civil it is, presently makes
this conclusion, surely God loves *me*, surely he hath made *me*
one of his, and will save *me*. This is now a wrong faith, as is
35 evident, in that it is placed upon a wrong object; for mark,
this faith is not placed assuredly on Gods grace *alone*, through
the *blood* and merits of Christ, being discovered effectually

to the soul, but upon God, through those things that God hath given it; as of *gifts*, either to preach, or pray, or great works, or the like, which will assuredly come to nought, as sure as God is in Heaven; if no better faith and ground of faith be found out for thy soul savingly to rest upon.   5

As to the second cause of the objection, which runs to this effect. God loves men upon the account of their *believing*. I answer, that God loves men before they *believe*, he loves them, he calls them, and gives them faith to believe. *But God who is rich in grace, with his great love, wherewith he loved us* (when? 10 when we believed or before), *even when we were dead in our sins* (and so far off from believers), *hath quickned us together with Christ, by grace you are saved*, Eph. 2. 4, 5.

Now also I suppose that thou wilt say in thy heart, I would you would shew us then, what is saving faith, which thing 15 it may be I may touch upon a while hence, in the next thing that I am to speak unto. O they that have that are safe indeed!

The second Thing.

The second thing that I am to speak unto is this: *Who* they are that are actually brought into this free and unchangeable 20 grace; and also *how* they are brought in.

Answ.   Indeed now we are come to the pinch of the whole discourse; and if God do but help me to run rightly thorow *this*, as I do verily believe he will, I may do thee, *Reader*, good and bring glory to my God.   25

The question containeth these two branches. First, *who* are brought in. Secondly, *how* they are brought in: the first is quickly answered. *Christ Jesus came into the world to save sinners*, *Jewish* sinners, *Gentile* sinners, *Old* sinners, *Young* sinners, *great* sinners, the *chiefest* of sinners, 1 *Tim*. 1. 14, 15. *Rom*. 30 5. 7, 8, 9, 10. 1 *Cor*. 6. 9, 10. *Mat*. 21. 31. *Publicans and harlots*, that is, whores and cheaters, exactors shall enter into the Kingdom of heaven. *For I came not* (saith Christ) *to call the righteous, but sinners to repentance*, Mark 2. 17.

A sinner in the Scripture is described in general to be a transgressor of the Law, 1 John. 3. 4. *Whosoever committeth sin transgresseth the Law; for sin is the transgression of the Law.*

But particularly, they are described in a more particular
5 way, as first, such as in whom dwelleth the devil, *Ephes*. 2. 2, 3. Secondly, such as will do the service of him, *John* 8. 44. Thirdly, such as are enemies to *God, Col*. 1. 21. Fourthly, such as are *drunkards, whoremasters, liars, perjured persons, covetous, revilers, extortioners, fornicators, swearers, possessed with devils,
10 thieves, idolaters, witches, sorcerers, conjurers, murderers, and the like; these be sinners, and such sinners that God hath prepared heaven, happinesse, pardon of sin, and an inheritance of God, with Christ, with Saints, with Angells, if they do come in, and accept of Grace, as I might prove at large: For
15 Gods grace is so great, that if they do come to him by Christ, presently all is forgiven them; therefore never object, that thy sins are too great to be pardoned: but *come taste and see how good the Lord is to any whosoever comes unto him.*

The second thing is, how are these brought into this ever-
20 lasting Covenant of Grace?

2. *Answ.* When God doth indeed and in truth bring in a sinner into this most blessed Covenant (*for so it is*), he usually goeth this way.

First, He slayes or *kills* the party to all things besides him-
25 self, and his Son Jesus Christ, and the comforts of the Spirit.

For the clearing of this, I shall shew you, first, with *what* God *kills*: secondly, *how* God *kills*; and thirdly, to what God kills those whom he makes alive in Jesus Christ.

For the first, When God brings *sinners* into the Covenant of
30 *Grace*, he doth first kill them with the Covenant of *Works*, which is the Morall Law, or Ten Commandments. This is *Pauls* doctrine, and also *Pauls* experience. It is his doctrine where he saith, *The ministration of death engraven in stones, the ministration of condemnation* (which is the Law, in that place
35 called the *Letter*), *kills*, 2 Cor 3. 6, 7, 8, 9. *The Letter* (saith he) *killeth*, or the Law, or the ministration of death, which in another place is called a sound of words, *Heb*. 12. 19. because

*1 Cor. 6. 9, 10.
2 Chron. 33. 1, 2, 3, 4, 5, 6, 7, 8, 9, 10, 11, 12, &c.
Acts 9. 1, 2, 3.
1 Tim. 1. 14, 15, 16.
Acts 19. 19.
Acts 2. 36, 37.

Come to the touchstone sinner.

they have no life in them, but rather death and damnation, through our inability to fulfill them (*Rom.* 8. 3.), doth kill, 2 *Cor.* 6.

Secondly, It is his experience, where he saith, *I was alive once* (that is, to my own things, *Phil.* 3. 7, 8, 9, 10.), *without the Law* (that is, before God did strike him dead by it), *but when the commandment came* (that is, to do and exercise its right office on me, which was to kill me, then) *sin revived, and I died* (and I was killed), *and the commandment* (or the Law) *which was ordained to be unto life, I found to be unto death: For sin taking occasion by the commandment, deceived me, and thereby slew me,* Rom. 7. 9, 10, 11. And indeed to speak my own experience, together with the experience of all the Saints, they can seal with me to this, more or lesse.

Quest. But how doth God *kill* with this Law or Covenant?

1. *Answ.* First, by opening to the soul the spirituality of it; *The Law is spirituall* (saith he), *but I am carnall, sold under sin,* Romans 7. 14. Now the spirituality of the Law is discovered this way.

First, by shewing to the soul, that every sinful thought is a sin against it. I sinner, when the Law doth come home indeed upon thy soul in the spirituality of it, it will discover such things to thee to be sins, that now thou lookest over, and regardest not; that is a remarkable saying of *Paul,* when he saith, *Sin revived, and I died;* sin revived, saith he, as if he had said, those things that before I did not value, nor regard, but looked upon them to be trifles, to be dead and forgotten; but when the Law was fastened on my soul, it did so *raise* them from the dead, *call* them to minde, so *muster* them before my face, and put such strength into them, that I was over mastered by them, by the gilt of them. *Sin revived,* by the commandment, or my sins had mighty strength, life, and abundance of force upon me, because of that; insomuch, that it *killed* me, *Matth.* 5. 28.

2. Secondly, It sheweth that every such sin deserveth eternall damnation: (Friends, I doubt there be but few of you that

16 marg. 1.] *om. 1685*   35 marg. 2.] *om. 1685*

have seen the spirituality of the *Law* of Works, but this is one thing in which it discovereth its Spirituality, and this is the proper work of the Law).

Thirdly, God with a discovery of this doth also discover 3. his own Divine, and Infinite *Justice* (of which the *Law* is a description), which backs what is discovered by the *Law*; and that by discovering of its Purity and Holiness, to be so Divine, so pure, so upright, and so far off from winking at the least sin, that he doth by that *Law*, without any favour, *condemn* the sinner for that sin, *Gal*. 3. 10. Now when he hath brought the soul into this Premunire, into this puzzle: Then,

2. He sheweth to the soul the nature and condition of the *Law*, as to its dealing with, or forbearing of the sinner, that hath sinned against it: which is to pass an eternal curse upon both soul and body, of the party so offending, saying to him, *Cursed be the man that continueth not in every thing that is written in the book of the Law to do it*: for saith the *Law*, this is *my* proper work. First, to shew thee thy sins, and when I have done that; then in the next place to condemn thee for them, and that without all remedy, as from *me*, or any thing within *my* bounds; for I am not to save any, to pardon any, nay, not to favour any in the least thing that have sinned against *me*: for God did not send *me* to make alive, but to discover sin, and to condemn for the same. Now so soon as this is presented to the conscience, in the next place, the Lord also by this *Law* doth shew that now there is no righteous act, according to the tenor of that Covenant, that can replieve him, or take him off from all this horrour and curse that lies upon him; because that is not an administration of pardon (as I said before) to forgive the sin; but an administration of damnation, because of transgression. O the very discovery of this, striketh the soul into a deadly swoun, even above half dead. But when God doth do the work indeed; he doth in the next place shew the soul that *he* is the man that is eternally under this Coven-ant by nature, and that it is thee that hath sinned against this *Law*, and doth by right deserve the curse and displeasure of

4 marg. 3.] *om. 1685*   25 Lord] Law *1685*

the same; and that all that ever *he* can do will not give satisfaction to that glorious justice that did give this *Law*; holy
actions, tears of blood, selling all, and giving it to the poor,
or whatever else can be done by *thee*, it comes all short, and
is all to no purpose (*Phil.* 3.). Ile warrant him, he that seeth 5
this, it will *kill* him to that which he was alive unto before,
though he had a thousand lives. Ah sinners, sinners, were
you but sensible indeed of the severity, and truth of this, it
would make you look about you to purpose. O how would it
make you strive to stop at that, that now you drink down 10
with delight? How many oaths would it make you bite
asunder? nay, it would make you bite your tongues, to think
that they should be used as instruments of the devil, to bring
your souls into such an unspeakable misery; then also, we
should not have you hang the salvation of your souls upon 15
such *slender pins* as now you do: no, no; but you would be in
another minde then. O then we should have you cry out, I
must have Christ, what shall I do for Christ? how shall I come
at Christ? would I was sure, truly sure of Christ, my soul is
gone, damned, cast away, and must for ever burn with the 20
devils; if I do not get precious Jesus Christ.

In the next place, when God hath done this, then he
further shews the soul, that Covenant which it is under by
nature, is distinct from the Covenant of Grace; and also they
that are under it, are by nature without any of the graces, 25
which they have that are under the Covenant of Grace: As
1. 2. first, that it hath no faith, *John* 16. 9. Secondly, no hope,
3. *Eph.* 2. 12. Thirdly, nor none of the spirit to work these
4. things in it by nature. Fourthly, Neither will that Covenant
5. give to them any peace with God. Fifthly, no promise of 30
6. safegard from his revenging *Law*, by *that* Covenant. Sixthly,
But lieth by nature liable to all the curses and condemnings,
7. and thunder-claps of this most fiery Covenant. Seventhly,
That it will accept of no sorrow, no repentance, no satis-

22 he] he the *1685*   27 marg. 1. 2.] *om. 1685*   28 marg. 3.] *om.*
1685   29 marg. 4.] *om. 1685*   in it] first *1685*   30 marg. 5.] *om.*
1685   31 marg. 6.] *om. 1685*   33 marg. 7.] *om. 1685*   Seventhly,]
7. *1659*

faction, as from *thee*. Eighthly, That it calls for no lesse then 8.
the shedding of *thy* blood. Ninthly, The damnation of *thy* 9.
soul and body. Tenthly, And if there be anything proffered 10.
to it by *thee*, as to the making of it amends, it throws it back
5 again as dirt in *thy* face, slighting all that *thou* canst bring.

Now when the soul is brought into this condition, then
it is indeed dead; *killed* to that, to which it was once alive.

And therefore in the next place to shew you to what it is
killed; and that is first to sin: O it dares not *sin*! it sees hell
10 fire is prepared for them that *sin*: Gods justice will not spare it
if it live in *sin*; the Law will damn it, if it live in *sin*; the Devill
will have it, if it follow its *sin*; O I say, it trembles at the very
thoughts of *sin*; I, if *sin* do but offer to tempt the soul, to draw
away the soul from God, it cries, it sighs, it shunneth the
15 very appearance of *sin*, it is odious unto it. If God would but
serve you thus that love your pleasures, you would not make
such a trifle of *sin*, as you do.

Secondly, It is *killed* to the *Law* of God, as it is the Covenant
of Works: O saith the soul, the Law hath killed me to its
20 self, *I through the Law am dead to the Law* (Gal. 2. 19.). The
Law is another thing then I did think it was; I thought it
would not have been so soul-destroying, so damning a *Law*;
I thought it would not have been so severe against me for
my little sins, for *my* playing, for *my* jeasting, for *my* dissembling,
25 quarrelling, and the like: I had some thoughts indeed, that it
would tew great sinners, but let me passe; and though it
condemned great sinners, yet it would passe *me* by: but now
would I were free from this Covenant, would I were free
from this Law. I will tell thee, that a soul thus worked upon,
30 is more afraid of the Covenant of *Works*, then he is of the
Devill; for he sees it is the Law that doth give him up into
his hands for *sin*: and if he was but clear from that, he should not
greatly need to fear the Devill. O now every particular command tears the caul of his heart; now every command is as

Here I am speaking of one that is effectually brought in.

1 Eighthly,] 8. *1659*   marg. 8.] *om. 1685*   2 Ninthly,] 9. *1659*   marg.
9.] *om. 1685*   3 Tenthly,] 10. *1659*   marg. 10.] *om. 1685*   10–11 it if it]
it if *1659*   11 the Law . . . *sin*] *om. 1685*   10–12 marg. Here I am . . .
brought in.] *om. 1685*

a great gun well charged against his soul; now he sees he had as good run into a *fire* to keep himself from *burning*, as to run to the *Law* to keep himself from *damning*; and this he sees really, I, and feels it too, to his own sorrow and perplexity.

Thirdly, The soul also now is *killed* to his own righteous- 5 nesse, and counts that but dung, but drosse, not worth the dirt hanging on shoes. O then sayes he, Thou *filthy righteousness* (Isa. 64. 6.), how hast thou deceived me? How hast thou beguiled my poor soul? How did I deceive my self with giving of a little alms? with abstaining from some grosse 10 pollutions? with walking in some ordinances, as to the outside of them? How hath my good words, good thinkings, good meanings (as the world calls them) deceived my ignorant soul? I want the righteousnesse of faith, the righteousnesse of God; for I see now there is no lesse will do me any good. 15

Fourthly, It is also *killed* to *its own* faith, *its* notion of the Gospel, *its own* hope, *its own* repentings, *its own* promises and resolutions to *its own* strength, *its own* vertue, or whatsoever it had before: now saith the soul, That faith I thought I had, it is but fancy; that hope I thought I had, I see it is but 20 hypocritical, but vain and groundlesse hope: now the soul sees it hath by nature no saving faith, no saving hope, no grace at all by nature, by the first Covenant. Now it crieth out, How many promises have I broken? and how many times have I resolved in vain? when I was sick at such a time, 25 and in such a straight, at such a place. Indeed I thought my self a wise man *once*, but I see my self a very fool *now*: O how ignorant am I of the Gospel *now*? and of the blessed experience of the work of God on a Christians heart? In a word, it sees it self beset by nature with *all* evil, and destitute of 30 *all* good, which is enough to kill the stoutest, hardest hearted sinner that ever lived on the earth. O Friends! should you be plainly dealt withal, by this discovery of the dealing of God with a sinner, when he makes him a Saint, and would seriously try your selves thereby (as God will try you one day), 35 how few would there be found of you, to be so much as

These things would be too tedious to enlarge upon.

16–18 marg. These things . . . enlarge upon.] *om. 1685*

acquainted with the work of God in the *Notion*? much lesse in the experimental knowledge of the same. And indeed God is fain to take this way with sinners, thus to kill them with the Old Covenant, to all things below a crucified Christ.

5   First, Because otherwise there would be none in the world that would look after this sweet Jesus Christ. There is but a few that go to heaven in all (comparatively), and them few, God is fain to deal with them in this manner, or else *his* heaven, *his* Christ, *his* glory, and everlasting happinesse must
10 abide by themselves for all sinners. Do you think that *Manasseh* would have regarded the Lord, had he not suffered his enemies to have prevailed against him? Do you think that *Ephraim* would have looked after salvation, had not God first confounded him with the gilt of the sins of his youth? What
15 do you think of *Paul*? What do you think of the Jaylour? What do you think of the three thousand? Was not this the way that the Lord was fain to take to make them close in with Jesus Christ? Was he not fain to kill them to every thing below a Christ, that they were driven to their wits ends? insomuch
20 that they were forced to cry out, *What shall we do to be saved*? I say, God might keep heaven and happiness to himself, if he should not go this way to work with sinners. O stout hearted rebels! O tender hearted God!

Secondly, because then, and not till then will sinners accept
25 of Jesus Christ on Gods terms. So long as sinners can make a life out of any thing below Christ, so long they will not close with Christ without indenting: but when the God of heaven hath *killed* them to every thing below himself, and his Son; then Christ will down on any terms in the world.
30 And indeed this is the very reason, why sinners when they hear of Christ; yet will not close in with him, there is something that they can take content in besides him. The prodigal so long as he could content himself with the husks that the swine did eat, so long he did keep away from his fathers house,
35 but when he could get no nourishment any where on this side of his Fathers house, then (saith he) and not till then, *I will arise and go to my father*, &c.

Six reasons of this discourse.

2 Chron. 33. from the 1. verse to the 16.

Jer. 31. 18.

Acts 9. 4, 5, 6.
Acts 16. 30, 31, 32.
Acts 2. 36, 37.

I say, this is the reason therefore why men come no faster, and close no readilier with the Son of God, but stand halting and indenting about the terms they must have Christ upon; for saith the drunkard, I look on Christ to be worth the having; but yet I am not willing to lose ALL for him, all but 5 my pot saith the drunkard, and all but the world saith the covetous. I will part with any thing but lust and pride, saith the wanton; but if Christ will not be had without, I forsake all, cast away all; then it must be with me as it was with the young man in the Gospel, such news will make me sorry at 10 the very heart.

But now when a man is soundly killed to all his sins, to all his righteousness, to all his comforts whatsoever, and sees that there is no way but the devil must have him, but he must be damned in hell, if he be not clothed with Jesus Christ; 15 Oh! then (saith he) give me Christ on any terms whatsoever he cost: though he cost me friends, though he cost me comforts, though he cost me all that ever I have; yet like the wise merchant in the Gospel they will sell all to get that pearl. I tell you when a soul is brought to see its want of 20 Christ aright, it will not be kept back, Father, Mother, Husband, Wife, Lands, Livings, nay, life and all shall go, rather then the soul will miss of Christ. I, and the soul counteth Christ a cheap Saviour, if it can get him upon any terms, now the soul indents no longer. Now Lord give me Christ 25 upon any terms whatsoever he cost; for I am a dead man, a damned man, a cast away, if I have not Christ. What say you, O you wounded sinners? Is not this true as I have said? would you not give ten thousand worlds if you had so many, so be you might be well answered, that your sins shall be 30 pardoned, and your souls and bodies justified, and glorified at the coming of the Lord Jesus Christ.

Thirdly, the Lord goeth this way for this reason also, that it might make the soul sensible what it cost Christ to redeem it from death and hell. When a man cometh to feel the sting 35 and guilt of sin, death and hell upon his conscience, then, and

2 readilier] *realier 1659, 1685*   11 the] my *1685*   36 of] or *1659*

not till then, can he tell what it cost Christ to redeem sinners.
O! saith the soul if a few sins are so terrible, and lay the soul
under such wrath and torment, what did Christ undergo?
who bare the sins of thousands, and thousands, and all at
5 once.

This also is one means to make souls tender of sin (it is the
burned childe that feareth the fire): to make them humble in a
sense of their own vileness, to make them count every thing
that God giveth them a mercy, to make much of the least
10 glimpse of the love of God, and to prize it above the whole
world. O sinners were you killed indeed, then heaven would
be heaven, and hell would be hell indeed; but because you are
not wrought upon in this manner, therefore you count the
wayes of God, as bad as a good man counteth the wayes of the
15 devil, and the wayes of the devil and hell as good as a Saint
doth count the wayes of God.

Fourthly, Again, God is fain to go this way, and all to
make sinners make sure of heaven. So long as souls are senseless of sin, and what a damnable state they are in by nature,
20 so long they will even dally with the kingdom of heaven,
and the salvation of their own poor souls: but when God
cometh and sheweth them where they are, and what is like
to become of them if they miss of the crucified Saviour, Oh
then, saith the soul, would I were sure of Jesus; what shall I
25 do to get assurance of Jesus? And thus is God forced as I
may say, to whip souls to Jesus Christ, they being so secure,
so senseless, and so much their own enemies as not to look
out after their own eternal advantage.

Fifthly, A fifth reason why God doth deal thus with sin-
30 ners, it is because he would bring Christ and the soul together in a right way. Christ and sinners would never come
together in a beloved posture, they would not so suitably
suit each other, if they were not brought together this way,
the sinner being *killed*.

35   O when the sinner is *killed*, and indeed struck dead to every
thing below a naked Jesus, how suitably then doth the soul
and Christ suit one with another. Then here is a *naked* sinner

for a *righteous* Jesus, a *poor* sinner to a *rich* Jesus, a *weak* sinner to a *strong* Jesus, a *blinde* sinner to a *seeing* Jesus, an *ignorant*, *careless* sinner to a *wise* and *carefull* Jesus. O how wise is God in dealing thus with the sinner, he strips him of his *own* knowledge, that he may fill him with *Christs*; he *killeth* him for 5 taking pleasure in *sin*, that he may take pleasure in Jesus Christ, &c.

Sixthly, But sixthly, God goeth this way with sinners, because he would have the *glory* of their salvation. Should not men and women be *killed* to their own things, they would do 10 sacrifice unto them, and instead of saying to the Lamb, THOU ART WORTHY, they would say their own arme, their own right hand hath saved them: but God will cut off boasting from ever entring within the borders of eternal glory: for he is resolved to have the glory of the beginning, 15 the middle, and the end, of the contriving, and saving, and giving salvation to them that enter into the joyes of everlasting glory. *That they may be called the trees of righteousness, the planting of the Lord, that he may be glorified*, Isa. 61. 3. I might have run thorow many things as to this: but I shall pass 20 them, and proceed.

Now secondly, the soul being thus *killed* to it's self, it's sins, it's righteousness, faith, hope, wisdom, promises, resolutions, and the rest of it's things which it trusted in by nature. In the next place, it hath also given unto it a most 25 glorious, perfect, and never-fading life, which is first a life imputed to it: yet so really, that the very thought of it in the soul hath so much operation and authority, especially when the meditation of it is mixed with faith, as to make it (though condemned by the Law) to triumph, and to look 30 its enemies in the face with comfort; notwithstanding the greatness of the multitude, the fierceness of their anger, and the continuation of their malice be never so hot against it.

This imputed life (for so it is) is the obedience of the 35 Son of God, as his righteousnesse, in his suffering, arising, ascending, interceding, and so consequently triumphing over

Marginal notes:
Rev. 5. 9.
Job. 40. 14.
Rom. 3. 27.
Ephes. 2. 8, 9.
Tit. 3. 5.

That soul that hath the right work of God upon its heart, is not onely killed to its self: but also made alive to Christ.

all the enemies of the soul, and given to me, as being wrought
on purpose for me. So that, is there righteousness in Christ?
that is mine: Is there perfection in that righteousnesse? that
is mine: did he bleed for sin? it was for mine: hath he over-
5 come the Law, the Devil, and Hell? the victory is mine, and I
am counted the conqueror; *Nay, more then a conquerour through
him that hath loved me*: and I do count this a most glorious life;
for by this means it is that I am in the first place proclaimed
both in heaven and earth guiltlesse, and such a one, who, as I
10 am in Christ, am not a sinner, and so not under the Law, to be
condemned; but as holy and righteous as the Son of God himself, because he himself is my holinesse and righteousnesse,
and so likewise having by this all things taken out of the
way that would condemn me.

15   Sometimes I blesse the Lord my soul hath had the life that
now I am speaking of, not onely imputed to me, but the very
glory of it upon my soul: For upon a time when I was under
many condemnings of heart, and feared because of my sins
my soul would misse of eternall glory; methought I felt in my
20 soul such a secret motion as this, *Thy righteousness is in heaven,*
together with the splendour and shining of the spirit of
grace in my soul, which gave me to see clearly, that my righteousnesse by which I should be justified (from all that could
condemn) was the Son of God himself, in his own person now
25 at the right hand of his Father representing me compleat
before the mercy-seat in his own self: so that I saw clearly,
that night and day, where ever I was, or what ever I was a
doing, still there was my righteousnesse just before the eyes
of divine glory; so that the Father could never finde fault
30 with me for any insufficiency that was in my righteousnesse,
being it was compleat; neither could he say, where is it?
because it was continually at his right hand.

Also at another time having contracted guilt upon my soul,
and having some distemper of body upon me, supposed that
35 death might now so seize upon, as to take me away from
among men: then thought I what shall I do now? is all right
with my soul? have I the right work of God on my soul?

Answering my self, No surely, and that because there were so many weaknesses in me; yea, so many weaknesses in my best duties: for thought I, how can such a one as I finde mercy, whose heart is so ready to evil, and so backward to that which is good (so far as it is naturall)? Thus musing, 5 being filled with fear to die, these words came in upon my

Rom. 3. soul, *Being justified freely by his grace, through the redemption which is in Christ*; as if God had said, Sinner, thou thinkest because that thou hast had so many infirmities and weaknesses in thy soul while thou hast been professing of me, therefore now 10 there can be no hopes of mercy: but be it known unto thee, that it was not any thing done by thee at the first, that moved me to have mercy upon thee; neither is it any thing that is done by thee now that shall make me either accept or reject thee; behold my Son who standeth by me, he is righteous, 15 he hath fulfilled my Law, and given me good satisfaction; on him therefore do I look, and on thee onely as thou art in him, and according to what he hath done, so will I deal with thee. This having stayed my heart, and taken off the guilt through the strength of its coming on my soul, anon after 20 came in that word as a second testimony: *He hath saved us, and called us with an holy calling, not according to the works of righteousness which we have done, but according to his own purpose and grace which was given us in Christ Jesus before the world began.* 25

And thus is the sinner made alive from the dead, being justi- fied by Grace through the righteousnesse of Christ which is unto all and upon all them that believe according to the

Gal. 2. 20. Scriptures. *And the life that I now live, it is by the faith of the Son of God, who loved me, and gave himself for me. I lay down my* 30

John 10. 10, *life for my sheep. I am come that you might have life, and that you*
15. *might have it more abundantly. For if while we were enemies, we were reconciled to God by the death of his Son: much more then*

Rom. 5. 10. *being reconciled, we shall be saved by his life. That as sin reigned*
21. *unto death, even so might Grace reign through righteousness unto* 35 *eternall life, by Jesus Christ our Lord.*

7 marg. Rom 3.] *om.* 1685   9 that] *om.* 1685

Secondly, This life is not onely imputed to him that is
wrought on by the spirit of Grace, that is, not onely counted
his; but also there is put into the soul an understanding enlightened on purpose to know the things of God, which is
5 Christ and his imputed righteousnesse (1 *John* 5. 20.), which
it never thought of nor understood before (1 *Cor.* 2. 9, 10, 11.),
which understanding being enlightened, and made to see
such things, that the soul cannot be contented without it
lay hold of, and apply Christ unto it self, so effectually; I say
10 that the soul shall be exceedingly revived in a very heavenly
measure, with the application of this imputed righteousnesse;
for thereby it knoweth it shall finde God speaking peace to it
self and with a fatherly affection say, *Be of good chear, thy sins
are forgiven thee*, the righteousnesse of my Son I bestow upon
15 thee: *For what the Law could not do in that it was weak through*   Rom. 8. 3, 4.
the (thy) *flesh, I have sent forth my onely Son and have condemned
thy sins in his flesh.* And though thou hast gone astray like a
lost sheep, yet on him I have laid thy iniquities; and though
thou thereby didst undo and break thy self for ever, yet by his
20 stripes I have healed thee. Thus I say the Lord causeth the
soul by faith to apply that which he doth by grace impute
unto it (for thus every soul more or less is dealt withal): the
soul being thus inlightned, thus quickned, thus made alive
from that dead state it was in before (or at least having the
25 beginnings of this life), it hath these several vertuous advantages, which they have not that are dead in their sins and
trespasses, and under the Law.

First, it seeth, what a sad condition all men by nature are
in, they being in that state which it self was in but a while
30 since: but now by grace it is a beginning to scrable out of it;
now it seeth the whole world lieth in wickedness (1 *John*
5. 19.), and so liable to eternal vengeance, because of their
wickedness. Ah friends, let me tell you, though you may be
ignorant of your state and condition, yet the poor groaning
35 hungering Saints of God do see what a sad, woful, miserable
state you are in, which sometimes makes them tremble to

18 thy] thine *1685*

think of your most lamentable latter end (you dying so) and also to *flye the faster to their Lord Jesus, for very fear that they also should be partakers of that most doleful doom: and this it hath by vertue of its own experience, knowing its self was but a while ago in the same condition, under the same condemnation. O! there is now a hearty blessing of God that ever he should shew to it its sad condition, and that he should incline its heart to seek after a better condition. O blessed be the Lord! saith the soul that ever he should awaken me, stir up me, and bring me out of that sad condition, that I once with them was in. It makes also the soul to wonder to see how foolishly and vainly the rest of its neighbours do spend their precious time, that they should be so void of understanding, so forgetful of their latter end, so senseless of the damning nature of their sins: O that their eyes was but in-lightened, to see where abouts they are! surely they would be of another minde then they are now in. Now the soul wonders to see what slender pins those poor creatures do hang the stress of the eternal salvation of their souls upon. O methinks! saith the soul, it makes me mourn to see that some should think that they were Born Christians, and others that their Baptisme makes them so, others depending barely upon a traditional, historical faith, which will leave their souls in the midst of perplexity. O that they should trust to such fables, fancies, and wicked slights of the devil, as their good doings, their good thinkings, their civil walking, and living with the world. O miserable profession, and the end thereof will be a miserable end.

But now, when the soul is thus wrought upon, it must be sure to look for the very gates of hell to be set open against it, with all their force and might to destroy it. Now hell rageth, the devil roareth, and all the world resolved to do the best they can, to bring the soul again into bondage, and ruine. Also the soul shall not want enemies, even in its own hearts lust, as covetousnesse, adultery, blasphemy, unbelief, hardness of heart, coldness, half-heartednesse, ignorance, with an

*Like as the children of Israel who fled for fear, when the ground opened its mouth to swallow up *Corah* and his company.

Psal. 103. 1, 2, 3.

innumerable company of attendants, hanging like so many But this is but for the exercise of its faith.
blocks at its heels, ready to sink it into the fire of hell every
moment, together with strange apprehensions of God, and
Christ, as if now they were absolutely turned to be its ene-
5 mies, which maketh it doubt of the certainty of its salvation:
For you must understand, that though a soul may in reality
have the righteousness of the Son of God imputed to it, and
also some faith in a very strong manner to lay hold upon it:
yet at another time through temptation they may fear, and
10 doubt again; insomuch that the soul may be put into a very
great *fear lest it should return again into the condition it *Jer. 32. 40.
once was in. O saith the soul when I think of my former state,
how miserable it was, it makes me tremble; and when I
think that I may fall into that condition again, how sad are
15 the thoughts of it to me! I would not be in that condition
again for all the world: and this fear riseth still higher and
higher, as the soul is sensible of Satans temptations, or of the
workings of its own corruptions. Ha! these filthy lusts, these
filthy corruptions. O that I was rid of them, that they were
20 consumed in a moment, that I could be quite rid of them,
they do *so* disturb my soul, *so* dishonour my God, *so* defile
my conscience, and sometimes *so* weaken my hands in the
way of God, and my comforts in the Lord; O how glad would
I be, if I might be stripped of them? *Rom.* 7. 24. Which fear
25 puts the soul upon flying to the Lord by prayer, for the cover-
ing of his imputed righteousness, and for strength against the
devils temptations, and its own corruptions; that God would
give down his holy spirit to strengthen it against the things
that do so anoy its soul, and so discourage it in its way, with
30 a resolution through grace, never to be contented, while it
doth finde in it self a triumphing over it by faith in the blood,
of a Crucified Jesus.

Secondly, The soul that hath been thus *killed* by the *Law*
to its things it formerly delighted in; now, O now it cannot
35 be contented with that slender groundlesse faith and hope

1–3 marg. But this . . . its faith.] *om. 1685*   17–18 the workings] its
working 1685   21 *so*] soul *1685*   23 would] should *1685*

that once it contented it self withall. No, no, but now it must be brought into the right saving knowledge of Jesus Christ, now it must have him discovered to the soul by the spirit, now it cannot be satisfied, because such and such do tell it is so. No, but now it will cry out, *Lord shew me continually in the light of thy Spirit through thy word, that Jesus that was born in the dayes of Cesar Augustus (when Mary a daughter of Judah went with Joseph to be taxed at Bethlehem), that he is the very Christ. Lord let me see it in the light of thy spirit, and in the operation thereof, and let me not be contented without such a faith that is so wrought: even by the discovery of his birth, crucifying, death, blood, resurrection, ascension, intercession, and second* (which is his personall) *coming again, that the very faith of it may fill my soul with comfort and holinesse*: and O how afraid the soul is, lest it should fall short of this faith, and of the hope that is begotten by such discoveries as these are! For the soul knoweth, that if it hath not this, it will not be able to stand neither in death nor judgement: and therefore saith the soul, *Lord, whatever other poor souls content themselves withall, let me have that which will stand me instead, and carry me through a dangerous world, that may help me to resist a cunning devill, that may help me to suck true soul satisfying consolation from Jesus Christ through thy promises by the might and power of thy Spirit*. And now when the poor soul at any time hath any discovery of the love of God through a bleeding, dying, risen, interceding Jesus, because it is not willing to be deceived; O how *wary is it of closing with it, for fear it should not be right, for fear it should not come from God? saith the soul, *Cannot the devil give one such comfort too? Cannot he transform himself thus into an Angel of light?* So that the soul (because it would be upon a sure ground) cries out, *Lord shew me thy salvation, and that not once or twice: but Lord let me have thy presence continually upon my heart, to day, and to morrow, and every day*; for the soul when it is rightly brought from under the Covenant of Works, and planted into the Covenant of grace, then it cannot be (unless it be under some desperate temptation) contented without the presence of God, teaching, comforting, stablishing, and helping of the

5

10

15

20

25

30

35

*But this may be its temptation taking place through the timerousness of the soul.

soul to grow in the things of the Lord Jesus Christ; because
it knoweth, that if God hath but withdrawn his presence in
any way from it (as he doth do sometimes for a while), that
then the devil will be sure to be near at hand, working with
5 his temptations, trying all wayes to get the soul into slavery
and sin again; also the corrupt principle that will be joyning
and combining with the wicked one, and will be willing to be
a Co-partner with him to bring the soul into mischief, which
puts the soul upon an earnest, continuall panting after more
10 of the strengthning, preserving, comforting, and teaching
presence of God, and for strong supplies of faith, that it may
effectually lay hold on him.

   Thirdly, The soul is quickned so, that it is not satisfied
now without it do in deed and in truth partake of the peace
15 of Gods Elect; now it is upon the examination of the reallity of
its joy and peace: Time was indeed that any thing would
serve its turn, any false conceits of its state to be good:
but now all kinde of peace will not serve its turn, all kinde
of joy will not be accepted with it; now it must joy in God
20 through Jesus Christ, now its peace must come through the
vertues of the blood of Christ, speaking peace to the conscience by taking away both the gilt and filth of sin by that
bloud, also by shewing the soul its free acceptance with
God through Christ, he having compleatly fulfilled all the
25 conditions of the first Covenant, and freely placed it into the
safety of what he hath done, and so presents the soul compleat
and spotless in the sight of God through his obedience. Now
I say, he hath *peace through the blood of his Cross*, and sees himself *reconciled to God by the death of his Son*, Col. 1. 20, 21. or else
30 his comfort will be questioned by him. It is not every promise
as cometh now upon his heart that will serve his turn: no,
but he must see whether the Babe Jesus be presented to the
soul in and through that promise; now if the Babe leap in his
womb, as I may so say, it is because the Lords promise
35 sounds aloud in his heart, coming to him big with the love

      21 vertues] vertue *1685*   22 filth] the filth *1685*   34 may so say]
   may say, so say *1685*

and pardoning grace of God in Jesus Christ; I say, this is the first and principle joy that the soul hath, that is quickned and brought into the Covenant of Grace.

Fourthly, now the man findes heavenly sanctification wrought in his soul, through the most precious blood of the 5 man whose name is Jesus Christ. *Jesus that he might sanctifie the people with his own blood, suffered without the gate.* Now the soul findes a change in the understanding, in the will, in the minde, in the affections, in the judgement, and also in the conscience; through the inward man a change, and through 10 the outward man a change, from head to foot, as we use to say. *For he that is in Christ,* and so in this Covenant of Grace, *is a new Creature,* 2 Cor. 5. 17. or hath been twice made, made, and made again. O now the soul is resolved for heaven and glory, now it crieth out, Lord, if there be a *right* eye that is 15 offensive to thee, pluck it out; or a *right* foot, cut it off; or a *right* hand, take it from me; now the soul doth begin to studdy how it may honour God, and bring praise to him. Now the soul is for a preparation, for the second coming of Christ, endeavouring to lay aside every thing that may 20 hinder: And for the closing in with those things that may make it in a beloved posture against that day.

Fifthly, And all this is from a Gospel Spirit, and not from a Legal, natural principle, for the soul hath these things as the fruits, and effects of its being separated unto the Covenant of 25 Grace, and so now possessed with that spirit that doth attend, yea, and dwell in them that are brought into the Covenant of Grace, from under the old Covenant; I say, these things do spring forth in the soul, from another root, and stock, then any of the actings as other men do; for the soul that is 30 thus wrought upon, is as well dead to the *Law* and the righteousness thereof (as the first Covenant), as well as to its *sins.*

Sixthly, Now the soul begins to have some blessed experience of the things of God, even of the glorious mysteries 35 of the Gospel.

John 6. 55.   1. Now it knoweth the meaning of those words. *My flesh*

is meat indeed, and my blood is drink indeed: and that by experience;
for the soul hath received peace of conscience through that
blood, by the effectual application of it to the soul. First, by
feeling the *guilt* of sin dye off from the conscience, by the
5 operation thereof. Secondly, by feeling the *power* thereof, to
take away the *curse* of the Law. Thirdly, by finding the very
strength of *hell* to fail, when once the blood of the man Jesus
Christ is received in reality upon the soul.

2. Now the soul also knoweth by experience the meaning
10 of that Scripture that saith, *Our old man is crucified with him,* Rom. 6. 6.
that the body of sin might be destroyed. Now it sees that when the
man Jesus did hang on the tree, on Mount *Calvary*, that then
the body of its sins was there hanged up, dead and buried with
him, though it was then unborne, so as never to be laid to
15 its charge, either here or hereafter; and also, so as never to
carry it captive into perpetual bondage, being it self overcome by him, even Christ the head of that poor creature. And
indeed this is the way for a soul, both to live comfortably,
as touching the *guilt* of sin; and also, as touching the power
20 of the *filth* of sin: for the soul that doth, or hath received this
indeed, and in truth, findes strength against them both, by,
and through that man, that did for him and the rest of his
fellow sinners, so gloriously overcome it, and hath given the
victory unto them, so that now they are said to be overcomers,
25 nay, *more then conquerours through him,* the one man Jesus
Christ, *Rom.* 8. 33, 34, 35, 36, 37.

3. Now the soul hath received a faith indeed, and a lively
hope indeed, such a one as now it can fetch strength from the
fulness of Christ, and from the merits of Christ.

30   4. Yea, now the soul can look on it self with one eye, and
look upon Christ with another; and say indeed it is true, I
am an empty soul, but Christ is a full Christ; I am a poor
sinner, but Christ is a rich Christ; I am a foolish sinner, but
Christ is a wise Christ; I am an unholy, ungodly, unsancti-
35 fied creature in my self, *But Christ is made of God, unto me,*
wisdome, righteousness, sanctification, and redemption, 1 Cor. 1. 30.

5. Now also that fiery Law, that it could not once endure,

nor could not once delight in; I say, now it can delight in it after the inward man, now this Law is its delight, it would always be walking in it, and always be delighting in it, being offended with any sin, or any corruption, that would be any wayes an hinderance to it, *Rom.* 7. 24, 25. And yet it will not abide, it will not endure that that, even that that Law should offer to take the work of its salvation out of Christs hand: no, if it once comes to do that, then out of doors it shall go, if it was as good again. For that soul that hath the right work of God indeed upon it, cries, not my prayers, not my tears, not my works, not my things, do they come from the work of the spirit of Christ it self within me; yet these shall not have the glory of my salvation: no, it is none but the blood of Christ, the death of Christ, of the man Christ Jesus of *Nazareth* the Carpenters Son (as they called him) that must have the Crown and Glory of my salvation. None but Christ; none but Christ; and thus the soul labours to give Christ the preeminence. *Col.* 1. 18.

Now before I go any further, I must needs speak a word from my own experience of the things of Christ; and the rather, because we have a company of silly ones in this day of ignorance, that do either comfort themselves with a notion without the power, or else do both reject the notion and the power of this most glorious Gospel: therefore, for the further conviction of the *Reader*, I shall tell him (with *David*) something of what the Lord hath done for my soul: and indeed a little of the experience of the things of Christ, is far more worth then all the world. It would be too tedious for me to tell thee (here) all from the first to the last, but something I shall tell thee, that thou mayest not think these things are fables.

Reader, when it pleased the Lord to begin to instruct my soul, he found me one of the black sinners of the world; he found me making a sport of oaths, and also of lies, and many

Something of the Authors experience.

a soul-poysoning meal did I make out of divers lusts, as
drinking, dancing, playing, pleasure with the wicked ones of
the world. The Lord finding of me in this *condition, did
open the glass of his Law unto me, wherein he shewed me so
5 clearly my sins, both the greatnesse of them, and also how
abominable they were in his sight, that I thought the very
clouds were charged with the wrath of God, and ready to
let fall the very fire of his jealousie upon me: yet for all this
I was so wedded to my sins, that thought I with my self, I
10 will have them, though I lose my soul (O wicked wretch
that I was); but God, the great, the rich, the infinite merciful
God, did not take this advantage of my soul, to cast me away,
and say, then take him devil, seeing he cares for me no more:
no, but he followed me still, and won upon my heart, by
15 giving of me some understanding, not onely into my miserable
state which I was very sensible of; but also that there might
be hopes of mercy, also taking away that love to lust, and
placing in the room thereof a love to religion; and thus the
Lord won over my heart to some desire after the means, to
20 hear the word, and to grow a stranger to my old companions,
and to accompany the people of God, together with giving
of me many sweet encouragements, from several promises
in the Scriptures: but after this, the Lord did wonderfully
set my sins upon my conscience, those sins especially, that I
25 had committed since the first convictions, temptations also
followed me very hard, and especially such temptations as did
tend to the making of me question the very way of salvation,
viz. whether Jesus Christ was the Saviour or no: and whether
I had best to venture my soul upon his blood for salvation,
30 or take some other course. But being through grace kept
close with God (in some measure) in prayer, and the rest of
the ordinances; but went about a year and upwards, without
any sound evidence as from God to my soul, touching the
salvation as comes by Jesus Christ. But at the last, as I may
35 say, when the set time was come, then the Lord (just before
the men called Quakers came into the Countrey) did set me
down so blessedly in the truth of the Doctrine of Jesus Christ,

*This conviction seized on my soul, one Sabbath day when I was at play, being one of the first that I had; which when it came, though it scared me with its terrour, yet through the temptation of the devil immediately striking in therewith, I did rub it off again, and became as vile for some time as I was before; like a wretch that I was.

that it made me marvail, to see first, how Jesus Christ was Born
of a Virgin, walked in the world a while with his Disciples,
afterwards hanged on the Cross, spilt his Blood, was Buried,
Rose again, Asscended above the Clouds and Heavens, there
lives to make intercession; and that he also will come again 5
at the last day to judge the World, and take his Saints unto
himself. These things, I say, I did see so evidently, even as if I
had stood by when he was in the world, and also when he was
caught up. I having such a change as this upon my soul, it
made me wonder; and musing with my self at the great 10
alteration that was in my spirit (for the Lord did also very
gloriously give me in his precious word to back the discovery
of the Son of God unto me, so that I can say through grace
it was according to the Scriptures, 1 *Cor.* 15. 1, 2, 3, 4), and
as I was musing with my self what these things should mean, 15
methought I heard such a word in my heart as this; *I have*
set thee down on purpose; for I have something more then ordinary
for thee to do; which made me the more marvel, saying, What,
my Lord, such a poor wretch as I? yet still this continued,
I have set thee down on purpose, and so forth, with more fresh in- 20
comes of the Lord Jesus, and the power of the blood of his
Cross upon my soul, even so evidently, that I saw (through
grace) that it was the blood shed on Mount *Calvary* that did
save and redeem sinners, as clearly, and as really with the
eyes of my soul, as ever (methoughts) I had seen a penny- 25
loaf bought with a penny; which things then discovered had
such operation upon my soul, that I do hope, they did
sweetly season every faculty thereof. Reader, I speak in the
presence of God, and he knows I lye not: much of this, and
such like dealings of his, could I tell thee of; but my business 30
at this time is not so to do, but onely to tell what operation
the blood of Christ hath had over, and upon my conscience,
and that at several times, and also when I have been in
several frames of spirit.

As first, sometimes I have been so loaden with my sins, 35
that I could not tell where to rest, nor what to do; yea, at such
times I thought it would have taken away my senses: yet

at that time, God through grace hath all on a sudden, so effectually applied the blood that was spilt at Mount *Calvary*, out of the side of Jesus, unto my poor, wounded, guilty conscience, that presently I have found such a sweet, sollid, 5 sober, heart comforting peace, that it hath made me, as if it had not been, and withall the same (I may say, and I ought to say, the power of it) hath had such a powerful operation upon my soul, that I have for a time been in a straight and trouble, to think that I should love and honour him no more, 10 the vertue of his blood hath so constrained me.

Again, sometimes methinks my sins have appeared so big to me, that I thought one of my sins have been as big as all the sins of all the men in the nation, I, and of other nations too. (Reader, these things be not fancies, for I have smarted 15 for this experience) but yet the least stream of the heart blood of this man Jesus, hath vanished all away, and hath made it to flie, to the astonishment of such a poor sinner; and as I said before, hath delivered me up into sweet and heavenly peace, and joy in the holy Ghost.

20 Again, sometimes when my heart hath been hard, dead, slothful, blinde and senseless (which indeed are sad frames for a poor Christian to be in) yet at such a time when I have been in such a case; then hath the blood of Christ, the precious blood of Christ, the admirable blood of the God of 25 Heaven, that run out of his body when it did hang on the Cross, so softened, livened, quickned, and inlightned my soul, that truly (Reader) I can say, O it makes me wonder!

Again, when I have been loaden with sin, and pestered I cannot 30 with several temptations, and in very sad manner, then have I stand here to tell thee had the triall of the vertue of Christs blood, with the triall of particular of the vertue of other things: and I have found that when temptations. tears would not do, prayers would not do, repentings and all other things could not reach my heart: O then one touch, 35 one drop, one shining of the vertue of the blood, of that blood that was let out with the spear; it hath in a very blessed

29–31 marg. I cannot . . . temptations.] *om.* 1685

manner delivered me, that it hath made me to marvel. O! methinks it hath come with such life, such power, with such irresistible, and marvellous glory, that it wipes off all the slurs, silences, all the out-cries, and quenches all the fiery darts, and all the flames of hell fire, that are begotten by the charges of the Law, Satan, and doubtful remembrances of my sinful life.

Friends, as *Peter* saith to the Church, so I say to you, I have not preached to you cunningly devised fables, in telling you of the blood of Christ, and what authority it hath had upon my conscience; O no: but as *Peter* saith touching the coming of the Lord Jesus into the world; so in some measure I can say of the blood of the Lord Jesus Christ, that was shed when he did come into the world. There is not onely my single testimony touching this; no, but there is all the Prophets do agree, in advancing this in writing, and also all the Saints do now declare the same, in speaking forth the amiableness, and many powerful vertues thereof. *As for thee, by the blood of thy Covenant* (saith God to Christ) *I have sent forth thy prisoners out of the pit, wherein was no water,* Zech. 9. 11. *We have redemption through his blood,* Ephes. 1. 7. Again, Col. 1. 14. *We have redemption through his blood. Our robes are washed, and made white in the blood of the Lamb,* Rev. 7. 14. *The devil is overcome through the blood of the Lamb,* Rev. 12. 11. Yea, *and conscience is purged too, and that through the blood of the Lamb.* Heb. 9. 14. *We have* Heb. 10. 19. *free recourse to the Throne of grace through the blood of Jesus.* I could bring thee a cloud of witnesses out of all the types and shadows, and out of the sundry Prophets, and much more out of the New Testament, but I forbear, because I would not be too tedious to thee Reader, in making too large a digression, though I have committed here in this Discourse no transgression; for the blood of Christ is precious blood, I *Pet.* 1. 18, 19.

In the next place I shall shew you the several priviledges, and advantages, that the man or woman hath, that is under this Covenant of Grace, over they have that are under the Covenant of the Law, and Works.

As first, the Covenant of Grace is not grounded upon our
obedience, but upon Gods love, even his pardoning love to us
through Christ Jesus. The first Covenant it stood to be broken
or kept by us, and Gods love or anger, to be lost, or enjoyed
5 thereafter, as we, as creatures behaved our selves: but now
the very ground of the Covenant of Grace is Gods love, 'tis
meer love through Jesus Christ, *Deut.* 7. 7, 8. *The Lord did not
set his love upon you, nor chuse you; because you were more in
number then other people; for you were the fewest of all people: but*
10 *because the Lord loves you, and because he will keep the oath which
he swore to your fathers.* Again, Isa. 63. 9. *In his love and in his
pitty he redeemed them, and the Angel of his presence saved them,*
That is Jesus Christ. And again, 2 Tim. 1. 9. *Who hath
saved us.—Not according to the works of righteousness which we*
15 *have done; but according to his own purpose and grace, which was
given to us in Christ Jesus, before the world began.*

Secondly, This love is not conveyed to us through what
we have done (as is afore proved), but through what he hath
done, with whom the Covenant was made, *which was given*
20 *us in Christ. According as he hath chosen us in Christ. Who hath
blessed us with all spirituall blessings in heavenly places in Christ.
God for Christs sake hath loved you* (2 Tim. 1. 9. Eph. 1. 3, 4.
Eph. 4. 32.). That is through Christs doings, through Christs
sufferings. Now if this be but rightly understood, it doth dis-
25 cover abundance of comfort to them that are within the
bounds of the Covenant of Grace. For

First, Here a believer seeth he shall stand, if Christs
doings and sufferings stand (which is a sure foundation) for
God dealeth with him through Christ. And so secondly, he
30 shall not fall, unless the sufferings and merits of Christ be
thrown over the bar, being found guilty (which will never be)
before the eyes of divine justice. For with him the Covenant
was made, and he was the surety of it, *Zech.* 9. 11. *Heb.* 7. 22.
That is, as the Covenant was made with him, so he stood
35 bound to fulfill the same. For you must understand that the
Covenant was made between the Father and the Son, long

7 7. 7, 8.] 7. 8, 9. *1659, 1685*

before it was accomplished, or manifestly sealed with Christs blood, it was made before the world began (*Tit.* 1. 2. *Ephes.* 1. 4. 1 *Pet.* 1. 18, 19, 20.). But the conditions thereof was not fulfilled, untill less then two thousand years ago; and all that while did Jesus stand bound as a surety (as I said before) is used to do, till the time in which the payment should be made. And it was by vertue of his suretiship (having bound himself by Covenant to do all things agreed on, by the Father and him) that all those of the election that were born before he came, that they might be saved, and did enter into rest. For the forgivenesse of sins that was past, though it was through the blood of Christ; yet it was also through the forbearance of God, *Rom.* 3. 25. That is, Christ becoming surety for those that died before his coming, that he would indeed and in truth, at the fulnesse of time (or at the time appointed, *Gal.* 4. 4.) give a compleat and full satisfaction for them according to the tenour, or condition of the Covenant.

Again secondly, The second Covenant, which believers are under, as the ground and foundation of it is safe; so the promises thereof are better, surer, freer, and fuller, *&c.*

First, they are better, if you compare the excellency of the one, with the excellency of the other. The first hath promised nothing but an earthly paradise, *Do this and thou shalt live.* Namely, here in an earthly paradise. But the other doth bring the promise of an heavenly paradise.

Secondly, As the Covenant of Works doth promise an earthly Paradise; yet it is a Paradise or blessing, though once obtained, yet might be lost again (for no longer then thou dost well, no longer art thou accepted by that); O but the promises in the New Covenant do bring unto us the benefit of an eternal inheritance (*Heb.* 9. 15.), *That they which are called might receive the promise of eternall inheritance.* O rare! it is an eternal inheritance.

Thirdly, the other, as it is not so good as this, so neither is it so sure as this, and therefore he calls the one, such a one as might be, and was shaken (*Heb.* 12. 27.): but this is said to be such a one that cannot be shaken. *And this word,* saith he, treating of the two Covenants from verse the 18. to the 24. *And this word, yet once more, signifies the removing of those things that are* (or may be) *shaken, as of things that are made, that those things that cannot be shaken* (which is the second Covenant), 5 *may remain*; for saith he, verse the 28. *which cannot be moved.* Therefore ye blessed Saints, seeing you have received a King-dom which cannot, *which cannot be moved*: (therefore) *Let us have grace whereby we may serve* (our) *God acceptably, with reverence and godly fear.* Thus in generall, but more particular.

10   First, They are surer, in that they are founded upon Gods love also, and they come to us without calling for those things at our hands, that may be a means of putting of a stop to our certain enjoying of them. The promises under, or of the Law, they might easily be stopped by our disobedience: but the 15 promises under the Gospel saith, *If heaven above can be measured, and the foundation of the earth searched out, then* (and not till then) *will I cast off all the seed of Israel for all that they have done.* Again, *I, even I am he that blotteth out thy transgressions for my* Isa. 43. 25. *own Names sake, and will not remember thy sins.* I will make thee a 20 partaker of my promise; and that I may so do, I will take away that which would hinder; *I will cast all your sins into the depths of the sea*, that my promise may be sure to *all* the seed. And therefore saith the Apostle, when he would shew us that the New Covenant promises was more sure then the Old; he 25 tells us plainly that the Law and Works are set aside, and they are meerly made ours through the righteousness of faith, which is the righteousness of Christ. *For the promise that Abraham should be heir of the world* (saith he), *was not to him, or to his seed through the Law* (or Works), *but through the righteous-* 30 *ness of faith. For if they which are of the Law* (or of Works) *be heirs, then faith is made void, and the promise made of none effect. Therefore it is of faith,—to the end the promise might be sure to all the seed*, Rom. 4. 13, 14, 16.

Secondly surer, because that as that is taken away that 35 should hinder, so they are committed to a faithful friend of ours in keeping: *For all the promises of God are in Christ; not yea and nay, but yea and amen*; certain and sure; sure because they are in the hand of our head, our friend, our brother, our husband, our flesh and bones, even in the heart and hand of our precious Jesus.

Thirdly, Because all the conditions of them are already fulfilled for us by Jesus Christ, as aforesaid, every promise that 5 is a new Covenant promise, if there be any condition in it, our undertaker hath accomplished that for us, and also giveth us such grace as to receive the sweetnesse as doth spring from them through his obedience to every thing required in them.

Fourthly, surer, because that as they are grounded upon the 10 love of God; every thing taken out of the way, in the hand of a sure friend: And as Christ hath fulfilled every condition as to justification that is contained therein; so the Lord hath solemnly sworn with an oath for our better confidence in this particular. *For when God made promise to Abraham* (and so to all 15 Saints), *because he could swear by no greater, he sware by himself, saying, Surely, blessing I will blesse thee, and multiplying I will multiply thee: and so after he had patiently endured, he obtained the promise. For men verily swear by the greater, and an oath for confirmation is to them an end of all strife* (that there might be no 20 more doubt or scruple concerning the certain fulfilling of the promise); *wherein God willing more abundantly to shew unto the heirs of promise the immutability of his counsell* (or certain, constant, unchangeable decree of God in making of the promise, for the comfort of his children), *confirmed it by an oath, that by* 25 *two immutable things* (his promise backt with an oath), *wherein it is impossible for God to lie, we might have strong consolation, who have fled for refuge to lay hold upon the hope set before us,* Heb. 6. 13, 14, 15, 16, 17, 18.

Fifthly, That they are better it appears also, in that they 30 are freer and fuller; that they are freer, it is evident, in that the one saith, no works no life: Do this, and then thou shalt live, if not, thou shalt be damned. But the other saith, we are saved by believing in what another hath done, without the works of the Law; *Now to him that worketh not, but believeth on* 35 *him that justifieth the ungodly, his faith is counted for righteousness,* Rom. 4. 4, 5. The one saith, pay me that thou owest; the other saith, I do frankly and freely forgive thee all. The one saith, because thou hast sinned thou shalt dye; the other saith, *because Christ lives thou shalt live also*, John 15.

Secondly, And as they are freer, so they are fuller; fuller of 5 encouragement, fuller of comfort; the one (to wit the Law) looks like *Pharaohs* seven ill favoured kine, more ready to eat one up, then to afford us any food. The other is like the full grape in the cluster, which for certain hath a glorious blessing in it. The one saith, if thou hast sinned, turn again; the other 10 saith, if thou hast sinned, thou shalt be damned, for all I have a promise in me.

Thirdly, they that are of the second, are better then they that are of the first; & it also appeareth in this. The promises of the Law, through them we have neither faith, nor hope, 15 nor the Spirit conveyed: But through the promises of the Gospel there is all these, 2 *Pet*. 1. 4. *Whereby are given unto us exceeding great and precious promises, that by these we might be partakers of the Divine nature.* O therefore *let us hold fast the profession of our faith without wavering; for he is faithfull that* 20 *promised*, Heb. 10. 23. *In hope of eternall life* (why so?) *because God that cannot lie, promised it before the world began*, Tit. 1. 2.

Fourthly, They that are in this Covenant are in a very happy state; for though there be several conditions in the Gospell to be done, yet Christ Jesus doth not look that they 25 should be done by man, as man, but by his own Spirit in them, as it is written, *Thou hast wrought all our works in us and for us.* Is there that condition, they must believe? why then, he will be both the *Author and finisher of their faith*, Heb. 12. 2, 3. Is there also hope to be in his children? he also doth, and hath 30 given *them good hope through his grace*. 2 *Thes*. 2. 26. Again, are the people of God to behave themselves to the glory of God the Father? Then he will work in them *both to will and to do of his own good pleasure*. Philippians 2. 13.

Fifthly, Again, as he works all our works in us and for us, 35 so also by vertue of this Covenant, we have another nature given unto us. Whereby, or by which we are made willing to

*1 Cor. 6. 20. be glorifying of God *both in our bodies, and in our spirits, which are his. *Thy people shall be willing in the day of thy power,* Psal. 110. 3.

Sixthly, In the next place all those that are under this second Covenant, are in a wonderful safe condition: For in 5 case they should slip, or fall, after their conversion into some sin, or sins (for who lives and sins not, *Prov.* 24. 16.), yet through the merits, and intercession of Christ Jesus, who is their undertaker in this Covenant, they shall have their sins pardoned, their wounds healed, and they raised up again; 10 which priviledge the children of the first Covenant have not, for if they sin, they are never afterwards regarded by that Covenant. *They break my Covenant, and I regarded them not, saith the Lord,* Heb. 8. 9. But when he comes to speak of the Covenant of Grace, speaking first of the publick person under the 15 name of *David,* he saith thus, **He shall cry unto me, Thou art my Father, my God, and the rock of my salvation. Also I will make him my first-born: higher then the kings of the earth. My mercy will I keep for him for evermore, and my Covenant shall stand fast with him. His seed also will I make to endure for ever, and his throne as the 20 dayes of heaven. If his Children forsake my Law, and walk not in my judgements: If they break my Statutes, and keep not my Command-ments; then will I visit their transgression with the rod, and their iniquity with stripes. Nevertheless my loving kindness will I not utterly take from him, nor suffer my faithfulness to fail. My Covenant will 25 I not break, nor alter the thing that is gone out of my lips. Once have I sworn by my holiness, that I will not lie unto David, His seed shall endure for ever, and his throne as the Sun before me; it shall be estab-lished for ever as the Moon, and as a faithfull witness in heaven.*

*Psal. 89. from the 26. verse to the 37.

Mark this ☞ *My Covenant shall stand fast with him,* mark that, As if God had 30 said, I did not make this Covenant with man, but with my Son, and with him I will perform it; and seeing he hath given me compleat satisfaction, though his children do through in-firmity transgress, yet my Covenant is not therefore broken,

1 marg. 1 Cor.] 2 Cor. *1659, 1685*   13–14 *saith the Lord*] om. *1685*
22 *judgements*] *judgement 1685*   24–6 *utterly take . . . will I not*] om. *1685*
30 marg. Mark this] om. *1685*

seeing he with whom it was made, standeth firme, according to the desire of my heart; so that my justice that is satisfied, and my Law hath nothing to say; for there is no want of perfection in the sacrifice of Christ.

5   If you love your souls and would have them live in the peace of God, to the which you are called in one body, even all believers; then I beseech you seriously to ponder, and labour to settle in your souls this one thing, that the new Covenant is not broken by our transgressions, and that be-
10 cause it was not made with us. The reason why the very Saints of God have so many ups and downs in this their travel towards heaven; it is because they are so weak in the faith of this one thing; for they think that if they fail in this or that particular performance, if their hearts be dead, and
15 cold, and their lusts mighty and strong; therefore now God is angry, and now he will shut them out of his favour, now the new Covenant is broken, and now Christ Jesus will stand their friend no longer; now also the devil hath power again, and now they must have their part in the resurrection of
20 damnation; when alas the Covenant is not for all this never the more broken, and so the Grace of God no more straightned then it was before. Therefore I say, when thou findest that thou art weak here, and failing there, backward to this good, and thy heart forward to that evil; then be sure that thou
25 keep a stedfast eye on the Mediator of this new Covenant; and be perswaded, that it is not onely made with him, and his part also fulfilled, but that he doth look upon his fulfilling of it, so as not to lay thy sins to thy charge, though he may as a father chastise thee for the same. *If his children forsake*
30 *my Law, and walk not in my judgements. If they break my statutes, and keep not my Commandments; then will I visit their transgressions with a rod, and their iniquities with stripes. Nevertheless,* mark, *nevertheless my loving kindness will I not utterly take from him: nor suffer my faithfulness to fail. My Covenant*
35 *will I not break, nor alter the thing that is gone out of my mouth.* And what was that? why, that *his seed shall endure for ever,*

13 in] of *1685*   24 that²] *om. 1685*

and his throne as the dayes of heaven. Psal. 89. 30, 31, 32, 33, 34, 35, 36.

Seventhly, Another priviledge that the Saints have by vertue of the new Covenant, is, that they have part of the possession, or hold of heaven and glory already: and that two manner of wayes. First the divine nature is conveyed from heaven into them. And secondly, the humane nature (*i.e.*) the nature of man is received up, and entertained in, and hath got possession of heaven.

Rom. 8. 8, 9, 10, 11.   1. We have the first-fruits of the spirit (saith the man of God), we have the earnest of the spirit which is instead of the whole, for it is the earnest of the whole. *Which is the earnest of our inheritance, untill the redemption of the purchased possession, unto the praise of his glory.* Eph. 1. 13, 14.

*1 Cor. 15. 20.   2. The nature of man, OUR nature is got into glory as the *first*-fruits of mankinde, as a fore-runner to take possession till we all come thither. For the man born at *Bethlehem* is ascended (which is part of the lump of mankinde) into glory, as a publick person, as the *first*-fruits, representing the *whole* of the children of God. So that in some sense it may be said, that the *Saints* have already taken possession of the kingdome of heaven, by *their* Jesus, *their* publick person; he being in

*John 14. 1, 2, 3, 4, 5.   *their* room entred to prepare *a place for *them*.

I beseech you consider: When Jesus Christ came down from glory, it was that he might bring *us* to glory; and that he might be sure not to fail, he clothed himself with *our* nature,

*Heb. 2. 14, 15.   as if one should take a piece out of the whole *lump instead of the whole (untill the other comes), and investeth in that glory which he was in before he came down from heaven: and thus is that saying to be understood, speaking of Christ and Saints, which saith, *And* (he) *hath raised us up together and made us sit together in heavenly places in Christ Jesus*, Eph. 2. 6.

*1 Pet. 1. 5.   Eighthly, Again, not onely thus, but all the *power of God, together with the rest of his glorious attributes are on *our* side, in that they dweil in *our* nature, which is the man Jesus, and doth ingage for *us*, poor, simple, empty, nothing

12 for it is . . . the whole] *om. 1685*   26 clothed] clotheth *1659*

creatures, as to our eternal happinesse. *For in him* (that is in Col. 2. 9, 10.
the man Christ, who is our nature, our head, our root, our
flesh, our bone) *dwelleth all the fulness of the God-head bodily*;
mark how they are joyned together, *In whom dwelleth the ful-*
5 *ness of the Godhead. And ye are compleat in him.* God dwelleth
compleatly in him, and you also are compleatly implanted in
him, which is the head of all principality and power, and all
this by the consent of the Father. *For it hath pleased the Father,*
that in him should all fulness dwell. Now mark, the God-head
10 doth not dwell in Christ Jesus for himself onely, but that it
may be in a way of righteousnesse conveyed to us, for our
comfort and help in all our wants. *All power is given unto me in*
heaven and in earth, saith he, *Mat. 28. 18.* And then followeth,
And loe I am with you alway, even unto the end of the world, ver. Psal. 68. 18.
15 20. *He hath received gifts for men, even for the rebellious. Of his* John 1. 16. Col. 1. 9.
fulness have we all received, and grace for grace. And this the
Saints cannot be deprived of, because the Covenant made
with Christ, in every tittle of it was so compleatly fulfilled
as to righteousness, both active and passive, that justice can-
20 not object any thing, holiness now can finde fault with nothing; nay, all the power of God cannot shake any thing that
hath been done for *us* by the *Mediator of the new Covenant*;
so that now there is no Covenant of Works to a Believer,
none of the commands, accusations, condemnations, or the
25 least tittle of the old Covenant to be charged on any of those
that are the children of the second Covenant, no sin to be
charged, because there is no Law to be pleaded, but all is
made up by our middle man Jesus Christ. O blessed Covenant!
O blessed priviledge! Be wise therefore O ye poor drooping
30 souls that are the sons of this second Covenant, And *stand fast*
in the liberty wherewith CHRIST hath made you free, and be not
again intangled (not terrified in your consciences) *with the yoke*
of bondage; neither the commands, accusations, or condemnations of the Law of the old Covenant, *Gal. 5. 1, 2.*
35   *Object.* If it be so, then one need not care what they do, The first objection.

14 ver.] *om. 1685*   28 Jesus Christ] Christ Jesus *1685*   35 marg.
The first objection.] *om. 1685*

they may sin and sin again, seeing Christ hath made satisfaction.

Answer. *Answ.* If I was to point out one that is under the power of the devil, and going poste haste to hell (for my life) I would look no further for such a man, then to him that would make such a use as this of the grace of God. What because Christ is a Saviour, thou wilt be a sinner; because his grace abounds, therefore thou wilt abound in sin. O wicked wretch! rake hell all over, and surely I think thy fellow will scarce be found: And let me tell thee this before I leave thee, as Gods Covenant with Christ for his Children (which are of faith) stands sure, immutable, unrevokable, and unchangeable; so also hath God taken such a course with thee, that unless thou canst make God forswear himself, it is impossible that thou shouldest go to heaven, dying in that condition. *They tempted me, proved me*, and turned the grace of God into lasciviousness (Compare *Heb.* 3. the 9, 10, 11. verses, with the 1 *Cor.* 10. Chap. from the 5. verse to the 10.). *So I sware*, mark that, *So I sware* (and that in my wrath too), *that they should never enter into my rest.* No, saith God, if Christ will not serve their turns, but they must have their sins too, take them devil; if heaven will not satisfie them, take them hell, devour them hell, scald them, fry them, burn them hell; God hath more places then one to put sinners into, if they do not like of heaven, he will fit them with hell; if they do not like Christ, they shall be forced to have the Devil. Therefore we must and will tell of the truth of the nature of the Covenant of the grace of God to his poor Saints, for their encouragement, & for their comfort, who would be glad to leap at Christ upon any terms: yet therewith we can tell how through grace, to tell the hogs and sons of this world, what a hogsty there is prepared for them, even such a one that God hath prepared to put the Devil and his Angels into, is fitly prepared for them, *Mat.* 25. 41.

The second objection. *Object.* But if Christ hath given God a full and compleat satisfaction, then though I do go on in sin, I need not fear,

---

3 marg. Answer.] *om. 1685*   is] was *1685*   17 the¹] *om. 1685*
34 marg. The second objection.] *om. 1685*

seeing God hath already been satisfied; it will be injustice in God to punish for those sins, for which he is already satisfied for by Christ.

   Answ. Rebell, rebell, there are some in Christ, and some out Answer. of him; they that are in him have their sins forgiven, and they themselves made new creatures, and have the spirit of the Son, which is a holy, loving, self-denying spirit. And they that are thus in Jesus Christ are so far off from delighting in sin, that sin is the greatest thing that troubleth them; and O how willingly would they be rid of the very thoughts of it, *Psal.* 119. 113. It is the grief of their souls (when they are in a right frame of spirit) that they can live no more to the honour and glory of God, then they do; and in all their prayers to God, the breathings of their souls is as much for sanctifying grace, as pardoning grace, that they might live a holy life; they would as willingly *live holy here, as they would be *Phil. 3. 6, 7, happy in the world to come; they would as willingly be 8, 9, 10, 11, cleansed from the filth of sin, as to have the guilt of it taken 12, 13, 14, away; they would as willingly glorifie God here, as they would 15, 16, 17, be glorified by him hereafter. 18, 19, 20, 21.

   2. But there are some, that are out of Christ, being under the Law, and as for all those, let them be civil or profane, they are such as God accounts wicked; and I say, as for those, if all the Angels in heaven can drag them before the judgement-seat of Christ, they shall be brought before it to answer for all their ungodly *deeds; and being condemned for them, if all *Jude 15. the fire in hell will burn them, they shall be burned there (if they dye in that condition). And therefore if you love your souls, do not give way to such a wicked spirit. *Let no man deceive you with* (such) *vain words* (as to think, because Christ hath made satisfaction to God for sin: therefore you may live in your sins. O no, God forbid that any should think so) *for because of these things cometh the wrath of God upon the children of disobedience,* Ephes. 5. 6.

   Thus have I (Reader) given thee a brief discourse, touching the Covenant of Works, and the Covenant of Grace, also of

4 marg. Answer.] *om. 1685*

the nature of the one, together with the nature of the other. I have also in this Discourse, endeavoured to shew you the condition of them that are under the Law, how sad it is, both from the nature of the Covenant they are under, and also by the carriage of God unto them by that Covenant. 5 And now because I would bring all into as little a compass as I can, I shall begin with the Use and Application of the whole in as brief a way as I can, desiring the Lord to bless it to thee.

The first use is a use of examination. And first of all, let us here begin to examine a little touching the Covenant you stand before God in, whether it be the 10 Covenant of Works, or the Covenant of Grace; and for the right doing of this, I shall lay down this proposition. Namely, that all men naturally come into the world under the first of these, which is called the old Covenant, or the Covenant of Works, which is the Law. *And were all by nature the children* 15 *of wrath, even as others,* which they could not be, had they not been under the Law; for there are none that are under the other Covenant, that are still the children of the wrath, but the children of faith, the children of the promise, the accepted children, the children not of the Bond-woman, but of the 20 free, *Gal.* 4, the 4. last verses.

Now here lieth the question. Which of these two Covenants art thou under, soul?

Answ. I hope I am under the Covenant of Grace.

Quest. But what ground hast thou to think that thou art 25 under that blessed Covenant? and not rather under the Covenant of Works, that strict, that soul-damning Covenant?

Answ. What ground? Why, I hope I am.

Quest. But what ground hast thou for this thy hope? For a hope without a ground is like a Castle built in the air, that will 30 never be able to do thee any good, but will prove like unto that spoken of in the eighth of *Job; Whose hope shall be cut off, and whose trust shall be* (like) *a spiders web. He shall lean upon his house but it shall not stand, he shall hold it fast* (as thou wouldest thy hope 'tis like), *but it shall not endure,* Job 8. 13, 14, 15.   35

9–11 marg. The first . . . examination.] *om. 1685*   20 Bond-woman] Bond-man *1685*

Answ. My hope is grounded upon the promises, what else should it be grounded upon?

Answ. Indeed to build my hope upon Christ Jesus, upon God in Christ, through the promise, and to have this hope
5 rightly, by the shedding abroad of the love of God in the heart, it is a right grounded hope, *Rom.* 5. 1, 2, 3, 4, 5.

Quest. But what promises in the Scripture do you finde your hope built upon? And how do you know whether you do build your hope upon the promises in the Gospel, the promises
10 of the new Covenant; and not rather on the promises of the old Covenant, for there are promises in that as well as in the other?

Answ. I hope that if I do well I shall be accepted; because God hath said I shall, *Gen.* 4. 7.

15 *Rep.* O soul, if thy hope be grounded there, thy hope is not grounded upon the Gospel promises, or the new Covenant, but verily upon the old; for these words was spoken to *Cain*, a Son of the old Covenant; and they themselves are the tenour and scope of that, for that runs thus. *Do this and thou*
20 *shalt live. The man that doth these things shall live by them. If thou do well, thou shalt be accepted.* Levit. 18. 5. Ezek. 20. 11. Rom. 10. 5. Gal. 3. 12. Gen. 4. 7.

Rep. Why, truly if a mans doing well, and living well, and his striving to serve God as well as he can, will not help him
25 to Christ, I do not know what will; I am sure sinning against God will not.

Quest. Did you never read that Scripture, which saith, *Israel which followed after the Law of righteousness, hath not attained to the Law of righteousness*? Rom. 9. 30, 31, 32.

30 *Object.* But doth not the Scripture say, *Blessed are they that keep his Commandments, that they may have right to the tree of life*? Rev. 22. 14.

Answ. There is first therefore to be enquired into, whether to keep his Commandments, be to strive to keep the Law, as it
35 is a Covenant of Works; or whether it be meant of the great Commandments of the New Testament, which are cited, 1 *John* 3. 22, 23. *And whatsoever we ask we receive of him, because*

we keep his Commandments, and do those things that are pleasing in his sight. But what do you mean *John*? do you mean the Covenant of the Law, or the Covenant of the Gospel? Why, *This is his Commandment* (saith he) *that we should believe on the name of his Son Jesus Christ, and to love one another* (as the fruits of this faith), 5 as he gave us Commandment. If it be the old Covenant, as a Covenant of Works, then the Gospel is but a lost thing. If it were of Works, then no more of Grace; therefore it is not the old Covenant, as the old Covenant.

Quest. But what do you mean by these words, the old Cove- 10 nant, as the old Covenant? explain your meaning.

Answ. My meaning is, that the Law is not to be looked upon for life, so as it was handed out from Mount *Sinai*, if ever thou wouldest indeed be saved; though after thou hast faith in Christ, thou mayest and must solace thy self in it, and take 15 pleasure therein, to express thy love to him, who hath already saved thee by his own blood, without thy obedience to the Law, either from *Sinai*, or elsewhere.

Quest. Do you think that I do mean that my righteousness will save me, without Christs? If so, you mistake me, for I 20 think not so: but this I say, I will labour to do what I can, and what I cannot do Christ will do for me.

Answ. Ah poor soul, this is the wrong way too, for this is to make Christ but a piece of a Saviour; thou wilt do something, and Christ shall do the rest, thou wilt set thy own 25 things in the first place, and if thou wantest at last, then thou wilt borrow of Christ, thou art such a one that doest Christ the greatest injury of all. First in that thou doest undervalue his merits, by preferring of thy own works before his. And secondly by mingling of thy works, thy dirty ragged right- 30 eousnesse with his.

Quest. Why, would you have us do nothing? Would you have us make Christ such a drudge as to do all, while we sit idling still?

Answ. Poor soul thou mistakest Jesus Christ, in saying thou 35 makest him a drudge, in letting him do all: I tell thee he

counts it a great glory to do all for thee, and it is a great dishonour unto him, for thee so much as to think otherwise.
And this the Saints of God that have experienced the work of
Grace upon their souls do count it also the same, *Rev. 5. 9.*
5 *Saying, Thou art worthy to take the book, and to open the seals thereof,*
ver. 12. *Worthy is the Lamb that was slain, to receive power, and
riches, and wisdom, and strength, and honour, and glory, and blessing,* And why so? read again the 9. ver. *For thou wast slain and
hast redeemed us to God by thy* (own) *blood.* See also Ephes. 1. 6, 7.
10 *To the praise of the glory of his grace: In whom we have redemption
through his blood.*

Rep. All this we confess that Jesus Christ died for us: but
he that thinks to be saved by Christ, and liveth in his sins,
shall never be saved.

15 *Answ.* I grant that. But this I say again, a man must not
make his good doings the lowest round of the ladder, by
which he goeth to heaven; that is, he that will, and shall go to
heaven, must wholly, and alone, without any of his own
things, venture his precious soul upon Jesus Christ and his
20 merits.

Quest. What, and come to Christ as a sinner?

Answ. Yea, with all thy sins upon thee, even as filthy as ever
thou canst.

Quest. But is not this the way to make Christ to loath us?
25 You know when Children fall down in the dirt, they do
usually before they go home, make their clothes as clean as
they can, for fear their Parents should chide them, and so I
think should we.

Answ. This comparison is wrongly applied, if you bring it to
30 shew us how we must do when we come to Christ. He that
can make himself clean hath no need of Christ; for the whole,
the clean, and righteous have no need of Christ, but those that
are foul and sick. Physicians you know if they love to be
honoured, they will not bid the Patients first make themselves
35 whole, and then come to them: no, but bid them come with
their sores all running on them, as the woman with her
bloody issue, *Mark* 5. And as *Mary Magdalen* with her Belly

full of Devils, and the Lepers all scabbed, and that is the right coming to Jesus Christ.

Reply. Well, I hope that Christ will save me, for his promises and mercy is very large, and as long as he hath promised to give us life, I fear my state the less.   5

Answ. It is very true, Christs promises are very large, blessed be the Lord for ever, and also so is his mercy; but notwithstanding all that, there is many go in at the broad gate; and therefore I say your business is seriously to enquire whether you are under the first or second Covenant; for 10 unless you are under the second, you will never be regarded of the Lord, for as much as you are a sinner, *Heb.* 8. 9. And the rather, because if God should be so good to you as to give you a share in the second, you shall have all your sins pardoned; and for certain have eternal life, though you have 15 been a great sinner.

But do not expect that thou shalt have any part or share in the large promises and mercy of God, for the benefit and comfort of thy poor soul, whilest thou art under the old Covenant, because so long thou art out of Christ, through 20 whom God conveyeth his mercy, grace, and love to sinners. *For all the promises of God in him are yea, and in him, Amen.* Indeed his mercy, grace, and love, is very great, but it's treasured up in him, given forth in him, through him. *But God who is rich in mercy, for his great love wherewith he loved us—that he might shew* 25 *the exceeding riches of his grace*: But which way? *In his kindness towards us through Christ Jesus.* But out of Christ thou shalt finde God, a just God, a sin revenging God, a God that will by no means spare the guilty; and be sure, that every one that is found out of Jesus Christ, will be found guilty in the 30 judgement day, upon whom the wrath of God shall smoke to their eternal ruine.

Now therefore consider of it, and take the counsel of the Apostle in 2 *Cor.* 13. 5. Which is to *examine thy self whether thou art in the faith*, and to prove thy own self, whether thou hast 35 received the Spirit of Christ into thy soul, whether thou hast been converted, whether thou hast been born again, and

made a new creature, whether thou hast had thy sins washed
away in the blood of Christ, whether thou hast been brought
from under the old Covenant into the new; and do not make a
slight examination, for thou hast a precious soul, either to be
5 saved or damned.

And that thou mayest not be deceived, consider that it is
one thing to be convinced, and another to be converted; one
thing to be wounded, and another to be killed; and so to be
made alive again by the faith of Jesus Christ. When men are
10 killed they are killed to all things they lived to before, both
sin and righteousness, as all their old faith, and supposed grace
that they thought they had. Indeed the old Covenant will
shew thee that thou art a sinner, and that a great one too; but
the old Covenant, the Law, will not shew thee without the
15 help of the spirit that thou art without all grace by nature:
no, but in the midst of thy troubles thou wilt keep thy self
from coming to Christ, by perswading thy soul, that thou
art come already, and hast some grace already. O therefore
be earnest in begging the spirit, that thy soul may be en-
20 lightned, and the wickedness of thy heart discovered, that
thou mayest see the miserable state that thou art in, by reason
of sin and unbelief, which is the great condemning sin:
and so in a sight and sense of thy sad condition (if God should
deal with thee in severity according to thy deservings) do
25 thou cry to God for faith in a Crucified Christ, that thou
mayest have all thy sins washed away in his blood, and such
a right work of Grace wrought in thy soul, that may stand in
the judgement-day.

Again secondly, in the next place, you know I told you The second
30 that a man might go a great way in a profession, and have use.
many excellent gifts, so as to do many wonderous works,
and yet be but under the Law; from hence you may learn, not
to judge your selves to be the children of God, because you 1 Cor. 1.
may have some gifts of knowledge or understanding more
35 then others: no, for thou mayest be the knowingest man in all
the Countrey, as to head-knowledge, and yet be but under

29 marg. The second use.] om. 1685   33 marg. 1.] 13. 1659

the Law, and so consequently under the curse, notwithstanding that.

Now seeing it is so, that men may have all this and yet perish; then what will become of those that do no good at all, and have no understanding, neither of their own sadness, nor 5 of Christs mercy. O sad! Read with understanding, *Isa.* 27. 11. *Therefore he that made them will have no mercy on them, and he that formed them, will shew them no favour.* See also 2 Thes. 1. 8, 9.

Now there is one thing, which for want of most people do 10 miscarry in a very sad manner; and that is because they are not able to distinguish between the nature of the Law, and the Gospel. O people, people, your being blinded here, as to the knowledge of this, is one great cause of the ruining of many: As *Paul* saith; *While Moses is read,* or while the Law is 15 *The Use.* discovered, *the vail is over their hearts,* 2 Cor. 3. 15. that is, the vail of ignorance is still upon their hearts, so that they cannot discerne either the nature of the Law, or the nature of the Gospel, they being so dark and blinde in their mindes, as you may see, if you compare it with Chap. 4. 3, 4. And truly I 20 am confident, that were you but well examined, I doubt many of you would be found so ignorant, that you would not be able to give a word of right answer concerning either the Law, or the Gospel. Nay my friends, set the case one should ask you what time you spend, what pains you take, to the 25 end you may understand the nature and difference of these two Covenants; would you not say (if you should speak the truth) that you did not so much as regard whether there was two or more? Would you not say, I did not think of Covenants or studdy the nature of them? I thought that if I had lived 30 honestly, and did as well as I could, that God would accept of me, and have mercy upon me, as he had on others. Ah friends, this is the cause of the ruine of thousands, for if they are *The Use.* blinded to this, both the right use of the Law, and also of the Gospel, is hid from their eyes; and so for certain they will be 35 in danger of perishing most miserably (poor souls that they

16 marg. *The Use.*] *om. 1685*   34 marg. *The Use.*] *om. 1685*

are), unless God of his meer mercy and love doth rend the vail from off their hearts; the vail of ignorance, for that is it which doth keep these poor souls in this besotted, and blinde-folded condition, in which if they dye, they may be lamented
5 for, but not helped; they may be pittied, but not preserved from the stroak of Gods everlasting vengeance.

In the next place, if you would indeed be delivered from the first into the second Covenant, I do admonish you to the observing of these following particulars.

10 First, have a care that you do not content your selves, though you do good works (that is, which in themselves are good) in, and with a Legal spirit, which are done these wayes as followeth.

First, if you do any thing commanded in Scripture, and in *Here I spoil*
15 your doing of it, do think that God is well pleased therewith, *a natural man.* because you, as you are religious men do do the same: upon this mistake was *Paul* himself in danger of being de- *The Use.* stroyed; for he thought because he was zealous, and one of the strictest sect for Religion, therefore God would have been
20 good unto him, and have accepted his doings, as it is clear, for he counted them his *gain*, *Philippians* 3. 4, 5, 6, 7, 8.

Now this is done thus. When a man doth think, that because he thinks he is more sincere, more liberal, with more difficulty, or to the weakning of his estate; I say, if a man
25 because of this, doth think that God accepteth his labour, it is done from an old Covenant Spirit.

Again, some men they think that they shall be heard, because they have prayer in their families, because they can pray long, and speak excellent expressions, or express them-
30 selves excellently in prayer, that because they have great enlargements in prayer: I say, that therefore to think that God doth delight in their doings, and accept their works, this is from a Legal spirit.

Again, some men think, that because their parents have *The Use.*
35 been religious before them, and have been indeed the people

14 marg. Here I . . . natural man.] *om. 1685*   17 marg. *The Use.*] *om.*
1685   34 marg. *The Use.*] *om. 1685*

of God, they think if they also do as to the outward observing
of that which they learned from their forerunners, that therefore God doth accept them: but this also is from a wrong
spirit; and yet how many are there in *England* at this day, that
think the better of themselves, meerly upon that account, I, 5
and think the people of God ought to think so too; not understanding that it is ordinary, for an *Eli* to have an *Hopni* and
a *Phinehas*, both sons of *Belial*: Also a good *Samuel* to have
a perverse off-spring; likewise *David* an *Absalom*. I say, their
being ignorant of, or else negligent in regarding this, they 10
do think that because they do spring from such and such, as
the Jews in their generations did, that therefore they have
a priviledge with God more then others, when there is no
such thing: but for certain, if the same faith be not in them,
which was in their forerunners, to lay hold of the Christ of 15
God, in the same spirit as they did, they must utterly perish,
for all their high conceits that they have of themselves.

Secondly, When people come into the presence of God,
without having their eye upon their Divine Majesty, through
the flesh and blood of the Son of *Mary*, the Son of God; then 20
also do they come before God, and do whatsoever they do
from a Legal Spirit, an old Covenant Spirit. As for instance,
you have some people, 'tis true, they will go to prayer (in
appearance very fervently) and will plead very hard with
God, that he would grant them their desires, pleading their 25
want, and the abundance thereof; they will also plead with
God his great mercy, and also his free promises: but yet they
neglecting the aforesaid body, or person of Christ, the
righteous Lamb of God to appear before him in: I say, in
thus doing, they do not appear before the Lord, no other- 30
wayes then in an old Covenant Spirit; for they go to God
onely as a mercifull Creator, and they themselves as his
Creatures: not as he is their Father in the Son, and they
his children by regeneration through the Lord Jesus. I,
and though they may call God their Father in the Notion 35
(not knowing what they say, onely having learned such

Marginal notes:
John 8. 33, 34, 35. Mat. 3. 7, 8, 9.

The Use.

things by tradition) as the Pharisees did; yet Christ will have
his time to say to them, even to their faces, as he did once to *The Use.*
the Jews, Your father (for all this your profession) is the devil,
to their own grief, and everlasting misery, *John* 8. 44.

5　　The third thing that is to be observed, if we would not be
under the Law, or do things in a Legal Spirit is this: to have a
care that we do none of the works of the holy Law of God, for
life, or acceptance with him; no, nor of the Gospel neither.
To do the works of the Law, to the end we may be accepted
10 of God, or that we may please him, and to have our desires of
him, is to do things from a Legal or old Covenant-Spirit, and
that is expresly laid down, where it is said, *To him that worketh,*
is the reward not reckoned of grace, but of debt; that is, he appears
before God through the Law, and his obedience to it (*Rom.*
15 4. 4, 5.). And again though they be in themselves Gospel
ordinances, as baptisme, breaking of bread, hearing, praying,
meditating, or the like: yet I say if they be not done in a right
spirit, they are thereby used as a hand by the devil, to pull
thee under the Covenant of Works; as in former times he
20 used circumcision, which was no part of the Covenant of *The Use.*
Works, the ten Commands, but a seal of the righteousness of
Faith: yet I say, they being done in a Legal Spirit, the soul Rom. 4.
was thereby brought under the Covenant of Works, and so
most miserably destroyed unawares to it self, and that be-
25 cause there was not a right understanding of the nature and
terms of the said Covenants. And so it is now. Souls being
ignorant of the nature of the old Covenant, do even by their
subjecting to several Gospel ordinances, run themselves under
the old Covenant, and fly off from Christ, even when they
30 think they are a coming closer to him: (O miserable!) If you
would know when or how this is done, whether in one particular or more, I shall shew you as followeth.

　　1. That man doth bring himself under the Covenant of
Works, by Gospel Ordinances, when he cannot be perswaded
35 that God will have mercy upon him, except he do yield

obedience to such or such a particular thing commanded in the word: this is the very same spirit that was in the false brethren *The Use.* spoken of (*Acts* 15. *Gal.* the whole Epistle), whose judgement was, that unless such and such things were done *they could not be saved.* As now adayes we have also some that say, unless your infants be baptized, they cannot be saved; and others say, unless you be rightly baptized, you have no ground to be assured that you are believers, or members of Churches; which is so far off from being so good as a Legal Spirit, that it is the spirit of Blasphemy; as is evident, because they do reckon that the Spirit, Righteousness, and Faith of Jesus, and the confession thereof, is not sufficient to declare men to be members of the Lord Jesus; when on the other side, though they be rank hypocrites, yet if they do yield an outward subjection to this or that, they are counted presently com-municable members; which doth clearly discover, that there is not so much honour given to the putting on the righteousness of the Son of God, as there is given to that which a man may do, and yet go to hell within an hour after; nay, in the very doing of it, doth shut himself for ever from Jesus Christ.

2. Men may do things from a Legal, or Old Covenant-*The Use.* Spirit, when they content themselves with their doing of such and such a thing; as prayers, reading, hearing, baptisme, breaking of bread, or the like; I say, when they can content themselves with the thing done, and sit down at ease and content, because the thing is done. As for instance, some men they being perswaded, that such and such a thing is their duty, and that unless they do do it, God will not be pleased with them, nor suffer them to be heirs of his kingdome: they from this spirit do rush into, and do the thing, which being done, they are content, as being perswaded, that now they are without doubt in a happy condition, because they have done such things, like unto the Pharisee, who because he had done this and the other thing, said therefore, in a bragging way. *Lord, I thank thee that I am not as this Publicane; for I have*

3 marg. *The Use.*] *om.* 1685   judgement] judgements 1659   4 were] was 1659   22 marg. *The Use.*] *om.* 1685

done thus and thus: when alas the Lord gives him never a good word for his labour, but rather a reproof.

3. That man doth act from a Legal Spirit, who maketh the strictness of his walking, the ground of his assurance for
5 eternal life. Some men all the ground they have to believe that they shall be saved, it is, because they walk not so loose as their neighbours, they are not so bad as others are, and therefore they question not but that they shall do well; now this is a false ground, and a thing that is verily Legal, and
10 savours onely of some slight and shallow apprehensions of the Old Covenant; I call them shallow apprehensions because they are not right and sound, and are such as will do the soul no good, but beguile it, in that the knowledge of the nature of this Covenant doth not appear to the soul, onely
15 some commanding power it hath on the soul, which the soul endeavouring to give up it self unto, it doth find some peace and content, and especially if it finde it self to be pretty will-ing to yield itself to its commands; and is not this the very ground of thy hoping that God will save thee from the wrath
20 to come? If one should ask thee what ground thou hast to think thou shalt be saved: wouldst thou not say? truly be- cause I have left my sins, and because I am more inclinable to do good, and to learn, and get more knowledge, I endeavour to walk in Church-order (as they call it) and therefore I hope
25 God hath done a good work for me, and I hope will save my soul? Alas, alas, this is a very trick of the devil, to make souls build the ground of their salvation upon this their strictness, and abstaining from the wickedness of their former lives, and because they desire to be stricter, and stricter. Now if you
30 would know such a man or woman, you shall finde them in this frame; namely, when they think their hearts are good, then they think also that Christ will have mercy upon them: but when their corruptions work, then they doubt and scruple, untill again they have their hearts more ready to do the
35 things contained in the Law and Ordinances of the Gospel. Again, such men do commonly chear up their hearts, and

6 marg. *The Use.*] *om. 1685*   25 marg. *The Use.*] *om. 1685*

encourage themselves still to hope all shall be well, and that because they are not so bad as the rest, but more inclinable then they, saying, *I am glad I am not as this Publicane, but better then he, more righteous then he*, Luke 18. 11.

4. That is a Legal and Old Covenant-Spirit, that secretly 5 perswades the soul, that if ever it will be saved by Christ, *The Use.* it must first be fitted for Christ, by its getting of a good heart and good intentions to do this and that for Christ: I say, that the soul when it comes to Christ may not be rejected, or turned off, when indeed and in truth, this is the very 10 way for the soul to turn it self from Jesus Christ, instead of turning to him; for such a soul looks upon Christ, rather to be a painted Saviour or a Cipher, then a very, and real Saviour. Friend, if thou canst fit thy self, what need hast thou of Christ? If thou canst get qualifications to carry to Christ, that 15 thou mightest be accepted, thou doest not look to be *accepted in the beloved*. Shall I tell thee? Thou art as if a man should say, I will make my self clean, and then I will go to Christ that he may wash me; or like to a man possessed, that will first cast the devils out of himself, and then come to Christ for 20 cure from him. Thou must therefore, if thou wilt so lay hold of Christ, as not to be rejected by him, I say thou must come to him as the basest in the world, more fitter to be damned, if thou hadst thy right, then to have the least smile, hope, or *The Use.* comfort from him: come with the fire of hell in thy conscience; 25 come with thy heart hard, dead, cold, full of wickedness and madness against thy own salvation; come as renouncing all thy tears, prayers, watchings, fastings; come as a blood-red sinner, do not stay from Christ, till thou hast a greater sense of thy own misery, nor of the reality of Gods mercy; do not 30 stay while thy heart is softer, and thy spirit in a better frame, but go against thy minde, and against the minde of the devil, and sin, throw thy self down at the foot of Christ, with a halter about thy neck, and say, Lord Jesus, hear a sinner, a hard-hearted sinner, a sinner that deserveth to be damned, 35

to be cast to hell; and resolve never to return, or to give over
crying unto him, till thou do finde, that he hath washed thy
conscience from dead works with his blood vertually, and
clothed thee with his own righteousness, and made thee com-
5 pleat in himself, this is the way to come to Christ.

Now a few words to the second Doctrine, and so I shall
draw towards a conclusion, the doctrine doth contain in it
very much comfort to thy soul, who art a new Covenant man,
or one of those who art under the new Covenant.

The use for the second Doctrine.

10   There is first pardon of sin. And secondly, the manifestation of the same. And thirdly, a power to cause thee to per-
severe through faith to the very end of thy life.

There is first pardon of sin which is not in the old Covenant; for in that there is nothing but commands, and if not
15 obeyed, condemned. O but there is pardon of sin, even of all
thy sins, against the first and second Covenant, under which
thou art, and that freely upon the account of Jesus Christ the
righteous, he having in thy name, nature, and in the room of
thy person, fulfilled all the whole Law in himself for thee, and
20 freely giveth it unto thee: O though the Law be a ministration of death and condemnation, yet the Gospel under which
thou art, is the ministration of life and salvation, 2 *Cor.* 3. 6,
7, 8, 9. Though they that live and dye under the first Covenant, God regardeth them not, *Heb.* 8. 9. Yet they that are
25 under the second are as the apple of his eye (*Deut.* 32. 10.
Psal. 17. 8. *Zech.* 2. 8.). Though they that are under the first,
the Law, *Are called to blackness and darkness, and tempest, the
sound of a Trumpet, and a burning Mountain, which sight was so
terrible that Moses said, I exceedingly fear, and quake* (Heb. 12. 18,
30 19, 20, 21.). *Yet you are come unto Mount Sion, to the City of the
living God, to the heavenly Jerusalem, and to an innumerable company of Angels. To the general assembly and Church of the first-
born, whose names are written in heaven, and to God the judge of all,
and to the spirits of just men made perfect. And to Jesus* (to blessed
35 Jesus) *the Mediator of the New Covenant, and to the blood of
sprinkling, which speaketh better things then that of Abel* (Heb.
12. 22, 23, 24.), even forgiveness of sins, *Eph.* 1. 7.

2. The Covenant that thou art under doth allow of repentance, in case thou chance to slip or fall, by sudden temptation (*Rev.* 2. 5.), but the Law allows of none (*Gal.* 3. 10.). The Covenant that thou art under allows thee strength also: But the Law, is onely a sound of words, commanding 5 words, but no power is given by them, to fulfill the things commanded, *Heb.* 12. 19. Thou that art under this second, art made a Son; but they that are under that first, are slaves and Vagabonds, *Gen.* 4. 12. Thou that art under this hast a Mediator, that is to stand between justice and thee, 1 *Tim.* 2. 5. 10 But they under the other, their Mediator is turned an accuser, and speaketh most bitter things against their souls (*John* 5. 45.). Again, the way that thou hast into Paradise, is a new and living way; mark, a living way (*Heb.* 10. 20.). But they that are under the Old Covenant, their way into paradise 15 is a killing and destroying way (*Gen.* 3. 24.). Again, thou hast the righteousness of God to appear before God withall (*Phil.* 3. 9.), but they under the Old Covenant have nothing but the righteousness of the Law, which *Paul* counts dirt and dung (*Phil.* 3. 7, 8.). Thou hast that which will make thee 20 perfect; but the other will not do so, *Heb.* 7. 19. *The Law makes nothing perfect: but the bringing in of a better hope* (which is the Son of God) *did, by which we draw nigh to God.*

3. The New Covenant promiseth thee a new heart (as I said before) (*Ezek.* 36. 26.), but the Old Covenant promiseth 25 none; and a new spirit, but the Old Covenant promiseth none. The New Covenant conveyeth faith (*Gal.* 3.), but the Old one conveyeth none. Through the New Covenant the love of God is conveyed into the heart (*Rom.* 5.), but through the Old Covenant there is conveyed none of it savingly 30 through Jesus Christ. The New Covenant doth not onely give a promise of life, but also with that, the assurance of life; but the Old one giveth none. The Old Covenant wrought wrath in us, and to us (*Rom.* 4. 15.), but the new One worketh love, *Gal.* 5. 6. Thus much for the first use.   35

Secondly, As all these, and many more priviledges, do come to thee through, or by the New Covenant: and that

thou mightest not doubt of the certainty of these glorious
priviledges, God hath so ordered it, that they do all come to
thee by way of purchase being obtained for thee, ready to thy
hand, by that one Man Jesus, who is the Mediator, or the
5 Person that hath principally to do, both with God and thy
Soul, in the things pertaining to this Covenant: so that now
thou mayest look on all the glorious things that are spoken of
in the New Covenant, and say all these must be mine; I must
have a share in them; Christ hath purchased them for me, and
10 given them to me. Now I need not to say, O! but how shall I
come by them? God is holy, I am a sinner; God is just, and I
have offended: no, but thou mayest say, though I am vile
and deserve nothing: yet Christ is holy, and he deserveth
all things; though I have so provoked God by breaking his
15 Law, that he could not in justice look upon me, yet Christ
hath so gloriously paid the debt, that now God can say,
welcome soul, I will give thee grace, I will give thee glory,
thou shalt lie in my bosom, and go no more out; my Son hath
pleased me, he hath satisfied the loud cries of the Law &
20 Justice, that called for speedy vengeance on thee. He hath
fulfilled the whole Law, he hath brought in everlasting right- Dan. 9. 24,
eousness, he hath overcome the devil, he hath washed away 25.
thy sins with his most precious blood, he hath destroyed the
power of death, and triumphs over all the enemies. This he
25 did in his own person, as a common Jesus, for all persons in
their stead, even for so many as shall come in to him; for his 1 Cor. 15.
victory I give to them, his righteousnesse I give to them, his 55, 56, 57.
merits I bestow on them, and look upon them holy, harmless,
undefiled, and for ever comely in my eye, through the victory
30 of the captain of their salvation.

And that thou mayest indeed and in truth, not onely hear
and read this glorious Doctrine, but be found one that hath
the life of it in thy heart, thou must be much in studying of
the two Covenants; the nature of the one and the nature
35 of the other, and the conditions of them that are under them
both. Also thou must be well grounded in the manner of the
victory and merits of Christ, how they are made thine. And

here thou must in the first place believe, *that the Babe that was Born of Mary, lay in a manger at Bethelhem, in the time of Cesar Augustus; that he, that Babe, that Child, was the very Christ.* Secondly, thou must believe that in the dayes of *Tiberias Cesar*, when *Herod* was *Tetrarch* of *Galilee*, and *Pontius Pilate* 5 governour of *Judea*, that in those dayes he was crucified, or hanged on a tree between two Thieves, which by computation, or according to the best account, is above sixteen hundred years since. Thirdly, thou must also believe that when he did hang upon that Cross of Wood, on the Mount *Calvary*, 10 that then he did dye there *for the sins of those that did dye before he was Crucified, also for their sins that was alive at the time of his Crucifying, and also that he did by that one death give satisfaction to God for all those that should be born and believe in him after his death, even unto the worlds end. I 15 say, this thou must believe upon pain of eternal damnation, that by that one death, that when he did dye, he did put an end to the curse of the Law, and sin, and at that time by his death on the Cross, and by his Resurrection out of *Josephs* Sepulchre, he did bring in a sufficient righteousnesse to 20 clothe thee withall compleatly. *For by one offering he hath for ever perfected them that are sanctified, not that he should often offer himself; for then must he often have suffered since the foundation of the world: but now ONCE in the end of the world hath he appeared to put (or do) away sin by the sacrifice of himself.* Namely, when 25 he hanged on the Cross. *For it is by the offering up of the body of* (this blessed) *Jesus Christ ONCE for all.* Indeed, *other priests may offer oftentimes, sacrifices and offerings which can never take away sins; but this man* (this Jesus, this annointed and appointed sacrifice) *when he had offered ONE sacrifice for sins,* 30 *for ever sat down on the right hand of God.*

But because thou in thy pursuit after the faith of the Gospel wilt be sure to meet with devils, hereticks, particular corruptions, as unbelief, ignorance, the spirit of works animated on by suggestions, false conclusions, with damnable 35 doctrines, I shall therefore briefly, besides what hath been

*This is the Doctrine that I will live and dye by, and be willing to be damned if it saves me not. I am not ashamed of the Gospel of Christ, for it is the power of God to salvation; therefore I preach Christ Crucified, to the Jews a stumbling block, and to the Greeks foolishnesse. Rom. 1. 1 Cor. 1. Heb. 10. 14. Heb. 9. 25, 26.

already said, speak a word or two more before I leave
thee, of further advice, especially concerning these two
things.

First, How thou art to conceive of the Saviour.

5   Secondly, How thou art to make application of him.

First, For the Saviour, thou must look upon him to be
very God and very man; not man onely, nor God onely, but
God and man in one person, both natures joyned together,
for the putting of him in a capacity to be a suitable Saviour:
10 suitable I say to answer both sides and parties with whom
he hath to do in the office of his Mediatorship, and being as
a Saviour.

Secondly, Thou must not onely do this, but thou must also
consider and believe, that even what was done by Jesus
15 Christ, *it was not done by one nature without the other: but thou*
must consider that both natures, both the God-head and the man-hood
did gloriously concur and joyn together, in the undertaking of the
salvation of our bodies and souls; not that the God-head undertook any
thing without the man-hood, neither did the man-hood do any thing
20 *without the vertue and union of the God-head; and thou must of neces-*
sity do this, otherwise thou canst not finde any sound ground and
footing for thy soul to rest upon.

For if thou look upon any of these asunder, that is to say,
the God-head without the man-hood, or the man-hood with-
25 out the God-head, thou wilt conclude that what was done by
the God-head, was not done for man, being done without the
man-hood; or else, that that which was done with the man-
hood could not answer Divine Justice, in not doing what it
did, by the vertue and in union with the God-head; for it was
30 the God-head that gave vertue and value to the suffering of
the man-hood, and the man-hood being joyned therewith,
that giveth us an interest into the heavenly glory and comforts of the God-head.

What ground can a man have to believe, that Christ is his
35 Saviour, if he do not believe that he suffered for sin in his
nature? And what ground also can a man have to think that
God the Father is satisfied, being infinite, if he believe not also

that he who gave the satisfaction was equal to him who was offended?

Therefore, Beloved, when you read of the offering of the body of the Son of man for our sins, then consider that he did it in union with, and by the help of the eternal God-head. 5 *How much more shall the blood of Christ, who through the eternall Spirit offered himself without spot to God, purge your consciences from dead works, &c.*

And when thou readest of the glorious works and splendour of the God-head in Christ, then consider that all that was 10 done by the God-head, it was done as it had union and communion with the man-hood. And then thou shalt see that the devil is overcome by God-man, sin, death, hell, the grave, and all overcome by Jesus God-man, and then thou shalt finde them overcome indeed. They must needs be overcome 15 when God doth overcome them; and we have good ground to hope the victory is ours, when in our nature they are overcome.

2. The second thing, is, how to apply, or to make application of this Christ to the soul. And for this there is to be 20 considered the following particulars.

First, That when Jesus Christ did thus appear being Born of *Mary*, he was looked upon by the Father, as if the sin of the whole world was upon him; nay further, God did look upon •2 Cor. 5. him, and account him the sin of man. *He hath made him to be 25 21. sin for us.* That is, God made his Son Jesus Christ our sin, or *reckoned* him to be, not onely a sinner, but the very bulk of sin of the whole world, and condemned him so severely as if he had been nothing but sin. *For what the Law could not do in that it was weak through the flesh, God sent forth his son in the 30 likeness of sinful flesh, and for sin condemned sin in the flesh.* That is, for our sins condemned his Son Jesus Christ: as if he had indeed and in truth been our very sin, and yet altogether without sin, 2 *Cor.* 5. 21. *Rom.* 8. 3. Therefore as to the taking away of thy curse, thou must reckon him to be made sin for thee. 35 And as to his being thy justification, thou must reckon him to be thy righteousnesse: for saith the Scripture, *He* (that is

God) *hath made HIM to be SIN for us, though he knew no sin, that WE might be made the RIGHTEOUSNESSE of God in HIM.*

Secondly, Consider for whose sakes all this glorious design of the Father and the Son was brought to pass, and that you 5 shall finde to be for man, for sinfull man, 2 *Cor.* 8. 9.

Thirdly, The terms on which it is made ours; and that you will finde to be a free gift, meerly arising from the tenderheartednesse of God. *You are justified freely by his grace through the redemption that is in Christ, whom God hath set forth to be a* 10 *propitiation through faith in his blood,* &c.

Fourthly, How men are to reckon it theirs, and that is upon the same terms which God doth offer it, which is freely, as they are worthless and undeserving creatures, as they are without all good, and also unable to do any good. 15 This I say, is the right way of applying the merits of Christ to thy soul, for they are freely given to thee a poor sinner, not for any thing that is in thee, or done by thee: but freely as thou art a sinner, and so standest in absolute need thereof.

And Christian, thou art not in this thing to follow thy 20 sense and feeling: but the very Word of God. The thing that doth do the people of God the greatest injury, it is their too little hearkening to what the Gospel saith, and their too much giving credit to what the Law, Sin, the Devil, and Conscience saith: and upon this very ground to conclude, 25 that because there is the certainty of guilt upon the soul, therefore there is also for certain by sin, damnation to be brought upon the soul. This is now to set the Word of God aside, and to give credit to what is formed by the contrary: but thou must give more credit to one syllable of the written 30 Word of the Gospel, then thou must give to all the Saints and Angels in Heaven and Earth; much more then to the devil and thy own guilty conscience.

Let me give you a parable, there was a certain man that had committed treason against his King; but for as much as 35 the King had compassion upon him, he sent him by the hand of a faithfull messenger, a pardon under his own hand and seal: but in the Countrey where this poor man dwelt, there was also many that sought to trouble him, by often putting of him in minde of his treason, and the Law that was to be executed on the offender. Now which way should this man so honour his King, but as by believing his hand-writing, which was the pardon: certainly he would honour him more 5 by so doing, then to regard all the clamours of his enemies continually against him.

Just thus it is here, thou having committed treason against the King of heaven, he through compassion for Christs sake hath sent thee a pardon: but the Devil, the Law, and thy Con- 10 science do continually seek to disturb thee, by bringing thy sins afresh into thy remembrance: but now wouldest thou
1 John 5. 10, honour thy King, why then, *He that believeth the RECORD that*
11. *God hath given of his Son, hath set to his SEAL that God is true.*
And this is the record, that God hath given to US eternal life, and 15
this life is in his Son. And therefore my Brethren, seeing God our Father hath sent us damnable traitors a pardon from heaven (even all the promises of the Gospel) and also hath sealed to the certainty of it with the heart-blood of his dear Son: let us not be daunted, though our enemies with 20 terrible voices do bring our former life never so often into our remembrance.

Object. But (saith the soul) how if after I have received a pardon I should commit treason again? what should I do then? 25

Answ. Set the case thou hast committed abundance of treason, he hath by him abundance of pardons. *Let the wicked forsake his way, and the unrighteous man his thoughts, and let him return to the Lord, and he will have mercy upon him, and to our God, for he will ABUNDANTLY pardon.* 30

Sometimes I my self have been in such a straight, that I have been (almost) driven to my wits ends with a sight and sense of the greatness of my sins: but calling to minde that God was God in his mercy, pitty, and love, as well as in his holiness, justice, *&c.* And again considering the ability of the 35 satisfaction that was given to Holiness and Justice, to the end there might be way made for sinners to lay hold of this mercy; I say, I considering this when tempted to doubt and despair, I have answered in this manner.

'Lord here is one of the greatest sinners that ever the ground 5 bare. A sinner against the Law, and a sinner against the Gospel. I have sinned against light, and I have sinned against mercy; and now Lord the guilt of them breaks my heart, the devil also he would have me despair, telling of me that thou art so far from hearing my prayers in this my distress, that 10 I cannot anger thee worse, then to call upon thee; for saith he, thou art resolved for ever to damn and not to grant me the least of thy favour: yet Lord I would fain have forgiveness. And thy word though much may be inferred from it against me; yet it saith, *If I come unto thee thou wilt in no wise cast me out.* 15 Lord, shall I honour thee most by believing thou canst pardon my sins, or by believing thou canst not? Shall I honour thee most by believing thou wilt pardon my sins, or by believing thou wilt not? Shall I honour the blood of thy Son also by despairing, that the vertue thereof is not sufficient, or by 20 believing that it is sufficient to purge me from all my blood-red and crimson sins? surely, thou that couldest finde so much mercy as to pardon *Manasseh, Mary Magdalen,* the three thousand murderours, persecuting *Paul,* murderous and adulterous *David,* and blaspheming *Peter,* thou that offeredst 25 mercy to *Simon Magus* a witch, and didst receive the Astro-logers and Conjurers in the nineteenth of *Acts,* thou hast mercy enough for one poor sinner. Lord, set the case my sins were bigger then all these, and I less deserved mercy then any of these: yet thou hast said in thy word, that he that *cometh* 30 *to thee, thou wilt in no wise cast out.'* And God hath given com-fort to my soul, even to such a sinner as I am: and I tell you, there is no way so to honour God, and to beat out the devil as to stick to the truth of Gods Word, and the merits of Christs blood by believing. *When Abraham believed* (even Rom. 4. 35 *against hope and reason) he gave glory to God. And this is our* I John 5. 4. *victory, even our faith. Believe and all things are possible to you. He that believeth shall be saved. He that believeth on the Son hath everlasting life, and shall never perish, neither shall any man pluck them out of my Fathers hand.*

And if thou dost indeed believe this, thou wilt not onely confess him as the Quakers do. That is, that he was born at *Bethlehem* of *Mary*, suffered on Mount *Calvary* under *Pontius* 5 *Pilate*, was Dead and Buried, Rose again, and Ascended, &c. For all this they confess, and in the midst of their confession they do verily deny that his death on that Mount *Calvary* did give satisfaction to God for the sins of the world; and that his Resurrection out of *Josephs* Sepulchre, is the cause of our 10 justification in the sight of God, Angels, and Devills: But I say, if thou doest believe these things indeed, thou doest believe that then, so long ago, even before thou wast born, he did bear thy sins in his own body, which then was Hanged on the Tree (and never before nor since), that thy old man 15 was then Crucified with him, namely, in the same body then Crucified, see 1 *Pet.* 2. 24. and *Rom.* 6. 6. This is non-sense to them that believe not: but if thou do indeed believe thou seest it so plain, and yet such a mystery, that it makes thee wonder.   20

But in the third place, this glorious Doctrine of the New Covenant, and the Mediator thereof, will serve for the comforting, and the maintaining of the comfort of the children of the New Covenant this way also; that is, that he did not onely dye and rise again, but that he did ascend in his own 25 person into heaven, to take possession thereof for *me*, to prepare a place there for *me*, standeth there in the second part of his suretiship to bring *me* safe in *my* coming thither, and to present *me* in a glorious manner, *Without spot or wrinkle or any such thing*; that he is there exercising of his 30 priestly office for *me*, pleading the perfection of his own righteousnesse for *me*, and the vertue of his blood for *me*. That he is there ready to answer the accusations of the Law, Devil, and sin for *me*. Here thou mayest through faith look the very devil in the face, and rejoyce, saying, O Satan! I have a precious 35 Jesus, a soul-comforting Jesus, a sin-pardoning Jesus. Here

2 *hand*] *Hands 1685*

thou mayest hear the biggest thunder-crack that the Law
can give, and yet not be daunted. Here thou mayest say,
O Law! thou mayest roar against sin: but thou canst not
reach *me*, thou mayest curse and condemn: but not *my soul*;
5 for I have a righteous Jesus, a holy Jesus, a soul saving Jesus:
and he hath delivered *me* from thy threats, from thy curses,
from thy condemnations; I am out of thy reach, and out of
thy bounds, I am brought into another Covenant, under
better promises, promises of life and salvation, free promises
10 to comfort *me* without my merit, even through the blood of
Jesus, the satisfaction given to God for *me* by him; therefore
though thou layest my sins to my charge, and sayest thou
wilt prove me guilty; yet so long as Christ is above ground,
and hath brought in everlasting righteousness, and given that
15 to *me*, I shall not fear thy threats, thy charges, thy soul-scaring
denounceations; my Christ is all, hath done all, and will
deliver *me* from all that thou, and whatsoever else can bring
an accusation against me. Thus also thou mayest say when
death assaulteth thee, *O death where is thy sting?* Thou mayest
20 bite indeed, but thou canst not devour; I have comfort by, and
through the one man Jesus, Jesus Christ he hath taken thee
captive, and taken away thy strength, he hath pierced thy
heart, and let out all thy soul-destroying poyson; therefore
though I see *thee*, I am not afraid of *thee*; though I feel *thee*,
25 I am not daunted, thou hast lost thy sting in the side of the
Lord Jesus; through him I overcome *thee*, and set foot upon
thee. Also O Satan! Though I hear thee grumble, and make
a hellish noise, and though thou threaten me very highly:
yet my soul shall triumph over *thee*, so long as Christ is alive,
30 and can be heard in heaven; so long as he hath broken thy
head, and won the field of thee; so long as thou art in prison,
and canst not have thy desire. I therefore, when I hear thy
voice, do pitch my thoughts on Christ my Saviour, and do
hearken what he will say, for he will speak comfort; he saith
35 he hath got the victory, and doth give to me the Crown, and
causeth me to triumph through his most glorious conquest.

12 thou¹] though *1659, 1685*

Nay, my brethren, the Saints under the Levitical Law, who had not the New Covenant sealed, or confirmed any further then by promise that it should be. I say, they when they thought of the glorious priviledges that God had promised should come, though at that time they were not come but seen afar off, how confidently were they perswaded of them, and embraced them, and was so fully satisfied as touching the certainty of them, that they did not stick at the parting* with all for the enjoyning of them. How many times doth *David* in the *Psalms* admire, triumph, and perswade others to do so also, through the faith that he had in the thing that was to be done. Also *Job*, in what faith doth he say he should see his Redeemer, though he had not then shed one drop of blood for him: yet because he had promised so to do; and this was signified* by the blood of bulls and goats. Also *Samuel*, *Isaiah*, *Jeremiah*, *Zechariah*, &c. how gloriously in confidence did they speak of Christ, and his death, bloud, conquest, and everlasting Priesthood, even before he did manifest himself in the flesh which he took of the Virgin. We that have lived since Christ, have more ground to hope then they under the Old Covenant had (though they had the word of the Just God for the ground of their faith). Mark, They had onely the promise that he should and would come; but we have the assured fulfilling of those promises, because he is come: they were told he should spill his blood, but we do see he hath spilt his bloud: They ventured all upon his standing surety for them, but we see he hath fulfilled, and that faithfully too, the office of his suretiship, in that according to the engagement he hath redeemed us poor sinners. They ventured on the New Covenant, though not actually sealed, onely *because they judged him faithfull that had promised*, but we have the Covenant sealed, all things are compleatly done, even as sure as the heart bloud of a crucified Jesus can make it.

There is as great a difference between their dispensation and ours for comfort, even as much as there is between the making of a bond with a promise to seal it, and the sealing

Shall not we then that see all things already done before us, make it a strong argument to increase our faith?
*Heb. 11.

*For they were as so many sure promises with a remembrance in them, also for the better satisfaction of them that believed them.

*Heb. 11. 11.

of the same. It was made indeed in their time, but it was not
sealed until the time the blood was shed on the Mount *Cal-*
vary; and that we might indeed have our faith mount up with
wings like an Eagle, he sheweth us what encouragement, and
5 ground of faith we have to conclude we shall be everlastingly
delivered; saying, *For where a testament* (or Covenant) *is, there*   Heb. 9. 16,
must of necessity be the death of the Testatour; for a testament is   17, 18.
of force after men are dead, otherwise it is of no strength at all
whilest the Testatour liveth; whereupon neither the first testament was
10 *dedicated without blood,* as Christs blood was the confirmation of
the New Covenant, yet it was not sealed in *Abraham, Isaac,* or
Jacobs dayes, to confirm the Covenant that God did tell them
of, and yet they believed; therefore we ought to give the
more earnest heed to (believe) the things that we have heard,
15 and not in any wise to let them be questioned; and the rather
because you see the testament is not onely now made, but confirmed: not onely spoken of, and promised, but verily sealed by
the death and bloud of Jesus, which is the Testatour thereof.

My Brethren, I would not have you ignorant of this one
20 thing, that though the Jews had the promise of a sacrifice,
of an everlasting high Priest that should deliver them, yet
they had but the promise; for Christ was not sacrificed, and
was not then come an high Priest of good things to come,
onely the type, the shadow, the figure, the ceremonies they
25 had, together with Christs engaging as surety to bring all
things to pass that was promised should come, and upon that
account received and saved.

It was with them and their dispensation as this similitude
gives you to understand. 'Set the case that there be two men
30 who make a covenant, that the one should give the other
ten thousand sheep, on condition the other give to him two
thousand pound: but forasmuch as the money is not to be
paid down presently; therefore if he that buyeth the sheep
will have any of them before the day of payment, the creditour
35 requesteth a surety, and upon the engagement of the surety
there is part of the sheep given to the debter, even before the

3 might] might have *1685*   31 to] *om. 1685*

day of payment, but the other at and after.' So it is here, Christ covenanted with his Father for his sheep (*I lay down my life for my sheep*, saith he), but the money was not to be paid down so soon as the bargain was made (as I have already said), yet some of the sheep were saved, even before 5 the money was paid, and that because of the suretiship of Christ: as it is written, *Being justified* (or saved) *freely by his grace, through the redemption* (or purchase) *of Jesus Christ, whom God hath set forth to be a propitiation through faith in his blood to declare himself righteous, in his forgiving the sins that are* 10 *past* (or the sinners who died in the faith, before Christ was crucified), *through Gods forbearing till the payment was paid; to declare, I say, at this time his righteousness, that he might be just, and the justifier of him that believeth in Jesus.*

Rom. 3. 24, 25, 26.

The end of my speaking of this, is to shew you that it is 15 not wisdom now to doubt whether God will save you or no, but to believe, because all things are finished as to our justification: The Covenant not onely made, but also sealed; the debt paid, the prison doors flung off of the hooks, with a proclamation from heaven of deliverance to the prisoners of 20 hope; saying, *Return to the strong hold ye prisoners of hope, even to day do I declare* (saith God) *that I will render unto thee double.* And saith Christ when he was come, *The spirit of the Lord is upon me, because he hath anointed me to preach the Gospel (that is, good tidings to the poor, that their sins shall be pardoned, that their* 25 *souls shall be saved).* He hath sent me to binde up the broken hearted, to preach deliverance to the Captives, and recovering of the sight of the blinde; to set at liberty them that are bruised, and to comfort them that mourne, to preach the acceptable year of the Lord. 30

Zech. 9. 12.

Luke 4. 18, 19.

Therefore here soul thou mayest come to Jesus Christ for any thing thou wantest, as to a common treasure-house, being the principal man for the distributing of the things made mention of in the New Covenant, he having them all in his own custody, by right of purchase: for he hath bought them 35 all, paid for them all. Doest thou want faith? then come for it to

the man Christ Jesus. *Heb.* 12. 2. Doest thou want the Spirit?
then ask it of Jesus? Doest thou want wisdom? Doest thou
want grace of any sort? Doest thou want a new heart? Doest
thou want strength against thy lusts, against the Devils
5 temptations? Doest thou want strength to carry thee thorow
afflictions of body, and afflictions of spirit? Through persecutions wouldest thou willingly hold out, stand to the last,
and be more then a conquerour? then be sure thou meditate
enough on the merits of the bloud of Jesus, how he hath
10 undertaken for thee, that he hath done the work of thy
salvation in thy room, that he is filled of God on purpose to
fill thee, and is willing to communicate whatsoever is in him,
or about him, to thee. Consider this, I say, and triumph in it.

Again, This may inform us of the safe state of the Saints,
15 as touching their perseverance, that they shall stand though
hell rages, though the devil roareth, and all the world en-
deavoureth the ruine of the Saints of God; though some
through ignorance of the vertue of the offering of the body of
Jesus Christ do say a man may be a child of God to day, and a
20 childe of the Devil to morrow, which is gross ignorance; for
what is the bloud of Christ, the death of Christ, the resurrection of Christ of no more vertue then to bring in for us an
uncertain salvation; or must the effectualness of Christs
merits, as touching our perseverance be helped on by the
25 doings of man, surely they that are predestinated, are also Rom. 8. 30.
justified; and they that are justified, they shall be glorified.
Saints, do not doubt of the salvation of your souls, unless you
do intend to undervalue Christs Blood; and do not think but
that he that hath begun the good work of his grace in you Phil. 1. 6.
30 will perfect it, to the second coming of our Lord Jesus.
Should not we as well as *Paul*, say, I am perswaded that
nothing shall separate us from the love of God which is in Rom. 8.
Christ Jesus? O let the Saints know! that unless the devil can
pluck Christ out of heaven, he cannot pull a true believer
35 out of Christ. When I say a true believer, I do mean such
a one as hath the faith of the operation of God in his soul.

Lastly, Is there such mercy as this? such priviledges as these? is there so much ground of comfort? and so much cause to be glad? is there so much store in Christ? and such a ready heart in him to give it to me? hath his bleeding wounds so much in them, as that the fruits thereof should be the sal- 5 vation of my soul? of my sinfull soul? as to save me sinfull, me rebellious, me desperate, me, what then? shall not I now be holy? shall not I now study, strive, and lay out my self for him that hath laid out himself soul and body for me? shall I now love ever a lust or sin? shall I now be ashamed of 10 the cause, wayes, people, or Saints of Jesus Christ? Shall I not now yield my members as instruments of righteousness, seeing my end is everlasting life? Shall Christ think nothing too dear for me? and shall I count any thing too dear for him? shall I grieve him with my foolish carriage? shall I slight his 15 counsel by following of my own will? Thus therefore the Doctrine of the New Covenant doth call for holiness, engage to holiness, and maketh the Children of that Covenant to take pleasure therein. Let no man therefore conclude on this, that the Doctrine of the Gospel is a licentious Doctrine: but if they 20 do, it is because they are fools, and such as have not tasted of the vertue of the Blood of Jesus Christ; neither did they ever feel the nature, and sway that the love of Christ hath in the hearts of his. And thus also you may see that the Doctrine of the Gospel is of great advantage to the people of God, 25 that are already come in, or to them that shall at the consideration hereof be willing to come in to partake of the glorious benefits of this glorious Covenant. But saith the poor soul,

Rom. 6. (margin, beside "now yield my members")

Object.	Alas I doubt this is too good for me. 30
Inquire.	Why so I pray you?
Object.	Alas because I am a sinner.
Reply.	Why, all this is bestowed upon none but sinners, as it is written. *While we were ungodly, Christ died for us*, Rom. 5. 6, 8. *He came into the world to save sinners*, 1 Tim. 1. 14, 15. 35
Object.	O but I am one of the chief of sinners.
Reply.	Why, this is for the chief of sinners (1 *Tim.* 1. 14, 15.).

Christ Jesus came into the world to save sinners, of whom I am chief
(saith *Paul*).

O but my sins are so big, that I cannot conceive how I Object.
should have mercy.

5   Why soul? didst thou ever kill any body? didst thou ever Reply. You
burn any of thy children in the fire to idols? hast thou been that are re-
solved to go
a witch? didst thou ever use enchantments and conjuration? on in your
didst thou ever curse and swear, and deny Christ? And yet if sins, meddle
not with this.
thou hast, there is yet hopes of pardon; yea, such sinners as
10 these have been pardoned, as appears by these and the like
Scriptures, 2 *Chron.* 33. 1, 2, 3, 4, 5, 6, 7, 8, 9. verses compared
with the 12, 13. Again, *Acts* 19. 19, 20. *Acts* 8. 22. compared
with verse 9. *Matth.* 26. 74, 75.

But though I have not sinned such kinde of sins; yet it Object.
15 may be I have sinned as bad.

That cannot likely be; yet though thou hast, still there is Answ.
ground of mercy for thee, for as much as thou art under the
promise, *John* 6. 37.

Alas man, I am afraid that I have sinned the unpardonable Object.
20 sin, and therefore there is no hope for me.

Doest thou know what the unpardonable sin (the sin Answ.
against the holy Ghost) is? and when it is committed?

It is a sin against light. Reply.

That is true: yet every sin against light, is not the sin Answ.
25 against the holy Ghost.

Say you so? Reply.

Yea, and I prove it thus. If every sin against light, had Answ.
been the sin that is unpardonable, then had *David* and *Peter*
and others sinned that sin: but though they did sin against
30 light, yet they did not sin that sin; therefore every sin
against light is not the sin against the holy Ghost, the unpardonable sin.

But the Scripture saith, *If we sin wilfully after we have re-* Object.
ceived the knowledge of the truth, there remaineth no more sacrifice for
35 *sin: but a certain fearful looking for of judgement, and fiery in-*
dignation, which shall devour the adversaries.

Do you know what that wilful sin is? Answ.

Reply.   Why, what is it? Is it not for a man to sin willingly after enlightning?

1 Answ.   Yes, yet doubtless every willing sin is not that; for then *David* had sinned it, when he lay with *Bathsheba*, and *Jonah* when he fled from the presence of the Lord, and *Solomon* also 5 when he had so many Concubines.

2 Answ.   But that sin is a sin that is of another nature, which is this; *For a man after he hath made some profession of salvation to come alone by the blood of Jesus, together with some light and power of the same upon his spirit: I say, for him after this, knowingly, wilfully,* 10 *and despitefully, to trample upon the blood of Christ shed on the Cross, and to count it an unholy thing, or no better then the blood of another man; and rather to venture his soul any other way, then to be saved by this precious blood.* And this must be done I say, after some light (*Heb.* 6. 4, 5.), *Despitefully* (Heb. 10. 29.), *Knowingly* 15 (2 Pet. 2. 21.) *and wilfully* (Heb. 10. 26. compared with ver. 29.) and that not in a hurry and sudden fit, as *Peters* was: but with some time before-hand to pause upon it first, with *Judas,* and also with a continued resolution, never to turn or be converted again. *For it is impossible to renew such again to* 20 *repentance,* they are so resolved, and so desperate, *Heb.* 6. 6.

Quest.   And how sayest thou now? didst thou ever after thou hadst received some blessed light from Christ, wilfully, despitefully, and knowingly, stamp, or trample the blood of the man Christ Jesus under thy feet? and art thou for ever 25 resolved so to do?

Answ.   O no, I would not do that wilfully, despitefully, and knowingly, not for all the world.

Inquire.   But yet I must tell you now you put me in minde of it, surely sometimes I have most horrible blasphemous thoughts 30 in me against God, Christ, and the Spirit: May not these be that sin too?

Answ.   Doest thou delight in them? are they such things as thou takest pleasure in?

Reply.   O no, neither would I do it for a thousand worlds, O 35 methinks they make me sometimes tremble to think of

1 Is it] It is *1659*   21 6. 6.] 6. *1659, 1685*   31 these] those *1685*

them: But how and if I should delight in them before I am
aware?

Beg of God for strength against them, and if at any time Answ.
thou findest thy wicked heart, to give way in the least thereto
5 (for that is likely enough), and though thou finde it may on a
sudden give way to that hell-bred wickedness that is in it:
yet do not despair, for as much as Christ hath said, *All manner*
of sins and blasphemies shall be forgiven to the sons of men. And who-
soever shall speak a word against the Son of man (that is Christ),
10 *as he may do with Peter,* through temptation, yet upon repentance, *it shall be forgiven him.* Mat. 12. 32.

But I thought it might have been committed all on a Object.
sudden, either by some blasphemous thought, or else by
committing some other horrible sin.

15 For certain this sin and the commission of it, doth lie in Answ.
a knowing, wilfull, malicious, or despiteful, together with a
final trampling the bloud of sweet Jesus under foot, *Heb.* 10.

But it seems to be rather a resisting of the Spirit, and the Object.
motions thereof, then this which you say; for first its proper
20 Title is the sin against the Holy Ghost. And again, *They have*
done despite unto the Spirit of Grace. So that it rather seems to be,
I say, that a resisting of the Spirit, and the movings thereof
is that sin.

For certain the sin is committed by them that do as before 1 Answ.
25 I have said, that is, by a finall, knowing, wilful, malicious
trampling under foot the bloud of Christ, which was shed on
Mount *Calvary,* when Jesus was there crucified. And though
it be called the sin against the Spirit, yet (as I said before)
every sin against the Spirit is not that: for if it was, then
30 every sin against the light and convictions of the Spirit would
be unpardonable: but that is an evident untruth for these
reasons. First, because there be those who have sinned against
the movings of the Spirit, and that knowingly too, and yet
did not commit that. As *Jonah,* who when God had expresly
35 by his Spirit bid him go to *Nineveh,* he runs thereupon quite
another way. Secondly, because the very people that have
sinned against the movings of the Spirit, are yet if they do

return received to mercy. Witness also *Jonah*, who though he had sinned against the movings of the Spirit of the Lord, in doing contrary thereunto: *Yet when he called* (as he saith) *to the Lord* (*out of the belly of hell*), *the Lord heard him, and gave him deliverance, and set him again about his work.* (Read the whole 5 story of that Prophet.)

2 Answ   But secondly, I shall shew you that it must needs be wilfully, knowingly, and a malicious rejecting of the man Christ Jesus as the Saviour: That is, counting his bloud, his righteousness, his intercession in his own person (for he that rejects 10 one rejects all) to be of no value, as to salvation. I say, this I shall shew you is the unpardonable sin. And then afterwards in brief shew you why it is called the sin against the Holy Ghost.

First, That man that doth reject, as aforesaid, the bloud, 15 death, righteousness, resurrection, ascension, and intercession of the man Christ, doth reject that sacrifice, that blood, that righteousness, that victory, that rest, that God alone hath appointed for salvation (John 1. 29.). *Behold the Lamb* (or sacrifice) *of God. We have redemption through his* 20 *blood* (Ephes. 1. 7.). *That I may be found in him,* (to wit) in Christs righteousness, with Christs own personal obedience to his Fathers will (*Phil.* 3. 7, 8, 9, 10.). By his resurrection comes justification, *Rom.* 4. 25. His intercession now in his own person in the Heavens, now absent from his Saints, is 25 the cause of the Saints perseverance, 2 *Cor.* 6, 7, 8. also *Rom.* 8. 33, 34, 35, 36, *&c.*

Secondly, They that reject this sacrifice, and the merits of this Christ, which he by himself hath brought in for sinners, hath rejected him through whom alone all the promises 30 of the New Testament, together with all the mercy discovered thereby, doth come unto poor creatures; *For all the promises in him are yea, and in him Amen, unto the glory of God.* 2 Cor. 1. 20. And all spirituall blessings are made over to us through him, *Ephes.* 1. 3, 4. That is through and in this man 35 (which is Christ) we have all our spirituall, heavenly, and eternall mercies.

Thirdly, He that doth knowingly, wilfully, and despitefully reject this man for salvation, doth sin the unpardonable
sin; because there is never another sacrifice to be offered.
There is no more offering for sin; there remaineth no more sacrifice for Heb. 10. 26.
5 *sin* (namely, then the offering of the body of Jesus Christ a Heb. 10. 18.
sacrifice *once for all*, Heb. 10. ver. 10. & 14. compared with
ver. 18. & 26.). No, but they that shall after light, and clear
conviction, reject the first offering of his body for salvation, do
crucifie him the second time, which irrecoverably merits their
10 own damnation: *For it is impossible for those who were once enlightened, and have tasted of the heavenly gift, and were made partakers of the Holy Ghost; and have tasted the good word of God, and
the powers of the world to come: If they shall fall away to renew them
again unto repentance, seeing they crucifie to themselves the Son of God*
15 *afresh, and put him to an open shame. If they fall away to renew them
again unto repentance*: And why so? seeing, saith the Apostle,
they do crucifie to themselves the Son of God afresh, and do
put him to open shame. O then! how miserably hath the
Devil deceived some? In that he hath got them to reject the
20 merits of the first offering of the Body of Christ (which was
for salvation), and got them to trust in a fresh crucifying of
Christ, which unavoidably brings their speedy damnation.

Fourthly, They that do reject this man, as aforesaid, do sin
the unpardonable sin; because in rejecting him, they do make
25 way for the justice of God to break out upon them, and to
handle them as it shall finde them: which will be in the first
place, sinners against the first Covenant, which is the soul-
damning Covenant; and also despising of (even the life, and
glory, and consolations, pardon, grace, and love that is dis-
30 covered in) the second Covenant, forasmuch as they reject
the Mediatour and Priest of the same, which is the man
Jesus. And the man that doth so, I would fain see how his
sins should be pardoned, and his soul saved, seeing the means
(which is the Son of man, the Son of *Mary*, and his merits)
35 is rejected. For saith he, *If you believe not that I am he, you shall,*
mark, *you shall*, do what you can, *you shall*, appear where you

35 he] add. *1685*

can, *you shall*, follow *Moses*, Law, or any holiness whatsoever, *you shall die in your sins*, Joh. 8. 24. So that I say, the sin that is called the unpardonable sin, is a knowing, wilful, & despiteful rejecting of the sacrificing of the Son of man the first time for sin. And now to shew you why it is called the sin against the Holy Ghost, as in these Scriptures, *Mat.* 12. *Heb.* 10. *Mark* 3.

First, Because they sin against the manifest light of the Spirit (as I said before), it is a sin against the light of the Spirit: That is, they have been formerly enlightened into the nature of the Gospel, and the merits of the man Christ, and his bloud, righteousness, intercession, &c. And also professed, and confessed the same, with some life and comfort in, and through the profession of him: yet now against all that light, maliciously, and with despite to all their former profession, turn their backs, and trample upon the same.

Secondly, It is called the sin against the Holy Ghost, because such a person doth (as I may say) lay violent hands on it; one that sets himself in opposition to, and is resolved to resist all the motions that do come in from the Spirit to perswade the contrary. For I do verily believe, that men in this very rejecting of the Son of God, after some knowledge of him, especially at their first resisting and refusing of him, they have certain motions of the Spirit of God to disswade them from so great a soul damning act: but they being filled with an over-powering measure of the spirit of the devil, do do despite unto these convictions and motions, by studying and contriving how they may answer them, and get from under the convincing nature of them; and therefore it is called a doing despite unto the Spirit of Grace, *Heb.* 10. 29. And so,

Thirdly, In that they do reject the beseechings of the Spirit, and all its gentle intreatings of the soul to tarry still in the same doctrine.

Fourthly, In that they do reject the very testimony of the Prophets, and Apostles, with Christ himself: I say, their Testimony through the Spirit; of the power, vertue,

sufficiency, and prevalency, of the Blood, 'Sacrifice, Death, Resurrection, Ascension, and Intercession of the man Christ Jesus, of which the Scriptures are full both in the Old and New Testament, as the Apostle saith, *For all the Prophets from*
5 *Samuel, with them that follow after, have shewed of these dayes.* That is, in which Christ should be a sacrifice for sin, *Acts* 3. 24. compared with ver. 6, 13, 14, 15, 18, 26. Again saith he, *He therefore that despiseth, despiseth not man, but God, who hath also given unto us his holy Spirit*, 1 Thes. 4. 8. That is, he rejecteth or
10 despiseth the very Testimony of the Spirit.

Fifthly, It is called the sin against the holy Ghost, because he that doth reject and disown the Doctrine of salvation by the man Christ Jesus, through believing in him, doth despise, resist, and reject the wisdome of the Spirit; for the wisdom
15 of Gods Spirit did never more appear, then in its finding out a way for sinners to be reconciled to God, by the death of this man; and therefore Christ as he is a sacrifice, is called *the wisdom of God*. And again when it doth reveal the Lord Jesus, it is called *the spirit of wisdom and revelation in the knowledge of him*,
20 Ephes. 1. 17.

Object. But (some may say) the slighting, or rejecting of the Son of man (Jesus of *Nazareth* the Son of *Mary*), cannot be the sin that is unpardonable, as is clear from that Scripture in the twelfth of *Matthew*, where he himself saith, *He that shall*
25 *speak a word against the Son of man, it shall be forgiven him: but he that shall sin against the holy Ghost, it shall not be forgiven him, neither in this world, nor in the world to come*, ver. 32. Now by this it is clear that the sin that is unpardonable is one thing, and the sin against the Son of man another; that sin that is
30 against the Son of man is pardonable: but if that was the sin against the holy Ghost it would not be pardonable; therefore the sin against the Son of man is not the sin against the holy Ghost, the unpardonable sin.

Answ. First, I do know full well that there are several per-
35 sons that have been pardoned, yet have sinned against the son of man; and that have for a time rejected him, as *Paul*. 1 *Tim.* 1. 13, 14. Also the Jews, *Acts* 2. 36, 37. But there was

an ignorant rejecting of him without the enlightning, and taste, and feeling of the power of the things of God made mention of in the sixth of *Hebrews*, the 3, 4, 5, 6. verses.

Secondly, There is, and hath been a higher manner of sinning against the Son of man, which also hath been, and is still pardonable; as in the case of *Peter*, who in a violent temptation, in a mighty hurry upon a sudden denied him, and that after the revelation of the Spirit of God from heaven to him, that he (Jesus) was the Son of God, *Matth.* 16. 16, 17, 18. This also is pardonable, if there be a coming up again to repentance (O rich grace! O wonderful grace! that God should be so full of love to his poor creatures, that though they do sin against the Son of God, either through ignorance, or some sudden violent charge breaking loose from hell upon them): but yet take it for certain that if a man do slight and reject the Son of God, and the Spirit, in that manner as I have before hinted, that is for a man after some great measure of the enlightning by the Spirit of God, and some profession of Jesus Christ, to be the Saviour, and his blood that was shed on the Mount without the Gates of Jerusalem to be the attonement; I say, he that shall after this, knowingly, wilfully, and out of malice and despite, reject, speak against, and trample that Doctrine under foot, resolving for ever so to do: and if he there continue, I will pawn my soul upon it, he hath sinned the unpardonable sin, and shall never be forgiven neither in this world nor in the world to come; or else those Scriptures that testifie the truth of this must be scrabled out, and must be looked upon for meer fables; which are these following. *For if after they have escaped the pollutions of the world, through the knowledge of our Lord and Saviour Jesus Christ* (which is the Son of man, *Matth.* 16. 13.), *and are again intangled therein, and overcome* (which must be by denying this Lord that bought them, 2 *Pet.* 2. 1.); *the latter end is worse with them then the beginning,* 2 Pet. 2. 20. *For it is impossible for those who were once enlightned and have tasted of the heavenly gift.—And have tasted the good word of God, and the powers of the world to come: If they shall fall away* (not onely fall, but fall away; that is, finally, *Heb.* 10. 19.) *it is impossible to renew them again unto repentance*; and the reason is rendred, *seeing they have crucified to themselves the Son of God* (which is the Son of man) *afresh, and put him* 5 *to an open shame*, Heb. 6. 4, 5, 6. Now if you would further know what it is to Crucifie the Son of God afresh: it is this. For to undervalue and trample under foot the merits and vertue of his blood for remission of sins, as is clearly manifested in the tenth of *Hebrews*, the 26, 27, 28. verses, where its said, 10 *For if we sin wilfully after we have received the knowledge of the truth, there remaineth no more sacrifice for sins; But a certain fearful looking for of judgement, and the fiery indignation, which shall devour the adversaries. He that despised Moses Law died without mercy: of how much sorer punishment suppose ye shall he be thought worthy,* 15 *that hath trodden under foot the Son of God* (there is the second Crucifying of Christ which the Quakers think to be saved by), *and hath counted the blood of the Covenant wherewith he was sanctified, an unholy thing.* And then followeth, *And hath done despite unto the Spirit of Grace*, verse the twenty ninth. All that *Paul* 20 had to keep him from this sin, it was his ignorance in persecuting the man, and merits of Jesus Christ, *Acts* 9. But I obtained mercy (saith he) because I did it ignorantly, 1 *Tim.* 1. 13. And *Peter*, though he did deny him knowingly, yet he did it unwillingly, and in a sudden and fearfull temptation, 25 and so by the intercession of Jesus escaped that danger. So I say, they that commit this sin, they do it after light knowingly, wilfully, and despitefully, and in the open view of the whole world, reject the Son of man for being their Lord and Saviour, and in that it is called the sin against the holy Ghost. 30 It is a name most fit for this sin to be called the sin against the holy Ghost for these reasons but now laid down; for this sin is immediately committed against the motions and convictions and light of that holy Spirit of God, that makes it its business to hand forth, and manifest the truth and reality 35 of the merits and vertues of the Lord Jesus the Son of man. And therefore beware Ranters and Quakers, for I am sure you are the nearest that sin by profession (which is indeed the right committing of it) of any persons that I do know at this day under the whole heavens; for as much as you will not venture the salvation of your souls on the blood shed on Mount *Calvary* (*Luke* 23. 33.), out of the side of that man that was offered up in sacrifice for all that did believe, in that his offering up of his body at that time (either before he offered it, or that have, do, or shall believe on it for the time since, together with that time that he offered it) though formerly you did profess that salvation was wrought out that way, by that sacrifice then offered, and also seemed to have some comfort thereby; yea, insomuch that some of you declared the same in the hearing of many, professing your selves to be believers of the same. O therefore! it is sad for you that were once thus enlightned, and have tasted these good things; and yet notwithstanding all your profession, you are now turned from the simplicity that is in Christ to another doctrine which will be to your destruction, if you continue in it; for without blood there is no remission, *Heb.* 9. 22.

Many other reasons might be given, but that I would not be too tedious: yet I would put in this caution, that if there be any souls that be but now willing to venture their salvation upon the merits of a naked Jesus, I do verily for the present believe, they have not sinned that sin; because there is still a promise holds forth it self to such a soul, where Christ saith, *He that comes to me, I will in no wise* (for nothing that he hath done) *cast him out*, *John* 6. 37. That promise is worthy to be written in letters of gold.

Object.   But alas though I should never sin that sin, yet I have other sins enough to damne me?

Answ.   What though thou hadst the sins of a thousand sinners; yet if thou come to Christ he will save thee, *Joh.* 6. 37. see also *Heb.* 7. 25.

Object.   Alas! but how should I come? I doubt I do not come as I should do; my heart is naught, and dead; and alas then how should I come?

Why, bethink thy self of all the sins that ever thou didst Answ. commit, and lay the weight of them all upon thy heart, till thou art down loaden with the same, and come to him in such a case as this, and he will give thee rest for thy soul, *Mat.*
5 11. the three last verses.

And again, if thou wouldest know how thou shouldest come, come as much undervaluing thy self as ever thou canst, saying, Lord, here is a sinner, the basest in all the countrey, if I had my deserts I had been damned in hell fire long ago:
10 Lord, I am not worthy to have the least corner in the King-dom of Heaven: and yet O that thou wouldest have mercy! Come like *Benhadads* servants to the King of *Israel*, with a 1 Kin. 20. rope about thy neck, and fling thy self down at Christs feet, 31, 32. and lie there a while, striving with him by thy prayers, and
15 Ile warrant thee speed, *Mat.* 11. 28, 29, 30. *John* 6. 37.

O! but I am not sanctified.   Object.

He will sanctifie thee, and be made thy sanctification also, Answ. 1 *Cor.* 6. 10, 11. 1. *Cor.* 1. 30.

O! but I cannot pray.   Object.
20 To pray, is not for thee to down on thy knees, and say over Answ. a many Scripture words onely; for that thou mayest do, and yet do nothing but bable: but if thou from a sense of thy baseness canst groan out thy hearts desire before the Lord, he will hear thee, and grant thy desire; for he can tell what is
25 the meaning of the groanings of the Spirit, *Rom.* 8. 26, 27.

O but I am afraid to pray, for fear my prayers should be Object. counted as sin in the sight of the great God.

That is a good sign that thy prayers are more then bare Answ. words, and have some prevalence at the Throne of Grace
30 through Christ Jesus, or else the Devill would never seek to labour to beat thee off from prayer, by undervaluing thy prayers, telling thee they are sin; for the best prayers he will call the worst, and the worst he will call the best, or else how should he be a liar?
35 But I am afraid the day of Grace is past, and if it should be Object. so, what should I do then?

Truly with some men indeed it doth fare thus, that the Answ.

day of grace is at an end before their lives are at an end. Or thus, the day of grace is past before the day of death is come (as Christ saith), *If thou hadst known, even thou, at least in this thy day, the things that belong unto thy peace (that is, the word of grace or reconciliation), but now it is hid from thine eyes*, Luke 19. 41, 42. But for the better satisfying of thee, as touching this thing, consider these following things.

First, doth the Lord knock still at the door of thy heart by his word and Spirit? If so, then the day of grace is not past with thy soul; for where he doth so knock, there he doth also proffer, and promise to come in and sup (that is, to communicate of his things unto them), which he would not do was the day of grace past with the soul, *Rev.* 3. 20.

But how should I know whether Christ do so knock at my heart, as to be desirous to come in? That I may know also whether the day of grace be past with me or no?

Consider these things.

First, doth the Lord make thee sensible of thy miserable state, without an interest in Jesus Christ? and that naturally thou hast no share in him, no faith in him, no communion with him, no delight in him, or love in the least to him? If he hath, and is doing of this, he hath, and is knocking at thy heart.

Secondly doth he together with this, put into thy heart an earnest desire after communion with him, together with holy resolutions not to be satisfied without reall communion with him?

Thirdly, doth he sometimes give thee some secret perswasions (though not scarcely discernable) that thou maiest attain, and get an interest in him?

Fourthly, doth he now and then glance in some of the promises into thy heart, causing them to leave some heavenly savour (though but for a very short time) on thy spirit?

Fifthly, doest thou at some time see some little excellency in Christ? and doth all this stir up in thy heart some breathings after him? If so, then fear not, the day of grace is not past with thy poor soul; for if the day of grace should be past

with such a soul as this, then that Scripture must be broken,
where Christ saith, *He that cometh unto me, I will in no wise*
(for no thing, by no means, upon no terms whatsoever)
cast out, John 6. 37.

5   But surely if the day of grace was not past with me, I Object.
should not be so long without an answer of Gods love to my
soul; that therefore doth make me mistrust my state the more,
is that I wait and wait, and yet am not delivered.

Hast thou waited on the Lord so long as the Lord hath Answ.
10 waited on thee? it may be the Lord hath waited on thee this
twenty or thirty, yea forty years, or more, and thou hast not
waited on him seven years; cast this into thy minde therefore
when Satan tells thee, that God doth not love thee, because
thou hast waited so long without an assurance (for it is his
15 temptation); for God did wait longer upon thee, and was fain
to send to thee by his Ambassadours, time after time: And
therefore say thou, *I will wait to see what the Lord will say unto
me*; and the rather because, *he will speak peace*, for he is the Lord
thereof.

20   But secondly, Know that it is not thy being under trouble
a long time, that will be an argument sufficient to prove that
thou art past hopes, Nay contrariwise; for Jesus Christ did
take our nature upon him, and also did undertake deliverance
for those, and bring it in for them *who were all their LIFE TIME*
25 *subject to bondage*, Heb. 2. 14, 15.

But alas I am not able to wait, all my strength is gone, Object.
I have waited so long I can wait no longer.

It may be thou hast concluded on this long ago, thinking Answ.
thou shouldest not be able to hold out any longer; no not
30 a year, a month, or a week, nay, it may be not so long. It
may be in the morning thou hast thought thou shouldest not
hold out till night, and at night till morning again: yet the
Lord hath supported thee, and kept thee in waiting upon him
many weeks, and years; therefore that is but the temptation
35 of the Devil to make thee think so, that he might drive thee
to despair of Gods mercy, and so to leave off following the
wayes of God, and to close in with thy sins again. O therefore

do not give way unto it: but believe that thou shalt *see the goodness of the Lord in the land of the living. Wait on the Lord, be of good courage, and he shall strengthen thine heart; wait, I say, on the Lord,* Psal. 27. 13, 14. And that thou mayest so do, consider these things.   5

First, If thou, after thou hast waited thus long, shouldest now give over, and wait no longer, thou wouldest lose all thy time and pains that thou hast taken in the way of God hitherto, and wilt be like to a man that because he sought long for Gold, and did not finde it; therefore turned back from seeking 10 after it, though he was hard by it, and had almost found it: and all because he was loath to look and seek a little further.

Secondly, Thou wilt not onely lose thy time, but also lose thy own soul; for salvation is no where else but in Jesus Christ, *Acts* 4. 12.   15

Thirdly, Thou wilt sin the highest sin that ever thou didst sin before, in drawing (finally) back, insomuch, that God may say, my soul shall have no pleasure in him, *Heb.* 10. 38.

But secondly, consider, thou sayest all my strength is gone, and therefore how should I wait? why at that time when thou 20 feelest, and findeth thy strength quite gone, even that is the time when the Lord will renew, and give thee fresh strength. *The youths shall faint and be weary, and the young men shall utterly fall: but they that wait upon the Lord, shall renew their strength, they shall mount up with wings as eagles, they shall run and not be 25 weary, they shall walk and not be faint,* Isa. 40. 30, 31.

Object.   But though I do wait, yet if I be not elected to eternal life, what good will all my waiting do me? *For it is not in him that willeth, nor in him that runneth, but of God that sheweth mercy.* Therefore I say, if I should not be elected, all is in vain.   30

1 Answ.   Why, in the first place, to be sure thy backsliding from God will not prove thy election, neither thy growing weary of waiting upon God.

2 Answ.   But secondly, Thou art it may be troubled to know whether thou art elected: And sayest thou; if I did but know that, that 35 would encourage me in my waiting on God. *Answ.* I believe

4 27. 13, 14.] 27. 23, 24. *1659, 1685*   28 waiting] waiting to *1659*

thee; but mark, thou shalt not know thy election in the firs
place, but in the second. That is to say, thou must first ge
acquaintance with God in Christ, which doth come by thy
giving credit to his promises, and records which he hath
5 given of Jesus Christ, his blood and righteousness, together
with the rest of his merits.

That is, before thou canst know whether thou art elected,
thou must believe in Jesus Christ so really, that thy faith
laying hold of, and drinking and eating the flesh and blood of
10 Christ, even so, that there shall be life begotten in thy soul
by the same. Life from the condemnings of the Law, Life from
the guilt of sin. Life over the filth of the same. Life also to
walk with God in his Son and wayes; the life of love to God
the Father, and Jesus Christ his Son, Saints, and wayes; and
15 that because they are holy, harmless, and such that are
altogether contrary to iniquity.

For these things must be in thy soul as a forerunner of thy
being made acquainted with the other. God hath these two
wayes to shew to his children their election.

20   First by Testimony of the Spirit. That is, the soul being
under trouble of Conscience, and grieved for sin, the Spirit
doth seal up the soul by its comfortable testimony; perswading of the soul, that God for Christs sake hath forgiven all
those sins, that lie so heavy on the conscience, and that do so
25 much perplex the soul, by shewing it that that Law which
doth utter such horrible curses against it, is by Christs blood
satisfied, and fulfilled, *Eph.* 1. 13, 14.

Secondly, By consequence; that is, the soul finding that
God hath been good unto it, in that he hath shewed it its
30 lost state, and miserable condition: and also that he hath
given it some comfortable hope that he will save it from the
same: I say, the soul from a right sight thereof, doth, or may,
draw this conclusion, that if God had not been minded to
have saved it, he would not have done for it such things as
35 these. But for the more surer dealing with thy soul, it is
not good to take any of these apart; that is, it is not good to

take the testimony of the Spirit (as thou supposest thou hast), from the fruits thereof, so as to conclude the testimony thou hast received, to be a sufficient ground without the other; (not that it is not, if it be the Testimony of the Spirit) but because the Devil doth also deceive souls by the workings 5 of his spirit in them, pretending that it is the Spirit of God. And again, thou shouldest not satisfie thy self, though thou do finde some seekings in thee after that which is good, without the testimony of the other, that is to say, of the spirit; for it is the testimony of two, that is to be taken for 10 truth: Therefore say I, as thou shouldest be much in praying for the Spirit to testifie assurance to thee, so also thou shouldest look to the end of it when thou thinkest thou hast it; which is this, to shew thee that it is alone for Christs sake, that thy sins are forgiven thee, and also thereby a constrain- 15 ing of thee to advance him, both by words, and works, in holiness and righteousness all the dayes of thy life. From hence thou mayest boldly conclude thy election, 1 *Thes.* *3, 4, 5, 6. Remembring without ceasing your work of faith, and labour of love, and patience of hope in our Lord Jesus Christ, in the* 20 *sight of God our Father: Knowing, brethren* (saith the Apostle) *beloved, your election of God.* But how? why by this, *For our Gospel came not to you in word onely, but also in power, and in the Holy Ghost, and in much assurance.—And ye became followers of us, and of the Lord, having received the word in much affliction, with* 25 *joy of the Holy Ghost: So that you were ensamples to all that believe in Macedonia and Achaia. And to wait for his Son from heaven, whom he raised from the dead, even Jesus which* (hath) *delivered us from the wrath to come,* ver. 10.

Object.　But alas for my part, instead of finding in me any thing 30 that is good, I finde in me all manner of wickedness, hardheartedness, hypocrisie, coldness of affection to Christ, very great unbelief, together with every thing that is base, and of an ill savour. What hope therefore can I have?

Answ.　If thou wast not such a one, thou hadst no need of mercy. 35 If thou wast whole, thou hadst no need of the Physician;

30 in] *om. 1659*

doest thou therefore see thy self in such a sad condition as this? Thou hast the more need to come to Christ, that thou mayest be not onely cleansed from these evils: but also that thou mayest be delivered from that wrath they will bring
5 upon thee (if thou do not get rid of them) to all eternity.

But how should I do? and what course should I take to be *Quest.* delivered from this sad and troublesome condition?

Doest thou see in thee all manner of wickedness? The best *Answ.* way that I can direct a soul in such a case, is to pitch a sted-
10 fast eye on him that is full, and to look so stedfastly upon him by faith, that thereby thou mayest even draw down of his fulness into thy heart; for that is the right way, and the way that was typed out (before Christ came in the flesh) in the time of *Moses*, when the Lord said unto him, *Make thee a*
15 *serpent of brass* (which was a type of Christ) *and set it upon a pole; and it shall come to pass that when a serpent hath bitten any man, that he may look thereon and live*, Numb. 21. 8.

Even so now in Gospel times, when any soul is bitten with the fiery serpents (their sins) that then the next way to be
20 healed, is for the soul to look upon the Son of man, who, as the serpent was, was hanged on a pole (or tree) that whosoever shall indeed look on him by faith, may be healed of all their distempers whatsoever, *John* 3. 14, 15.

As now to instance in some things. First, is thy heart
25 hard? why then, behold how full of bowels and compassion is the heart of Christ towards thee, which may be seen in his coming down from heaven to spill his heart blood for thee.

2. Is thy heart slothful and idle? then see how active the Lord Jesus is for thee, in that he did not onely die for thee:
30 but also in that he hath been ever since his ascension into heaven, making intercession for thee, *Heb.* 7. 25.

3. Doest thou see and finde in thee iniquity and un-righteousness? Then look up to heaven and see there a righteous person, even thy righteous Jesus Christ, now pre-
35 senting thee in his own perfections before the Throne of his Fathers Glory, 1 *Cor.* 1. 30.

4. Doest thou see that thou art very much void of right

sanctification? then look up and thou shalt see that thy sanctification is in the presence of God a compleat sanctification, representing all the Saints as (righteous, so) sanctified ones in the presence of the great God of heaven. And so whatever thou wantest, be sure to strive to pitch thy faith upon the Son of God, and behold him stedfastly, and thou shalt by so doing finde a mighty change in thy soul. *For when we behold him, as in a glass, even the glory of the Lord, we are changed* (namely by beholding) *from glory to glory, even as by the Spirit of the Lord,* 2 Cor. 3. 18. This is the true way to get both comfort to thy soul, and also sanctification, and right holiness into thy soul.

Poor souls that are under the distemper of a guilty conscience, and under the workings of much corruption, do not go the nearest way to heaven, if they do not in the first place look upon themselves as cursed sinners by the Law; and yet at that time they are blessed, for ever blessed Saints by the merits of Jesus Christ. *O wretched man that I am,* saith *Paul,* and yet O blessed man that I am through my Lord Jesus Christ: for that is the scope of the Scripture, *Rom.* 7. 24, 25.

Object.   But alas I am blinde and cannot see, what shall I do now?

Answ.   Why truly thou must go to him that can make the eyes that are blinde to see (even to our Lord Jesus) by prayer, saying as the poor blinde man did, *Lord that I might receive my sight,* and so continue begging with him, till thou do receive sight, even a sight of Jesus Christ, his death, blood, resurrection, ascension, intercession, and that for thee, even for thee.

Rev. 3. 18.   And the rather, because first he hath invited thee to come and buy such eye-salve of him that may make thee see. Secondly, because thou shalt never have any true comfort till thou doest thus come to see, and behold the Lamb of

John 1. 29. God that hath taken away thy sins. Thirdly, because that thereby thou wilt be able (through grace) to step over, and turn aside from the severall stumbling-blocks that Satan, together with his instruments, hath laid in our way, which

otherwise thou wilt not be able to shun, but wilt certainly
fall when others stand, and groap and stumble, when others
go upright, to the great prejudice of thy poor soul.

But alas I have nothing to carry with me, how then should Object.
5 I go?

Hast thou no sins? If thou hast, carry them, and exchange Answ.
them for his righteousness; because he hath said, *Cast thy* Psal. 55. 22.
burthen upon the Lord, and he will sustein thee; and again, because
he hath said, Though thou be heavy laden, yet if thou do but
10 come to him he will give thee rest, *Mat.* 11. 28.

But (you will say) Satan telleth me that I am so cold in Object.
prayers, so weak in believing, so great a sinner, that I do go
so slothfully on in the way of God, that I am so apt to slip at
every temptation, and to be entangled therewith, together
15 with other things, so that I shall never be able to attain those
blessed things that are held forth to sinners by Jesus Christ:
and therefore my trouble is much upon this account also,
and many times I fear that will come upon me which Satan
suggesteth to me; that is, I shall miss of eternall life.

20 As to the latter part of the Objection, that thou shalt 1 Answ.
never attain to everlasting life. That is obtained for thee
already, without thy doing, either thy praying, striving, or
wrestling against sin. If we speak properly, it is Christ that
hath in his own body abolished death on the Cross, and
25 brought light, life, and glory to us, through this his thus
doing. But this is the thing that thou aimest at, that thou
shalt never have a share in this life already obtained for so
many as do come by faith to Jesus Christ: and all because thou
art so slothful, so cold, so weak, so great a sinner, so subject
30 to slip and commit infirmities.

I answer, Didst thou never learn for to out-shoot the Devil 2 Answ.
in his own bow, and to cut off his head with his own sword,
as *David* served *Goliah* who was a Type of him.

O how should a poor soul do this? this is rare indeed.   Quest.

35 Why truly thus, Doth Satan tell thee thou prayest but Answ.
faintly, and with very cold devotion; answer him thus, and

say, I am glad you told me, for this will make me trust the more to Christs prayers, and the less to my own; also I will endeavour hence forward to groan, to sigh, and to be so fervent in my crying at the Throne of Grace, that I will, if I can, make the heavens rattle again, with the mighty groans 5 thereof. And whereas thou sayest that I am so weak in believing, I am glad you minde me of it, I hope it will hence forward stir me up to cry the more heartily to God for strong faith, and make me the more restless till I have it. And seeing thou tellest me that I run so softly, and that I shall go near to 10 miss of glory; this also shall be through grace to my advantage, and cause me to press the more earnestly towards the mark, for the price of the high calling of God in Christ Jesus. And seeing thou doest tell me that my sins are wonderous great; hereby thou bringest the remembrance of the 15 unsupportable vengeance of God into my minde, if I die out of Jesus Christ, and also the necessity of the bloud, death, and merits of Christ to help me; I hope it will make me flye the faster, and presse the harder after an interest in him; and the rather because (as thou tellest me) my state will be unspeak- 20 able miserable without him. And so all along, if he tell thee of thy deadness, dulness, coldness, or unbelief, or the greatness of thy sins; answer him, and say, I am glad you told me, I hope it will be a means to make me run faster, seek earnestlier, and to be the more restless after Jesus Christ. If thou 25 didst but get this art, as to out-run him in his own shoes (as I may say), and to make his own darts to pierce himself, then thou mightest also say, now doth Satans temptations as well as all other things work together for my good, for my advantage, *Rom.* 8. 28.   30

Object.   But I do finde so many weaknesses in every duty that I do perform, as when I pray, when I read, when I hear, or any other duty, that it maketh me out of conceit with my self, it maketh me think that my duties are nothing worth.

Answ.   I answer, It may be it is thy mercy that thou art sensible 35 of infirmities in thy best things thou doest, I, a greater mercy then thou art aware of.

Can it be a mercy for me to be troubled with my corrup- tions? Can it be a priviledge for me to be anoyed with in- firmities, and to have my best duties infected with it? How can it possibly be?

5 Verily thy sins appearing in thy best duties, do work for thy advantage these wayes. First, in that thou findest ground enough thereby to make thee humble; and when thou hast done all, yet to count thy self but an unprofitable Servant. And secondly, thou by this means art taken off from leaning 10 on any thing below a naked Jesus for eternall life. It is like if thou wast not sensible of many by-thoughts and wicked- nesses in thy best performances, thou wouldest go near to be some proud abominable Hypocrite, or a silly proud dis- sembling wretch at the best, such a one as would send thy 15 soul to the devil in a bundle of thy own righteousness: but now thou, through grace, seest that all and every thing thou doest, there is sin enough in it to condemn thee. This in the first place makes thee have a care of trusting in thy own doings. And secondly, sheweth thee that there is nothing in 20 thy self which will do thee any good, by working in thee, as to the meritorious cause of thy salvation: No, but thou must have a share in the birth of Jesus, in the death of Jesus, in the blood, resurrection, ascension, and intercession of a crucified Jesus. And how sayest thou? doth not thy finding of 25 this in thee, cause thee to flie from a depending on thy own doings? And doth it not also make thee the more earnestly to groan after the Lord Jesus? Yea, and let me tell thee also, it will be a cause to make thee admire the freeness and tender- heartedness of Christ to thee, when he shall lift up the light 30 of his countenance upon thee, because he hath regarded such a one as *thou*, sinful *thou*: And therefore in this sense it will be a mercy to the Saints, that they do finde the reliques of sin still struggling in their hearts: But this is not simply the nature of sin, but the mercy and wisdom of God, who 35 causeth *all things to work together for the good of those that love and fear God*, Rom. 8. And therefore whatever thou findest in thy soul, though it be sin of never so black a soul-scaring nature,

let it move thee to run the faster to the Lord Jesus Christ, and thou shalt not be ashamed, that is, of thy running to him.

But secondly, When thou doest apprehend that thou art defiled, and also thy best duties annoyed with many weak- 5 nesses, let that Scripture come into thy thoughts, which saith, *Of him are ye in Christ Jesus, who of God is made unto us wisdom, righteousness, sanctification, and redemption.* And if thou shalt understand that, what thou canst not finde in thy self, thou shalt finde in Christ. Art thou a fool in thy self? then 10 Christ is made of God thy wisdom. Art thou unrighteous in thy self? Christ is made of God thy righteousness. Doest thou finde that there is but very little sanctifying Grace in thy soul? still here is Christ made thy sanctification; and all this in his own person without thee, without thy wisdom, without 15 thy righteousness, without thy sanctification, without in his own person in thy Fathers presence, appearing there perfect wisdom, righteousness, and sanctification in his own person, I say, as a publick person for thee: So that thou mayest believe and say to thy soul, My soul, though thou doest finde 20 innumerable infirmities in thy self, and in thy actions; yet look upon thy Jesus, the man Jesus, he is wisdom, and that for thee, to govern thee, to take care for thee, and to order all things for the best for thee. He is also thy righteousness now at Gods right hand alwayes shining before the eyes of his 25 glory: So that there it is unmoveable, though thou art in never such a sad condition, yet thy righteousness, which is the Son of God, God-man, shines as bright as ever, and is as much accepted of God as ever: (O this sometimes hath been life to me). And so, whatever thou O my soul findest wanting 30 in thy self, through faith, thou shalt see all laid up for thee in Jesus Christ, whether it be wisdom, righteousness, sanctification, or redemption. Nay, not onely so: but as I said before, he is all these in his own person without thee in the presence of his Father for thee.   35

Object.   But now if any should say in their hearts, O but I am one of the Old Covenant men I doubt; that is, I doubt I am not

within this glorious Covenant of Grace. And how if I should
not?

Well, thou fearest that thou art one of the Old Covenant, Answ.
a son of the Bond-woman. In the first place know that thou
5 wast one of them by nature; for all by nature are under that
Covenant: but set the case that thou art to this day under
that, yet let me tell thee in the first place, there is hopes for
thee; for there is a gap open, a way made for souls to come
from under the Covenant of works, by Christ, *For he hath*
10 *broken down the middle wall of partition between us and you.* And Ephes. 2. 14.
therefore if thou wouldest be saved thou mayest come to
Christ. If thou wantest a righteousness (as I said before)
there is one in Christ. If thou wouldest be washed, thou
mayest come to Christ, and if thou wouldest be justified,
15 there is justification enough in the Lord Jesus Christ. That's
the first.

And secondly, thou canst not be so willing to come to 2 Answ.
Christ, as he is willing thou shouldest come to him; witness
his coming down from heaven, his humiliation, his spilling
20 of his blood from both his *Cheeks, by sweat under the bur- *Luke 23. 44.
den of sin, and his shedding of it by the spear, when he hanged
on the Cross. It appears also by his promises, by his invita-
tions, by his sending forth his messengers to preach the same
to poor sinners, and threatneth damnation upon this very
25 account, namely, the neglect of him; and declares that all the
thousands, and ten thousands of sins in the world, should not
be able to damn those that believed in him; that he would
pardon all, forgive and pass by all if they would but come unto
him: moreover, promiseth to cast out none, no, not the
30 poorest, vilest, contemptiblest creature in the whole world.
Come unto me all (every one, though you be never so many,
never so vile, though your load be never so heavy and intollerable, though you deserve no help, not the least help,
no mercy, not the least compassion) yet *cast your burthen upon*
35 *me, and you shall finde rest for your souls.* Come unto me and I
will heal you, love you, teach you, and tell you the way to

17 marg. 2 Answ.] *Ans. 2. (placed in text) 1685*

the kingdome of heaven: Come unto me and I will succor you, help you, and keep you from all devils and their temptations, from the Law and its curses, and from being for ever overcome with any evil whatsoever. Come unto me for what you need, and tell me what you would have, or what you 5 would have me do for you, and all my strength, love, wisdom, and interest that I have with my Father shall be laid out for you. Come unto me your sweet Jesus, your loving and tenderhearted Jesus, your everlasting and sin-pardoning Jesus. Come unto me and I will wash you, and put my righteousness 10 upon you, pray to my Father for you, and send my Spirit into you that you might be saved. Therefore,

Consider besides this, what a priviledge thou shalt have at the day of judgement above thousands, if thou do indeed and in truth close in with this Jesus and accept of him; for thou 15 shalt not have a priviledge in this life onely, but in the life everlasting, even at the time of Christs second coming from heaven; for then when there shall be the whole world gathered together, and all the good Angels, bad Angels, Saints, and Reprobates, when all thy friends, and kindred, with thy 20 neighbours on thy right hand and on the left shall be with thee, beholding of the wonderful glory and majesty of the Son of God; then shall the Son of Glory, even Jesus, in the very view and sight of them all, smile and look kindly upon thee; when a smile or a kinde look from Christ shall be worth 25 more then ten thousand worlds, then thou shalt have it. You know it is counted an honour for a poor man to be favourably looked upon by a Judge, or a King in the sight of Lords, Earles, Dukes, and Princes; why thus it will be with thee in the sight of all the Princely Saints, Angels, and Devils, in the sight of 30 all the great Nobles in the world; then even thou that closest in with Christ, be thou rich or poor, be thou bond or free, wise or foolish, if thou close in with him, he will say unto thee, *Well done good and faithful servant*, even in the midst of the whole world, they that love thee shall see it, and they that 35 hate thee shall all to their shame behold it; for if thou fear him here in secret, he will make it manifest even at that day upon the house top.

Secondly, not onely thus; but thou shalt also be lovingly received, and tenderly embraced of him at that day, when Christ hath thousands of gallant Saints, as old *Abraham, Isaac, Jacob, David, Isaiah, Jeremiah,* together with all the Prophets and Apostles, and Martyrs, attending on him; together with many thousands of glittering Angels ministering before him: besides, when the ungodly shall appear there with their pale faces, with their guilty consciences, and trembling souls, that would then give thousands and ten thousands of worlds (if they had so many), if they could enjoy but one loving look from Christ. I say then, then shalt thou have the hand of Christ reached to thee kindely to receive thee, saying, Come thou blessed, step up hither; thou wast willing to leave all for me, and now will I give all to thee; here is a Throne, a Crown, a Kingdom, take them; thou wast not ashamed of me when thou wast in the world among my enemies, and now will not I be ashamed of thee before thine enemies, but will in the view of all these devils and damned reprobates promote thee to honour and dignity. *Come ye blessed of my Father, inherit the Kingdom prepared for you from the foundation of the world*: Thou shalt see that those who have served me in truth, shall lose nothing by the means: No, but ye shall be as pillars in my Temple, and inheritours of my glory, and shall have a place to walk in among my Saints and Angels, *Zech*. 3. 7. O! who would not be in this condition? Who would not be in this glory? It will be such a soul-ravishing glory, that I am ready to think the whole reprobate world will be ready to run mad* to think that they should *Deut. 28. miss of it; then will the vilest drunkard, swearer, liar, and 34. unclean person willingly cry, *Lord, Lord, open to us*; yet be denied of entrance, and thou in the mean time embraced, entertained, made welcome, have a fair mitre set upon thy head, and clothed with immortal glory, *Zech*. 3. 5. O therefore let all this move thee, and be of weight upon thy soul to close in with Jesus, this tender-hearted Jesus. And if yet for all what I have said, thy sins do still stick with thee, and thou findest thy hellish heart loath to let them go, think with thy self in this manner. Shall I have my sins, and lose my soul? Will they do me any good when Christ comes? Would not heaven be better to me then my sins? And the company 5 of God, Christ, Saints, and Angels be better then the company of *Cain*, *Judas*, *Balaam*, with the Devils in the furnace of fire? Canst thou now that readest or hearest these lines, turn thy back, and go on in thy sins? Canst thou set so light of heaven, of God, of Christ, and the salvation of thy poor, 10 yet precious soul? Canst thou hear of Christ, his bloody sweat, and death, and not be taken with it, and not be grieved for it, and also converted by it? If so, I might lay thee down severall considerations to stir thee up to mend thy pace towards heaven; but I shall not: there is enough written already 15 to leave thy soul without excuse, and to bring thee down with a vengeance into hell fire, devouring fire, the lake of fire, eternall, everlasting fire; Oh! to make thee swim and roul up and down in the flames of the furnace of fire.

The End.

1 do] doth *1659*

I WILL PRAY WITH THE
SPIRIT

I WILL PRAY WITH THE SPIRIT

Note on the Text

THREE editions of *I Will Pray with the Spirit* were published in Bunyan's lifetime, the first probably in 1662, the second in 1663, and the third in 1685. There is also an undated copy of the third edition. The second edition was printed for Bunyan in London in 1663. The third edition was also printed for the author in London and, according to the dated copy, in 1685. No printer is indicated for either the 1663 or 1685 editions, possibly because of the illegal nature of the work as an anti-Prayer Book tract. F. M. Harrison also suggests that Bunyan 'may have desired to use the profits from its sale to provide for himself and family, whilst debarred from pursuing his trade'.[1] No copy of the first edition is known.

THE SECOND EDITION

Title-page: [within rules] *I will Pray with the Spirit, and I* | *will Pray with the Understanding* | *also:* | Or, A | DISCOURSE | Touching | PRAYER, | From 1 *Cor.* 14. 15. | Wherein is briefly discovered, | 1. What Prayer is. | 2. What it is to pray with the Spirit. | 3. What it is to pray with the Spirit, | and with the Understanding also. | [rule] | By JOHN BUNYAN. | [rule] | *The Second Edition.* | [rule] | *But, we know not what we should pray for* | *as we ought; onely the Spirit helpeth* | *our infirmities,* Rom. 8. 26. | [rule] | *London,* Printed for the Author, 1663.

The British Museum and Bodleian copies of the second edition have an additional title-page (π1). In the British Museum copy π1 is now bound so that it precedes A1^r, whereas in the Bodleian copy π1 is bound up at the end of the volume. Both these and the Pierpont Morgan copy lack E12. Progressive damage to P in l. 7, to the third *i* in '*infirmities*' in l. 18, and to the side rules indicates that π1 is the later state. The rule above the imprint line is damaged in A1^r and π1. The inclusion of two

---

[1] Harrison, pp. xiv–xv.

title-pages may be due to the fact that extra copies were run off to serve as advertisements—a practice not unusual at this time. Some of these extra pages were probably then bound up with copies of the tract. The inclusion of two title-pages is not unique to this tract. The British Museum copies of the 1684 second edition and the 1686 third edition of *Come, & Welcome, to Jesus Christ* each has two title-pages.

Transcription of π1: [within rules] *I will pray with the Spirit, and I | will pray with the Understanding | also:* | OR, | A DISCOVRSE | Touching | PRAYER. | From 1 *Cor.* 14. 15. | Wherein is briefly discovered. | 1. VVhat PRAYER is. | 2. What it is to pray with the Spirit. | 3. What it is to pray with the Spirit, | and with the Understanding also. | [rule] | By JOHN BUNYAN. | [rule] | *The Second Edition.* | [rule] | *But, we know not what we should pray for | as we ought; onely the Spirit helpeth | our infirmities,* Rom. 8. 26. | [rule] | London, Printed for the Author.

Collation: 12⁰: π1 A–D¹² E¹² ⟨–E12⟩. Pages: 118; 2 additional pages in the British Museum and Bodleian copies for π1.

Contents: A1ʳ title-page, A1ᵛ blank, A2ʳ–E10ʳ text, E10ʳ–E11ʳ conclusion, π1ʳ alternate title-page, π1ᵛ blank. Double rules precede the Scripture text on A2ʳ. A rule precedes 'The Conclusion.' on A10ʳ. A rule also precedes the catchword 'Here' on C5ʳ, and follows the running title at the top of C5ᵛ. The conclusion is followed, at the bottom of E11ʳ, with '*Grace be with thee.*| THE END.' The conclusion itself is printed in larger type, probably to make more effective use of the allotted sheets. It may have been added while the book was going through the press. The few misprints may be noted. Page 84 appears as 4. Page 9, l. 18 has 'it in' for 'in it'; p. 16, l. 17 has '*mouth*' for '*youth*'; p. 30 has 'Apostles speak' for 'Apostle speaks'; p. 41, l. 4 has 'comes' for 'becomes'; p. 42, l. 17 has 'Gods' for 'God'; p. 42, l. 23 has 'to' for 'so'; p. 45, l. 26 has 'or' for 'of'; p. 71, ll. 9–10 has '*direction*' for '*directions*'; p. 80, l. 3 has 'his' for 'is'; p. 111, l. 11 has 'you' for 'your'.

Running Titles: pp. 4–117, 'I will pray with the Spirit, *&c.*' The *&c.* is romanized on pp. 6, 7, 10–27, 30, 31, 34–49, 51–3, 56–8, 60–73, 75–7, 80–2, 84–97, 99–101, 104–6, 108–17. Page 27 has the misprint '*wi h*'. Page 104 has the misprint '&c:' in the British Museum and Bodleian copies, but not the Pierpont Morgan copy. The latter appears to be a later state.

Catchwords: (selected) A12ᵛ and B12ᵛ self C12ᵛ *Answer*. D12ᵛ the E10ᵛ VIII.

Copies Collated: British Museum; Bodleian, Oxford (π 1 bound after E11); Pierpont Morgan (–π 1).

THE THIRD EDITION

Title-page: [within rules] *I will Pray with the Spirit, and I will* | *Pray with the Understanding also.* | Or, A | Discourse | Touching | PRAYER. | From 1 *Cor.* 14. 15. | Wherein is briefly discovered, | 1. What Prayer is. | 2. What it is to Pray with the Spirit. | 3. What it is to Pray with the Spirit, | and with the Understanding also. | [rule] | By JOHN BUNYAN. | [rule] *The Third Edition.* | [thin rule] | *But we know not what we should pray for as we* | *ought; only the Spirit helpeth our infirmities,* | Rom. 8: 26: | [rule] | *London,* Printed for the Author.

Collation: 12⁰: A–D¹², ⟨E¹¹⟩. Pages: 1–116 ⟨117–18⟩.

Contents: A1ʳ title-page, A1ᵛ blank, A2ʳ–E10ʳ text, E10ʳ–⟨E11ʳ ᵒʳ ᵛ⟩ conclusion. A double rule precedes the Scripture text on A2ʳ. A rule precedes the catchword 'Here' on C5ʳ, and a rule follows the running title on C5ᵛ. 'The Conclusion.' on E10ʳ is preceded by a rule. The conclusion is printed in larger type, as in the second edition, but E10ᵛ (and therefore the missing E11) has been reset to take up more space. The few misprints may be noted. Page 24, l. 26 has 'is' for 'his'; the pointing finger on p. 42, l. 8 is omitted; the word 'but' is omitted on p. 53, l. 1; p. 54, l. 9 has 'farther' for 'further'; p. 56, l. 4 has 'a' for 'an'.

Running Titles: pp. 4–116 (117?), 'I *will pray with the Spirit,* &c.' The &c. is italicized on pp. 36, 50, 84, 108.

Catchwords: (selected) A12ᵛ and B12ᵛ self) C12ᵛ *Answer.* D12ᵛ the E10ᵛ which.

Copy Collated: British Museum. This copy is undated. An undated copy in the Stadtbibliothek, Frankfurt, was lost in the Second World War. A dated copy in the Offor collection was destroyed in the 1865 fire.[1]

There are no substantial changes in the third edition. The obvious misprints in the second edition are corrected, but the numerous inaccurate Scriptural citations are not. Bunyan did not take the time to correct these or to make any changes in the text. It is interesting in view of the close thematic relation of the two works to note that the third edition of *I Will Pray with the Spirit* was published in the same year (1685) as the second edition of *Law and*

[1] Harrison, pp. xiv–xv.

Grace. This text is based on the British Museum copy of the second edition; it follows the principles used in connection with *Law and Grace.*

A fourth edition of *I Will Pray with the Spirit* was published for Nathaniel Ponder in 1692. Charles Doe also included the tract in his *1692 Folio.*

I will pray with the Spirit, and I will pray with the understanding also :

OR,

A DISCOVRSE

Touching

PRAYER.

From 1 *Cor.* 14.15.

Wherein is briefly discovered,

1. VVhat PRAYER is.
2. What it is to pray with the Spirit.
3. What it is to pray with the Spirit, and with the Understanding also.

By JOHN BUNYAN.

The Second Edition.

But, we know not what we should pray for as we ought ; onely the Spirit helpeth our infirmities, Rom. 8.26.

London, Printed for the Author.

Additional title-page to second edition of
I Will Pray with the Spirit

I will pray with the Spirit, and I will pray with the Understanding also.

Prayer is an Ordinance of God, and that to be used both in Publick and Private; yea, such an Ordinance, as brings those that have the Spirit of Supplication, into great familiarity with God; and is also so prevalent an action, that it getteth
5 of God, both for the person that prayeth, and for them that are prayed for, great things. It is the opener of the heart of God, and a means by which the soul, though empty, is filled. By Prayer the Christian can open his heart to God as to a Friend, and obtain fresh testimony of God's Friendship to
10 him. I might spend many words in distinguishing between publick and private Prayer; as also between that in the Heart, and that with the vocal Voice: Something also might be spoken to distinguish between the Gifts and Graces of Prayer; but eschewing this method, my business shall be at this time,
15 only to shew you the very heart of Prayer, without which all your lifting up, both of hands, and eyes, and voices, will be to no purpose at all. *I will pray with the Spirit.*

The method that I shall go in at this time, shall be,

First, To shew you what true Prayer is.

20 *Secondly,* To shew you what it is to pray with the Spirit.

Thirdly, What it is to pray with the Spirit, and Understanding also.

And so, *fourthly,* to make some short Use and Application of what shall be spoken.

25 I. *What Prayer is.*

For the *first,* What Prayer is.

Prayer is a sincere, sensible, affectionate pouring out of the heart or soul to God through Christ, in the strength and assistance of the holy Spirit, for such things as God hath
30 promised, or, according to the Word, for the good of the Church, with submission, in Faith, to the Will of God.

In this Description are these seven things.

1. It is a sincere,

2. A sensible,

3. An affectionate pouring out of the soul to God through Christ,

4. By the strength or assistance of the Spirit,

5. For such things as God hath promised, or, according to his Word,

6. For the good of the Church,

7. With submission in Faith to the Will of God.

For the *First* of these, *It is a sincere* pouring out of the soul to God.

Sincerity is such a Grace as runs through all the Graces of God in us, and through all the actings of a Christian, and hath the sway in them too, or else their actings are not any thing regarded of God, and so of & in Prayer, of which particularly *David* speaketh, when he mentioneth Prayer, *Psal.* 66. 17, 18. *I cryed unto the Lord with my mouth, & he was extolled with my tongue. If I regard iniquity in my heart, the Lord will not hear my prayer*, Psal. 17. 1, 2, 3, 4. Part of the exercise of Prayer is *sincerity*, without which God looks not upon it as Prayer in a good sense: *Then shall you seek me and find me, when you shall search for me with your whole heart*, Jer. 29. 12, 13.

The want of this made the Lord reject their prayers in *Hos.* 7. 14. where he saith, *They have not cryed unto me with their heart* (that is, in *sincerity*) *when they howled upon their beds*. But for a pretence, for a shew in hypocrisie, to be seen of men, and applauded for the same, they pray.

Sincerity was that which Christ commended in *Nathaniel*, when he was under the fig-tree; *Behold an Israelite indeed, in whom there is no guile*. Probably this good man was pouring out of his soul to God in Prayer under the fig-tree, and that in a sincere and unfained spirit before the Lord. The Prayer that hath this in it, as one of the principal ingredients, is the Prayer that God looks at. Thus, *the Prayer of the Upright is his delight*, Prov. 15. 8.

And why must *Sincerity* be one of the essentials of Prayer

which is accepted of God, but because *sincerity* carries the soul
in all simplicity to open its heart to God, and to tell him the
case plainly without equivocation; to condemn it self plainly
without dissembling; to cry to God heartily without com-
5 plementing. *I have surely heard* Ephraim *bemoning himself thus:*
Thou hast chastized me, and I was chastized, as a bullock unac-
customed to the yoak, Jer. 31. 18. *Sincerity* is the same in a corner
alone as it is before the face of all the world. It knows not
how to wear two vizards, one for an appearance before men,
10 and another for a short snatch in a corner; but it must have
God, and be with him in the duty of Prayer. It is not a lip-
labour that it doth regard, for it is the heart that God looks
at, and that which *sincerity* looks at, and that which Prayer
comes from, if it be that Prayer which is accompanied with
15 *sincerity.*

Secondly, It is a sincere *and sensible* pouring out of the heart
or soul. It is not, as many take it to be, even a few babling,
prating, complementory expressions, but a *sensible feeling* there
is in the heart. Prayer hath in it a sensibleness of divers things:
20 Sometimes sence of sin, sometimes of mercy received, sometimes of the readiness of God to give mercy, &c.

First, a sence of the want of mercy, by reason of the danger
of sin. The soul, I say, feels, and from feeling, sighs, groans,
and breaks at the heart. For right Prayer bubleth out of the
25 heart when it is over-pressed with grief and bitterness, as
blood is forced out of the flesh, by reason of some heavy burthen that lyeth upon it, I *Sam.* I. 10. *David* roars, cryes, weeps,
faints at the heart, fails at the eyes, loseth his moisture, &c.
Psal. 69. 3. & 38. 8, 9, 10. *Hezekiah* mourns like a dove, *Isa.*
30 38. 14. *Ephraim* bemoans himself, *Jer.* 31. 18. *Peter* weeps bitterly, *Mat.* 26. 75. Christ hath (*Heb.* 5. 7.) strong cryings and
tears; and all this from a sence of the justice of God, the guilt
of sin, the pains of Hell and destruction. *The sorrows of Death*
compassed me about, the pains of Hell got hold upon me, and I found
35 *trouble and sorrow. Then cryed I unto the Lord,* Psal. 116. 3, 4.
And in another place, *Psal.* 77. 2. *My sore ran in the night.*

11 a] *om. 1685*   31 75.] 57. *1663, 1685*

Again, *Psal*. 38. 6. *I am bowed down greatly, I go mourning all the day long*. In all these instances, and in hundreds more that might be named, you may see, that Prayer carrieth in it a sensible feeling disposition, and that first from a sence of sin.

2dly, Sometimes there is a sweet sence of mercy received; encouraging, comforting, strengthening, enlivening, enlightening mercy, &c.

Thus *David* pours out his soul to bless and praise, and admire the great God for his loving kindness to such poor vile wretches. *Psal*. 103. 1, 2. *Bless the Lord, O my soul, and all that is within me bless his holy Name. Bless the Lord, O my soul, and forget not all his benefits. Who forgiveth all thine iniquities, who healeth all thy diseases, and crowneth thee with loving kindness and tender mercies; who redeemeth thy life from destruction, who satisfieth thy mouth with good things, so that thy youth is renewed as the Eagles.* And thus is the Prayer of Saints sometimes turned into praise and thanksgiving, and yet are Prayers still.

This is a Mystery, God's people pray with their praises, as it is written, *Phil*. 4. 6. *Be careful for nothing, but in every thing by Prayer, with supplication and thanksgiving, let your requests be made known to God.* A sensible thanksgiving for mercies received, *is a mighty Prayer in the sight of God*; it prevails with him unspeakably.

3dly, In Prayer, there is sometimes in the soul, a sence of Mercy to be received. This again sets the soul all on a flame. *Thou, O Lord God* (saith *David*, 2 *Sam*. 7. 27.), *hast revealed unto thy Servant, saying, I will build thee an house; therefore hath thy Servant found in his heart to pray unto thee.*

This provoked *Jacob, David, Daniel*, with others, even a sence of Mercies to be received, as you may see, *Gen*. 32. 9, 10, 11, 12. *Dan*. 9. 2, 3, 4. which caused them, not by fits and starts, nor yet in a foolish frothy way to babble over a few words written in a paper; but mightily, fervently, and continually, to groan out their conditions before the Lord, as being sensible; sensible, I say, of their wants, their misery, and the willingness of God to shew mercy.

A good sence of sin, and the wrath of God, with some

encouragement from God to come unto him, is a better Common Prayer-Book, than that which is taken out of the Papistical *Mass-Book; being the Scraps and Fragments of the devices of some Popes, some Friars, and I wot not what.

*See Mr. Fox *his cita-tion of the* Mass, *in the* last Volume *of* the Book of Martyrs.

5 3. Prayer is a sincere, sensible, *and an affectionate* pouring out of the soul to God. O the heat, strength, life, vigor, and *affection* that is in right Prayer.

As the heart panteth after the Water-brooks, so longeth my soul after thee, O God, Psal. 42. 1. *I have longed for thy Precepts; I*
10 *have longed after thy Salvation,* Psal. 119. 40. *My soul longeth, yea, fainteth for the Courts of the Lord; my heart and my flesh cryeth out for the living God,* Psal. 84. 2. *My soul breaketh for the longing that it hath unto thy Judgements at all times,* Psal. 119. 20. Mark ye here, *My soul longeth, it longeth, it longeth,* &c. Oh what
15 affection is here discovered in Prayer!

The like you have in *Daniel,* Dan. 9. 19. *O Lord hear, O Lord forgive, O Lord hearken and do; defer not for thy Names sake, O my God.* Every syllable carrieth a mighty *vehemency* in it.

This is called the *fervent,* or the *working* Prayer, by *James,*
20 Jam. 5. And so again, *Luke* 22. 44. *And being in an Agony, he prayed more earnestly;* or had his affections more and more drawn out after God for his helping hand.

Oh how wide are the most of men with their Prayers, from this Prayer, that is Prayer in God's account. Alas, the greatest
25 part of men make no conscience at all of the duty; and as for them that do, it is to be feared, that many of them are very great strangers to a sincere, sensible, and *affectionate* pouring out their hearts or souls to God; but even content themselves with a little lip-labour, & bodily exercise, mumbling over
30 a few imaginary Prayers.

When the Affections are indeed engaged in Prayer, then, then the whole man is engaged, and that in such sort, that the soul will spend it self to nothing, as it were, rather than it will go without that good desired, even communion and
35 solace with Christ. And hence it is, that the Saints have spent their strengths, and lost their lives, rather than go

34 desired] desire *1685*

without the blessing, *Psal*. 69. 3. *Psal*. 38. 9, 10. *Gen*. 32. 24, 25, 26.

All this is too too evident by the ignorance, prophaness, and spirit of envy, that reigns in the hearts of those men that are so hot for the Forms, and not the Power of prayer: Scarce 5 one of forty among them, know what it is to be born again, to have communion with the Father through the Son; to feel the power of Grace sanctifying their hearts: but for all their prayers, they still live cursed, drunken, whorish, and abomi- nable Lives, full of Malice, Envy, Deceit, Persecuting of the 10 dear Children of God. Oh what a dreadful after-clap is coming upon them! which all their hypocritical assembling them- selves together, with all their prayers, shall never be able to help them against, or shelter them from.

Again, *It is a pouring out of the Heart or Soul*: There is in 15 Prayer, an unbosoming of a man's self, an opening of the Heart to God, an affectionate pouring out of the Soul in requests, sighs, and groans. *All my desires are before thee* (saith David, *Psal*. 38. 9.) *my groanings are not hid from thee*. And again, *My soul thirsteth for God, even for the living God: When shall I* 20 *come and appear before God? When I remember these things, I pour out my soul in me*, *Psal*. 42. 2, 3. Mark; I pour out my Soul: It is an Expression signifying, that in Prayer, there goeth the very life and whole strength to God. As in another place, *Psal*. 62. 8. *Trust in him at all times, ye people, pour out your* 25 *hearts before him*. This is the Prayer to which the Promise is made, for the delivering of a poor Creature out of captivity and thraldom. *If from thence thou shalt seek the Lord, thou shalt find him, if thou seek him with all thy heart, and with all thy soul*, *Deut*. 4. 29.   30

Again, It is a pouring out of the heart or soul *to God*. This sheweth also the Excellency of the Spirit of prayer: it is the great *God* to which it retires; *When shall I come and appear before God?* And it argueth, that the Soul that thus prayeth indeed, sees an emptiness in all things *under heaven*; That in 35 *God* alone there is rest and satisfaction for the Soul. *Now she*

29 *seek*] *seekest 1663*

that is a Widow, and desolate, trusteth in God, 1 Tim. 5. 5. So
saith David, *In thee, O Lord, do I put my trust, let me never be put
to confusion; deliver me in thy Righteousness, and cause me to escape;
incline thine ear to me, and save me: be thou my strong habitation,*
5 *whereunto I may continually resort: For thou art my rock and my
fortress; deliver me, O God, out of the hand of the unrighteous and
cruel man: For thou art my hope, O Lord my God, thou art my
trust from my youth.* Many in a wording way, speak of *God,*
but right Prayer makes God his hope, stay, and *all.* Right
10 *Prayer* sees nothing substantial, & worth the looking after,
but *God:* And that (as I said before) it doth in a *sincere,
sensible, and affectionate way.*

    Again, It is a sincere, sensible, affectionate pouring out of the
heart, or soul to God, *through Christ.* This, *through Christ,* must
15 needs be added, or else it is to be questioned, whether it be
Prayer, though in appearance it be never so eminent, or eloquent.

    Christ is the *way* through whom the Soul hath admittance to
God, *John* 14. 6. and without whom, it is impossible that so
much, as one desire, should come into the eares of the Lord of
20 Sabbath. *If you ask any thing in my Name, whatsoever you ask the
Father in my Name, I will do it,* Joh. 14. 13, 14. This was *Daniels*
way in praying for the People of God; he did it in the Name
of Christ, *Now therefore, O our God, hear the prayer of thy servant,
and his supplications, and cause thy face to shine upon thy Sanctuary
25 that is desolate, for the Lords sake,* Dan. 9. 17. And so *David, for
thy Names sake* (that is, for thy Christs sake), *pardon mine
iniquity, for it is great,* Psal. 25. 11.

    But now, it is not every one that maketh mention of
Christ's Name in prayer, that doth indeed and in truth effec-
30 tually pray to God in the Name of Christ, or *through him.* This
coming to God *through Christ,* is the hardest part that is
found in *Prayer:* A man may more easily be sensible of his
works, I, and sincerely too desire mercy, and yet not be able
to come to God by Christ. That man that comes to God by
35 Christ, he must *first* have the knowledge of him: *For he
that comes to God, must believe that he is,* Heb. 11. 6. And so he

that comes to God through Christ, must be enabled to know Christ. *Lord* (saith *Moses*, Exod. 33. 13.) *shew me thy Way, that I may know thee.*

This Christ, none but the Father can reveale, *Mat.* 11. 27. *Mat.* 16. 16. And to come through Christ, is for the soul to be enabled of God, to shroud it self under the shadow of the Lord Jesus, as a man shroudeth himself under a thing for safeguard.

Hence it is that *David* so often terms Christ his *shield, buckler, tower, fortress, rock of defence, &c.* Psal. 18. 2. Psal. 27. 1. Psal. 28. 1. not only because by him he overcame his enemies, but because through him he found favour with God the Father. And so he saith to *Abraham*, Gen. 15. 1. *Fear not, I am thy shield, &c.*

The man then that comes to God through Christ, must have faith by which he puts on Christ, and in him appears before God. Now he that hath Faith, is born of God (*John* 3. 5, 7.) born again, and so become one of the Sons of God (*John* 1. 12.) by virtue of which he is joyned to Christ, and made a *member of him*, Ephes. 5. 30. And therefore, *Secondly,* He, as a member of Christ, comes to God, I say, as a member of him, so that God looks on that man as part of Christ, part of his Body, flesh and bones, united to him by election, conversion, illumination, the Spirit being conveyed into the heart of that poor man by God; so that now he comes to God in Christ's merits, in his blood, righteousness, victory, intercession, and so stands before him; being accepted in his beloved, *Ephes.* 1. 6. And because this poor creature is thus a member of the Lord Jesus, and under this consideration, hath admittance to come to God: therefore, by vertue of this union, also, is the holy Spirit, conveyed into him, whereby he is able to pour out himself (to wit) his soul before God, with his audience. And this leads me to the next, or fourth particular.

4. Prayer is a sincere, sensible, affectionate pouring out of the heart or soul to God through Christ, *by the strength or assistance of the Spirit.* For these things do so depend one upon

another, that it is impossible that it should be Prayer without
there be a joynt concurrence of them: for though it be never
so famous, yet without these things, it is only such Prayer as
is rejected of God. For without a sincere, sensible, affectionate
5 pouring out of the heart to God, it is but lip-labour; and if it
be not through Christ, it falleth far short of ever sounding
well in the ears of God. So also, if it be not in the strength and
assistance of the Spirit, it is but like the Sons of *Aaron*,
offering with strange fire, *Levit.* 10. 1, 2. But I shall speak more
10 to this under the second head; and therefore in the mean
time, That which is not petitioned through the teaching and
assistance of the Spirit, it is not possible that it should be
according to the will of God, *Rom.* 8. 26, 27.

But to proceed.

15   5. Prayer is a sincere, sensible, affectionate pouring out of
the heart or soul to God, through Christ, *in the strength and
assistance of the Spirit, for such things as God hath promised,* &c.
Mat. 6. 6, 7, 8. Prayer it is, when it is within the compass of
God's word; and it is blasphemy, or at best, vain babling,
20 when the Petition is beside the Book.

David therefore still in his prayer, kept his eye on the Word
of God. *My soul,* saith he, *cleaveth to the dust; quicken me according to thy word,* Psal. 119. 25, 28. And again, Psal. 119. 41, 42,
58, 65, 74, 81, 82, 107, 147, 154, 169, 170. *My soul melteth for
25 heaviness; strengthen me according to thy Word.* And, *Remember thy
word unto thy servant, on which thou hast caused me to hope.* And
indeed, the holy Ghost doth not immediately quicken and
stir up the heart of the Christian without, but by, with,
and through the word, by bringing that to the heart, and by
30 opening of that whereby the man is provoked to go to the
Lord, and to tell him, how it is with him; and also to argue,
and supplicate, according to the Word.

Thus it was with *Daniel,* that mighty Prophet of the Lord.
He understanding by Books, that the Captivity of the Chil-
35 dren of *Israel* was hard at an end; Then according unto that
word, he maketh his prayer to God.

11 teaching] teachings *1685*   35 unto] to *1685*

I Daniel (saith he, *Dan.* 9. 2, 3.), *understood by Books* (viz. the Writings of *Jeremiah*), *the number of the years whereof the Word of the Lord came to Jeremiah, that he would accomplish seventy years in the desolation of Jerusalem. And I set my face to the Lord God, to seek by prayer and supplication, with fasting, and sackcloth* 5 *and ashes.* So that, I say, as the Spirit is the helper and the governour of the Soul, when it prayeth according to the Will of God; so it guideth by and according to the Word of God, and his Promise. Hence it is that our Lord Jesus Christ himself did make a stop, although his Life lay at stake for it. 10 *I could now pray to my Father, & he should give me more than twelve legions of Angels; but how then must the Scripture be fulfilled, that thus it must be?* Mat. 26. 53, 54. As who should say, were there but a word for it in the Scripture, I should soon be out of the hands of mine enemies, I should be helpt by 15 Angels; but the Scripture will not warrant this kind of praying, for that saith otherwise: It is a praying then according to the word & promise. The Spirit by the Word must direct, as well in the manner, as in the matter of Prayer. *I will pray with the Spirit, and I will pray with the Understanding* 20 *also.* But there is no understanding without the Word; *For if they reject the Word of the Lord, what wisdom is in them?* Jer. 8. 9.

6. *For the good of the Church.* This clause reacheth in whatsoever tendeth either to the honour of God, Christ's advancement, or his Peoples benefit. For God, and Christ, and his 25 People, are so linked together, that if the Good of one be prayed for, to wit, the Church, the glory of God, and advancement of Christ must needs be included. For as Christ is in the Father, so the Saints are in Christ, *John* 17. 23. And he that toucheth the Saints, toucheth the Apple of God's Eye, 30 *Deut.* 32. 10. *Psal.* 17. 8. *Zach.* 2. 8. And therefore pray for the *Peace of Jerusalem,* and you pray for all that is required of you, *Psal.* 122. 6. *Psal.* 51. 8. *Isa.* 62. 6, 7. For *Jerusalem* will never be in perfect peace, until she be in Heaven; and there is nothing that Christ doth more desire, than to have her there. 35 That also is the place, that God through Christ hath given to her. He then that prayeth for the peace and good of *Sion,*

or the Church, doth ask that in prayer which Christ hath
purchased with his Blood; and also, that which the Father
hath given to him as the price thereof. Now he that prayeth
for this, must pray for abundance of Grace for the Church,
5 for help against all its temptations, that God would let nothing be too hard for it, and that all things might work together
for its good; that God would keep them blameless and harmless, the Sons of God, to his glory, in the midst of a crooked
and perverse Nation. And this is the substance of Christ's
10 own Prayer in the seventeenth of *John*. And all *Paul's* Prayers
did run that way, as one of his Prayers do eminently shew, in
Ephes. 1. 16, to the 21. and *Chap.* 3. ver. 14, to the 19th. with
Col. 1. 9, 10, 11, 12, 13. And *Phil.* 1. 9, 10, 11. he saith, *And
this I pray, that your love may abound yet more and more in all
15 knowledge, and in all judgement; that ye may approve things that are
excellent; that you may be sincere, and without offence until the day
of Christ. Being filled with the fruits of Righteousness which are by
Jesus Christ, to the glory and praise of God.*

But a short Prayer you see, and yet full of good desires for
20 the Church, from the beginning to the end: That it may
stand and go on, and that in the most excellent frame of
spirit, even without blame, sincere, and without offence, until
the day of Christ, let its temptations or persecutions be what
they will. And because, as I said, Prayer doth submit to the
25 will of God, and say, *Thy Will be done*, as Christ hath taught
us, *Matth.* 6. 10. therefore the People of the Lord in humility
are to lay themselves and their prayers, and all that they have,
at the foot of their God, to be disposed of by him as he in his
heavenly wisdom seeth best; Yet not doubting but God will
30 answer the desire of his People, that way that shall be most
for their advantage, and his glory. When the Saints therefore
do pray with submission to the Will of God, it doth not
argue that they are to doubt or question Gods love and kindness to them. But because they at all times are not so wise,
35 but that sometimes Satan may get that advantage of them,
as to tempt them to pray for that, which if they had it, would
neither prove to God's glory, nor his Peoples good: 1 *John*

5. 14, 15. Yet this is the confidence we have in him, that if we ask any thing according to his Will, he heareth us: And if we know that he heareth us, whatsoever we ask, we know that we have the Petition that we ask of him; that is, we asking in the Spirit of grace and supplication. For, as I said before, that Petition that is not put 5 up in and through the Spirit, it is not to be answered, because it is beside the Will of God. For the Spirit only knoweth that, and so consequently knoweth how to pray according to that Will of God. *For what man knoweth the things of a man, save the spirit of a man that is in him? even so the things of God knoweth* 10 *no man, but the Spirit of God,* 1 Cor. 2. 11. But more of this hereafter.

Thus you see, first, what Prayer is. Now to proceed.

II. *I will pray with the Spirit.*

Now to pray with the Spirit; for that's the praying man, 15 and none else, so as to be accepted of God: It is for a man (as aforesaid) sincerely and sensibly, with affection to come to God through Christ, &c. which sincere, sensible, and affectionate coming, must be by the working of God's Spirit.

There is no man, nor Church in the world, that can come to 20 God in Prayer but by the assistance of the holy Spirit; *For* (Eph. 2. 18.) *through Christ we all have access by one Spirit unto the Father.* Wherefore *Paul* saith, *We know not what we should pray for as we ought; but the Spirit it self maketh intercession for us, with groanings which cannot be uttered. And he that searcheth the* 25 *heart, knoweth the meaning of the Spirit, because he maketh intercession for the Saints according to the will of God.* And because there is in this Scripture so full a discovery of the Spirit of Prayer, and of mans inability to pray without it; therefore I shall in a few words comment upon it.   30

Rom. 15. 16. *For we.*] Consider first the person speaking, even *Paul,* and in his person all the Apostles. We Apostles, we extraordinary Officers, the wise Master-builders, that have some of us been caught up into *Paradise,* 1 *Cor.* 3. 10. 2 *Cor.* 12. 4. *We know not what we should pray for.*   35

Surely there is no man but will confess, that *Paul* and his
Companions were as able to have done any work for God, as
any *Pope* or proud *Prelate* in the Church of *Rome*, and could as
well have made a **Common-Prayer Book*, as those who at first **See Mr.*
5 composed this; as being not a whit behind them, either in Fox's *Acts*
grace or gifts. *and Monu-*
 ments. Volume
 2.

For we know not what we should pray for.] We know not the
Matter of the things for which we should pray, neither the
Object to whom we pray, nor the *Medium* by, or through whom
10 we pray; none of these things know we, but by the help and
assistance of the Spirit, *Mat.* 11. 27. 1 *Cor.* 2. 9, 10, 11. Should
we pray for Communion with God through Christ; should
we pray for Faith, for Justification by Grace, and a truly
sanctified heart? None of these things know we. For, *As no man*
15 *knoweth the things of a man, save the spirit of a man that is in him;*
even so the things of God knoweth no man, but the Spirit of God,
1 *Cor.* 2. 11. But here (alas!) the Apostle speaks of inward
and spiritual things, which the world knows not, *Isa.* 29. 11.

Again, As they know not the *Matter, &c.* of Prayer, with-
20 out the help of the Spirit, so neither know they the *Manner*
thereof without the same; and therefore he addeth, *We know*
not what we should pray for as we ought; but, *the Spirit helpeth*
our infirmities, with sighs and groans which cannot be uttered. Mark
here, they could not so well and so fully come off in the
25 manner of performing this duty, as these in our dayes think
they can.

The Apostles when they were at the best, yea, when the
holy Ghost assisted them, yet then they were fain to come off
with sighs and groans; falling short of expressing their mind,
30 but with *sighs* and *groans*, which *cannot be uttered*.

But here now, the wise men of our dayes are so well
skill'd, as that they have both the *Manner* and *Matter* of their
Prayers at their finger ends; setting such a Prayer for such a
day, and that twenty years before it comes. One for *Christmass*,
35 another for *Easter*, and six dayes after that. They have also
bounded how many syllables must be said in every one of

17 Apostle speaks] Apostles speak *1663*

them at their publick Exercises. For each Saints day also, they have them ready for the generations yet unborn to say. They can tell you also, when you shall kneel, when you should stand, when you should abide in your seats, when you should go up into the Chancel, and what you should do when you 5 come there. All which the Apostles came short of, as not being able to compose so profound a manner. And that for this reason included in this Scripture, because the fear of God tyed them to pray *as they ought*.

For we know not what we should pray for as we ought.] Mark this, 10 *As we ought*. For the not thinking of this word, or at least, the not understanding it, in the spirit and truth of it, hath occasioned these men to devise, as *Jeroboam* did (1 *King*. 12. 26, 27, 28, 29, 30, 31, 32, 33.) another way of Worship, both for *matter* and *manner*, than is revealed in the Word of 15 God. But saith *Paul*, *We must pray as we ought*; and this we cannot do by all the art, skill, cunning and device of Men or Angels. *For we know not what we should pray for as we ought, but the Spirit*; nay further, it must be *the Spirit it self* that helpeth our infirmities; not the Spirit and man's lusts. What man of 20 his own brain may imagine and devise, is one thing; and what they are commanded and ought to do, is another. *Many ask and have not, because they ask amiss*, *Jam*. 4. 3. and so are never the nearer the injoying of those things they petition for. It is not to pray at random, that will put off God, or cause him to answer. 25

While Prayer is making, God is searching the heart, to see from what root and spirit it doth arise. *And he that searcheth the heart, knoweth* (that is, approveth only) *the meaning of the Spirit, because he maketh intercession for the Saints according to the will of God*, 1 *John* 5. 14. For in that which is according to his 30 Will only he heareth us, and in nothing else. And it is the Spirit only that can teach us so to ask; it onely being able to search out all things, *even the deep things of God*. Without which Spirit, though we had a thousand *Common-Prayer-Books*, yet we know not what we should pray for as we ought, being 35 accompanied with those infirmities that make us absolutely uncapable of such a work. Which infirmities, although it is a hard thing to name them all, yet some of them are these that follow.

First, Without the Spirit, man is so infirm, that he cannot with all other means whatsoever, be enabled to think one right saving thought of God, of Christ, or of his blessed things; and therefore he saith of the wicked, *God is not in all their thoughts,* Psal. 10. 4, Unless it be that they *imagine him altogether such a one as themselves,* Psal. 50. 20. *For every imagination of the thought of their heart, is only evil, and that continually,* Gen. 6. 5. Gen. 8. 21.

They then, not being able to conceive aright of God to whom they pray, of Christ through whom they pray, nor of the things for which they pray, as is before shewed, how shall they be able to address themselves to God, without the Spirit help this infirmity?

Peradventure you will say, By the help of the *Common-Prayer-Book*: but, that cannot do it unless it can open the eyes, and reveal to the soul all these things before touched. Which, that it cannot, it is evident; because that is the work of the Spirit only: The Spirit it self is the revealer of these things to poor souls, and that which doth give us to understand them; wherefore, Christ tells his Disciples, when he promised to send the Spirit, the Comforter, *He shall take of mine, and shew unto you;* as if he had said, I know you are naturally dark and ignorant, as to the understanding any of my things; though ye try this course and the other, yet your ignorance will still remain; the vail is spread over your heart, and there is none can take away the same, nor give you spiritual understanding, *but the Spirit.* The *Common-Prayer-Book* will not do it, neither can any man expect that it should be instrumental that way, it being none of God's Ordinances; but a thing since the Scriptures were written, patched together, one piece at one time, and another at another; a meer humane invention and institution, which God is so far from owning of, that he expresly forbids it, with any other such like, and that by manyfold sayings in his most holy and blessed Word. See *Mark* 7. vers. 7, 8. and *Col.* 2. vers. 16. 17, 18, 19, 20, 21, 22, 23. *Deut.*

12. 30, 31, 32. *Prov.* 30. 6. *Deut.* 4. 2. *Rev.* 22. 18. For right prayer, must as well in the outward part of it, in the outward expression, as in the inward intention, come from what the soul doth apprehend in the Light of the Spirit; otherwise it is condemned as vain and an abomination (*Mark* 7.); because 5 the heart and tongue do not go along joyntly in the same, *Prov.* 21. 9. *Isa.* 29. 13. neither indeed can they, unless the Spirit help our infirmities. And this *David* knew full well, which did make him cry, *Lord, open thou my lips, and my mouth shall shew forth thy praise*, Psal. 51. 10, 11.   10

I suppose, there is none can imagine, but that *David* could speak, and express himself as well as others, nay, as any in our generation, as is clearly manifested by his word, and his works. Nevertheless, when this good man, this Prophet, comes into God's Worship, then the Lord must help, or he 15 can do nothing; *Lord open thou my lips, and then my mouth shall shew forth thy praise.* He could not speak one right word, except the Spirit it self gave utterance: *For we know not what we should pray for as we ought: but the Spirit it self helpeth our infirmities.*

But *Secondly*, It must be a praying with the Spirit, that is 20 the effectual praying; because, without that, as men are senceless, so hypocritical, cold, and unseemly in their prayers; and so, they with their prayers, are both rendred abominable to God, *Mat.* 23. 14. *Mark* 12. 40. It is not the excellency of the voice, nor the seeming affection, and earnestness of him that 25 prayeth, that is any thing regarded of God without it, *Luke* 18. 11, 12. *Isa.* 58. 2, 3. For man, as man, is so full of all manner of wickedness, that as he cannot keep a word, or thought, so *much less a piece of prayer clean*, and *acceptable to God through Christ*. And for this cause, the Pharisees, with their prayers, 30 were rejected. No question, but they were excellently able to express themselves in words, and also for length of time too they were very notable; but they had not the Spirit of Jesus Christ to help them, and therefore they did what they did with their infirmities or weaknesses only, and so fell short of 35 a sincere, sensible, affectionate pouring out of their souls to

27 as] *om. 1685*

God through the strength of the Spirit. That is the prayer that goeth to Heaven, that is sent thither in the strength of the Spirit. For,

Thirdly, Nothing but the Spirit can shew a man clearly his 5 misery by nature, and so put a man into a posture of prayer. Talk is but talk, as we use to say, and so it is but mouth-worship, if there be not a sence of misery, and that effectually too.

O the cursed hypocrisie that is in most hearts, and that 10 accompanieth many thousands of praying men, that would be so looked upon in this day, and all for want of a sence of their misery! But now the Spirit, that will sweetly shew the soul its misery, where it is, and what is like to become of it; also the intolerableness of that condition: For it is the Spirit that 15 doth effectually *convince of sin and misery, without the Lord Jesus*, John 16. 7, 8, 9. and so puts the soul into a sweet, serious, sensible, affectionate way of praying to God according to his Word.

Fourthly, If men did see their sins, yet without the help of 20 the Spirit, they would not pray: For they would run away from God, with *Cain* and *Judas*, and utterly despair of mercy, were it not for the Spirit. When a man is indeed sensible of his sin, and God's curse, then it is an hard thing to perswade him to pray; For saith his heart, *There is no hope, It is in vain* 25 *to seek God*, Jer. 2. 25. Jer. 18. 12. I am so vile, so wretched, and so cursed a creature, that I shall never be regarded. Now here comes the Spirit, and stayeth the soul, helpeth it to hold up its face to God, by letting into the heart some small sence of mercy, to encourage it to go to God; and hence it is called the 30 *Comforter*, John 14. 26.

Fifthly, It must be in, or with the Spirit; For without that, no man can know how he should come to God the right way. Men may easily say, they come to God in his Son: but it is the hardest thing of a thousand to come to God aright and in his 35 own way, without the Spirit. *It is the Spirit that searcheth all things, yea, the deep things of God*, 1 Cor. 2. 10. It is the Spirit that must shew us the way of coming to God, and also what there is in God that makes him desireable. *I beseech thee* (saith *Moses*) *shew me thy way, that I may know thee*, Exod. 33. 13. And *Joh*. 16. 14. *He shall take of mine, and shall shew it unto you.*   5

Sixthly, Because without the Spirit, though a man did see his misery, and also the way to come to God; yet he would never be able to claim a share in either God, Christ, or Mercy, with Gods approbation. O how great a task is it, for a poor soul that becomes sensible of sin, and the wrath of God, to say 10 in Faith, but this one word, *Father*! I tell you, how ever hypocrites think, yet the Christian, that is so indeed, finds all the difficulty in this very thing, it cannot say, God is its *Father*.

Oh! saith he, I dare not call him Father; and hence it is, that the Spirit must be sent into the hearts of Gods people 15 for this very thing, to cry, *Father*, Gal. 4. 6. it being too great a work for any man to do *knowingly*, and *believingly*, without it. When I say, *knowingly*, I mean, knowing what it is to be a Child of God, and to be born again. And when I say, *believingly*, I mean, for the soul to believe, and that from good 20 experience, that the work of Grace is wrought in him: this is the right calling of God *Father*; and not as many do, to say in a babling way, the Lords Prayer (so called) by heart, as it lyeth in the words of the Book. No, here is the life of Prayer, when in, or with the Spirit, a man being made sensible of 25 sin, and how to come to the Lord for mercy; he comes, I say, in the strength of the Spirit, and cryeth, *Father*.

☞   That one word spoken in Faith, is better than a thousand prayers, as men call them, written and read, in a formal, cold, luke-warm way.   30

Oh how far short are those people of being sensible of this, who count it enough to teach themselves and children, to say the Lords Prayer, the Creed, with other sayings; when as God knows they are senceless of themselves, their misery, or what it is to be brought to God through Christ!   35

Ah poor souls! study your misery, and cry to God to shew

10 becomes] comes *1663*   God] Gods *1663*

you your confused blindness and ignorance, before you be so rife in calling God your Father, or learning your children either so to say. And know, that to say, God is your Father, in a way of prayer, or conference, without an experiment of 5 the work of grace on your souls, it is to say, you are *Jews*, and are not, and so to lie.

You say, Our Father, God saith you blaspheme. You say, you are *Jews*, that is, true Christians: God saith, you lie. *Behold I will make them of the Synagogue of Satan, which say, they* 10 *are Jews, and are not, but do lie. And I know the blasphemy of them that say, they are Jews, and are not, but are the Synagogue of Satan,* Rev. 3. 9. Rev. 2. 9.

And so much the greater the sin is, by how much the more the sinner boasts it with a pretended sanctity, as the *Jews* 15 did to Christ, in *John* 8. 41, to 45. which made Christ even in plain terms to tell them their doom, for all their hypocritical pretences. And yet forsooth, every cursed whoremaster, thief and drunkard, swearer, and perjured person, they that have not only been such in times past, but are even so still; these, 20 I say, by some must be counted the only honest men, and all because, with their blasphemous throats and hypocritical hearts, they will come to Church and say, *Our Father*. Nay further, these men, though every time they say to God, our Father, do most abominably blaspheme, yet they must be 25 compelled thus to do. And because others that are of more sober Principles, scruple the truth of such vain Traditions; therefore they must be looked upon to be the only Enemies of God and the Nation, *Isa.* 53. 10. when as it is their own cursed Superstition, that doth set the great God against them, and 30 cause him to count them for his enemies. And yet, just like to *Bonner*, that blood-red Persecutor, they commend (I say) these wretches, although never so vile (if they close in with their Traditions) to be good Churchmen, the honest sub- jects; while God's People are (as it hath alwayes been, *Ezra* 35 4. 12, to 16.) looked upon to be a turbulent, seditious, and factious people.

Therefore give me leave a little to reason with thee, thou poor, blind, ignorant Sot; It may be, thy great prayer is to say, *Our Father which art in Heaven, &c.* Dost thou know the meaning of the very first words of this Prayer? Canst thou indeed, with the rest of the Saints, cry, *Our Father*? Art thou 5 truly born again? hast thou received the Spirit of Adoption? dost thou see thy self in Christ? and canst thou come to God as a Member of him? Or, art thou ignorant of these things, and yet darest say, *Our Father*? Is not the Devil thy Father (*John* 8. 44.), and dost thou not do the deeds of the flesh? and 10 yet darest thou say to God, *Our Father*? Nay, art thou not a desperate Persecutor of the Children of God? hast thou not cursed them in thy heart many a time? And yet, dost thou out of thy blasphemous throat suffer these words to come, even, *Our Father*?   15

He is their Father, whom thou hatest and persecutest.

But as the Devil presented himself amongst the Sons of God, *Job* 1. when they were to present themselves before the Father, even our Father; so is it now: because the Saints are commanded to say, *Our Father*; therefore all the blind ignorant 20 rabble in the world, they must also use the same words, *Our Father*.

Secondly, And dost thou indeed say, *Hallowed be thy Name,* with thy heart? Dost thou study by all honest and lawful wayes, to advance the Name, Holiness and Majesty of God? 25 Doth thy heart and conversation agree with this passage? Dost thou strive to imitate Christ in all the works of Righteousness, which God doth command of thee, and prompt thee forwards to? It is so, if thou beest one that canst truly with God's allowance cry, *Our Father*.   30

Or, is it not the least of thy thoughts all the day? and dost thou not clearly make it appear that thou art a cursed Hypocrite, by condemning that with thy daily practice, which thou pretendest in thy praying with thy dissembling tongue?

Thirdly, Wouldest thou have the *Kingdom of God come indeed,* 35 and also his Will to be done in Earth as it is in Heaven? Nay,

27–8 the works . . . doth command] thy works . . . hath commanded *1685*

notwithstanding, thou, according to the form, sayest, *Thy Kingdom come*; yet, would it not make thee ready to run mad, to hear the Trumpet sound, to see the Dead arise, and thy self just now to go and appear before God, to reckon for all
5 the deeds thou hast done in the Body? Nay, are not the very thoughts of it altogether displeasing to thee? And if God's Will should be done on Earth as it is in Heaven, must it not be thy ruine?

There is never a Rebel in Heaven, against God; and if
10 he should so deal on Earth, must he not whirle thee down to Hell?

And so of the rest of the Petitions.

Ah! how sadly would even those men look, and with what terror would they walk up and down the world, if they did
15 but know the lying and blaspheming that proceedeth out of their mouth, even in their most pretended sanctity?

The Lord awaken you, and learn your poor souls, in all humility, to take heed, that you be not rash and unadvised with your heart, and much more with your mouth; when you
20 appear before God (as the wise man saith) *Be not rash with thy mouth, and let not thine heart be hasty to utter any thing*; especially to call God *Father*, without some blessed experience when thou comest before God. But I pass this.

Seventhly, It must be a praying with the Spirit if it be ac-
25 cepted; because, there is nothing but the Spirit can lift up the soul or heart to God in Prayer. *The preparation of the heart in man, and the answer of the tongue is from the Lord, Prov.* 16. 1. That is, In every work for God (and especially in Prayer) if the heart run with the tongue, it must be prepared by the Spirit
30 of God.

Indeed the tongue is very apt (of it self) to run without either Fear or Wisdom. But when it is the answer of the heart, and that such an heart as is prepared by the Spirit of God; then it speaketh so as God commands and doth desire.
35 They are mighty words of *David*, where he saith, *That he lifteth his heart and his soul to God*, Psal. 25. 1.

34 speaketh] speaks *1685*

It is a great work for any man without the strength of the Spirit; and therefore I conceive that this is one of the great reasons why the Spirit of God is called a Spirit of *Supplication*, *Zech.* 12. 10. because it is that which helpeth the heart when it supplicates indeed, to do it.   5

And therefore saith *Paul*, Ephes. 6. 18.—*Praying with all Prayer and Supplication in the Spirit.* And so in my Text, *I will pray with the Spirit.*

Prayer, without the heart be in it, is like a sound without life; and a heart, without it be lifted up of the Spirit, will 10 never pray to God.

Eighthly, As the heart must be lifted up by the Spirit if it pray aright; so also it must be held up by the Spirit when it is up, if it continue to pray aright.

I do not know what, or how, it is with others hearts, 15 whether they be lifted up by the Spirit of God, and so continued, or no: But this I am sure of;

First, That it is impossible that all the Prayer-Books that men have made in the world, should lift up or prepare the heart; that is the work of the great God himself.   20

And in the *Second* place, I am sure, that they are as far from keeping it up, when it is up.

And indeed, here is the life of Prayer, to have the heart kept with God in the duty.

Exod. 17. 12. It was a great matter for *Moses* to keep his 25 *hands* lifted up to God in Prayer; but how much more then to keep the heart in it!

The want of this is that which God complains of, *Ezek.* 33. *That they draw nigh to him with their mouth, and honour him with their lips, but their hearts were far from him,* (but chiefly) 30 *they that walk after the Commandments and Traditions of men:* as the scope of *Matth.* 15. 8, 9. doth testifie.

And verily, may I but speak my own Experience, and from that tell you the difficulty of Praying to God as I ought; it is enough to make your poor, blind, carnal men, to entertain 35 strange thoughts of me. For, as for my heart, when I go to pray, I find it so loth to go to God, and when it is with him, so loth to stay with him, that many times I am forced in my Prayers; *first*, to beg of God that he would take mine heart, and set it on himself in Christ, and when it is there, that 5 he would keep it there (*Psal.* 86. 11.). Nay, many times I know not what to pray for, I am so blind, nor how to pray I am so ignorant; *onely* (blessed be Grace) *the Spirit helps our infirmities.*

Oh the starting-holes that the heart hath in the time of 10 Prayer! none knows how many by-wayes the heart hath, and back-lains, to slip away from the presence of God. How much pride also, if enabled with expressions? how much hypocrisie, if before others? And how little conscience is there made of Prayer between God and the Soul in secret, unless the *Spirit* 15 *of Supplication* be there to help?

When the Spirit gets into the heart then there is Prayer indeed, and not till then.

Ninthly, The soul that doth rightly pray, it must be in and with the help and strength of the Spirit; because it is im-20 possible that a man should express himself in Prayer without it: when I say it is impossible for a man to express himself in prayer without it, I mean that it is impossible that the heart in a sincere and sensible, affectionate way, should pour out it self before God, with those groans and sighs that come from 25 a truly praying heart, without the assistance of the Spirit. It is not the mouth that is the main thing to be looked at in Prayer, but whether the heart be so full of affection and earnest-ness in Prayer with God, that it is impossible to express their sence and desire. For then a man desires indeed, when his 30 desires are so strong, many and mighty, that all the words, tears and groans that can come from the heart, cannot utter them. *The Spirit helpeth our infirmities, and maketh intercession for us with sighs and groans that cannot be uttered.*

That is but poor prayer, which is only discovered in so 35 many words.

A man that truly prayes one Prayer, shall after that never be able

27 but] *om. 1685*

to expresse with his mouth or pen, the unutterable desires, sence, affection and longing, that went to God in that Prayer.

The best Prayers have often more groans than words; and those words that it hath, are but a lean and shallow representation of the heart, life, and spirit of that Prayer. You do not find any words of Prayer that we reade of, come out of the mouth of *Moses*, when he was going out of *Egypt*, and was followed by *Pharoah, Exod.* 14. 15. and yet he made Heaven ring again with his cry: But it was the unexpressible, and unsearchable groans, and cryings of his soul, in and with the Spirit.

God is *the God of Spirits*, Numb. 16. 22. and his eyes look further than the outside of any duty whatsoever, 1 *Sam.* 16. 7.

I doubt this is but little thought on by the most of them that would be looked upon as a praying people.

The nearer a man comes in any work that God commands him, to the doing of it according to his will; so much the more hard and difficult it is. And the reason is, because man, as man, is not able to do it.

But Prayer (as aforesaid) is not only a duty, but one of the most eminent duties; and therefore so much the more difficult. Therefore *Paul* knew what he said, when he said, *I will pray with the Spirit*. He knew well, it was not what others writ or said, that could make him a praying person; nothing lesse than the Spirit could do it.

Tenthly, It must be with the Spirit, or else, as there will be a failing in the act it self, so there will be a failing, yea a fainting in the prosecution of the work. Prayer is an Ordinance of God, that must continue with a soul so long as it is on this side glory.

But as I said before, it is not possible for a man to get up his heart to God in Prayer; so it is as difficult to keep it there, without the assistance of the Spirit.

And if so, then for a man to continue from time to time in Prayer with God, it must of necessity be with the Spirit.

Christ tells us, That *men ought always to pray, and not to faint*, Luke 18. 1, 2. And again tells us, that this is one definition of an Hypocrite, That either *he will not continue in Prayer*,

or else, if he do, it will *not be in the power* (*Job* 27. 10.), that is,
in the Spirit of Prayer, but in the Form, *for a pretence only*,
Mat. 23. 14.

It is the easiest thing of an hundred, to fall from the Power
5 to the Form; but it is the hardest thing of many, to keep in the
Life, Spirit and Power of any one duty, especially Prayer: That
is such a work, that a man without the help of the Spirit cannot
so much as pray once; much less, continue without it in a sweet
praying frame, and in praying, so to pray, as to have his
10 Prayers to ascend into the ears of the Lord God of Sabbaoth.

Jacob did not only *begin*, but held it; *I will not let thee go,
unless thou bless me*, Gen. 32.

So did the rest of the Godly, *Hos.* 12. 4. But this could not
be without the Spirit of Prayer. *It is through the Spirit that we
15 have access to the Father*, Ephes. 2. 18.

That same is a remarkable place in *Jude*, when he stirreth
up the Saints by the Judgement of God upon the Wicked, to
stand fast, and continue or hold out in the Faith of the Gospel,
as one excellent means thereto, without which he knew they
20 would *never* be able to do it. Saith he, *Build up your selves in your
most holy Faith, praying in the holy Ghost*, Jude 20. As if he had
said, *Brethren, as eternal Life is laid up for the persons that hold out
only, so you cannot hold out, unless you continue praying in the Spirit.*

The great cheat that the Devil and Antichrist deludes the
25 World withal, it is to make them continue in the form of any
Duty, the Form of Preaching, of Hearing, of Praying, &c.
*These are they that have a Form of Godliness, but deny the Power;
from such turn away*, 2 Tim. 3. 5.

Here followeth the Third Thing; to wit,
30   *What it is to pray with the Spirit, and with Understanding.*

And now to the next thing, What it is *to pray with the Spirit*,
and *to pray with the Understanding also*. For the Apostle put
a clear distinction between *praying with the Spirit*, and *praying
with the Spirit and Understanding*. Therefore when he saith, he
35 *will pray with the Spirit*, he addeth, and *I will pray with the*

Understanding [*also*]. This distinction was occasioned through the *Corinthians* not observing, that it was their duty to do what they did to the Edification of themselves, and others too; whereas they did it for their own commendations. So I judge. For many of them having extraordinary gifts, *as to 5 speak with divers tongues, &c.* therefore they were more for those mighty gifts, than they were for the edifying of their Brethren; which was the cause that *Paul* wrote this Chapter to them, to let them understand, that though extraordinary gifts were excellent, yet, to do what they did to the edification of the 10 Church, was more excellent. *For* (saith the Apostle) *if I will pray in an unknown tongue, my spirit prayeth, but my understanding* (and also the understanding of others) *is unfruitful.* Therefore, *I will pray with the Spirit, and I will pray with the Understanding also,* 1 Cor. 14. 4, 5,—12, 13, 14, 15, *&c.* reade the scope of the 15 whole Chapter.

It is expedient then that the *Understanding* should be occupied in Prayer, as well as the heart and mouth; *I will pray with the Spirit, and I will pray with the Understanding also.* That which is done with Understanding, is done more effectually, 20 sensibly and heartily (as I shall further shew anon), than that which is done without it. Which made the Apostle pray for the *Colossians, That God would fill them with the knowledge of his Will, in all wisdom, and spiritual understanding,* Col. 1. 9. And for the Ephesians, *That God would give unto them the Spirit 25 of Wisdom and Revelation in the knowledge of him,* Ephes. 1. 17. And so for the Philippians, *That God would make them abound in knowledge, and in all judgment,* Phil. 1. 9.

A suitable understanding is good in every thing a man undertakes, either Civil or Spiritual; and therefore it must be 30 desired by all them that would be a Praying people.

In my speaking to this, I shall shew you what it is to pray with Understanding.

Understanding is to be taken both for speaking in our *mother-tongue*; and also *experimentally.*   35

I shall pass the first, and treat only on the second.

For the making of right Prayers, it is to be required that

there should be a good or spiritual understanding in all them
who pray to God.

First, To pray with Understanding, *is to pray as being instructed by the Spirit, in the understanding of the want of those*
5 *things which the soul is to pray for.*

Though a man be in never so much need of pardon of sin,
and deliverance from wrath to come, yet if he understand not
this, he will either not desire them at all, or else be so cold
and lukewarm in his desires after them, that God will even
10 loath their frame of spirit in asking for them. Thus it was
with the Church of the *Laodiceans,* they wanted knowledge
or spiritual understanding; They knew not that they were
poor, wretched, blind and naked: The cause whereof, made them,
and all their services, so loathsome to Christ, that he threatens
15 *to spue them out of his mouth,* Rev. 3. 16.

Men without understanding, may say the same words in
prayer as others do, but if there be an understanding in the
one, and none in the other; there is, Oh there is a mighty difference in speaking the very same words! The one speaking
20 it from a spiritual understanding of those things, that he in
words desires; and the other words it only, and there is all.

Secondly, Spiritual understanding, *Espieth in the heart of God,*
a readiness and willingness to give those things to the soul, that it
stands in need of.

25 *David* by this could guess at the very *thoughts* of God
towards him, *Psal.* 40. 5.

And thus it was with the woman of *Canaan* (*Mat.* 15. 22, 23,
24, 25, 26, 27, 28.) she did by Faith and a right Understanding, discern (beyond all the rough carriage of Christ) tender-
30 ness and willingness in his heart to save, which caused her
to be vehement and earnest, yea, restless, until she did
enjoy the mercy she stood in need of.

An understanding of the willingness that is in the heart of
God to save sinners, there is nothing will press the soul more
35 to seek after God, and to cry for pardon, than it. If a man
should see a Pearle, worth an hundred pounds, lye in a ditch,
yet, if he understood not the value of it, he would lightly

pass it by; but if he once get the knowledge of it, he would venture up to the neck for it.

So it is with souls concerning the things of God; If a man once get an understanding of the worth of them, then his heart, nay, the very strength of his soul runs after them, and 5 he will never leave crying till he have them.

The two blind men in the Gospel, because they did certainly know that Jesus who was going by them, was both able & willing to heal such infirmities as they were afflicted with, therefore they cryed, *and the more they were rebuked,* 10 *the more they cryed,* Mat. 20. 29, 30, 31.

Thirdly, The understanding being spiritually enlightned, *hereby there is the way* (as aforesaid) *discovered, through which the soul should come unto God;* which gives great encouragement unto it.   15

It is else with a poor soul, as with one who hath a work to do, and if it be not done, the danger is great; if it be done, so is the advantage: but he knows not how to begin, nor how to proceed, and so through discouragement, lets all alone, and runs the hazard.   20

Fourthly, The enlightened Understanding, *sees largeness enough in the Promises to encourage it to pray,* which still adds to it strength to strength. As when men promise such and such things to all that will come for them, it is great encouragement to those that know what promises are made, to come 25 and ask for them.

Fifthly, The Understanding being enlightned, *way is made for the soul to come to God with suitable arguments.*

Sometimes in a way of expostulation, as *Jacob, Gen.* 32. 9. Sometimes in way of supplication; yet not in a verbal way 30 only, but even from the heart there is forced by the Spirit, through the understanding, such effectual Arguments, as moveth the heart of God.

When *Ephraim* gets a right Understanding of his own unseemly carriages towards the Lord, then he begins to *bemoan* 35 *himself,* Jer. 31. 18, 19, 20. and in bemoaning of himself, he useth such Arguments with the Lord, that it affects his heart, draws out forgiveness, and makes *Ephraim* pleasant in his eyes, through Jesus Christ our Lord. *I have surely heard Ephraim bemoaning himself thus* (saith God) *Thou hast chastised me, and I was chastised; as a bullock unaccustomed to the yoak:* 5 *turn thou me, and I shall be turned; for thou art the Lord my God. Surely after I was turned, I repented, and after I was instructed* (or had a right understanding of my self) *I smote upon my thigh. I was ashamed, yea, even confounded, because I did bear the reproach of my youth.*

10   These be *Ephraim's* complaints and bemoanings of himself; at which the Lord breaks forth into these heart-melting expressions, saying,

   Is Ephraim my dear Son? Is he a pleasant Child? For since I spake unto him, I do earnestly remember him still; therefore my 15 *bowels are troubled for him: I will surely have mercy upon him, saith the Lord.*

   Thus you see, that as it is required to pray with the Spirit, so it is to pray with the Understanding also.

   And to illustrate what hath been spoken by a similitude; 20 Set the case there should come two a begging to your door, the one is a poor, lame, wounded, and almost starved creature; the other is a healthful lusty person.

   These two use the same words in their begging, the one saith he is almost starved, so doth the other; but yet the man 25 that is indeed the poor, lame, or maimed person, he speaks with more sence, feeling and understanding of the misery that is mentioned in their begging, than the other can do; and it is discovered more by his affectionate speaking, his bemoaning himself: His pain and poverty makes him speak 30 more in a spirit of lamentation than the other, and he shall be pittied sooner than the other, by all those that have the least dram of natural affection or pitty.

   Just thus it is with God.

   There are some who out of custome and formality, go and 35 pray; there are others, who go in the bitterness of their spirit: The one he prayes out of bare notion, and naked knowledge; the other hath his words forced from him by the anguish of his soul. Surely, that is the man that God will look at, even *him that is of a humble and contrite spirit, and that trembleth at his word*, Isa. 66. 2.

Sixthly, An Understanding well enlightened, is of admirable use also, *both as to the matter and manner of Prayer.*   5

He that hath his understanding well exercised, to discern between good and evil, and in it placed a sence, either of the misery of man, or the mercy of God; that soul hath no need of the Writings of other men, to teach him by Forms of Prayer: For as he that feels the pain, needs not to be learned to cry, 10 *Oh*! Even so he that hath his Understanding opened by the Spirit, needs not so to be taught of other mens prayers, as that he cannot pray without them: the present sence, feeling, and pressure that lyeth upon his spirit, provokes him to groan out his requests unto the Lord.   15

When *David* had the pains of hell catching hold on him, and the sorrows of hell compassing him about, he needed not a *Bishop in a Surplice*, to learn him to say, *O Lord I beseech thee deliver my soul*, Psal. 116. 3, 4. Or to look into a Book, to teach him in a Form to pour out his heart before God.   20

It is the nature of the heart of sick men, in their pain and sickness, to vent it self for ease, by dolorous groans and complaints to them that stand by.

Thus it was with *David*, in *Psal*. 38. to the 12. *vers*. And thus, Blessed be the Lord, it is with them that are indued with 25 the Grace of God.

Seventhly, It is necessary that there be an enlightened Understanding, to the end that the soul be kept in a continuation of the duty of Prayer.

The People of God are not ignorant how many wiles, 30 tricks, and temptations the Devil hath to make a poor soul, who is truly willing to have the Lord Jesus Christ, and that upon Christ's terms too; I say, to tempt that soul to be weary of seeking the face of God, and to think that God is not willing to have mercy on such a one as him. I, saith Satan, 35 thou mayest pray indeed, but thou shalt not prevail. Thou seest thine heart is hard, cold, dull and dead, thou dost not pray with the Spirit, thou dost not pray in good earnest, thy thoughts are running after other things, when thou pretendest to pray to God. Away hypocrite, go no further, it is but in vain to strive any longer.

5　Here now, if the soul be not well informed in its understanding, it will presently cry out, *The Lord hath forsaken me, and my God hath forgotten me,* Isa. 49. 14. Whereas the soul rightly informed and enlightned, saith, *Well, I will seek the Lord, and wait; I will not leave off, though the Lord keep silence, and speak*
10　*not one word of comfort,* Isa. 49. 14.

He loved *Jacob* dearly, and yet he made him wrestle before he had the blessing, *Gen.* 32. 25, 26, 27.

Seeming delays in God are no tokens of his displeasure; he may hide his face from his dearest Saints, *Isa.* 8. 17. He loves
15　to keep his People praying, and to find them ever knocking at the gate of Heaven: It may be, sayes the soul, the Lord tries me, or he loves to hear me groan out my condition before him.

The woman of *Canaan* would not take seeming denyals for
20　real ones; she knew the Lord was gracious, *Luke* 18. 1, to 6. And the Lord will avenge his People, though he bear long with them. The Lord hath waited longer upon me, than I have waited on him: And thus it was with *David, I waited patiently,* saith he: That is, It was long before the Lord answer-
25　ed me, though at the last *he enclined his ear unto me, and heard my cry,* Psal. 40. 1.

And the most excellent remedy for this, is an understanding well informed and enlightened.

Alas, how many poor souls are there in the world, that
30　truly fear the Lord; who, because they are not well informed in their understanding, are oft ready to give up all for lost, upon almost every trick and temptation of Satan! The Lord pitty them, and help them to pray with the Spirit, and with the Understanding also.

35　Much of mine own experience could I here discover; when I have been in my fits of agony of spirit, I have been strongly

7 49. 14.] 45. 27. *1663, 1685*　　36 agony] agonies *1663*

perswaded to leave off, and to seek the Lord no longer; but
being made to understand, what great sinners the Lord hath
had mercy upon; and how large his Promises were still to
sinners; and that it was not the whole, but the sick, not the
righteous, but the sinner, not the full, but the empty, that 5
he extended his Grace and Mercy unto.

This made me, through the assistance of his holy Spirit, to
cleave to him, to hang upon him, and yet to cry, though for
the present he made no answer; and the Lord help all his
poor tempted and afflicted People to do the like, and to con- 10
tinue, though it be long, according to the saying of the Prophet, *Hab.* 2. 3. And to help them (to that end) to pray not
by the inventions of men, and their stinted Forms, but with
the Spirit, and with the Understanding also.

And now to answer a Query or two, and so to pass on to the 15
next thing.

Query 1.

*But what would you have us poor creatures to do, that cannot
tell how to pray; the Lord knows, I know not either how to pray, or
what to pray for?*   20

Answer.

Poor heart! Thou canst not (thou complainest) pray. Canst
thou see thy misery? Hath God shewed thee that thou art by
nature under the Curse of his Law? If so, do not mistake, I
know thou dost groan, and that most bitterly. I am perswa- 25
ded, thou canst scarcely be found doing any thing in thy
calling, but Prayer breaks from thy heart, *Rom.* 8. 26. Have
not thy groans gone up to Heaven from every corner of thy
house? I know 'tis thus; and so also, doth thine own sorrowful
heart witness thy tears, thy forgetfulness of thy calling, 30
&c? Is not thy heart so full of desires after the things of
another World, that many times thou dost even forget the
things of this World? Prethee read this Scripture, *Job.* 23. 12.

Query 2.

Yea, but when I go into secret, and intend to pour out my soul before God, I can scarce say any thing at all.

Answer.

5   Ah sweet soul! It is not thy words, that God so much regards, as that he will not mind thee, except thou comest before him with some eloquent Oration. His eye is on the brokenness of thine heart, and that it is, that makes the very bowels of the Lord run over, *A broken and a contrite heart, O God, thou*
10 *wilt not despise,* Psal. 51. 17.

2. The stopping of thy words may arise from over much trouble in thy heart. *David* was so troubled sometimes, *that he could not speak,* Psal. 77. 3, 4. But this may comfort all such sorrowful hearts as thou art, that though thou canst not
15 through the anguish of thy spirit speak much, yet the holy Spirit stirs up in thine heart groans and sighs, so much the more vehement; when the mouth is hindred, yet the Spirit is not.

Moses, as aforesaid, made Heaven ring again with his Prayers, when (that we read of) not one word come out of his
20 mouth. But,

3. If thou wouldst more fully express thy self before the Lord; study,

　　First, Thy filthy Estate.

　　Secondly, Gods Promises.
25   *Thirdly,* The Heart of Christ.

Which thou mayest know or discern;

1. By his condescention and bloodshed.

2. By the mercy he hath extended to great sinners formerly; and plead thine own vileness by way of bemoaning,
30 Christs blood by way of expostulation; and in thy prayers, let the mercy that he hath extended to other great sinners, together with his rich promises of grace, be much upon thy heart. Yet let me counsel thee.

1. Take heed that thou content not thy self with words.

12 thy] the *1685*

2. That thou do not think that God looks only at them neither. But,

3. However, whether thy words be few or many, let thine heart go with them; *And then shalt thou seek him, and find him, when thou shalt seek him with thy whole heart,* Jer. 29. 13.   5

Object. 1.

But though you have seemed to speak against any other way of praying but by the Spirit, yet here you your self can give directions how to pray.

Answ.   10

We ought to prompt one another forward to Prayer, though we ought not to make for each other Forms of Prayer.

To exhort to pray with Christian direction is one thing, and to make stinted Formes for the tying up of the Spirit of God to them, is another thing.   15

The Apostle gives them no form to pray withal, yet directs to Prayer, *Ephes.* 6. 18. *Rom.* 15. 30, 31, 32.

Let no man therefore conclude, that because we may with allowance give instructions and directions to pray; that therefore it is lawful to make for each other Forms of Prayer.   20

Object. 2.

But if we do not use Forms of Prayer, how shall we teach our Children to pray?

Answ.

My judgement is, that men go the wrong way to learn 25 their Children to pray, in going about so soon to learn them any set company of words, as is the common use of poor creatures to do.

For to me it seems to be a better way for people betimes to tell their Children what cursed creatures they are, and how 30 they are under the wrath of God by reason of original and actual sin: also to tell them the nature of God's wrath, and

8 *directions*] *direction 1663*

the duration of the misery; which if they conscientiously do, they would sooner learn their Children to pray than they do.

The way that men learn to pray, it is by conviction for sin; and this is the way to make our sweet babes do so too. But 5 the other way, namely, to be busie in learning Children forms of prayer, before they know any thing else, it is the next way to make them cursed hypocrites, and to puff them up with pride. Learn therefore your Children to know their wretched state, and condition; tell them of hell fire, and their sins, of 10 damnation, and salvation: the way to escape the one, and to enjoy the other (if you know it your selves) and this will make tears run down your sweet babes eyes, and hearty groans flow from their hearts; and then also you may tell them to whom they should pray, and through whom they 15 should pray; you may tell them also of Gods promises, and his former grace extended to sinners, according to the word.

Ah! poor sweet babes, the Lord open their eyes, and make them holy Christians. Saith *David, Come ye Children, hearken unto me, and I will teach you the fear of the Lord,* Psalm 34. 11. 20 He doth not say, I will nuzle you up in a form of Prayer; but, *I will teach you the fear of the Lord;* Which is to see their sad states by nature, and to be instructed in the Truth of the Gospel, which doth through the Spirit beget Prayer in every one that in Truth learns it: And the more you learn them this, 25 the more will their hearts run out to God in Prayer.

God did never account *Paul* a praying man, until he was a *convinced and converted man, Acts* 9. 11. no more will it be with any else.

Object. 3.

30 *But we find that the Disciples desired that Christ would teach them to pray, as* John *also taught his Disciples; and, that thereupon he taught them that form, called the* Lord's Prayer.

Answ.

First, To be taught by Christ, is that which not only they, 35 but we desire; and seeing he is not here in his person to teach us, the Lord teach us by his Word and Spirit; for the Spirit is it which he hath said he would send to supply in his room when he went away, as it is, *John* 14. 16. and 16. 7.

Secondly, As to that called *a Form,* I cannot think that Christ intended it as a stinted Form of Prayer.   5

First, Because he himself layeth it down diversly, as is to be seen, if you compare *Matth.* 6. with *Luke* 11. Whereas, if he intended it as a set-form, it must not have been so laid down: for a set-form is so many words and no more.

Secondly, We do not find that the Apostles did ever observe 10 it as such, neither did they admonish others so to do: Search all their Epistles: Yet surely they, both for knowledge to discern, and faithfulness to practise, were as eminent as any He ever since in the World which would impose it.

But in a word; Christ by those words, *Our Father, &c.* doth 15 instruct his People what Rules they should observe in their Prayers to God.

1. That they should pray in Faith.

2. To God in the Heavens.

3. For such things as are according to his Will, &c. *Pray* 20 *thus*; or, *after this manner.*

Object. 4.

But Christ bids, Pray for the Spirit: This implieth, that men without the Spirit, may notwithstanding pray, and be heard: See Luke 11. 9, 10, 11, 12, 13.   25

Answ. 1. The speech of Christ there is directed to his own, *vers.* 1.

2. Christ his telling of them, that God would give his holy Spirit to them that ask him, is to be understood of giving more of the holy Spirit; For still they are the Disciples spoken to, 30 which had a measure of the Spirit already; for he saith, When ye pray, say, *Our Father,* ver. 2. *I say unto you,* vers. 8. And, *I say unto you,* vers. 9. *If ye then, being evil, know how to give good things to your children, how much more shall your heavenly Father give the holy Spirit to them that ask him?*   35

28 his] is *1685*   32 Father] Father, &c. *1685*

Christians ought to pray for the Spirit, that is, for more of it, though God hath endued them with it already.

Quest.

Then would you have none pray, but those that know they are the
5 *Disciples of Christ?*

Answ. Yes.

1. Let every soul that would be saved, pour out it self to God, although it cannot, through temptation, conclude it self a Child of God. And,

10   2. I know if the Grace of God be in thee, it will be as natural to thee to groan out thy condition, as it is for a sucking Childe to cry for the breast.

Prayer is one of the first things that discovereth a man to be a Christian, *Acts* 9. 12. But yet if it be right, it is such Prayer
15 as followeth.

First, To desire God in Christ, for Himself, for his Holiness, Love, Wisdom and Glory. For right Prayer, as it runs onely to God through Christ, so it centers in him; and in him alone; *Whom have I in Heaven but thee? and there is none in Earth*
20 *that I desire* (long for, or seek after) *besides thee,* Psal. 73. 25.

Secondly, That the soul might enjoy continual Communion with him, both here and hereafter. *I shall be satisfied, when I awake, with thine Image, or in thy likeness,* Psal. 17. 15. *For in thee we groan earnestly,* &c. 2 *Cor.* 5. 2.

25   *Thirdly,* Right Prayer is accompanied with a continual labour after that which is prayed for. *My soul waiteth for the Lord, more than they that watch for the morning,* Psal. 130. 6. *I will arise now, and seek him whom my soul loveth,* Cant. 3. 2.

For mark, I beseech you, there is two things that provoke
30 to Prayer: One is, a detestation to sin, and the things of this life; The other is, a longing desire after Communion with God, in an holy and undefiled state and inheritance.

Compare but this one thing with most of the Prayers that are made by men, and you shall finde them but mock-prayers,
35 and the breathings of an abominable spirit; for even the most of men, either not pray at all, or else only endeavour to

mock God and the world by so doing: for, do but compare their prayer, and the course of their lives together, and you may easily see that the thing included in their prayer is the least looked after by their lives. Oh sad Hypocrites!

Thus have I briefly shewed you,   5

1. What Prayer is.

2. What it is to pray with the Spirit.

3. What it is to pray with the Spirit, and with the Understanding also.

I shall now speak a word or two of Application, and so 10 conclude, with,

1. *A word of Information.*

2. *A word of Encouragement.*

3. *A word of Rebuke.*

USE I.   15

A Word of Information.

For the first, to inform you, That as Prayer is the duty of every one of the Children of God, and carried on by the Spirit of Christ in the soul: So every one that doth but offer to take upon him to pray to the Lord, had need be very wary, 20 and go about that work *especially*, with the Dread of God, as well as with hopes of the Mercy of God through Jesus Christ.

Prayer is an Ordinance of God, in which a man draws very near to God; and therefore it calleth for so much the more of the assistance of the Grace of God, to help a soul to pray, as 25 becomes one that is in the presence of him.

It is a shame for a man to behave himself irreverently before a King, but a sin to do so before God. And as a King (if wise) is not pleased with an Oration made up with unseemly words and gestures; *So God takes no pleasure in the sacrifice of fools*, 30 Eccles. 5. 1, 4.

It is not long discourses, nor eloquent tongues, that are the things which are pleasing in the ears of the Lord; but *a humble, broken and contrite heart* (*Psal.* 51. 17. *Isa.* 57. 15.), that is sweet in the nostrils of the heavenly Maiesty.   35

Therefore for information, know, that there are these *Five Things* that are obstructions to Prayer, and even make void the requests of the creature.

First.

5   When men regard iniquity in their hearts, at the time of their Prayers before God. *If I regard iniquity in my heart, the Lord will not hear my Prayer*, Psal. 66. 18. For the preventing of temptation, that by the misunderstanding of this, may seize thy heart; when there is a secret love to that very thing, which
10 thou with thy dissembling lips dost ask for strength against. For this is the wickedness of man's heart, that it will even love, and hold fast that, which with the mouth it prayeth against; and of this sort are they, *that honour God with their mouth, but their heart is far from him*, Ezek. 33. 31.
15   O how ugly would it be in our eyes, if we should see a beggar ask an alms, with intention to throw it to the dogs! Or, that should say with one breath, Pray you bestow this upon me; and with the next, I beseech you give it me not. And yet thus it is with these kind of persons; with their mouth they
20 say, *Thy will be done*; and with their hearts nothing less. With their mouth say, *Hallowed be thy Name*; and with their hearts and lives, they delight to dishonour him all the day long.

These be the prayers that become sin, *Psal.* 109. 7. and though they put them up often, yet the Lord will never answer
25 them, 2 *Sam.* 22. 42.

Secondly.

When men pray for a shew to be heard, and thought some body in Religion, and the like.

These prayers also fall far short of God's approbation, and
30 are never like to be answered, in reference unto eternal life.

There are two sorts of men that pray to this end.

1. Your Trencher-Chaplains, that trust themselves into great mens Families, pretending the Worship of God, when in truth the great business is their own Bellies: which were

notably painted out by *Ahab's* Prophets, 1 *King*. 18. 19. and also *Nebuchadnezzars* wise men, *Dan.* 2. who though they pretended great devotion, yet their lusts and their bellies were the great things aimed at by them in all their pieces of devotion.   5

2. Them also that seek repute and applause for their eloquent terms, and seek more to tickle the ears and heads of their hearers, than any thing else. These be they that *pray to be heard and seen of men, and have all their reward already*, Mat. 6. 5.   10

These persons are discovered thus.

1. They eye only their Auditory in their expressions.

2. They look for Commendations when they have done.

3. Their hearts either rise or fall according to their praise or enlargement.   15

4. The length of their Prayer pleaseth them; and that it might be long, they will vainly repeat things over and over, *Matth.* 6. 7. They study for enlargements, but look not from what heart they come. They look for returns, but it is the windy applause of men; and therefore they love not to be in a 20 chamber, but among company; and if at any time conscience thrusts them into their closet, yet hypocrisie will cause them to be heard in the streets; and when their mouthes have done going, their prayers are ended; for they wait not *to hearken what the Lord will say*, Psal. 85. 8.   25

Thirdly.

A third sort of prayer that will not be accepted of God, it is, When either they pray for wrong things; or, if for right things, yet, that the thing prayed for, might be spent upon their lusts, and laid out to wrong ends: *Some have not, be-* 30 *cause they ask not*, saith James; *and others ask and have not, because they ask amiss, that they may consume it upon their lusts*, James 4. 2, 3, 4.

Ends contrary to God's Will, is a great Argument with God to frustrate the Petitions presented before him. Hence it is, 35 that so many pray for this and that, and yet receive it not;

God answereth them onely with silence, they have their
words for their labour, and that is all.

Object.

But God heareth some persons, though their hearts be not right
5 *with him, as he did* Israel, in giving Quails, *Psal.* 106. 14.
though they spent them upon their lusts.

Answer.

If he doth, it is in Judgment, not in Mercy: He gave them
their desire indeed, but they had better have been without
10 it, for *he sent leanness into their souls,* Psal. 106. 15. Wo be to that
man that God answereth thus.

Fourthly.

Another sort of prayers there are that are not answered,
and those are such as are made by men, and presented to God
15 in their own persons only, without their appearing in the Lord
Jesus. For, though God hath appointed Prayer, and promised
to hear the Prayer of the creature, yet not the prayer of any
creature that comes not in Christ. If you *ask any thing in My
Name, &c.* John 14. 13. And, *Whether ye eat or drink, or whatso-*
20 *ever ye do, do all in the Name of the Lord Jesus Christ,* Col. 3. 17.
If you ask any thing in my Name, I will do it, Joh. 14. 14.

Though you be never so devout, zealous, earnest and constant in prayer, yet, it is in Christ only that you must be
heard and accepted. But alas, the most of men know not what
25 it is to come to him in the Name of the Lord Jesus, which is
the reason they either live wicked, pray wicked, and also die
wicked. Or else,

2. That they attain to nothing else but what a meer natural
man may attain unto, as to be exact in word and deed be-
30 twixt man and man, and only with the righteousness of the
Law, to appear before God.

Fifthly.

The last thing that hindreth Prayer, is, The *Form* of it
without the *Power.* It is an easie thing for men to be very hot

for such things, as Forms of Prayer, as they are written in a
Book, but yet they are altogether forgetful to enquire with
themselves, whether they have the Spirit and Power of
Prayer. These men they are like a painted man, and their
Prayers are like a false voice; they in person appear as Hypo- 5
crites, and their Prayers are an Abomination, *Prov.* 28. 9.
When they say they have been pouring out their souls to
God, he saith, they have been *howling like dogs*, Hos. 7. 14.

When therefore thou intendest, or art minded to pray to
the Lord of Heaven and Earth, consider these following 10
Particulars.

1. Consider seriously what thou wantest; do not as many,
who in their words onely beat the air, and ask for such things
as indeed they do not desire, nor see that they stand in need
thereof.   15

2. When thou seest what thou wantest, keep to that, and
take heed thou pray sensibly.

Object.

But I have a sence of nothing; Then, by your Argument, I must
not pray at all.   20

Answer.

First, If thou findest thy self sensless in some sad measure,
yet thou canst not complain of that senslesness, but by being
sensible.

There is a sense of senslesness, according to thy sense then, 25
that thou hast of the need of any thing, so pray (*Luke* 8. 9.),
and if thou art sensible of thy senslesness, pray the Lord to
make thee sensible of what-ever thou findest thine heart
sensless of. This was the usual practice of the holy men of
God; *Lord make me to know mine end*, saith *David*, Psal. 39. 4. 30
Lord, open to us this Parable, said the Disciples, *Luke* 8. 9.

And to this is annexed the Promise, *Call upon me, and I will*
hear thee, and shew thee great and mighty things that thou knowest
not, Jer. 33. 3. that thou art not sensible of. But,

Secondly, Take heed that thine heart go to God as well as 35

thy mouth; let not thy mouth go any further than thou
strivest to draw thine heart along with it. *David* would lift
his heart and soul to the Lord, and good reason: for so far as a
man's mouth goeth along without his heart, so far it is but
5 lip-labour only; and though God calleth for, and accepteth
the calves of the lips, yet the lips, without the heart, argueth
not only senslesness, but our being without sense of our
senslesness; and therefore if thou hast a mind to enlarge in
Prayer before God, see that it be with thy heart.

10   *Thirdly*, Take heed of affecting expressions, and so to
please thy self with the use of them, that thou forget not the
Life of Prayer.

I shall conclude this Use with a Caution or two.

First, *Take heed thou do not throw off Prayer, through sudden*
15 *perswasions that thou hast not the Spirit, neither prayest thereby.*

It is the great work of the Devil to do his best, or rather
worst, against the best prayers. He will flatter your false
dissembling hypocrites, and feed them with a thousand
fancies of well-doing, when their very duties of Prayer, and
20 all other, stink in the nostrils of God; When he standeth at a
poor *Joshua's hand to resist him* (Isa. 66. 5. Zech. 3. 1.), that is, to
perswade him, that neither his person nor performances are
accepted of God.

Take heed therefore of such false conclusions and ground-
25 less discouragements; And though such perswasions do come
in upon thy spirit, be so far from being discouraged by them,
that thou use them to put thee upon further sincerity and
restlesness of spirit in thy approaching to God.

Secondly, *As such sudden temptations should not stop thee from*
30 *Prayer and pouring out thy soul to God; so neither should thine own*
hearts corruption hinder thee.

It may be thou mayest find in thee all those things before-
mentioned, and that they will be endeavouring to put forth
themselves in thy praying to him: thy business then is to
35 judge them, to pray against them, and to lay thy self so
much the more at the foot of God, in a sence of thy own
vileness, and rather make an argument from thy vileness and

corruption of heart, to plead with God for justifying and sanctifying grace, than an argument of discouragement and dispair.

David went this way; *O Lord*, saith he, *pardon mine iniquity, for it is great*, Psal. 25.   5

USE II.

A Word of Encouragement.

Secondly, To speak a word by way of Encouragement (to the poor tempted and cast-down soul) to pray to God through Christ. Though all Prayer that is accepted of God in re- 10 ference to eternal life must be in the Spirit, for that onely maketh intercession for us according to the Will of God, *Rom.* 8. 27. Yet, because many poor souls may have the holy Spirit working on them, and stirring of them to groan unto the Lord for mercy, though through unbelief they do not, 15 nor for the present cannot believe that they are the People of God, such as he delights in; yet forasmuch as the truth of Grace may be in them, therefore I shall, to encourage them, lay down further these few particulars.

1. That Scripture in *Luke* 11. 8. is very encouraging to any 20 poor soul that doth hunger after Christ Jesus. In the 5th, 6th, and 7th verses, he speaketh a parable of a man that went to his friend to borrow three loaves, who, because he was in bed, denied him, yet for his importunity-sake he did arise and give him; clearly signifying, that though poor souls through 25 the weakness of their faith cannot see that they are the friends of God, yet they should never leave asking, seeking, and knocking at God's door for mercy, *Mat.* 7. 7, 8.

Mark, saith Christ, *I say unto you, Although he will not arise and give him, because he is his friend, yet because of his importunity* 30 (or restless desires) *he will arise and give him as many as he needeth.*

Poor heart! thou cryest out that God will not regard thee, thou dost not find that thou art a friend to him, but rather an enemy in thine heart *by wicked works, Col.* 1. 21. and thou art as though thou didst hear the Lord saying to thee, *Trouble me* 35

not, I cannot give unto thee; as he in the parable; Yet I say, continue knocking, crying, moaning and bewailing thy self:
*I tell thee, though he will not arise and give thee, because thou art
his friend; yet because of thy importunity he will arise and give thee*
5 *as many as thou needest.*

The same in effect you have discovered, *Luke* 18. in the
parable of the unjust Judge, and the poor Widow; her importunity prevailed with him.

And verily, mine own experience tells me, that there is
10 nothing that doth more prevail with God, than importunity.

Is it not so with you in respect of your beggars that come to
your door? though you have no heart to give them any thing
at their first asking, yet, if they follow you, bemoaning themselves, and will take no nay without an alms, you will give
15 them; for their continual begging overcometh you.

Are there bowels in you that are wicked, and will they be
wrought upon by an importuning beggar? *Go thou and do the
like*, Luke 11. 11.

It is a prevailing motive, and that by good experience;
20 *He will arise and give thee as many as thou needest.*

2. Another Encouragement for a poor trembling convinced soul, is, To consider the place, throne, or seat, on
which the great God hath placed himself to hear the petitions
and prayers of poor creatures; and that is *a Throne of Grace*,
25 Heb. 4. 16. *The Mercy-Seat*, Exod. 25. 22. Which signifieth,
that in the dayes of the Gospel God hath taken up his Seat,
his abiding-place, in mercy and forgiveness; and from thence
he doth intend to hear the sinner, and to commune with him,
as he saith, *Exod.* 25. 22. (speaking before of the Mercy-
30 Seat) *And there will I meet with thee.* Mark; It is upon the Mercy-
Seat; *There will I meet with thee, and there will I commune with
thee, from above the Mercy-seat.*

Poor souls! they are very apt to entertain strange thoughts
of God, and his carriage towards them, and suddenly to
35 conclude, that God will have no regard unto them; when
yet he is upon the Mercy-Seat, and hath taken up his place

2 bewailing thy] bewailing of thy *1685*

on purpose there, to the end he may hear and regard the prayers of poor creatures.

If he had said, I will commune with thee from my Throne of Judgement; then indeed you might have trembled and fled from the face of the great and glorious Majesty. But when he 5 saith, he will hear and commune with souls upon the Throne of Grace, or from the Mercy-Seat; this should encourage thee, and cause thee to hope, nay to come boldly to the Throne of Grace, that thou mayest obtain mercy, and find Grace to help in time of need, *Heb.* 4. 16.   10

3. There is yet another Encouragement to continue in Prayer with God, and that is this.

As there is a Mercy-Seat, from whence God is willing to commune with poor sinners; so there is also by this Mercy-seat, *Jesus Christ who continually besprinkleth it with his blood.*   15

Hence it is called, *The Blood of sprinkling*, Heb. 12. 24.

When the High Priest under the Law was to go into the Holiest, where the Mercy-seat was, *he might not go in without blood*, Heb. 9. 7.

Qu. *Why so?*   20

Answ. Because, though God was upon the Mercy-Seat, yet he was perfectly just as well as merciful.

The Blood was to stop Justice from running out upon the persons concerned in the Intercession of the High Priest, as in *Levit.* 16. 13, 14, 15, 16. To signifie, that all thine unworthi- 25 ness that thou fearest, should not hinder thee from coming to God in Christ, for mercy.

☞   Thou cryest out, that thou art vile, and therefore God will not regard thy Prayers. 'Tis true, if thou delight in thy vileness, and come to God out of a meer pretence. But if from a 30 sence of thy vileness thou dost pour out thy heart to God, desiring to be saved from the guilt, and cleansed from the filth, with all thy heart; fear not, thy vileness will not cause the Lord to stop his ear from hearing of thee.

The value of the blood of Christ which is sprinkled 35 upon the Mercy-seat, stops the course of Justice, and opens a flood-gate for the mercy of the Lord to be extended unto thee.

Thou hast *therefore*, as aforesaid, *boldness to enter into the Holiest, by the Blood of Jesus, that hath made a new and living way for thee, thou shalt not dye*, Heb. 10. 19, 20.

Besides, Jesus is there, not only to sprinkle the Mercy-seat with his blood; but he speaks, and his blood speaks; he hath audience, and his blood hath audience; Insomuch, that God saith, when he doth but *see the blood, he will pass over you, and the plague shall not be upon you*, &c. Exod. 12. 13.

I shall not detain you any longer. Be sober and humble; Go to the Father in the name of the Son, and tell him your case, in the assistance of the Spirit, and you will then feel the benefit of praying with the Spirit, and with Understanding also.

USE III.

A Word of reproof.

This speaks sadly to you who never pray at all.

I will pray, saith the Apostle, and so saith the heart of them that are Christians.

Thou then art not a Christian that art not a praying person.

The promise is, *That every one that is righteous shall pray*, Psal. 32. 6.

Thou then art a wicked wretch that prayest not.

Jacob got the name of *Israel* by wrestling with God, *Gen.* 32. And all his Children bare that name with him, *Gal.* 6.

But the People that forget prayer, that call not on the name of the Lord, they have prayer made for them, but it is such as this, *Pour out thy fury upon the heathen, O Lord, and upon the people that call not upon thy name*, Jer. 10. 25.

How likest thou this, O thou that art so far off from pouring out thine heart before God, that thou goest to bed like a dog, and risest like an hog, or a sot, and forgettest to call upon God?

What wilt thou do when thou shalt be damned in Hell, because thou couldst not find in thine heart to ask for Heaven?

Who will grieve for thy sorrow, that didst not count mercy worth asking for?

I tell thee, the ravens, the dogs, *&c.* shall rise up in judgement against thee, for they will according to their kind, make signs, and a noise for something to refresh them when they want it; but thou hast not the heart to ask for Heaven, though thou must eternally perish in Hell, if thou hast it not.

2. This rebukes you that make it your business to slight, mock at, and undervalue the Spirit, and praying by that.

What will you do, when God shall come to reckon for these things?

You count it high Treason to speak but a word against the King. Nay, you tremble at the thoughts of it; and yet in the mean time you will blaspheme the Spirit of the Lord.

Is God indeed to be dallied with, and will the end be pleasant unto you?

Did God send his holy Spirit into the hearts of his People to that end, that you should taunt at it? is this to serve God? And doth this demonstrate the Reformation of your Church? Nay, is it not the mark of implacable Reprobates?

O fearful! can you not be content to be damned for your sins against the Law, but you must sin against the Holy Ghost?

Must the holy, harmless, and undefiled Spirit of Grace; the nature of God, the promise of Christ, the comforter of his Children; that without which, no man can do any service acceptable to the Father; Must this, I say, be the burthen of your Song, to taunt, deride, and mock at?

If God sent *Corah and his company headlong to hell, for speaking against Moses and Aaron,* Numb. 16. do you that mock at the Spirit of Christ, think to escape unpunished? *Heb.* 10. 29.

Did you never reade what God did to *Ananias* and *Saphira,* for telling but one lye against it? *Acts* 5. 1, 2, 3, 4, 5, 6, 7.

Also to *Simon Magus,* for but undervaluing of it, *Acts* 8. 18, 19, 20, 21.

And will thy sin be a virtue, or go unrewarded with vengeance, that makest it thy business to rage against, and oppose its Office, Service, and Help, that it giveth unto the Children of God?

It is a fearful thing to do despite unto the Spirit of Grace: compare *Mat.* 12. 31 with *Mark* 3. 30.

5   3. As this is the doom of those who do openly blaspheme the holy Ghost, in a way of disdain and reproach to its office and service: So also it is sad for you, who resist this Spirit of Prayer, by a Form of man's inventing. A very juggle of the Devil, that the Traditions of men should be of better esteem,

10 and more to be owned, than the Spirit of Prayer.

What is this less than that accursed Abomination of *Jeroboam*, which kept many from going to *Jerusalem*, the place and way of God's Appointment to worship, 1 *Kings* 12. 26, *&c.* And by that means brought such displeasure from God upon

15 them, as to this day is not appeased?

One would think that God's Judgements of old upon the Hypocrites of that day, should make them that have heard of such things, take heed and fear to do so.

Yet the Doctors of our day are so far from taking of warning

20 by the punishment of others, that they do most desperately rush into the same transgression (*viz.*) To set up an Institution of man, neither commanded nor commended of God: and whosoever will not obey herein, they must be driven either out of the Land, or the World.

25   Hath God required these things at your hands? If he hath, shew us where. If not (as I am sure he hath not) Then what cursed presumption is it in any, Pope, Bishop, or other, to command that in the Worship of God which he hath not required?

30   Nay, further: It is not that part only of the Form, which is several Texts of Scripture, that we are commanded to say; but even all must be confessed as the Divine Worship of God, notwithstanding those absurdities contained therein, which because they are at large discovered by others, I omit the

35 rehearsal of them.

Again, Though a man be willing to live never so peaceably; yet because he cannot for Conscience sake own that, for one of the most eminent parts of God's Worship, which he never commanded: therefore must that man be looked upon as factious, seditious, erroneous, heretical; a disparagement to the Church, a seducer of the people, and what not? Lord, what will be the fruit of these things! when for the Doctrine 5 of God there is imposed (that is more than taught) the Traditions of men?

Thus is the Spirit of Prayer disowned, and the Form imposed; the Spirit debased, and the Form extolled: they that pray with the Spirit, though never so humble and holy, 10 counted *Phanaticks*; and they that pray with the Form, though with that only, counted the *Vertuous*. And how will the favourites of such a practice, answer that Scripture, which commandeth, that the Church *should turn away from such as have a Form of Godliness, but deny the Power thereof?* 2 Tim. 3. 5. 15

And if I should say, That men that do these things aforesaid, do advance a Form of Prayer of other mens making, above the Spirit of Prayer, it would not take long time to prove it.

For, he that advanceth the *Book of Common-Prayer*, above the *Spirit of Prayer*, he doth advance a Form of mens making 20 above it.

But this do all those who banish, or desire to banish them that pray with the Spirit of Prayer, while they hug and imbrace them that pray by that Form onely, and that because they do it. 25

Therefore they love and advance the Form of their own, or others inventing, before the Spirit of Prayer, which is God's special and gracious Appointment.

If you desire the clearing of the *Minor*, look into the Goals in *England*, and into the Alehouses of the same: and I believe, 30 you will find those that plead for the Spirit of Prayer in the Goal, and them that look after the Form of mens Inventions only, in the Alehouse.

It is evident also, by the silencing of God's dear Ministers, though never so powerfully enabled by the Spirit of Prayer; 35 if they, in conscience, cannot admit of that Form of *Common-Prayer*.

If this be not an exalting the *Common-Prayer-Book* above either praying by the Spirit, or preaching the Word, I have taken my mark amiss.

It is not pleasant for me to dwell on this; the Lord in 5 mercy turn the hearts of the people to seek more after the Spirit of Prayer; and in the strength of that, to pour out their souls before the Lord.

Only let me say, It is a sad sign, that that, which is one of the most eminent parts of the pretended Worship of God, 10 is Antichristian; when it hath nothing but Tradition of men, and the strength of Persecution to uphold, or plead for it.

The Conclusion.

*I shall conclude this Discourse with this Word of Advice to all Gods
People.*

15 ### I.

Believe, that as sure as you are in the Way of God, you must meet with Temptations.

II.

The first day therefore that thou dost enter into Christ his 20 Congregation, look for them.

III.

When they do come, beg of God to carry thee through them.

IV.

25 Be jealous of thine own heart, that it deceive thee not in thy Evidences for Heaven, nor in thy walking with God in this world.

19 that] *om. 1685*

V.

Take heed of the flatteries of false Brethren.

VI.

Keep in the Life and Power of Truth.

VII.

Look most at the things which are not seen.

5

VIII.

Take heed of little sins.

IX.

Keep the Promise warm upon thy heart.

10

X.

Renew thy acts of Faith in the Blood of Christ.

XI.

Consider the Work of thy Generation.

XII.

15

Count to run with the foremost therein.

Grace be with thee.

THE END.

NOTES TO *LAW AND GRACE*

p. 11, l. 6. *the Law*: the Mosaic Law, the Old Covenant, the Law of Works.

p. 11, l. 16. *the second*: the Covenant of Grace.

p. 11, l. 23. *what they lie under*. Cf. *P.P.*, p. 20: 'So *Christian* turned out of his way to go to Mr. *Legality's* house for help: but behold, when he was got now hard by the *Hill*, it seemed so high, and also that side of it that was next the way side, did hang so much over, that Christian was afraid to venture further, lest the *Hill* should fall on his head . . .'

p. 12, l. 2. *experimentally*: experientially.

p. 12, l. 14. *dark*: unclear.

p. 12, l. 23. *the Commandement*: the Mosaic Law, properly ('spiritually') understood.

p. 13, l. 1. Matt. ix. 12.

p. 14, l. 5. *the biggest sinner in the world*: a Pauline allusion (1 Tim i. 15) developed by Bunyan in *Good News*.

p. 14, ll. 16–19. Luke xv. 24; Eph. ii. 3; 1 Pet. ii. 25.

p. 14, l. 36. *besides the Book*: preaching non-Biblical concepts.

p. 15, ll. 25–6. 1 Tim. i. 7.

p. 16, l. 1. *jasle, justle*: jostle.

p. 16, ll. 17–20. *I never went to School to* Aristotle *or* Plato, *but was brought up at my fathers house, in a very mean condition, among a company of poor Countrey-men.* Bunyan did attend school. See *G.A.*, § 3 (p. 5): 'But yet notwithstanding the meanness and inconsiderableness of my parents, it pleased God to put it into their heart, to put me to School . . .' It is not known where Bunyan attended school. If he was educated at a grammar school, it probably was that at Houghton Conquest. See Sharrock, p. 11; and Ola E. Winslow, *John Bunyan* (New York, 1961), p. 14.

p. 16, l. 21. *home sayings*. Cf. *G.A.*, p. 3, ll. 20–1, and the accompanying note on p. 132.

p. 16, l. 24. *seeing*: knowledgeable.

p. 16, l. 24. *coming short*: dealing with the subject incompletely.

p. 17, l. 32. *my common Providences*: the general call of God to all men, as distinguished from the irresistible call to the elect. See Greaves, pp. 62–3.

p. 21, l. 3. *the Apostle*: Paul.

p. 21, ll. 10–12. Rom. iii. 10.

p. 22, ll. 3–4. Rom. vi. 14.

p. 24, ll. 20–1. Abrahams *two Sons which he had by* Agar *and* Sarah. The son by Hagar was Ishmael; that by Sarah, his wife, was Isaac. See Gen. xvi–xvii.

p. 28, ll. 10–11. Gen. ii. 17.

p. 28, l. 23. *our publick person*. Christ is, for Bunyan, a public person in that his work was done for the entirety of God's elect. As a public person Christ suffered the penalty prescribed by God for sinners, the benefits of which were applicable to the elect. Cf., e.g., *Light*, p. 83; and *Righteousness, 1692 Folio*, p. 79. A different interpretation was offered by Baxter, who acknowledged that Christ was a '*Publick Root*', but rejected the idea that he suffered 'by *representing our persons . . .*'. Rather he was a public person in his capacity as a mediator between God and man. *Catholick Theologie* (1675), Bk. I, pt. 2, p. 16 and chaps. xli, xlii, xliii.

p. 32, ll. 18–21. Jas. ii. 11.

p. 32, l. 28. Gal. iii. 10.

p. 33, ll. 21–2. *walk up to the Law*: live according to the dictates of the Mosaic Law.

p. 33, l. 30. *bate*: mitigate, assuage.

p. 34, ll. 18–19. Prov. xxiv. 9.

p. 35, ll. 13–17, marg. Dod *upon the Commandments*: John Dod and Robert Cleaver, *A Plain and Familiar Exposition of the Ten Commandements. With a Methodicall Short Catechisme, Containing Briefly the Principall Grounds of Christian Religion* (3rd ed., 1606). There were numerous subsequent editions, and a slightly shorter first (1603) edition.

p. 35, ll. 33–5. *these words spoken by me, will prove an instrument for the directing of thy heart, to the right remedy, for the salvation of thy soul*. Cf. the role of the Evangelist in *P.P.*, pp. 9–10.

p. 37, ll. 5–6. Gal. iii. 12.

p. 38, l. 12. *I*: Aye.

p. 38, l. 23. *unrevokable*. Cf. Lewis Machin, *The Dumbe Knight* (1608), Act III (sig. E3ʳ): 'My vow is past, and is like fate still unrevocable.' *O.E.D.*

p. 39, l. 22. *satisfie the cries*. Bunyan, like many of his fellow writers, accepted the satisfaction theory of the Atonement. See Greaves, pp. 36–41.

p. 40, ll. 19–21. *the justice of God is as unchangeable as his love; his justice cannot change it's nature.* Cf. Bunyan's *Ebal and Gerizzim, or, One Thing is Needful* (3rd ed., 1688), p. 23:

> . . . God as he is Love,
> So he is Justice, therefore cannot move,
> Or in the least be brought to favour those,
> His Holiness and Justice doth oppose.

p. 41, ll. 10–11. *runnings out*: execution.

p. 41, ll. 31–2. John x. 35.

p. 42, l. 9. *irrecoverable*: irrevocable.

p. 43, l. 18. *dagg*: pierce, stab.

p. 44, l. 24. Allusion to Matt. xxv. 21.

p. 44, l. 34. *strength to stand*: the ability to obey the Law.

p. 45, ll. 25–6. 1 Tim. i. 7.

p. 46, ll. 5–7. Rom. iii. 20.

p. 47, ll. 14–15. Rom. vi. 14.

p. 47, l. 29. Rom. xiv. 4.

p. 53, ll. 24–5. *brag and cranck*: boastful and merry. Cf. similar usages as given in the *O.E.D.*, s.vv.; J. Philippson, *A Famouse Chronicle of Oure Time*, trans. John Daus (1560), fol. 119ᵛ: 'They are as bragge and as proude as pecockes.' William Gurnall, *The Christian in Compleat Armour* (5th ed., 1669), p. 114: 'Would not our bloud much more grow too rank, and we too cranck and wanton, if we should feed long on such luscious food?'

p. 55, l. 9. *walk up*: live.

p. 55, l. 12. *clear it*: explain it.

p. 55, ll. 15–16. *for my part I do know it is so.* Cf. the fuller account of his personal endeavours to find inner peace by living in accord with the Mosaic Law, and the consequent failure, *G.A.*, §§ 28–36 (pp. 12–14).

p. 55, l. 34. *a common person.* Both Adam and Jesus were often regarded in the seventeenth century as 'common persons', i.e. persons whose actions had affected all men (Adam) or all the elect (Jesus). Thus Thomas Goodwin wrote: Christ 'did collect and gather together in one body all the people of God; that is, did sustain their persons, stood in their stead, as one common person in whom they were all met, representing them equally and alike unto God, and so reconciled them to God in one body'. (*The Works of Thomas Goodwin, D.D.* (Edinburgh, 1861–6), ii. 386). The key Scriptural passage upon which this conception is based is 1 Cor. xv. 22. See above, note to p. 28, l. 23. 'Common' and 'public' are used interchangeably.

p. 56, ll. 28–30. Gal. iii. 10.

p. 56, ll. 35–6. Jas. iii. 2.

p. 58, ll. 15–16. *up to the nail-head*: in its totality, completely. Cf. the proverbial expression, 'drive the nail to the head', Tilley, p. 488.

p. 60, l. 2. *home*: an answer that strikes home; appropriately, directly.

p. 61, ll. 25–8. Matt. xxv. 1–2.

p. 61, l. 26. *a visible company of professors of Christ*: the Independent and Baptist concept of the Church Militant. See Geoffrey F. Nuttall, *Visible Saints* (Oxford, 1957); and Greaves, pp. 123–32.

p. 61, l. 27. ten Virgins. Cf. the different use of virgins in *P.P.*, pp. 46 ff.

p. 62, ll. 4–5. *they may attain to a great deal of honour in the said company of professors*. The *Church Book* provides examples of professing Christians who had to be expelled from the church. Cf., e.g., pp. 53, 54, 66.

p. 65, ll. 33–4. *as perfect a Gospel order, as to matter of practice and discipline in Church Affairs*: i.e. those in the Independent and Baptist traditions, especially those of the open communion variety.

p. 66, ll. 10–11. *satisfaction, as to justification any other wayes*. Bunyan expounds the doctrine of justification by faith alone in *Defence, Saved*, and *Righteousness*.

p. 67, ll. 2–3. *lay hold on*: take possession of. Cf. p. 79, ll. 31–2; p. 81, l. 31.

p. 68, l. 34–p. 69, l. 1. *doth go so hardly down*: is so difficult to accept.

p. 69, l. 23. *ripe*: knowledgeable, prepared.

p. 69, l. 25. *heart-work*. In *P.P.* (p. 85), Faithful says:

> *How* Talkative *at first lifts up his Plumes!*
> *How bravely doth he speak! how he presumes*
> *To drive down all before him! but so soon*
> *As* Faithful *talks of* Heartwork, *like the Moon*
> *That's past the full, into the wain he goes;*
> *And so will all, but he that* Heartwork *knows.*

p. 70, ll. 17–18. *the sounding of a Drum, Brass, or the tinckling of a Cimball*: an allusion to 1 Cor. xiii. 1. Cf. *G.A.*, § 298 (p. 91): 'A tinkling Cymbal is an instrument of Musick with which a skilful player can make such melodious and heart-inflaming Musick, that all who hear him play, can scarcely hold from dancing . . .'

p. 70, l. 30. *reprobates*. Bunyan accepted the Calvinist doctrine of predestination. See Greaves, pp. 51–8.

p. 71, ll. 19–20. Matt. xxii. 12.

p. 71, ll. 24–5. *standing on the left hand of Christ*. The reprobate stand on the left; the elect, on the right.

p. 72, l. 4. *ordinances*. Those in the Puritan tradition commonly used this term for the two sacraments, but, as Bunyan here indicates, it was also used to refer to other duties of the Christian life as well. In this sense it refers generally to those things which God has commanded. Unlike most other writers, however, Bunyan does not draw a distinct line between the sacraments as special means of grace and the rest of the ordinances. For similar usages of 'ordinance' in the broad sense see, e.g., Thomas Gouge, *The Principles of Christian Religion* (1675), pp. 15–16; and Richard Baxter, *A Christian Directory* (1673), Pt. I, p. 100. But Baxter carefully distinguishes between sacraments as a special means of grace and the other ordinances. *Confirmation and Restauration* (1658), p. 90. Also cf. the *Westminster Confession*, XXVII, iv.

p. 72, l. 18. Society: church.

p. 72, ll. 23–4. Allusion to Matt. xviii. 6.

p. 73, l. 5. *whereon you hang your souls*: in what you place your faith.

p. 74, marg. Bunyan subsequently amplified his concept of the New Testament ordinances 'in their [rightful] places' in *A Confession of My Faith* (1672). His argument that baptism by water was not a *sine qua non* for church membership was attacked by the Baptists Thomas Paul, William Kiffin, and John Denne. Bunyan retorted with his *Differences* and *Principles*.

p. 74, l. 16. *Galatians*. The early Christians in Galatia were involved in the controversy over whether Gentile Christians were obliged to undergo circumcision. It was this dispute that prompted Paul to write his epistle to these Christians, in which he contrasted law and grace.

p. 74, l. 29. *prayer it is a Gospel command*. Cf. below, Bunyan's tract on prayer, *I Will Pray with the Spirit*.

p. 75, l. 10. Matt. xxv. 21.

p. 76, l. 23. *use*: practical application.

p. 76, ll. 32–3. Matt. ix. 17.

p. 77, l. 27 *split*: fig., shipwreck.

p. 79, ll. 31–2. *closing with*: believing in.

p. 80, ll. 33–4. *clear out*: explain.

p. 85, l. 34. The alternative reading of verse 4 in the second edition is incorrect.

p. 86, ll. 12–13. *by imputation*. See Bunyan's tract *Righteousness*, and his refutation of Edward Fowler's *The Design of Christianity* in *Defence*. See Greaves, pp. 77–85.

p. 88, ll. 21 ff., marg. David *in this place signifieth Christ*. The use of David as a type of Christ was common in Protestant thought. Cf., e.g., John Calvin, *Institutes of the Christian Religion*, II. vi. 2.

p. 88, ll. 25–6. Isa. lii. 3.

p. 91, l. 30. *types*; p. 93, l. 11. *the type, the shadow*. The use of typology was widespread in the seventeenth century. It was based on the belief that Old

Testament persons and events foreshadowed the historic events of Jesus' life and the founding of the Christian church. Cf. *P.P.*, p. 4:

> ... *was not Gods Laws,*
> *His Gospel-laws in older time held forth*
> *By Types, Shadows and Metaphors?*

Bunyan's most extensive use of typology occurs in *Solomon*. Among the standard contemporary sources on typology are Samuel Mather, *The Figures or Types of the Old Testament* (1683); Thomas Worden, *The Types Unvailed* (1664); and B[enjamin]K[each], Τροπολογία: *A Key to Open Scripture Metaphors* (1682).

p. 92, l. 21–2. Jer. xxxi. 32–3.

p. 93, l. 34. *dark sayings and figures*: difficult types.

p. 94, l. 4. *made Christ*: made with Christ.

p. 95, ll. 15–18. Luke xix. 10, ix. 56; Mark x. 45.

p. 95, ll. 26–31. Heb. x. 5.

p. 96, ll. 6–9. Heb. xiii. 20.

p. 96, ll. 25–6. 1 Cor. xv. 55–6.

p. 96, ll. 29–30. 1 Cor. xv. 57.

p. 97, l. 13. *typed out by the Levitical Law*: types were provided in the laws or the book of Leviticus.

p. 101, ll. 20–3. John iii. 16–17.

p. 102, ll. 6–9. John vi. 37.

p. 102, ll. 21–2. John iii. 16.

p. 104, ll. 3–4. *on a goar blood*: besmeared with blood.

p. 107, ll. 19–20. *The Rock was not so rent*: an allusion to Matt. xxvii. 51.

p. 108, l. 18. Heb. ix. 22.

p. 109, l. 7. *bate.* See note to p. 33, l. 30.

p. 109, ll. 33–4. Matt. xx. 28.

p. 111, l. 10. *bowels*: compassion. Cf. *P.P.*, p. 183: 'Her Bowels yearned over *Christiana* . . .' Cf. also ibid., p. 186: 'Bowels becometh Pilgrims.'

p. 111, l. 23. blaunches: white spots on the skin.

p. 118, l. 32. *strikes* hands: shakes hands. In *H.W.* the King and his Son, making plans for the future relief of Mansoul, seal their bargain in this manner: 'This Son of Shaddai, I say, having stricken hands with his Father . . .' (1682), pp. 36–8.

p. 119, ll. 7–8. Ps. xxiv. 7.

p. 119, ll. 11–12. *against we come after*: for we who follow.

p. 119, l. 18. *stand*: take the time.

p. 120, ll. 17–24. Col. i. 20–2.

p. 122, l. 10. *like so many Lions*. Cf. the use of lions in *P.P.*, pp. 43, 45–6, 218–19, 242, 251.

p. 123, ll. 5–6. Rom. viii. 33–4.

p. 123, l. 18. 1 Tim. i. 16? or i. 17?

p. 124, l. 11. *appear*: happen.

p. 124, l. 16. *musick*. Bunyan had a marked liking for music, which is especially reflected throughout *P.P.* Note, for example, Mercie's exclamation to Christiana (p. 222): 'Wonderful! Musick in the House, Musick in the Heart, and Musick also in Heaven . . .'

p. 125, l. 6. *to all the great sinners to whom mercy was proffered*: a theme with personal interest for Bunyan, who developed it in his *Good News*. Cf. above, p. 14, l. 5.

p. 126, ll. 20–3. In *H.W.* Bunyan makes Mr. Justice the ensign of Captain Execution. The Captain's escutcheon is a fruitless tree with an axe at its root, vividly portraying the relation of justice to future punishment. Similarly the red flag of Captain Judgement, whose escutcheon was the burning, fiery furnace, is placed on Mount Justice at the command of Prince Emanuel. (1682), pp. 106–7.

p. 128, ll. 3–9. John v. 26–9.

p. 129, ll. 8–9. Gen. iii. 15, where an indirect promise is made to the seed of Adam and Eve.

p. 129, ll. 15–16. Cf. Luke xxii. 54–62.

p. 129, ll. 17–19. Cf. Acts ix.

p. 132, l. 7. *pitched*: bestowed.

p. 132, l. 24. *changeable*. The second edition is incorrect in altering this to *unchangeable*.

p. 133, l. 22. Hymeneus *and* Philetus. See 2 Tim. ii. 16–18.

p. 133, ll. 28–9. Mark xvi. 16.

p. 137, ll. 17–18. Ps. xxxiv. 8.

p. 137, marg. *the touchstone*. Cf. the title of John Flavell's *Touchstone of Sincerity* (1679).

p. 137, l. 32. Pauls *doctrine, and also* Pauls *experience*. Bunyan had a very high regard for Paul, whom he regarded as a 'man of men, who had so much Grace, revelation of grace, and Communion with Christ, that sometimes he knew not whether he was in or out of the body . . .' *A Holy Life* (1684), p. 71.

Bunyan records a similar experience of his own in his spritual autobiography: 'I had two or three times, at or about my deliverance from this temptation, such strange apprehensions of the Grace of God, that I could hardly bear up under it; it was so out of measure amazing, when I thought it could reach me, that I do think, if that sense of it had abode long upon me, it would have made me uncapable for business.' *G.A.*, § 252 (p. 78).

p. 138, l. 12. *to speak my own experience.* Cf. Geoffrey F. Nuttall: 'The appeal to individual, personal experience, is . . . the authentic voice of the seventeenth century . . .' *The Holy Spirit in Puritan Faith and Experience* (Oxford, 1946), pp. 26–7. Bunyan is referring specifically to the experience of grace in his own soul. To become a member of the Bedford congregation it was essential to recount one's experience of grace, *Church Book*, p. 17. This was common practice in Separatist churches. Cf. John Rogers: *Every one to be* ADMITTED, *gives out some* EXPERIMENTAL *Evidences of the* work *of* GRACE *upon his* SOUL *(for the* Church *to judge of) whereby he (or she) is* convinced *that he is* re- generate, *and* received *of God . . .' Ohel or Beth-shemesh. A Tabernacle for the Sun* (1653), p. 354.

p. 138, l. 25. Rom. vii. 9.

p. 139, l. 11. *Premunire*: 'The offense, which was not a capital one, of obeying other authority in preference to that of the crown. It originated from the exorbitant power claimed and exercised in England by the pope of Rome, and it took its name from the words of the writ which initiated a prosecution for the offense, "praemunire facias," etc. . . .' *Ballentine's Law Dictionary* (3rd ed., San Francisco, 1969), p. 973.

p. 139, l. 27. *replieve* = replevy. 'To secure the possession of personal property by means of an action of replevin', i.e. 'an action in which the owner or one who has a general or special property in a thing taken or detained by another seeks to recover possession in specie, and sometimes the recovery of damages as an incident of the cause.' *Ballentine's Law Dictionary*, pp. 1094–5. But there is another, less specialized usage in the seventeenth century, meaning 'to bail out'. Cf. John Preston, *Mt. Ebal* (1638): 'If a condemned person . . . should be repleeved or ransomed by another.' *O.E.D.*, s.v.

p. 140, l. 33. *thunder-claps of this most fiery Covenant.* Cf. *P.P.*, p. 20: 'There came also flashes of fire out of the Hill, that made *Christian* afraid . . .'

p. 141, l. 24. my *playing.* Bunyan was playing cat on a Sunday afternoon, when, according to his account, a voice from heaven questioned him about his sinful life . . . *G.A.*, § 22 (p. 10).

p. 141, l. 26. *tew*: flog, thrash. Cf. a similar usage as given in the *O.E.D.*, s.v. John Wilson, *Andronicus Comnenius* (1664), p. 21: 'He does so tew the Pope; That man of sin, The Whore of *Babylon.*'

p. 141, l. 34. *the caul*: the membranes. Cf. *P.P.*, p. 178: 'It returned upon her like a flash of lightning, and rent the Caul of her Heart in sunder.' (See also the accompanying note on p. 340.)

p. 142, l. 1. *a great gun well charged against his soul.* Cf. the development of this imagery in *H.W.*, pp. 73–4, 137. Bunyan did, of course, undertake military service during the Civil War. The 'great gun' was a culverin, a large cannon that was very long in proportion to its bore.

p. 143, l. 27. *indenting*: making stipulations, contracting. The term can be used in a legal sense, and has legal origins.

p. 143, l. 29. *will down*: will be accepted.

p. 143, l. 37. Luke xv. 18.

p. 145, l. 6. *tender of*: sensitive to.

p. 147, ll. 6–7. Rom. viii. 37.

p. 147, ll. 17–26. Bunyan subsequently described this experience in more detail in *G.A.*, §§ 229–30 (p. 72): 'But one day, as I was passing in the field, and that too with some dashes on my Conscience, fearing lest yet all was not right, suddenly this sentence fell upon my Soul, *Thy righteousness is in Heaven* ... Now did my chains fall off my Legs indeed, I was loosed from my affliction and irons, my temptations also fled away . . .'

p. 147, l. 33–p. 148, l. 25. This experience is described again in *G.A.*, §§ 255–9 (pp. 79–81). Bunyan described himself as 'inclining to a Consumption' (§ 255) when 'I sunk and fell in my Spirit, and was giving up all for lost; but as I was walking up and down in the house, as a man in a most woful state, that word of God took hold of my heart, *Ye are justified freely by his grace, through the redemption that is in Christ Jesus . . .*' (§ 257).

p. 148, ll. 21–5. 2 Tim. i. 9.

p. 149, ll. 3–4. *there is put into the soul an understanding enlightened on purpose to know the things of God.* Bunyan's religious epistemology was in the sectarian tradition, which embraced the fundamental principle that religious knowledge was derived from the Holy Spirit, not the use of human reason. Puritans (in the narrow sense, excluding sectaries) juxtaposed Spirit and reason in their epistemology. Baxter succinctly stated the Puritan position: 'The Spirit and reason are not to be . . . disjoined, much less opposed. As reason sufficeth not without the Spirit, being dark and asleep; so the Spirit worketh not on the will but by reason . . .' The contrasting sectarian position is exemplified in a sermon of Peter Sterry: 'To seek out spirituall things by the s[c]ent and sagacity of reason: were to plough with an Oxe & an Asse . . . You cannot understand spirituall things Rationally.' (Cited in Nuttall, *The Holy Spirit in Puritan Faith and Experience*, pp. 47, 37.)

p. 149, ll. 13–14. Matt. ix. 2.

p. 149, ll. 17–20. Cf. Isa. liii. 5–6.

p. 149, l. 30. *scrable*: scramble. Cf. *G.A.*, § 198 (p. 62): 'I did liken myself in this condition unto the case of some Child that was fallen into a Mill-pit, who though it could make some shift to scrable and spraul in the water, yet because it could find neither hold for hand nor foot, therefore at last it must die in that condition.' Cf. also *P.P.*, p. 126: '*Little-faith* came to himself, and getting up, made shift to scrabble on his way.'

p. 150, marg. For the story of Korah see Num. xvi, and *P.P.*, p. 109.

p. 150, l. 22. Baptisme *makes them so.* The position repudiated by Bunyan is asserted, e.g., by Baxter: 'Baptism doth but make us Christians . . .' *A Christian Directory* (1673), pt. 2, p. 806.

p. 152, l. 7. Cesar Augustus. Octavian governed the Roman Empire virtually alone following his defeat of Marcus Antonius at the Battle of Actium in 31 B.C. until his death in A.D. 14. Cf. Luke ii. 1.

p. 153, l. 14. *without*: unless.

p. 154, ll. 6–7. Heb. xiii. 12.

p. 156, ll. 28–9. *It would be too tedious for me to tell thee (here) all from the first to the last.* As early as 1659 Bunyan was apparently planning to write his spiritual autobiography. This is possibly borne out by a passage in *G.A.*, where he recalls himself thinking: 'Well, I would I had a pen and ink here, I would write this down before I go any further . . .' § 92 (p. 30). Although on this occasion he lacked writing implements, the idea of recording his experience was obviously in his mind for some years before 1659.

p. 156, l. 33. *one of the black sinners of the world.* Cf. *G.A.*, § 11 (p. 7): 'I could my self sin with the greatest delight and ease . . .'

p. 156, l. 34. *making a sport of oaths.* Cf. *G.A.*, § 26 (p. 11): 'But one day, as I was standing at a Neighbours Shop-window, and there cursing and swearing, and playing the Mad-man, after my wonted manner, there sate within the woman of the house, and heard me; who, though she was a very loose and ungodly Wretch, yet protested that I swore and cursed at that most fearful rate, that she was made to tremble to hear me . . .' Cf. § 28 (p. 12).

p. 157, l. 2. *dancing.* Cf. *G.A.*, § 35 (p. 14): 'Another thing was my dancing, I was a full year before I could quite leave it . . .' But also see *G.A.*, p. 137, note to § 35.

p. 157, l. 2. *playing.* Cf. *G.A.*, § 21 (p. 10): 'To my old custom of sports and gaming I returned with great delight.' Cf. § 24 (p. 11).

p. 157, ll. 2–3. *pleasure with the wicked ones of the world.* Cf. *G.A.*, § 11 (p. 7): 'I could . . . take pleasure in the vileness of my companions . . .'

p. 157, marg. Cf. above, p. 141, l. 24 and note.

p. 157, l. 4. *the glass of his Law.* Cf. above, p. 13, l. 37.

p. 157, ll. 9–10. *I will have them, though I lose my soul.* Cf. *G.A.*, § 23 (p. 10): 'I resolved in my mind I would go on in sin . . .'

p. 157, ll. 17–18. *taking away that love to lust, and placing in the room thereof a love to religion.* Cf. *G.A.*, § 30 (p. 12): 'Wherefore I fell to some outward Reformation, both in my words and life . . .'

p. 157, l. 20. *to grow a stranger to my old companions.* Cf. *G.A.*, § 43 (p. 16): 'There was a young man in our Town, to whom my heart before was knit more than to any other, but he being a most wicked Creature for cursing and swearing, and whoring, I shook him off and forsook his company . . .'

p. 157 ll. 35–6. *just before the men called Quakers came into the Countrey.* One of the first Quaker evangelists in Bedfordshire was William Dewsbury, who arrived in 1654. See Sharrock, p. 36.

p. 158 ll. 1–9. *to see first, how Jesus Christ was Born of a Virgin, . . . caught up.* Cf. *G.A.*, § 120 (pp. 37–8); 'Me thought I saw with great evidence . . . the wonderful work of God in giving Jesus Christ to save us, from his conception and birth, even to his second coming to judgement: me thought I was as if I had seen him born, as if I had seen him grow up, as if I had seen him walk thorow this world, from the Cradle to his Cross . . .' Bunyan's faith provided a contemporaneity that ultimately gave his preaching a sound ring of conviction.

p. 158, ll. 11–13. *the Lord did . . . give me in his precious word to back the discovery of the Son of God unto me.* The passage from *G.A.* just cited (§ 120) states that the evidence was 'from the relation of the four Evangelists'.

p. 158, ll. 29–34. See above, p. 156, ll. 28–9.

p. 159, ll. 14–15. *I have smarted for this experience.* Cf. the similar usage in *G.A.*, § 276 (p. 85): 'I preached what I felt, what I smartingly did feel . . .'

p. 159, ll. 35–6. Allusion to John ix. 34.

p. 160, ll. 8–12. Allusion to 2 Pet. i. 16.

p. 160, l. 36. *over*: as compared with those.

p. 161, l. 31. *thrown over the bar*: rejected (especially in a legal context).

p. 162, l. 23. Luke x. 28.

p. 163, ll. 15–17. Jer. xxxi. 37.

p. 163, ll. 21–2. Mic. vii. 19.

p. 163, ll. 36–7. 2 Cor. i. 20.

p. 165, l. 6. See Gen. xli.

p. 165, l. 26. Isa. xxvi. 12.

p. 165, l. 30. 2 Thess. ii. 16.

p. 167, ll. 20–1. *the Covenant is not for all this never the more broken.* In *P.P.* (pp. 32–3) Bunyan illustrates this point when Interpreter takes Christian to view the fire (the work of grace in the believer). Although the devil can be

seen casting water on the fire, it cannot be quenched because Christ continually but secretly fuels the fire with oil. Those who doubt the truth of the
doctrine of perseverance are informed in *H.W.* that their leader is Captain
Brimstone (1682 ed., p. 294). In *Saviour* Bunyan writes: 'My sins break not the
Covenant: but them not withstanding, God's Covenant stands fast with him
. . .' *1692 Folio*, p. 395.

p. 169, l. 19. *righteousness, both active and passive*. The active righteousness or
obedience of Jesus was his fulfilment of the precepts of the Mosaic Law.
His passive righteousness or obedience was his substitutionary death, due to
sinners for their transgressions of the Law. See *Pharisee*, p. 99.

p. 172, l. 6. *a compass*: space.

p. 172, ll. 15–16. Eph. ii. 3.

p. 175, l. 16. *round*: rung.

p. 176, l. 8. *there is many go in at the broad gate*. The proper entrance is a narrow
one. See the development of this metaphor in *Strait Gate*. In *P.P.* (pp. 10,
22–5) the metaphor appears as the Wicket Gate. In *G.A.*, § 54 (pp. 19–20),
Bunyan describes his vision of a group of people in the sun and his attempt to
get through the wall to join them in the warmth. 'At the last I saw as it were,
a narrow gap, like a little door-way in the wall, thorow which I attempted to
pass: but the passage being very straight, and narrow, I made many offers to
get in, but all in vain . . .' (See the note to § 53 on p. 138.)

p. 176, l. 22. 2 Cor. i. 20.

p. 176, ll. 24–7. Eph. ii. 4, 7.

p. 177, l. 29–p. 178, l. 2. Cf. the figure of Talkative in *P.P.*, pp. 75 ff., 80 ff.

p. 179, ll. 18–19. *one of the strictest sect*: a Pharisee.

p. 180, ll. 7–8. See 1 Sam. i–iv, for the story of Eli's sons.

p. 180, ll. 8–9. See 1 Sam. viii. 1–3.

p. 180, l. 9. See 2 Sam. xiii–xviii, for the story of Absalom.

p. 182, ll. 5–6. *unless your infants be baptized, they cannot be saved*. The paedo-
baptist position was not always asserted as stringently, though the practical
tendency was to accept this position. See above, note to p. 150, l. 22.

p. 182, ll. 7–8. *unless you be rightly baptized, you have no ground to be assured that
you are believers, or members of Churches*. Bunyan is here referring to the Baptist
position, which he repeatedly rejected in his controversy with Baptist writers
in the early 1670s. See above, note to p. 74, marg., and Greaves, pp. 135–44.

p. 182, l. 11. *the Spirit*. The only baptism Bunyan believed necessary was the
baptism of the Holy Spirit.

p. 182, ll. 15–16. *communicable members*: church members in good standing,
able to partake of the Lord's Supper.

p. 182, l. 35–p. 183, l. 1. Luke xviii. 11–12.

p. 183, l. 24. *walk in Church-order*: fulfil the requisite conditions for church membership and worship in accordance with the precepts of the church.

p. 184, l. 13. *a painted Saviour or a Cipher*: a feigned Saviour or a valueless symbol.

p. 184, ll. 16–17. Eph. i. 6.

p. 187, ll. 25–6. *in their stead*: in their place.

p. 188, ll. 4–5. Tiberias Cesar. Tiberius was Emperor from A.D. 14 to 37.

p. 188, ll. 19–20. Josephs *Sepulchre*. Jesus was buried in the tomb of Joseph of Arimathea (Matt. xxvii. 57–60).

p. 188, ll. 20–1. *righteousnesse to clothe thee withall compleatly*. Cf. *P.P.*, p. 41: 'And as for this Coat that is on my back, it was given me by the Lord of the place whither I go; and that . . . to cover my nakedness with. And I take it as a token of his kindness to me, for I had nothing but rags before . . .'

p. 188, ll. 21–31. Heb. x. 14, ix. 25–6, x. 10–12.

p. 188, ll. 34–5. *annimated on*: encouraged, incited.

p. 189, ll. 6–8. The orthodox doctrine of the person of Christ, as established by the Councils of Nicaea and Chalcedon.

p. 189, ll. 23–33. Throughout the treatise Bunyan has put forth an essentially Anselmic doctrine of a satisfactional atonement, a major exception being the omission of the concept of supererogation. Bunyan provides a simple summary of his doctrine on these lines. It is characteristic of his attempt to make the often complex doctrines of Christian theology intelligible to the common man.

p. 190, ll. 6–8. Heb. ix. 14.

p. 190, ll. 11–12. *union and communion*: Bunyan's favourite phrase to express the orthodox doctrine of the union of the divine and human natures in Christ.

p. 191, ll. 8–10. Rom. iii. 24–5.

p. 191, ll. 29–30. *one syllable of the written Word*. An indication of the 'literal-mindedness' of Bunyan. Cf. Sharrock's comments, *G.A.*, p. xxi.

p. 192, ll. 27–30. Isa. lv. 7.

p. 193, ll. 14, 29–30. John vi. 37.

p. 193, l. 36–p. 194, l. 2. Mark ix. 23, xvi. 16; John iii. 16, x. 28.

p. 194, ll. 3–11. Bunyan attacked Quaker beliefs in his first two tracts, *Truths* and *Vindication*. He subsequently appended a list of eight errors to his *Defence*, in which he compared the beliefs of the Quaker William Penn with those of the Anglican Edward Fowler.

p. 194, ll. 29–30. Eph. v. 27.

p. 195, ll. 1–2. *the biggest thunder-crack that the Law can give*. Cf. above, p. 140. l. 33.

p. 195, l. 13. *above ground*: has been resurrected from the grave.

p. 195, l. 19. I Cor. xv. 55.

p. 196, l. 1. *under the Levitical Law*: those who lived before the advent of Jesus: under the Mosaic Law.

p. 196, ll. 8–9. *not stick at the parting with all for the enjoyning of them*: not hesitate to rely on faith rather than legal works in order to take part in the privileges promised by God.

p. 197, ll. 3–4. Isa. xl. 31.

p. 198, ll. 2–3. John x. 15.

p. 198, l. 36–p. 199, l. 1. *Doest thou want faith, then come for it to the man Christ Jesus*. Bunyan is a firm adherent of the concept that faith is a divine gift, implanted in man by God. Yet he openly encourages his readers to undertake action that will enable them to receive this gift. See, e.g., p. 218, ll. 22–8.

p. 199, l. 8. Allusion to Rom. viii. 37.

p. 199, ll. 17–20. 'Some' are the Arminians especially, who rejected the doctrine of the absolute perseverance of the saints. Cf. John Goodwin, *et al.*, Εἰρηνομαχία. *The Agreement & Distance of Brethren* (1652), pp. 66–7: 'They [Calvinists] hold, that persons once true Beleevers, and truly justified, can never fall away from their Faith, either totally, or finally: we hold, that even such persons may fall away in both considerations.'

p. 199, ll. 31–3. Rom. viii. 38–9.

p. 200, ll. 11–13. Rom. vi. 13, 22.

p. 201, l. 12. i.e. 2 Chron. xxxiii. 12, 13.

p. 201, l. 21. *the unpardonable sin*. Bunyan at one point in his life believed that he had committed this sin. See *G.A.*, §§ 148 ff. (pp. 45 ff.), also the note to § 148 on pp. 145–6.

p. 201, ll. 33–6. Heb. x. 26–7.

p. 203, ll. 7–8. Matt. xii. 31.

p. 203, ll. 20–1. Heb. x. 29.

p. 203, ll. 34–6. See Jonah i. 1–3.

p. 204, ll. 1–5. See Jonah ii. 1–2 ff.

p. 205, ll. 10–16. Heb. vi. 4–6.

p. 208, l. 24. *pawn my soul upon it*: use my soul as a pawn that; wager my soul that.

p. 208, l. 27. *scrabled out*: scratched out, erased.

p. 209, l. 2. Heb. x. 29?

p. 209, l. 36. The Ranters were an Antinomian sect who stressed reliance on the Inner Light, rejected the authority of Scripture and the ministry, and were reputedly involved in extremes of sexual behaviour.

Early in his spiritual quest Bunyan read some books written by Ranters, but felt himself unable to judge the validity of their doctrines. He fared better when one of his companions professed Ranter beliefs, but lived licentiously and proclaimed atheism. Subsequently Bunyan met other Ranters, who characteristically sought to persuade him of the complete freedom of the new covenant. Bunyan, however, though ultimately contrasting the old and new covenants, refused to abandon the principles of the moral law. See *G.A.*, §§ 44–5 (pp. 16–17) and note to § 44 on pp. 137–8. For the views of the Ranters see, e.g., Jacob Barthumley, *The Light and Dark Sides of God* (1650); Abiezer Coppe, *A Fiery Flying Roll* (1649); and Joseph Salmon, *Heights in Depths, and Depths in Heights* (1651).

p. 211, l. 12. *Come like* Benhadads *servants*: come humbly. 1 Kings xx. 31–2.

p. 211, l. 15. *Ile warrant thee speed*: I encourage you to hurry.

p. 211, ll. 20–5. Bunyan expresses a clear-cut preference for extempore prayer. See *I Will Pray with the Spirit*, below pp. 235–86.

p. 211, l. 35. *But I am afraid the day of Grace is past*. Cf. *G.A.*, § 66 (p. 22): 'But how if the day of grace should be past and gone?' Virtually all the objections and queries posed by Bunyan in this theological treatise stem from his own religious experience.

the day of Grace. The phrase refers to a period of time in which God graciously offers the sinner the opportunity to believe and repent. In Bunyan's theology it has no real significance, for the elect will be saved in their day of grace, but the reprobate *cannot* be saved regardless of the length of such a day or period of time.

p. 212, l. 31. *glance in*: flash.

p. 213, l. 18. Ps. lxxxv. 8.

p. 214, ll. 28–9. Rom. ix. 16.

p. 214, ll. 34–5. *Thou art it may be troubled to know whether thou art elected*. Cf. *G.A.*, § 59 (p. 21): 'This would still stick with me, How can you tell you are Elected?'

p. 216, ll. 19–29. 1 Thess. i. 3–7, 10.

p. 218, ll. 24–5. Mark x. 51.

p. 220, ll. 12–14. Phil. iii. 14.

p. 222, ll. 7–8. 1. Cor. i. 30.

p. 223, l. 8. *there is a gap open*. See above, note to p. 176, l. 8.

p. 223, ll. 31, 34–5. Matt. xi. 28–9.

p. 224, l. 34. Matt. xxv. 21.

p. 225, ll. 21–3. Matt. xxv. 34.

p. 225, l. 32. Matt. xxv. 11.

p. 236, ll. 18–20. Ps. lxvi. 17–18.

p. 236, ll. 30–1. John i. 47.

p. 237, ll. 4–5. *complementing*: flattering. Bunyan may be using the word in a dual sense, meaning the employing of ceremonies as well as flattering.

p. 237, l. 9. *vizards*: countenances.

p. 238, ll. 10–15. Ps. ciii. 1–5.

p. 239, l. 3, marg. See especially John Foxe's principal treatment of the mass in his *Actes and Monuments*, ed. Stephen Reed Cattley, vi (1838), 356–83.

p. 239, ll. 19–20. Jas. v. 17.

p. 241, ll. 2–8. Ps. lxxi. 1–5.

p. 243, ll. 25–6. Ps. cxix, 49.

p. 246, ll. 23–7. Rom. viii. 26–7.

p. 248, ll. 27–30. Rom. viii. 27.

p. 248, l. 33. I Cor. ii. 10.

p. 249, ll. 7–8. Ps. l. 21.

p. 249, ll. 23–4. John xvi. 15.

p. 250, l. 7. Prov. xxi. 2?

p. 250, ll. 16–17. Ps. li. 15.

p. 250, ll. 29–30. I Pet. ii. 5.

p. 253, l. 31. Bonner: Edmund Bonner (c. 1500–69) was Bishop of London from 1539 to 1550 and from 1554 to 1559. He was instrumental in achieving the reconciliation of England with the Papacy under Mary, and was an enforcer of the laws against heresy.

p. 254, l. 3. Matt. vi. 9.

p. 255, ll. 20–1. Eccles. v. 2.

p. 257, ll. 32–3. Rom. viii. 26.

p. 258, l. 37. This is a general reference to Job xxvii. 9–10.

p. 259, ll. 11–12. Gen. xxxii. 26.

p. 261, ll. 13, 15. Rev. iii. 16–17.

p. 265, ll. 8–10. Isa. xlix. 14 applies to the quotation in ll. 6–7, which is followed by a non-existent reference, i.e. Isa. 45. 27.

p. 273, l. 32. *Trencher-Chaplains*: domestic chaplains. Cf. John Boys, *An Exposi-*

tion of the Dominical Epistles (1610). in *Works* (1630), 511: 'It is the fashion of parasites and trencher-Chaplaines to flatter, or at the least humour great men at their table.' *O.E.D.*

p. 274, l. 12. *Auditory*: audience.

p. 278, ll. 4–5. Ps. xxv. 11.

p. 279, l. 20. Luke xi. 8.

p. 283, l. 4. Mark iii. 29–30.